Po

L

Also by Christopher Knight and Robert Lomas

The Hiram Key
The Second Messiah
Uriel's Machine

By Robert Lomas

The Invisible College
The Man who Invented the Twentieth Century

By Robert Lomas and G. A. Lancaster

Forecasting for Sales and Material Management

The Book of Hiram

THE BOOK OF HIRAM

FREEMASONRY, VENUS AND THE SECRET KEY
TO THE LIFE OF JESUS

Christopher Knight and Robert Lomas

For more information visit these websites:
www.knight-lomas.com
www.robertlomas.com
www.bradford.ac.uk/webofhiram

C

CENTURY · LONDON

First published in the United Kingdom in 2003 by Century
The Random House Group Limited
20 Vauxhall Bridge Road, London SW1V 2SA

Random House Australia (Pty) Limited
20 Alfred Street, Milsons Point, Sydney,
New South Wales 2061, Australia

Random House New Zealand Limited
18 Poland Road, Glenfield
Auckland 10, New Zealand

Random House South Africa (Pty) Limited
Endulini, 5a Jubilee Road, Parktown 2193, South Africa

The Random House Group Limited Reg. No. 954009

www.randomhouse.co.uk

A CIP catalogue record for this book is available
from the British Library

Papers used by Random House are natural, recyclable products made from wood grown in sustainable forests. The manufacturing processes conform to the environmental regulations of the country of origin

ISBN 0 7126 94382

Typeset by Palimpsest Book Production, Polmont, Stirlingshire
Printed and bound in Great Britain by
Mackays of Chatham Ltd, Chatham, Kent

For Caroline – CK

To my wife and children in
thanks for their continual support – RL

Acknowledgements

This book could not have been written without the help and assistance of the many Masons, and family members of long-dead Masons, who have made available copies of forgotten ritual books. There are too many of you to thank individually but we are extremely grateful for all the material you have provided to enable us to create *The Masonic Testament*.

We would also like to thank:

The Brethren and staff of the Grand Lodge of Antient Free and Accepted Masons of Scotland for their advice and assistance.

Jenny Finder and her library staff at the Bradford University School of Management for their continuing good-natured support, and ability to procure long-lost books.

Tim Bentley and Stan Houghton of Bradford University Computer Centre for their help in setting up the Web of Hiram.

Geraint Lomas and Josh Gourlay for their tireless efforts in scanning and proof-reading vast tracts of ritual for the Web of Hiram.

Niven and Ian Sinclair, of the Niven Sinclair Library and Study Centre at Noss Head, Wick, for sharing their knowledge and introducing us to Ashley Cowie.

Ashley Cowie for sharing his discovery of the Rosslyn Lozenge Pattern.

Professor Philip Davies of Sheffield University for his expert and on-going Biblical advice.

Professor Jim Charlesworth of Princeton University for his support in proposing an excavation at Rosslyn.

Dr Jack Millar of Cambridge University for his insightful comments about the structure of Rosslyn.

Robin Heath for his helpful discussions on deciphering the travels of Enoch.

Corin Wilson for his encouragement to investigate astrology with an open mind.

Alan Butler for his assistance with matters astronomical and megalithic.

Tony Batters for his expertise and enthusiasm.

Our agent Bill Hamilton of A. M. Heath Ltd, whose enthusiasm and focus helped keep us on track during the conception and protracted birth of this book.

Our editor Mark Booth, whose guidance on how to present a very complex story has been invaluable.

All the folk at Random House who did all the tedious production tasks which are so necessary to turn a manuscript into a finished book. In particular we would like to single out for special thanks Hannah Black who organised the team, Steve Cox who slugged away copy-editing and Carolyn McAndrew who proof-read it all.

Contents

INTRODUCTION

It is now thirteen years since we joined forces to research the origins and meaning of the weird rituals used by Freemasons. For the first five years we had no intention of sharing our findings with anyone – inside or outside of Freemasonry. But because what we found appeared to be of great importance we decided to write a book about our voyage of discovery, and much to our surprise *The Hiram Key* became an immediate bestseller that went on to be translated into well over thirty languages.

The rituals of Freemasonry form the most ancient oral tradition of the Western world. Our quest was far from over with the publication of our first book, and we went on to write two further books that led us through history right back to the astronomy-based culture of prehistoric Britain. We found that the Freemasonic rituals formed an almost forgotten pathway through the past, linking together people and events that had previously been assumed to be unconnected. Many of our findings have challenged old ideas, but we have been pleased to receive the support of many leading scholars in various aspects of our work.

We have been fortunate to receive a great deal of help over the years, and our quest has made startling progress. However, there are two areas where we have found unexpected opposition. The first stems from the Roman Catholic Church. The second concerns our attempts to facilitate an archaeological investigation of a medieval building in Scotland that has become central to our investigation.

We became aware of hostility from the Catholic establishment from an early stage. Shortly after *The Hiram Key* hit the shops a small piece appeared in the *Catholic Herald* which was both balanced and open-minded. We were initially impressed by the paper's ability to be objective about a book that took an innovative approach to interpreting the history of Jesus Christ. But in the next edition a second review appeared that spanned two pages, complete with photographs copied from our book and a banner headline proclaiming 'Chris and Bob's Bogus Adventure'. This time the article was far from balanced, full of venom for our book, for us as individuals and anyone else who was a 'drunken' Freemason. The aim was not to debate or even mention our findings, but to ridicule us and our views from start to finish.

Our next book received the same treatment in a double-page spread filled with aggression that avoided any comment on the key issues we had raised. Again it was clear that the reviewer had read the book with little care, because the rare references made, even to insignificant parts of the content, were completely wrong.

When our third book came out we were waiting with interest to read the next attack from this corner of the Roman Catholic establishment. We were not disappointed. The producers of the *Catholic Herald* published a substantial review of *Uriel's Machine* with a bold headline that shouted 'Bogus Archaeology'. This article told its readers at length that our work was complete nonsense, without ever mentioning our claims or even attempting to refute any evidence.

We find it strange that a British Roman Catholic newspaper chose to run extensive reviews on three successive books, solely in order to label them utterly bogus. Surely if a book is complete rubbish you ignore it, rather than waste time telling your readers how awful it is.

Uriel's Machine had received favourable reviews from many newspapers, but then one appeared that was as aggressive and disingenuous as the *Catholic Herald* piece. Shortly after the book came out we were interviewed by someone else who used exactly the same theme for an article later carried in the *Daily Telegraph*. Perhaps the strikingly similar approach was simply chance, but we later found that one-time religious correspondent Damian Thompson was no stranger to the *Catholic Herald*.

After spending the first quarter of an hour demonstrating his comprehensive inability to operate a minidisc recorder, Thompson spent the rest of the two-hour interview repeatedly shouting: 'But you can't do science like that.' He admitted his ignorance of astronomy and mathematics; but being quite unable to understand the calculation methodology we employed did not deter him from dismissing our findings as wrong – simply because he said they were. When his article appeared it made no reference to our core thesis but juxtaposed weird claims from other people's books with references to us, thus creating the false impression that we had said these things, or supported them in some way. The lengthy headline read:

> *Minoans built Stonehenge, Atlantis is based in Antarctica, Jesus was buried in France. Welcome to the best selling world of bogus archaeology.*

Strange claims indeed; none of which we would accept. Thompson went on to try and discredit our work by stating that *The Hiram Key* had been 'rubbished by historians and critics alike'. He evidenced this claimed universal rebuttal of our earlier work by quoting a headline from just one publication. That headline was 'Chris and Bob's Bogus Adventure'. Of course the quotation, with the now familiar 'bogus' theme, came from none other than *The Catholic Herald*.

Could we be on to something so important that some people believed we must be discredited?

In April 1998 Chris was speaking at a Masonic symposium in Perugia, Italy. One evening before the event the organiser, Professor Giancarlo Seri, received a phone call from Rome. On the line was a senior figure from the Roman Catholic Church asking if it was true that one of the authors of *The Hiram Key* was to address Italian Freemasons. Professor Seri told him it was, asked the caller if he had read the book and, if so, what he thought of it. The clergyman's reply was frank: 'Yes, I have read it. It is an excellent book but there are certain things which should not be said.' He did not say it was inaccurate (let alone bogus), indeed his only objection to our work appeared to be that we were telling people about it.

We have great respect for the Roman Catholic Church, but we also believe that nobody has the right to prohibit the investigation of alternative explanations of the past. In its dark period the Church tolerated no deviation from its account of the way the world is, murdering whole populations if it suspected them of harbouring ideas different to those it preached. From Galileo onwards it has been fighting a losing battle, but today it reluctantly accepts concepts such as Darwinian evolution.

3

So what is it about our humble research into the origins of Masonic ritual that seems to have touched such a very delicate nerve? We decided to find out, and this book describes our search.

The second issue that we have to contend with is the resistance to a proper archaeological examination of the fifteenth-century Rosslyn Chapel that lies in the Lothian Hills just a little south of Edinburgh. In *The Hiram Key*, our quest ended at this late medieval building in Scotland that we reasoned might well contain documents originally buried under the Jerusalem Temple at the time when the earliest of the Gospels of the New Testament were being written down. We put forward an argument that Rosslyn Chapel, as it is now called, is the repository of the most important Dead Sea Scrolls, which are likely to contain direct references to a messianic individual who is now remembered under his Greek designation of 'Jesus Christ'.

We appreciate that this is, at first view, a strange claim but it is very well supported by evidence. The key points are:

1 The Copper Scroll found amongst the Dead Sea Scrolls at Qumran lists the scrolls and Temple treasures that were buried beneath the Jerusalem Temple in, or immediately prior to, 68 CE.

2 It is known that the nine Crusader founders of the Order of the Knights Templar continuously excavated under the ruins of that Temple between 1118 and 1128 CE.

3 A nineteenth-century British army expedition that excavated under the Temple found nothing but the workings of the Knights Templar and some artefacts left by them.

4 The older rituals of Freemasonry state that these knights found documents under the ruins of the Temple in Jerusalem and brought them to the St Clair estates in Kilwinning, Scotland, in 1140 CE.

5 Rosslyn was built by a member of the St Clair family, between 1441 and 1490 CE.

6 The same family later became the most senior Freemasons in the world as hereditary Grand Master Masons.

7 The ground plan of Rosslyn is a carefully designed copy of the layout of Herod's Temple in Jerusalem.

8 Dr Jack Miller, head of studies in geology from Cambridge University, confirmed that Rosslyn is built from exactly the same stone as the Jerusalem Temple.

9 The west wall of the 'chapel' is a copy of the west wall of the Jerusalem Temple, rather than an abandoned attempt to build a great collegiate church. Dr Miller also demonstrated that this oversized west wall was a copy of a ruin, and that it could not possibly be a part of any intended building.

10 Professor the Reverend James Charlesworth of Princeton University, Dead Sea Scroll expert and Albright Professor of Archaeology in Jerusalem, subsequently pointed out that the west wall exhibits deliberate design features to make it look like the architecture of the Jerusalem Temple.

11 Other experts, such as biblical scholar Professor Philip Davies, have pointed out that the building is clearly not Christian and that most of the hundreds of carved figures inside are holding either books or scrolls.

12 The only original inscription in the whole building is a single passage from the Book of Esdras which refers to the rebuilding of the Jerusalem Temple by Zerubbabel.

13 The foundations are recorded to have taken four years to lay out, and it is also known that the builder kept four large chests of documents in the nearby castle. These documents were more important to him than the women of his family, because when a fire broke out he insisted that these chests were rescued before his womenfolk.

14 A carving on the south wall proves a connection with Freemasonry. The layout of the pillars inside corresponds to the rituals of Freemasonry and is associated with ritual that states this is 'the key to finding the precious thing'.

When *The Hiram Key* was published one of the trustees of Rosslyn publicly stated that they would support an archaeological dig at the site if a team of world-class scholars, including leading Scottish academics, was assembled. After we took Professor Charlesworth to Rosslyn, he did exactly that and put a detailed proposal for an investigation to the trustees in early 1999. To the best of our knowledge no response has been received.

We have come to the conclusion that a proper archaeological investigation of Rosslyn is not going to happen in the near future, and hence we are not going to be able to recover the concealed documents and the secret teachings we believe they contain. The challenge we face is to get around this problem.

Our starting point is the vast amount of old Masonic ritual that has been given to us over the years by supportive Freemasons. We set about the huge task of sorting and organising as much early Masonic material as we could, and then Robert proceeded to create a major website to allow this material to be viewed in a number of different sequences. The website has proved to be an invaluable research tool for investigating the complex, convoluted and mainly discarded myths of Freemasonry.

Once all of this old Freemasonic ritual was assembled into a form where it could be scanned and searched simply, the underlying story emerged with a new clarity. A strange historical tale had been recorded in an almost random fashion across many Masonic degrees, often with considerable repetition. The historical content enabled the material to be sorted into chronological sequence to create a book, similar to a Testament of the Bible, with much that mirrors the two existing Testaments but also containing additional information only recorded in other contemporary Jewish documents such as the works of the first-century historian, Josephus. But there was also a third layer of information that does not appear anywhere else at all. This, therefore, has to be either simple invention or some lost strand of knowledge that can shed a great deal of light on both the Old and the New Testament. We have become convinced that it is the latter of these two options.

As we started to plan *The Book of Hiram* we decided to restructure this material into a document that we called *The Masonic Testament*. This forms Part Two of this book and it is made up of passages from Freemasonic ritual assembled in chronological order. The original ritual words are used as far as possible with only linking words added to allow the underlying story to be revealed. We see it as something akin to a missing book of the Bible.

We have used *The Masonic Testament* as a source document in Part One of this book and footnoted it with the abbreviation MT followed by the chapter and verse concerned. (e.g. MT 16:38 for Chapter 16 Verse 38).

Readers can check the validity of *The Masonic Testament* by looking up the precise words of each paragraph at a publicly accessible website Robert has created at the University of Bradford. It can be found at http://www.bradford.ac.uk/webofhiram.

This academic resource that we have called *The Web of Hiram* has now been taken on to be maintained by the University of Bradford as a research tool available to everyone.

The website provides the supporting evidence for our claims, and for the first time allows any reader with access to the Net to see the detail behind the story we tell. Now that readers can judge our claims for themselves, it is no longer necessary to rely on the opinions of third parties.

Our findings to date have led us to believe that there is a knowledge of ancient science at the heart of the almost lost rituals of Freemasonry. In this, the final phase of our quest, we set out to find this missing science that appears to worry the Roman Catholic Church so much.

Part One

Part One

Chapter One

THE DEATH OF THE BUILDERS

THE OLDEST MYSTERIES OF NATURE AND SCIENCE

Freemasonry is dying.

For most people life is far more complicated than it was just a generation ago. We work harder and we have more disposable income. Long-term commitments are usually avoided at all costs. In an age when employment comes packaged as a series of renewable contracts and even marriage is out of vogue, it is not surprising that men no longer queue up to sign on for a lifetime of acting out odd-ball rituals in a local hall with no windows. Candidates for the Craft are expected to enter into a lifelong relationship with a lodge before learning what Freemasonry is. They are given no advance warning of what they will be expected to do, or what benefit it will be to them. It is little wonder that the Grand Lodges who govern Freemasonry around the world are having difficulty in selling a proposition that does not meet any of the normal criteria of a marketable product.

An obvious question is 'Does the demise of this secretive Order really matter?' Maybe it should be allowed to quietly wither away. But, as we will demonstrate in this book, Freemasonry is a major untapped source of information about our past that is in grave danger of being lost for ever. To lose the information buried within its rituals before it is properly understood would be throwing away one of the true treasures of the Western world.

11

We both joined Freemasonry for the same reason: curiosity. We wanted to know what was going on inside this secretive gentlemen's club and the only way to find out was to join. We independently reasoned that becoming part of something so unknown was not too great a risk, as we could leave if we found it distasteful or simply boring. The rituals were every bit as strange as we imagined, but slowly it became evident that nobody, no matter how senior, could give us any clue what Masonry was really about. The charitable work the Order espoused was impressive, and the morality taught within the rituals was of the highest order, but that did not begin to explain why Freemasons practise such bizarre rituals, which claim to be extremely ancient and to contain unusual lessons, referred to as mysteries.

When we joined Freemasonry the first mystery imparted to us was that the technology of building in stone is a sacred act that serves as a metaphor to aid spiritual understanding. Indeed, during the most important section of our First Degree we were explicitly told that our initiation into Freemasonry was identical to the laying of the foundation stone of a spiritual building. The ritual says:

> It is customary at the erection of all stately and superb edifices, to
> lay the first or foundation stone in the North-East corner of the
> building. You, being newly initiated into Masonry are placed in the
> North-East part of the lodge, figuratively to represent that stone;
> and from the foundation laid this evening may you raise a super-
> structure, perfect in all parts and honourable to the builder.

Back in 1989, when we joined forces to investigate the origins of Masonic ritual, our initial belief was that the whole thing was probably developed from bits and bats of esoteric tradition by a stream of romantic thinkers between the sixteenth and nineteenth centuries. It was not many months before we started to suspect that this casual assumption was way off course.

A MATTER OF DEATH AND LIFE

Despite the widely held view that Freemasonry is an international brotherhood wielding unseen power and influence for the benefit of its members, the reality is that it is not a single organisation any more than the Christian Church or the communist movement. It is a loose idea, based on hundreds of esoteric rituals that claim varying amounts of antiquity. By general consensus the United Grand Lodge of England (UGLE) is the senior Masonic authority in the world, and yet it recognises only four of the many degrees in existence as being 'true Freemasonry'.

The term organisation seems inappropriate to a worldwide body that is so disparate and under-structured. Even the UGLE has no record of the membership of the thousands of lodges it directly controls in England and Wales, let alone the various Grand Lodges around the world that are affiliated to it. This absence of any information on members of the Craft (as it is known within the brotherhood) resembles the classical cell structure adopted by many secret organisations. Terrorist groups for instance operate on a tiered, need-to-know basis where each member is given the identity only of the few individuals with whom he has to have direct contact. This protects the organisation from suffering serial damage should any outsider infiltrate its ranks.

Modern Freemasonry is often described as a 'secret society', but it has sometimes preferred to describe itself as 'a society with secrets'. These are portrayed by UGLE as being only a handful of unimportant ceremonial niceties such as passwords and grips (distinctive handshakes) which are supposedly intended to prevent non-Freemasons gaining admittance to a lodge.

There are traditional penalties in each of the principal degrees of Freemasonry whereby the candidate swears to keep the secrets about to be imparted to him away from anyone who is not a member of that particular degree. These penalties were dropped from the UGLE-approved rituals a few years ago, but they remain in many other Grand Lodges, including that of Scotland. The obligations entered into are not insignificant, as they include having one's tongue or heart torn out, the throat cut and the body dismembered in a variety of imaginative ways.

According to the officially approved history of Masonry nothing is known for sure about the brotherhood prior to the installation of Anthony Sayer as Grand Master on Midsummer's day 1717, when a group of London-based Freemasons established a Grand Lodge. However there was nothing particularly 'Grand' about a handful of men from four pubs agreeing to get together as a formal unit, especially as Freemasonry was alive and well in many other towns and cities, especially in Scotland.

The self-inflicted amnesia about early Freemasonry that struck this little band of Londoners was entirely understandable. Just three years earlier the German-speaking George of Hanover had become king of Great Britain, displacing the rulers of the Catholic House of Stuart. The supporters of the deposed Stuarts (the Jacobites) hatched a number of plots to overthrow the new Protestant dynasty. In 1715 a group of Jacobite nobles led an uprising in Scotland and marched into England in support of James II's son, James Francis Edward Stuart, later known as the Old Pretender. After an indecisive battle with the government forces, the Jacobites surrendered at Preston in Lancashire.

Freemasonry was known to be closely associated with the Stuarts, and with Scotland in general, so to admit to being a member of the Order was tantamount to admitting support for a terrorist organisation dedicated to the overthrow of the king. In the same year as the Grand Lodge of London was formed the so-called Triple Alliance was negotiated between Great Britain, France and the Netherlands to guarantee the succession of the reigning monarchs in their respective countries. With the Jacobite struggle apparently lost, this was not a good time to be branded an enemy of the state. What better time to make sure you kept no central records of membership? The famous architect and founder member of the Royal Society, Sir Christopher Wren, was Grand Master of Freemasonry prior to 1717, but he, and many others like him, simply walked away from the Order rather than risk social exclusion or even arrest.[1] For some reason, the records of UGLE were amended, at the outbreak of the First World War, to remove the identification of Wren's Grand Mastership. Today it is officially denied.

Once English Freemasonry disowned its Jacobite heritage the need for secrecy was gone, and the lack of a central membership list today surely reflects an absence of need rather than deliberate policy. When the UGLE wishes to communicate with its rank and file it speaks to the various Provincial Grand Lodges, who write to the individual lodge secretaries, who in turn pass the correspondence on to the humble Masons convened in their lodges.

Being Freemasons ourselves, we are bound by our obligations to keep the secrets of Freemasonry. Some fellow Freemasons criticised us for revealing details of rituals when we published *The Hiram Key*. Indeed we described parts of several rituals, particularly key elements of the all-important third degree of the Order. However, we were extremely careful to obey the precise ruling of our own Grand Lodge here in England and Wales, and did not reveal any of the grips and passwords that constitute the present-day 'secrets' of the Order.

[1] Anderson, James: *The Book of Constitutions of the Grand Lodge of London*, 1738

Whilst most Freemasons are happy to admit their membership, some prefer to keep the whole subject private and, in the face of prejudice in the workplace, others find it necessary to sometimes deny that they are members. In our view the impression of secrecy that surrounds individual Freemasons is brought about by their embarrassment in talking about the nature of the rituals that, in the cold light of day, sound odd in the extreme. If asked what such strange rituals are all about, they have to confess that they do not know.

In other words we believe the compelling reason for silence amongst Masons is not so much a compulsion to adhere to their sacred vows or a fear of macabre retribution from their fellows; it is more the fact that they do not understand a word of the ceremonies they participate in, and their main fear is that people will laugh at the bizarre rituals they continue to perform.

It seems certain that Freemasonry once espoused some high purpose, but today it is a rapidly shrinking social club for elderly gentlemen. In the United Kingdom it provides an opportunity to indulge in some amateur theatricals, followed by a meal and plenty of beer, although in the United States of America alcohol is not permitted at Masonic meetings. The complex and obscure ritual has to be memorised through years of word-perfect repetition, but only small parts of the ceremony can be understood as simple allegorical messages concerning uprightness of moral character. The rest is a strange mixture of meaningless words and painstakingly detailed re-enactments of events that occurred in the distant past.

The three principal degrees consist of the Entered Apprentice (the initiation), Fellowcraft (known as the passing degree), and Master Mason (known as the raising degree). Within these degrees the 'true secrets' of the order are said to have been lost, and substituted secrets introduced in their place until such time as the real secrets are rediscovered.

THE DARKNESS OF THE THIRD DEGREE

In the first degree of Freemasonry the candidate is brought into the Craft in what is referred to as a state of 'naked indigence' at the lowest level of existence like a newborn baby. The details of the ritual may vary but its message remains constant. Here we talk about the tradition we both know. The Candidate is dressed in a rough white smock and properly prepared, complete with noose and blindfold, before being taken into the temple to

15

be made an Entered Apprentice Freemason. Here he will kneel in front of the leader of the lodge for that year (the Worshipful Master), with the twin pillars of King Solomon's Temple to either side of him. At a key point in the ceremony, after receiving his new rank, he is placed in the northeast of the temple to be given instruction. This position marks the path of light from the rising Sun on the day of the summer solstice, which is known to Freemasons as the Feast of St John, one of the two most important days in the Masonic calendar. The St John referred to here is John the Baptist, who was said to have been conceived on the autumn equinox and born on midsummer's day.

Some months later the candidate is put through his second degree. At the appropriate moment he is placed at the southeast of the temple to receive the next level of instruction, which is said to mark the progress he has made in the science. Standing at this position the candidate is on the line of the first light from the winter solstice sunrise. This day in late December is the other great day in Freemasonry, and it too is called the Feast of St John, but this time it belongs to St John the Divine, the author of the Book of Revelation.

Once the candidate has symbolically received instruction at dawn on both the summer and winter solstices he is ready to be made a Master Mason by being put through the third degree. This is a different experience right from the outset.

The candidate is once again dressed in the rough white smock, with both of his trouser legs rolled up and both sides of his chest exposed. He is not blindfolded, but as the temple door swings open to admit him he can see that the room is in total darkness except for a small shielded candle burning on the Worshipful Master's pedestal in the east. At first the change from light outside to darkness inside leaves the candidate blinded, and he has to rely on the two deacons to steer his path across the temple floor.

In this degree the most important section takes place in the east, between the two pillars of Boaz and Jachin that once marked the extremities of the Sun's passage north and south at the solstices in front of the Temple of Yahweh in Jerusalem. Here the candidate is told the story of the murder of Hiram Abif, who, it is revealed, was the architect of King Solomon's Temple some three thousand years ago. Strangely, the Worshipful Master makes reference to this otherwise unknown individual as though the average person should be aware of him when he says to the candidate:

. . . the annals of Freemasonry afford a glorious example in the unshaken fidelity and untimely death of our Grand Master Hiram Abif, who lost his life just before the completion of King Solomon's Temple, at the construction of which as you are doubtless aware, he was the principal architect.

When we first heard this assumption we found it strange, and in *The Hiram Key* we said that the character of Hiram Abif does not seem to exist outside of the rituals of Freemasonry. This observation caused a number of people to write to us to tell us we were mistaken, so let us here look more closely at what evidence there is in the Old Testament about the architect of Solomon's Temple. First we are told that the Phoenician king of Tyre named Hiram supplied the design, workers and many materials for Solomon's building works. This king's name is variously spelt as Hiram, Hirom and Huram, and was probably originally 'Ahi-ram'. Josephus says that letters between Solomon and this king were preserved in the Tyrian archives.[2] He also quotes the historians Dius and Menander of Ephesus, who say that Hiram was the son of King Abi-baal.

There was also another Hiram involved in the creation of the Temple. This Hiram was a worker in metals who set up a foundry in the Jordan valley between Succoth and Zeredatha, where he cast the two great pillars of Boaz and Jachin as well as other great ornaments of the Temple, including the huge vessel known as the 'molten sea'. This character is referred to in 2 Chr. 2: 11–14, where Hiram, king of Tyre, writes to Solomon to tell him that this Hiram is a son of the daughters of the tribe of Dan, but in 1 Kgs 7: 14 we are told that he was a widow's son of a different tribe, that of Naphtali.

Could this artisan in metals be considered the architect of the Temple? An architect is the designer of the overall building, not the manufacturer of its ornamentation, but in the Revised Standard Version of the Bible this builder is referred to as Huram-abi, which is indeed close to the name Hiram Abif.

A further piece of information emerged in March 1999 when visiting the library of Scottish Grand Lodge with the famous biblical scholar, Professor Philip Davies. On this occasion we were looking at an uncatalogued volume written almost two hundred years ago by Dr Anderson

[2] Josephus, *Antiquities of the Jews, ch. viii*

(writer of the first book of Constitutions of UGLE and a member of the Lodge of Aberdeen) in which this Masonic historian explained the name of Hiram Abif, which was given in a Hebrew version of 2 Chr. 4: 16 as follows:

Shelomoh lammelech Abhif Churam ghafah

As Philip studied the words his lips puckered in concentration before he stated that this appeared to suggest that this Hiram was father to King Solomon. But as everyone knows, David was Solomon's father, so Philip's only thought to make sense of what he saw was to suggest that perhaps it might mean that Hiram was the king's father-in-law.

On the balance of probabilities we now accept that the character referred to in Masonic ritual as Hiram Abif could be the worker in metals supplied to work on Solomon's Temple by Hiram, King of Tyre. However, this potential identification does nothing to explain his relationship to King Solomon or to illuminate why this legend is so important within Freemasonic lore.

In the Third Degree the candidate is told how a group of fifteen stonemasons wanted to extract the genuine secrets of a master mason from their master, Hiram Abif, so they planned to ambush him when he paused from his labours to give praise to a god referred to as the 'Most High'. The words of the ritual state:

> On the eve of carrying their conspiracy into execution, twelve of
> the fifteen recanted, but three of a more determined and atrocious
> character than the rest persisted in their impious designs, for which
> purpose they placed themselves respectively at the south, west and
> east gates of the Temple, whither our Master Hiram Abif had
> retired to pay his adoration to the Most High, as was his wonton
> custom, it being the hour of high twelve.

Whilst this is taken to be a reference to the deity Yahweh, who is now elevated to the point that we call him simply 'God', it is far more likely that this Canaanite artisan was worshipping the Sun god at his zenith in the sky; hence the description 'Most High'. Whilst the proposed Temple was to house the 'new' god of the Jews, who was temporarily living in a tent, He was not seen as particularly important even to Solomon, who later stopped worshipping Him altogether.

However, Hiram's choice of deity will undoubtedly not trouble the candidate too much, because at this point of the ritual he suddenly realises that he is about to become a murder victim. As the Worshipful Master tells how Hiram was struck a blow to the forehead at the south gate a blow is tapped to the side of the candidate's head, and the process repeated at the west gate. Then at the east gate the coup de grâce is delivered and the candidate is struck a 'fatal' blow to the centre of the head. This can be done gently or vigorously. Scottish Freemasons are particularly famous for entering into the full spirit of the occasion, and many a poor candidate has been hurled to the floor in fear of his life.

The candidate is held straight so that he hinges backwards onto a funeral shroud previously placed on the floor that is immediately draped around him so only his eyes are uncovered. At this point the Masons of the lodge walk around the edge of the 'grave', and finally three attempts are made to retrieve the brother from the arms of death. The first two fail because they use methods from the previous degrees, but the third technique, peculiar to the third degree, succeeds.

With the assistance of the deacons the 'cadaver' is 'resurrected' from his tomb with a special grip applied by the Worshipful Master. Still in near-total darkness, the body swings upwards to be held in a complicated ceremonial position, an embrace where the Master and Candidate touch each other at five distinct points. The ritual name for this embrace is the 'Five Points of Fellowship'. Whilst in this position an incantation is spoken into the ear of the candidate, who is then shown the black grave just behind and to the west of him, which has a real human skull and crossed thigh bones placed upon it to represent the candidate's own mortal remains. Next, the Worshipful Master directs the candidate's gaze towards the east, where he can see a five-pointed star shining in the darkness between the twin pillars of Boaz and Jachin. This star, he is told, is 'the bright star of the morning' – which is the planet Venus rising some minutes ahead of the Sun at dawn.

From this moment onwards, the man raised from the darkness of his figurative tomb will be a Master Mason for the rest of his life. It is important to note that whilst the candidate represented the character of Hiram Abif up to the point of the ritual slaying, there is no suggestion that Hiram was ever resurrected. The most important information given to the newly 'raised' Mason is that the genuine secrets of a Master Mason were lost 'with the death of our Grand Master Hiram Abif'. The currently worked rituals of the Three Degrees of the Craft do not shed any light on this matter, and for quite a while we believed that the original rituals which had discussed these matters must have been completely destroyed during the period of censorship that followed the creation of the United Grand Lodge of England, in 1813. (These events are described in *The Second Messiah*[3] and *The Invisible College*.[4])

WEAVING THE WEB OF HIRAM

When we wrote *The Hiram Key* we had only the vaguest notion of the content of many of the so-called 'Higher Degrees' of Freemasonry, but after the publication of this book we were contacted by hundreds of people with new information. Some would arrive by post, and sometimes when we were speaking at lodge meetings we would be given old documents of ritual that had been kept in dusty drawers for generations. Whilst researching *The Second Messiah* we came across a particularly significant source of material that pushed our researches forward in a lecture entitled 'Freemasonry and Catholicism' written by a Balkan scholar from Bosnia-Herzegovina by the name of Dimitrije Mitrinovic.

Mitrinovic came to live in London around the time of the First World War and he went on to become a leading figure in the 'Bloomsbury Group', a collective of intellectuals who took their name from the district near the British Museum in central London where most of the members lived. The statement which had attracted our attention was this:

> *Christ betrayed the secret word of Masonry . . . to the people, and he proclaimed it in Jerusalem, but in saying the Senate word to folk, he was before his time . . . Let Masons receive Christ back into Masonry . . . Masonry has been the expression of Christianity for the last 2000 years.*[5]

Mitrinovic was not a Freemason and it had taken us seven years of wide-ranging research, using our specialist Masonic knowledge, to come to this view, so we wondered how he had reached the same conclusion. In due course we discovered that it was from extensive study of a considerable

[3] Knight, C & Lomas, R: *The Second Messiah*, Arrow, 1998
[4] Lomas, Robert: *The Invisible College*, Headline, 2002
[5] Mitrinovic, D: Freemasonry and Catholicism in the New Order. Lectures 1926–1950, JB Priestley Library, University of Bradford, 1995

personal library he had built up, and we set out to find his books. We eventually tracked the collection down and found that they had been stacked in boxes after Mitrinovic died and stored in the back of his niece's garage for over forty years. When eventually the time came to clear out his old books, wanting to give Mitrinovic's library a good home she decided to donate them to a university. Fortunately the university that offered to house them was Bradford, where Robert teaches.

Back in 1997, when we first became interested in Mitrinovic's books, they were not on public display because the new extension to the JB Priestley Library had not then been completed. Like many other more obscure books they were temporarily stored in the basement of the library in an area known as 'the stack'. This consisted of a large windowless storeroom with a series of racked bookshelves set on rails in the floor. To access the inner shelves the outer bookcases, which were ten feet high and thirty feet long, had to be cranked aside, using a large handle. When Robert requested access to the collection it took him nearly half an hour just to trundle aside the eight outer bookcases which had to be moved to reach the volumes assembled by Mitrinovic.

In *The Second Messiah* we discussed the implications of some of the Masonic commentaries that Mitrinovic had saved, but it was later, once his collection was properly shelved and catalogued, making it accessible without having to squirm into a narrow steel tunnel to reach them, that other Masonic treasures came to light. Among the more general tomes were early copies of Masonic rituals which are no longer in use. One ritual book dated from the early nineteenth century and contained full details, illustrated with beautiful woodcuts, of all the degrees of the Ancient and Accepted Scottish Rite of Freemasonry. It was written by EA McClenachan, who was the father of the famous late nineteenth-century Masonic scholar Charles T McClenachan. This book alone was a wonderful find, as it contained accounts of rituals which had not been subjected to the hugely damaging modifications conducted at the behest of the Duke of Sussex, the First Grand Master of the United Grand Lodge of England in 1813.

Browsing through the rituals in this fascinating book we noticed a section on the Royal Arch of Enoch. Now we knew that the book of the prophet Enoch was lost in the early Christian period and not rediscovered until 1774. Yet the preface of this book claimed that the rituals it contained dated back to at least 1740, and we could see that they went into great detail about the importance of Enoch and his role in foretelling the coming of the Flood. These themes were not widely accepted until the discovery of multiple copies of the Book of Enoch during the twentieth century, a point we will discuss more fully later. How did these old myths come to hold such pride of place amongst these discarded rituals unless they were a survival of an ancient verbal tradition?

Whilst researching *Uriel's Machine* we had become aware that a Masonic ritual relating to Enoch existed, but it had not been worked for over two hundred years, since the time of the Duke of Sussex. Now as we read the original workings we found a description of a strange triangular pedestal, with sides of exactly the same length and angles of 60 degrees, making it equilateral. This shape was described as the 'Delta of Enoch' and was explained as the symbol by which the Mighty Architect of the Universe chose to reveal Himself to Enoch. The pedestal was said to have been an important part of the furniture of the original Temple which Enoch built on the site which is now known as Temple Mount in Jerusalem. The ritual explained how Solomon's workers found this threefold altar in a buried vault beneath the abandoned ruins of an earlier temple which Solomon at first attributed to 'pagans' who occupied the site before his father David seized it.

At the time this meant little to us, but we were later to discover that the symbol of the equilateral triangle was of immense significance within the early Canaanite religion of the Jebusites, who built Jerusalem. What did strike us, as we read this two-hundred-year-old printed ritual book, was that it seemed to be extremely familiar with early Jewish traditions and legends that were only recovered and confirmed in detail during archaeological excavations carried out within the last fifty years. This printed version of an older verbal ritual seemed to be preserving the story of a tradition of Canaanite temple building which was not recorded either in the Bible or in other early sources we were familiar with.

When we read it we did not know of any earlier temples in Jerusalem that pre-dated Solomon's, but we were soon to find that there is very good archaeological evidence for just such a Canaanite tradition. We wondered what other lost traditions these old rituals might contain, and just how we could systemise our investigation of the various themes of early ritual.

Over recent years we have built up a considerable collection of old rituals and lectures, but in paper form. Now books, although often very beautiful objects, are not simple to search or sequence for their information content, so we decided that we needed to create an electronic version of the material. Robert set about the task of scanning the oldest versions of each degree to incorporate them into the website we called *The Web of Hiram*. As his work of digitising the ritual proceeded, it was clear both that there was a complex story being told throughout the sequence of degrees, and that it was not being told in chronological order. This realisation led us to try to reconstruct the complete story which had once been told by Masonic ritual. It took a long time to complete the task but, as we will show, we have reconstructed an alternative account of history as told in the discarded and censored rituals of Freemasonry. It is told in the *Masonic Testament* to be found in Part Two of the book. The website that Robert created has now been adopted by Bradford University and is freely available for anyone interested in the, arguably, more authentic rituals of Freemasonry.

Another of our early discoveries was that the ritual of the Ancient and Accepted rite mentioned a question which had been bothering us. What happened after the death of Hiram Abif, when the true secrets of Masonry were lost?

Our reconstruction of the alternative account of history contained in Freemasonic ritual that we were now calling *The Masonic Testament* makes this comment about the two men who retained the true secrets of the ritual: [*Masonic Testament* 7:5]

> *Each Mason will apply our symbols and ceremonies according to*
> *his faith. In no other way could Masonry possess its universality –*
> *that character which has ever been peculiar to it from its origin,*
> *and which enabled two kings, worshippers of different Deities, to*
> *sit together as Grand Masters while the walls of the first Temple*
> *arose; and the men of Gebal, who bowed down to the Phoenician*
> *gods, to work by the side of the Hebrews, to whom those gods*
> *were an abomination.*

From this comment we began to suspect that there must have been a tradition of some tension between the religions of Solomon and the king of Tyre which might be reflected in the ritual. According to Masonic tradition both of them accepted the Third Degree ritual as a suitable substitution for the lost secrets, '*until time should again reveal the real ones*'. We were convinced that the implication of this ritual statement is that both surviving Grand Masters approved of the words and actions of the ritual.

We were beginning to suspect that a key point of this degree is the fact that the death and resurrection of the man takes place on a line with his feet in the east and head in the west. When the candidate is 'raised' from his tomb his head rises in a curve towards the east to meet Venus, which is also rising above the horizon. The east–west line marks the equinox, the point of equilibrium between the two solstices when there are twelve hours of day and twelve of darkness.

The three degrees of Craft Freemasonry could therefore be seen as entirely astronomical. First the total novice is given information on the line of the Sun at dawn on the summer solstice, then he is advanced to the second degree on the line of the winter solstice, and finally he is made a Master Mason on the line that precisely bisects the previous two: the equinoctial line that occurs once in spring and once in the autumn. As we were to discover, this is entirely consistent with the purpose of King Solomon's Temple and of Phoenician structures that long pre-dated it.

The Master of the lodge sits in the east between the two free-standing pillars called Boaz and Jachin in the Bible. He marks the rising Sun, and the planet Venus rises behind him just before dawn when a candidate is 'raised from his tomb'. The Senior Warden sits in the west to mark the setting Sun and the Junior Warden is in the south representing the Sun at noon. In English lodges there is normally a blazing Sun in the centre of the ceiling with a five-pointed star around it and the letter 'G' inside it, signifying God. This association between the Sun and God is evident throughout Masonic ritual, when He is sometimes referred to as the 'Most High' – literally the most high in the heavens.

There are two officers known as deacons who move around the Masonic Temple with the candidate but are officially stationed in the northeast and the southwest along the line of the summer solstice sunrise. They each carry with them a long rod, usually known as a 'wand', which we believe was once used to mark the angle of the sunrise and sunset by the shadow it cast. It is recorded that the deacons of the earliest Scottish lodges were sent for to align churches. In our book, *Uriel's Machine*, we said that we believed that churches were once aligned eastwards where the break of day at the location was deemed to be 'east'. The first shadow cast from the deacon's wand would be taken as the line of the north wall. We further speculated that it should be possible to work out the name of an old church by considering the local topography and then calculating the two days of the year that corresponds to the angle of the north wall. The church would have been named after one of the saints whose day it was. For example, a church aligned to either solstice is very likely to be called St John's Church.[6]

The picture we have formed is that the rituals of Craft Masonry are based upon astronomy and they have a heritage that is well over five thousand years old. We have found a chain of belief that has survived being passed through several different cultures to end up in modern Masonic Temples, where it is now faithfully recited without any understanding.

CONCLUSIONS

It is over six years since we published *The Hiram Key*, and over the course of researching two further books together we have accumulated a considerable amount of extra material which throws a great deal of light on questions we were originally forced to leave unanswered.

To try and deduce what might really be hidden under Rosslyn we have collected as many early Masonic rituals as we can, and Robert created an interlinked website to allow us to view the material in a variety of different sequences. We intend to use this invaluable research tool to investigate the complex, convoluted and mainly discarded myths of Freemasonry in a degree of detail never before attempted.

When we distil Freemasonry down to its key components we are left with the following ideas:

- The technology of building in stone is viewed as a spiritual act.

- The layout of the Masonic temple and the rituals are based upon astronomy.

- God is associated with the Sun.

- The helical rising of the planet Venus at the equinox marks restored life.

[6] The University of Hong Kong, Department of Earth Sciences, cited our research in this area. See Ali, JR & Cunih, P: 'The Orientation of Churches: Some New Evidence', *The Antiquaries Journal*, 81 (2001), pp. 155–93.

- The summer and winter solstices are important.

- The study of nature and science is important.

These are not common ideas today, but there was a culture in prehistory that appears to have been built on exactly these notions. They are known as the Grooved Ware People.

Chapter Two

THE GROOVED WARE
PEOPLE

THE FIRST STONEMASONS

Neolithic people first arrived in the British islands, around the northern coast of Scotland, about 9,000 years ago, before the North Sea plain was flooded and while it was still possible to walk overland from Norway. These people arrived soon after the glaciers of the last ice age retreated, uncovering ice-free land. When the sea level rose the lands became separate, but the Neolithic Scandinavians and the early Scottish population share a common ancestry.[1]

The Neolithic period marked the end of the Stone Age. In the western fringes of Europe these people are better remembered as being megalithic builders – the word means 'massive stones'. These early stonemasons inhabited what is now Wales, Scotland, Ireland, England, France, parts of southern Scandinavia and northern Spain as well as Malta. Today, people go about their daily business in these countries without a thought for the unknown people who once owned the land. England alone still has over 40,000 known megalithic sites that have survived for more than five thousand years. We can appreciate how impressive this is if we ask ourselves what will remain of our own civilisation in 5,000 years' time when flimsy, modern buildings are so often demolished within a single generation.

The climate in the British Isles at the time was far warmer than today,

[1] Wickham-Jones, CR: *Scotland's First Settlers*, Historic Scotland, 1994

and the land became covered in dense forests, making overland travel very difficult. The megalithic people, however, were both boat-builders and sailors, making great use of the sea as their highway. They colonised the many islands off the coast of Scotland, and there is plenty of evidence that they were trading widely. For example, quarried stone found only on the island of Rum was used in buildings on the mainland and on other islands of the Inner Hebrides. This maritime trading link appears to have extended to Scandinavia from the time of the earliest settlements.[2]

We know surprisingly little about the megalithic people of the British Isles, because they had no system of writing that we can still read. So we have no formal information about their culture, such as we find with later groups such as the Sumerians and the ancient Egyptians. Archaeologists call them simply the 'Grooved Ware People' after the grooved designs that they etched into their clay pots. However, they did leave behind them a system of symbols that amounts to proto-writing, some of which can be understood because of its astronomical references.

Most people are aware of the splendid stone circles that they erected, but they also constructed the earliest surviving stone buildings in the world, structures typically a thousand years older than the cities of Sumer. The perceived quality of the stonework varied considerably from apparently unworked upright slabs to beautifully engineered vaulted chambers such as Maes Howe in Orkney, whose standard of construction has been described as 'one of the supreme achievements of Neolithic Europe'.[3] Until relatively recently these buildings were thought to be younger than Middle Eastern structures, but a new chronology has now been established based on calibrated radio-carbon dating.[4] This has raised questions about the people who built the structures. As archaeologist Dr Euan Mackie comments:

> If the European megaliths, and even the Maltese temples, are older than the oldest towns then it is difficult to see how urban societies could have played any significant part in the great social processes which were under way in Atlantic Europe between 4500 and 2500 BC . . . there must have been specialised, proto-urban or urban stratified societies in existence before the earliest megaliths appeared.[5]

2 Wickham-Jones, CR: *Scotland's First Settlers*
3 Henshall, AS: 'The Chambered Cairns', in *The Prehistory of Orkney*, Edinburgh University Press, 1993
4 Renfrew, C: *Before Civilisation*, Jonathan Cape, 1973
5 Mackie, E: *The Megalithic Builders*, Phaidon Press, 1977

The structures these people built included standing stones in various formations, tunnel mounds, earth mounds and ditches. They extend all the way along the coasts of Europe from southern Spain up as far as Scandinavia, also appearing on the northern Mediterranean coast as well as in southern Italy and in Malta. There is even evidence that these types of stone structure were built in parts of North Africa, including Egypt and in Israel. The whole of the British Isles is covered with them.

Tunnel graves are an early type of structure whose contents often lend themselves to carbon dating, and we know that the megalithic mounds of Brittany pre-date 4000 BCE.[6] There have always been stories about the effects of light in these tunnel mounds, but only recently has a new branch of archaeology appeared known as archaeoastronomy, which studies their astronomical alignments.

In 1901 Sir Norman Lockyer, who was at that time the editor of the prestigious scientific publication *Nature*, studied the temples of ancient Egypt and noticed that many were built so as to allow the Sun to shine on important parts of the interior on special days of the year. He surveyed a number of sites in Britain including Stonehenge and arrived at the conclusion that some of the alignments he observed formed part of a calendar which was based on the solstices and the equinoxes.[7] After some considerable time spent studying British monuments Lockyer published his suggestion that megalithic tombs were built primarily as observatories or even as houses for astronomer priests, and burials were later inserted by new immigrants who imitated them and built round barrows for the dead, without living chambers for the priests.[8] As always with new ideas that open up existing conventions, Lockyer was dismissed as making a 'wild assertion' by fellow scientists of the time.

An important megalithic settlement had been discovered half a century before Lockyer put forward his theory, when a severe storm washed away part of a sand dune on Orkney Mainland, and revealed ancient stone dwellings. The site, known as Skara Brae, was not properly excavated until archaeologist Professor Gordon Childe started a dig in 1920. What he found is generally accepted as the best-preserved prehistoric village in northern Europe. Skara Brae had been continuously occupied for approximately 600

[6] Renfrew, C: *Before Civilisation*
[7] Lockyer, N: *Stonehenge and other British Stone Monuments Astronomically Considered*, Macmillan, 1909
[8] Lockyer N: 'Some Questions for Archaeologists', *Nature*, vol. 73, 1906, p. 280

years from around 3100 to 2500 BCE, and appears to be quarters for trainee astronomer-priests – just as Lockyer had predicted.[9]

Most of the household furniture, as well as the houses, was made of stone rather than wood, which means that a great deal of material has survived. The built-in fireplaces, dressers, tables and stone beds have been preserved. The site consists of seven near-identical apartments and what may have been a workshop, or a brewery,[10] and it is thought likely that there were more apartments that have been eroded into the sea.

It is known that there was no supply of wood to burn, so firewood had to be brought in by boat from the Scottish mainland. It is also evident from the study of bones that meat was shipped in, pre-butchered, which indicates that the inhabitants were considered to be important people who deserved to be carefully looked after.[11]

Euan Mackie believes that a class of magi must have developed out of this Orcadian society established by the Grooved Ware People:

A quite different kind of stratified Neolithic society can be postulated . . . in which a small elite class of professional priests, wise men and rulers were supported with tribute and taxes by a predominantly rural peasant population. Such a society could have achieved all that Thom has suggested it did because the members of the elite would have been free from the need to obtain their own food and build their own dwellings and could have devoted their entire time to religious, scientific or other intellectual pursuits . . . the process of transforming primitive Neolithic peasant communities into more advanced, stratified societies with skilled leaders and wise men as well as other specialists, may well have begun much earlier. If our hypothesis of a Religious Revolution is approximately correct it began with the progressively wider establishment of professional priesthoods in early Neolithic times, from about 4500 BC.[12]

This vision implies the existence of some type of formal training for these specialists. It is impossible to prove but, given the concentration of

[9] Mackie, E: *The Megalithic Builders*
[10] Dinely, M, 'The First Orkney Brewery', Orkney Science Festival, 2001
[11] Mackie, E: *The Megalithic Builders*
[12] Mackie, E: *The Megalithic Builders.*

Megalithic structures across Orkney, it seems reasonable to suppose that Skara Brae might have been a kind of Neolithic university.

THE RIDDLE OF THE MEGALITHIC YARD

No archaeologist would today deny that many megalithic sites are built with alignments to the solstices and equinoxes as well as towards key rising and setting points of the Moon and other heavenly bodies. The man who, almost single-handedly, founded archaeoastronomy as a true science was Alexander Thom, a distinguished professor of engineering at Oxford University. Thom, who spent fifty years of his life surveying and studying megalithic sites, made one of the most astounding breakthroughs in the field of archaeology.

Thom first become interested in megalithic structures as a young man in his native Scotland. He began his surveying work because he suspected that the sites did have astronomical alignments. His painstaking measurement of site after site slowly produced data that indicated that these prehistoric builders, from the islands off northern Scotland right down to Brittany in France, had shared a standard unit of measurement. It was surprising enough that they were so well organised as to agree an international standard unit, but the sheer precision with which the unit had been applied was truly amazing. The Megalithic Yard, as Thom called it, was clarified over the years he spent surveying, and eventually he defined it as being equal to 0.82966 metres.[13]

The belief amongst archaeologists at the time was that the inhabitants of the British Isles in the Neolithic period were a backward people, and the idea that they might have used mathematics or had a precise standard unit of measurement was thought to be ridiculous. Thom's work was initially ignored by the archaeological establishment, but thanks to an objective study by statisticians it became accepted among numerate scientists that a system of measurement was in use over large expanses of prehistoric Europe. However, it is still ignored by some less well informed archaeologists, who proffer ludicrous notions such as the idea that this highly respected professor of engineering had fooled himself by identifying nothing more than the average pace of a megalithic builder. Had these critics taken the time to check their supposed counter-

[13] Thom, A: *Megalithic Sites in Britain,* Oxford University Press, 1967

explanation by experiment they would have realised that they were talking nonsense.

The existence of an ancient standard unit of length demonstrates that a shared mathematics was in use over a remarkably large geographical range. Professor Thom was convinced that he had found a genuine mathematical artefact in the Megalithic Yard, but he died without ever understanding how on earth these people had been able to reproduce such a precise measurement. We have been able to solve this riddle because we came to it from a very unexpected direction. Our interest was a 2,200-year-old Jewish text found amongst the Dead Sea Scrolls in the ancient settlement known as Qumran, and we could never have guessed how this would lead us to the origin of the Megalithic Yard.

The Book of Enoch, popular in the first couple of centuries of the Christian era, soon became completely lost and was not found again until Scottish Freemason James Bruce went in search of it during the eighteenth century. He found what he was looking for, hidden away in Ethiopia, and when he translated it people were sure that this must be a heavily corrupted version, as it contained very strange material, including a whole section on incomprehensible astronomy.

The finding of several copies of this ancient text among the Dead Sea Scrolls demonstrated that Bruce had found an entirely authentic version. In the section entitled 'The Book of the Heavenly Luminaries' the reader is told how the early biblical hero Enoch was taken on a journey northwards to be shown the secrets of astronomy. From the dates of the year given and the length of daylight seen, it is possible to reconstruct the latitude at which the observer must have been standing. In *Uriel's Machine* we explained how this information led us to believe that the descriptions attributed to Enoch refer to a journey to the megalithic structures at Stonehenge in England and Newgrange in Ireland.

We also knew that Jewish tradition places Enoch over five thousand years ago, when these megalithic sites were active. This analysis sounded strange to some people because they view history as discreet units, separated by time and geography. The *Catholic Herald* informed its readers in very colourful language that this was 'bogus' research. Its correspondent Damian Thompson told us we were wrong. When we asked him why, he had to admit that he did not understand the calculations – but we had to be wrong because our conclusions sounded strange.

But we were not alone. We were later to find out that someone else, working independently of us, had also arrived at a broadly similar conclusion about the travels of Enoch. Robin Heath, a scientist, academic and writer, had been interested in tracing the development of civilisation from western Europe to the so-called first civilisations of the Middle East. His research, conducted over many years, led him to conclude that the megalithic culture of western Europe was an important influence on the development of civilisation in the Middle East. In his own words:

> *Despite the research of many people indicating that the megalith builders were practising high astronomy and geometry before 3000 BC, it still remains true that this culture is wholly undervalued as a vital component of our history.*[14]

Robin Heath is the son of the late Professor AE Heath of Oxford University. Prof. Heath helped set up the Rationalist Press Association, which encouraged research into the origins of scientific thought. As a child Robin Heath met Prof. Alexander Thom, who also worked at Oxford University and was a friend of his father. Robin became fascinated by Thom's work on megalithic measurement systems, and when he retired as Head of Department at a South Wales Technical Institute he decided to look more closely at the megalithic culture which Alexander Thom had discussed with him so many years before.

In particular Heath was interested in investigating if there were common links to be found between the measurement systems of ancient cultures. As he said:

> *The megalithic culture was until quite recently never considered to be other than an isolated phenomenon, a cultural oddity, and any possible links with other cultures were vehemently denied.*[15]

In particular he looked at the units of length used by the Egyptian and Sumerian cultures and used statistical tests to see if they were related to the Megalithic Yard. Making use of Thom's highly accurate survey of Stonehenge, he noticed overlaps between Egyptian units of measurement – the royal cubit and the pharaonic inch – the Sumerian foot and the Megalithic Yard, a unit used throughout Western Europe. He comments on what he found:

[14] Heath, R: *Sun, Moon and Stonehenge. Proof of High Culture in Ancient Britain*, Bluestone Press, 1998
[15] Heath, R: *Sun, Moon and Stonehenge. Proof of High Culture in Ancient Britain*

What we had no right to expect was that the [pharaonic] inch and the Megalithic yard are connected, through the [Sumerian] foot one might say, thus apparently linking Egyptian culture with the Stonehenge 'Wessex' culture.

This observation led him to further observe that the geometry of the henge platform at Stonehenge, a structure known to have been built by the Grooved Ware People, used area measurement systems, based on an ancient Egyptian unit of area called the aroura and the modern acre, which had also been used in building the Great Pyramids at Giza. He said of this:

Here we have a physical artefact representing historically validated measurement techniques, which are taken to be Egyptian in origin.

He went on to add that this interpretation had to be called into question, as the ditch and henge at Stonehenge pre-dated the Great Pyramids by hundreds of years.[16]

As Health hunted for a viable alternative explanation for this overlap of measurement systems he had noticed the length-of-day remarks in the Book of Enoch and also Enoch's comments about being taken to the far north. In Heath's own words:

Who says that there are no accounts of the European megalithic culture and its astronomy in the Middle East cultural record?[17]

Analysing the data on length of day he concluded:

It appears that Enoch's observations were taken at or very near the latitude of Stonehenge. The day/night ratio gradient is the same as for Stonehenge, and if the definition of 'night' was taken to be half hour different from sunrise/set, such as the time the first stars became visible, then the graph for Enoch's observations and for Stonehenge would exactly coincide. Enoch's writings, long assumed to contain only Jewish and/or Middle Eastern wisdom, suggest an influence from 'a great and glorious device' found at a latitude near to that of Stonehenge.[18]

[16] Heath, R: *Sun, Moon and Stonehenge. Proof of High Culture in Ancient Britain*
[17] Heath, R: *Sun, Moon and Stonehenge. Proof of High Culture in Ancient Britain*
[18] Heath, R: *Sun, Moon and Stonehenge. Proof of High Culture in Ancient Britain*

Robert e-mailed Robin Heath and asked him his views on the possibility of Enoch visiting Newgrange as well as Stonehenge. He wrote back saying:

my interest with Enoch was astronomy vis à vis the calendar. During some interminable and unutterably boring maths lecture, whilst my lads were doing an examination, I sketched out a BASIC program to 'do' the latitude from his data. Enoch kindly gives us four repeats of each quarter of the sine wave[19] that he is fumbling with, and I thought that this was reasonably good proof that the data would fit accurately to the original.

There are problems with the data. When is 'night' defined? It seemed a little post modern to ascribe 20 minutes after lighting up times, à la Highway Code, and being a bit of a dab hand at astronomy, I decided to plumb for half an hour after sunset and before dawn as a definition of 'night'. I ran the program that night at home, sometime in 1988, debugged it for about an hour and came up with the revelation that Enoch wasn't in the Middle East. I later ran the problem to my Navigation III students and they concluded that Enoch was observing through portals somewhere between 50 and 55 degrees, presumably north because the days lengthen in the spring time he describes, and the Sun, of course, 'mounts up' at midsummer.[20]

In *Uriel's Machine* we had concluded that the Book of Enoch was describing a location that fitted the range of latitudes occupied by the Grooved Ware People, who had built astronomically aligned megalithic structures such as the rings of Brodgar and Stenness, Maes Howe and Callanish in the north of Scotland, Newgrange, Knowth and Dowth in the Boyne Valley of Ireland, Barcliod yr Grawes and Bryn Celli Ddu in north-west Wales, and Stonehenge, Avebury, Silbury Hill and Durrington Walls in the south of England. We had concluded that it was more than just a coincidence that the Book of the Heavenly Luminaries is a dissertation on

---

[19] The length of daylight at any particular latitude varies in a predictable pattern because of the way the Earth's axis is tilted relative to the Sun's rays. The way in which the day lengthens and shortens can be written down in a mathematical formula called a Sine wave. This knowledge and the formula which can be deduced from measurements of the time of daylight underlay Heath's calculations.

[20] Robin Heath: private communication, 2001

ancient astronomy and the latitudes that Enoch inadvertently describes within it coincide with the world's earliest known astronomical observatories.[21]

But how do our investigations into the ancient Jewish document known as the Book of Enoch lead us to solve the riddle of the Megalithic Yard? In the end we found that the unit was derived from observing three factors: the spin of the Earth on its axis, the orbit of the Earth around the Sun, and the mass of the planet. Whilst these are obviously complex matters, we found that anyone can reproduce a Megalithic Yard in one day using astronomical observation, a length of rope, two rods, a piece of twine and a stone with a hole in its centre. A full description of the technique for making your own Megalithic Yard can be found in Appendix 1.

When we announced that we had rediscovered the method of creating the Megalithic Yard some people thought we were mad. Indeed, one highly respected professor of astronomy who was there when we presented our findings at the Orkney Science Festival admitted that he put us down as being mad – until he checked our findings. Then Professor Archie Roy described our results on the origins of the Megalithic Yard as 'true science', adding that the discovery 'opened up a new chapter in our understanding of Megalithic Man'.

THE CRYSTAL PALACE

There are many impressive megalithic structures in the Boyne Valley of Ireland, but one is particularly large. Newgrange is a 280,000-ton structure that started to be built around 3500 BCE – more than a thousand years before the Egyptians cleared the sands of the Giza Plateau for the Great Pyramid of Kufu and over two and a half thousand years before Hiram's team of builders laid the foundation stone of King Solomon's Temple. The mound is made of river-rolled granite stones and the east-facing wall is faced with gleaming white quartz. The design of this building is unique, and yet it perfectly fits the building described in the Book of Enoch and is at a location that corresponds with the day and night data recorded in the book.

When we first visited Newgrange together, we missed a turning and ended up stopping by the roadside to look across the bright curve of the

---

[21] Knight, C & Lomas, R: *Uriel's Machine*, Arrow, 1999

River Boyne, towards the sparkling white sunlit frontage. The effect was nothing less than stunning. Had we not known what we were looking at it could have been taken as an ultra-modern building, having all the scale and dramatic presence of a Le Corbusier creation. The Book of Enoch describes a night visit to a large, impressive structure at this latitude which was lit by a string of burning torches:

> And I went in till I drew nigh to a wall which is built of crystals and surrounded by tongues of fire: and it began to affrighten me. And I went into the tongues of fire and drew nigh to a large house which was built of crystals: and the walls of the house were like a tessellated floor of crystals.

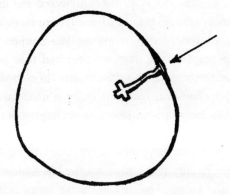

Plan of Newgrange showing how it was designed to allow the light of Venus to enter the inner chamber at the winter solstice.

In plan view the structure is made up of a series of sections of parabolas which make it almost circular, with a diameter of around a hundred metres. There are a number of carefully worked stones along a tunnel nineteen metres long leading from the entrance in the middle of the white wall to a chamber deep inside the mound. In front of the entrance stands an enormous stone which is carved with interlacing spirals, jagged V-shaped series of lines and nests of diamond lozenge figures. These are typical Grooved Ware symbols, but interestingly they can also be found in pre-dynastic Egyptian artefacts.

As we reported in *Uriel's Machine* we came to the conclusion that the spiral symbol represents a quarter of a year, it represents the path of the Sun over a transition from one solstice to the next equinox. The double spiral is the shape you get if you set up a vertical marker and put a dot on the point of the shadow at midday from June to December. Join the dots together and you get the double spiral, the symbol carved into the middle of the entrance stone at Newgrange, a symbol that occurs on many Grooved Ware sites in western Europe.

We knew that the symbol was widely used both on marker stones and on pottery, but we were fascinated to think that whereas we could find examples of pre-dynastic Egyptian pottery using Grooved Ware symbols, nobody has found any Egyptian artefacts in Britain. The indication is that ideas developed by the Grooved Ware People in and around the British Isles may have been introduced into Egypt before the establishment of the first dynasty and the beginnings of recorded history.

We also realised that the use of spiral symbols at Newgrange makes sense, because the structure is a tunnel mound that has a central chamber accessed via an entrance tunnel aligned to a special sunrise. On the morning of the winter solstice, when the sun rises as far south as it ever goes, its light penetrates the narrow tunnel with its rising double curve, to emerge as a tight beam that spills an intense glow as it strikes the rear wall of the inner chamber. That has to be a deliberate design feature of the building, because a special slot was cut above the entrance to let the light in.

The narrow tunnel into the mound is lined with enormous slabs of solid rock. There were twenty-two stones on the left-hand side of the tunnel as we walked in, and twenty-one stones on the other side of the passage for us to count as we came back out. The chamber is in the form of a cross, and in each of the arms is a beautifully worked stone basin, except that the right-hand alcove also has an extra smaller basin standing inside the larger one. There are two depressions in this small basin.

Newgrange was built by a group of people who were good enough farmers to be able to feed the specialist group of builders who engineered this massive structure. Indeed, when the mound was tidied up some of the turf was tested and it was discovered that it came from fields that once grew spelt (an early type of grain crop) but were then left to revert to a wild state, suggesting early use of crop rotation.[22]

The builders of Newgrange organised a significant workforce to create this structure, which is a mound 250 feet in diameter. The workers showed sufficient skill to construct a corbelled roof chamber and align an

[22] O'Kelly, Michael J: *Newgrange, Archaeology, Art and Legend*, Thames and Hudson, 1982

eighty-foot-long passage in such a way that it lies exactly along the line of the rising Sun at the winter solstice. This construction alone is a splendid achievement, but there are two other mounds of similar size and magnificence from the same period and in the same part of the Boyne Valley, all within sight of each other. The mound at Knowth has now been excavated by Professor George Eogan, and is partially open to the public, but the other passage mound at Dowth has yet to be excavated.

We calculated that the people who built these structures on the banks of the river Boyne invested a staggering two million man-hours in construction time, demonstrating that more than five and a half thousand years ago they must have lived in a complex society nearly a thousand years before the city states of Sumer and Egypt began.[23] However, there is an important aspect of Newgrange that had been missed by the experts involved with the excavations. It was designed to capture the light of Venus once every eight years.

During a visit to Newgrange the guide switched on a spotlight erected in the tunnel to imitate the Sun's rays as they enter at dawn on the winter solstice. We noticed at once that the beam was about three feet off centre to the right, and we asked the guide why these expert megalithic builders had caused it to happen that way. The answer was not satisfactory. It stated that the inaccuracy was the result of the 'precession of the equinoxes', and that it would have been straight five and a half thousand years ago when the small long-term tilt of the Earth was some 70° different. We pointed out that the precession of the equinoxes was a wobble of the planet on its axis which caused the stars to appear to rotate in a cycle that takes more than twenty-five millennia. This could have no effect on the angle of the Sun's rays entering this chamber at dawn. The movement of the Sun's declination is only likely to be affected by the much slower precession of the ecliptic, the plane of the Earth's orbit about the Sun. The period of this movement is three times longer than the precession of the equinoxes, and it has not moved significantly since Newgrange was built. We conclude that the alignment was deliberate rather than the result of a change in the Earth's relationship with the Sun. Either the misalignment was a design fault, or the angle of the solstice sunbeam was not their primary concern.

It might never have occurred to us to think about Venus if not for the fact that Robert spent several years investigating a megalithic site called

[23] Knight, C & Lomas, R: *Uriel's Machine, The Ancient Origins of Science*

Bryn Celli Ddu, some fifty miles from the mouth of the river Boyne across the Irish sea on Anglesey. His prolonged study revealed that this small structure, dating from the same period as Newgrange, provided a large number of astronomical alignments which were clearly intentional. These included:

1   Sight Lines which have been chosen to maximise Moon observations and which yield sufficient information to predict eclipses.

2   The alignment of the passage and its cup marking sequences which highlight the equinoxes and the summer solstice.

3   A shadow gauge which indicates where you are in the solar year at any time.

4   An internal pillar and an aligned lightbox (a slot in the wall of the chamber which allows light to enter) which are positioned to accurately measure the Venus cycle and mark the winter solstice.

The pillar and lightbox had been aligned before the chamber was built. The base of the lightbox, the part which throws the dagger of light onto the pillar, was formed by the upper edge of the large slab which makes up the southerly wall of the chamber. First the pillar was erected and then the stone positioned to the south of it. A notch was cut in the top right-hand side of the slab and the stone's position was adjusted until the shadow of this notch fell onto the pillar when the Sun was in the southwest.

Now the height of the Sun in the sky varies with the seasons. In summer the Sun is high in the sky whilst during the winter it is much lower. This means that the higher the Sun is in the sky, the lower down the pillar its shadow would fall. The position of the pillar and slab were adjusted until the shadow of the notch just reached the top of the pillar when the Sun was at its lower position in the sky. This occurs at midwinter, at the time of the winter solstice. This could easily have been set up so that the shadow fell on the pillar at 12 noon when the Sun was at its highest point, but the ancient designers of this structure had something else in mind. The slab and pillar are set so the light of the Sun falls on the pillar when the Sun is three hours passed its highest point.

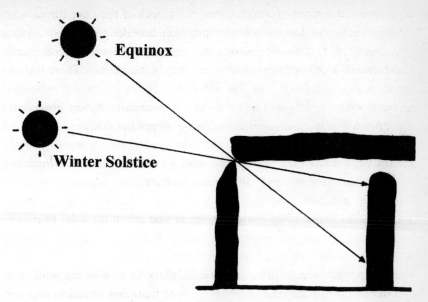

The 'light slot' at the Megalithic observatory now known as Bryn Celli Ddu on Anglesey which shows how it was designed to give a calendar reading. The slot is positioned to allow a narrow, horizontal beam of sunlight to enter and strike a pillar inside the chamber. This pillar was marked to show the range of the sun's maximum daily height in the sky between the winter solstice and the equinox so that the priest concerned just had to read the position of the bar of light to know the date.

Once the positions of the pillar and south slab were set, the chamber was constructed around the pillar. The existing position was chosen so that two hours after sunset Venus is in the same part of the sky that the setting winter Sun has vacated, and so the light of Venus could now also cast a shadow on the pillar. The positions of first the Sun and then the Venus shadow make it possible to measure the exact position of Venus in the evening sky. Now this was an important measurement for these ancient astronomers, because when viewed from Earth, the planet Venus is the most accurate indicator of the time of year available in the solar system. Every eight years it marks a point when the solar calendar, the lunar calendar and the sidereal calendar all coincide to within a few minutes. After exactly forty years, when Venus completes five of its eight-year cycles, it synchronises to within fractions of a second, providing a calendar and clock that was used to set the time of day until the 1950s when even more accurate atomic clocks were invented.

Put simply: Venus is the metronome of our world. Understand its

41

movements and you can understand such vital functions as the seasons and the tides. It makes you master of your environment both in terms of farming and seamanship, and thereby ensures that you eat well and trade efficiently. In many ways it is the centrepiece of civilisation.

Against the background of the zodiac Venus completes a five-pointed star shape every eight years and returns to its precise starting place after forty years. Whilst studying this Anglesey observatory Robert developed an analytical procedure to predict the times Venus should appear on the pillar of Bryn Celli Ddu. His predictions were accurate when tested by observation, so he next applied the same methodology to Newgrange. His calculations matched closely the physical measurements recorded by Dr Tom Ray, who first studied the alignment of the light box to the rising solstice Sun, and when Ray's temperature and pressure adjustments were taken into consideration they matched exactly.[24]

Venus appears as a morning star around the time of winter solstice four years out of every eight (the other four years it appears as an evening star following the setting Sun down). Some years it is brighter than others, and its closeness to the Sun varies throughout the cycle. Here is the pattern of Venus at the time of the winter solstice.

Year	Position	Brightness	Rising time before Sun	Declination
1	morning	99.5%	24 min.	-23:16
2	morning	36%	254 min.	-13:02
3	evening	86%		
4	morning	91%	126 min.	-20:07
5	evening	17.5%		
6	evening	97.5%		
7	morning	72.3%	224 min.	-15:11
8	evening	63.2%		

This table shows the basic eight-year cycle of Venus. The first column shows the year of the cycle. The next column shows whether Venus is appearing as the morning or the evening star. In years one, two, four and seven, Venus

[24] Ray, TH: An Investigation of the Solar Alignment of Newgrange, *Nature*, vol. 337, no. 26, 345–346, Jan. 1989

is a morning star rising before the Sun. On the other four years of the cycle it is an evening star, following the Sun down. Column three describes the brightness of Venus – how bright it appears in the sky depends on where it is relative to the Sun, the angle of reflection controlling how much light it can reflect towards the Earth. Its brightness is shown as a percentage of the maximum possible brightness it can ever achieve. Column four gives the time before sunrise that Venus appears in the eastern sky. Column five gives the declination of Venus at those times when it is a morning star at the winter solstice. This cycle repeats closely every eight years and repeats exactly every forty years. A new cycle started in the year 1 CE and another will begin in the year 2009 CE.

We knew that there were four possible occasions throughout the eight-year cycle when the light of Venus rose before the Sun during the winter solstice at Newgrange. However, it is not at the same distance from the Sun in each of the morning star phases, as the table of brightness and declination shows. Only on one of these occasions does Venus pass across the aperture of the Newgrange dormer slot, and it turns out that on this occasion it is at its brightest. On this morning, exactly 24 minutes before sunlight enters the chamber, the light of the Sun bounces off the surface of the planet Venus and enters the chamber at Newgrange as a collimated beam through the dormer. For about fifteen minutes the chamber will be brightly illuminated by the light of a full Venus, the third brightest object in the sky, and the light of Venus will be in the centre of the chamber. As Venus first appears its light will be red, as the bright light of the planet will be refracted by its low position on the horizon. This light will then turn steely blue-white as the planet rises.

On all the other occasions Venus is rising too far to the north for its light to enter the carefully designed dormer slot at Newgrange. However, when it does enter the slot and travel up the long collimated tunnel it will appear like the beam of a searchlight. Even in the open countryside the light from Venus is so strong that it will cast a discernible shadow on a moonless night, and it can often be seen in broad daylight, even when it is close to the Sun, which blinds out the light from the stars and other planets.

The effect at those prehistoric winter solstices must have been dramatic. The chamber is pitch-black, then as the brilliance of Venus makes one of its eight-year penetrations the light creates an unearthly glow, slowly turning from fiery red to become almost as bright as daylight but without colour. Then as the Sun rises some quarter of an hour later the cold, monochrome light dissolves into golden sunlight before returning to near total darkness again. Anyone in that chamber before dawn on every eighth winter solstice would have every reason to believe that they were communing with the gods.

Once we realised that the rising Venus was fundamental to Newgrange we noticed that the lintel over the lightbox has eight symbols carved into it. Each of these is a rectangle with a times cross within it, which has generally been identified as signifying 'one year' by representing the solstice rising and setting points. These eight one-year symbols could only have been carved here to announce to those ancient magi capable of reading this proto-writing that a special event happened inside the chamber once every eight years. If only we could understand more of the inscriptions used by the Grooved Ware People we strongly suspect that they would tell us that a god enters through this slot.

VENUS AND RESURRECTION

There were two further aspects of these megalithic structures of the Boyne Valley that were relevant to our current investigation. First, there is a strong sexual content to the artefacts found here, including beautifully carved stone phalluses. It is known from later writing, by Tacitus and other Roman authors, that sexual festivals were held in public by the much later Celtic people who are likely to have inherited their ancient traditions from the Grooved Ware People. The other, more speculative thought that we had considered in relation to Newgrange is the idea that the chambers may have been used for a ritual that was believed to have powers of reincarnation.

Chris had been struck by just how much the tunnel and the three-part chamber in the centre of this domed mount is reminiscent of the reproductive organs of a human female. We knew that many ancient people thought of the cycle of the seasons as the gods in heaven fertilising the Earth to give birth to cattle and plants. Could the shaft of light entering the uppermost of the double entrance have been viewed as a god's phallus penetrating this spectacular pudenda of the Earth, the life-bringing seed of heaven spilling down into this womb-chamber and all within it? We thought this seemed entirely likely for a number of reasons, particularly the fact that Tacitus reported that the Celts enjoyed a spring sexual festival, and then their women gave birth at the winter solstice.

We then considered how several cultures, including the Jews, believed that people from their own prehistory used to live for periods way beyond normal lifespans. It is almost certain that the character known as Enoch is a composite made up of distant cultural memories that belong to the groups of people who long pre-dated the emergence of the Hebrew people. As such his life cannot be dated in an historical way, but it is the dates ascribed to such mythical figures that we think are important. We found that there is indeed an accepted dating for Enoch's time on Earth in Jewish lore. A leading biblical scholar of the early twentieth century calls him 'A son of Jared, and father of Methuselah. He was born, by ordinary Hebrew computation, about B.C. 3382'.[25] The Old Testament is known to have been woven together from at least three separate traditions, and this one comes from the 'priestly tradition' usually known simply as 'P'. Enoch is said to have lived on Earth for 365 years before being 'trans-lated' to heaven in 3017 BCE as a living man. Such a dating is surprisingly early, being nearly one and a half millennia before Abraham and two thousand years before Moses. However, it is all the more interesting to us because it places Enoch on Earth at exactly the time that Newgrange was designed and built.

At first view, this dating does not correspond with the fact that the Old Testament places Enoch before the Flood – he was Noah's great-grand-father. Whilst our own investigations have shown that there was a global flood in the 8th millennium BCE,[26] the authors of the books of the Old Testament considered that Noah's flood had occurred around 2400 BCE, so the chronology of Enoch is consistent within Hebrew myth.

A further interesting point regarding Enoch is the meaning of his name. Enoch is said to translate into English as 'initiated' – suggesting that he had undergone some ritual that gave him secret information.[27] This is exactly what appears to be described in the Book of Enoch, when Uriel explains the workings of astronomy to the confused man from the Middle East.

From all of the available evidence we could imagine a belief that when a king or other major dignitary died their remains were kept in whole, or in part, and taken into the chamber on the day before the winter solstice.

[25] Hunter, RH: *Cassell's Concise Bible Dictionary*, Cassell & Co. Ltd, 1996
[26] Knight, C & Lomas, R: *Uriel's Machine. The Ancient Origins of Science*
[27] Hunter, RH: *Cassell's Concise Bible Dictionary*

Alongside this a woman, previously inseminated at the festival held at the vernal equinox and now heavily pregnant, was also taken into the chamber with the remains of the deceased to await the coming of the light of Venus. The ghostly light in the chamber would have been deemed to reincarnate the spirits of the dead within the birthing infant. Minutes later the warm glow of the life-giving Sun would celebrate the resurrection of the deceased person in their new form as a child.

Maybe the bowls found in the alcoves of the chamber were to contain the ashes, bones or other remnants of the dead as they awaited the light of resurrection.

Such a ritual process would have been believed to provide the community with a flow of reincarnated souls, allowing them to accept that their leaders were transcending the power of death over their brutally short lives. Certain key individuals could have been thought to be immortal through this ability to return with their knowledge of science to lead their people through adversity. They could have taken the name of the dead person and inherited their worldly goods. Their lives could have been structured as a continuation of the previous person's existence.

From our own experiences we know that as a child grows to adulthood, and on into middle age, accounts of events that are told to us as small children become impossible to separate from our first-hand experiences. We often become convinced that the memory we have comes from experiencing an event, rather than being told about it. We can imagine how, through repeated instruction from the priest and at their mother's knee, a 'reincarnated' individual could come to believe that they could remember their previous existence. Remember too that it is what Professor Robert Thouless described as a standard technique of religious indoctrination to bring a young person 'to believe in a prescribed religion and the otherwise preposterous myths that go with it'.[28]

We discovered a further ground for belief in our theory of reincarnation when we inspected the carvings within the chamber. There is a large triple spiral motif cut into the great stone at the entrance to Newgrange and another at a hidden part of the inner chamber where only the reflected light of Venus can strike. There is no other symbol near to it. We already knew that a single spiral is drawn by the Sun's movement every three

[28] Thouless, Robert H: *An Introduction to the Psychology of Religion*, Cambridge Univ. Press, Cambridge, 1971

months, so we reasoned that a symbol made up of three spirals must equal nine months. And nine months is the human gestation period. So the triple spiral symbol placed at such a key place within the chamber could well be written evidence that it was a birthing chamber, and its Venus alignment suggested to us that our resurrection theory might well be right.

It is certainly true that virtually every civilisation after the Grooved Ware People has associated Venus with love, sex and reproduction. But Venus is much more than a symbol of birth and rebirth.

CONCLUSIONS

Robin Heath, working independently of us, arrived at a similar conclusion, that the megalithic culture of western Europe was an important influence on the development of civilisation in the Middle East.

The central themes of the Grooved Ware People are as follows:

- They were the first people to develop a technology for building in stone.

- They measured and recorded the movements of the Sun.

- They knew of the importance of the rising and setting of the planet Venus.

- They celebrated the equinoxes and the summer and winter solstices.

- They are the first people known to have studied the science of astronomy.

- They probably held a belief in the resurrection of the dead, associated with Venus.

The rising Venus was fundamental to the Grooved Ware People who lived around the Irish Sea 5,500 years ago. And these people developed a proto-writing to record the special dawn-rising Venus event that happened inside the chamber once every eight years. We have come to believe that the Grooved Ware People associated Venus with love, sex and reproduction. They also developed a standard unit of measure, so demonstrating the use of a shared mathematics over a large geographical area extending from the islands off northern Scotland to the Breton coast of western France.

Chapter Three

THE LIGHT OF SECRET KNOWLEDGE

THE KNIGHTS OF SOLOMON'S TEMPLE

The ideas we had uncovered about the Grooved Ware People are such a close fit to the ideas that are central to Freemasonry that it would not be unreasonable to anticipate some kind of link between the two. However, we had only come to consider the Grooved Ware People because we had originally worked backwards to them. Now we set ourselves the task to reverse-engineer our original work and see if the case stands up to heavier scrutiny.

Our original investigations had established a route backwards from Freemasonry through the medieval order of the Knights Templar, back to Jerusalem at the time of Christ and back again to the formation of Judaism. At first view it might seem improbable that the early Jews were influenced by the Neolithic peoples of Western Europe who pre-dated them by around two thousand years, but we were to find some intriguing potential connections. We have found that there is a connection between the ancient Jewish text known as the Book of Enoch and the astronomically aligned sites of Neolithic Britain. And this conclusion has been independently arrived at by scientist Dr Robin Heath.

Then we came across a statement on the website (http://www.geo cities.com/hiberi/yair.html) of an Israeli historical investigator, Yair Davidy, which we found totally riveting:

Megalithic monuments and dolmens were once found throughout

*the Land of Israel although many have been destroyed and most of
those remaining are in the Golan and east of the Jordan where
they are known to the Arabs as -Kubur Beni Israil-, i.e. 'Graves of
the Children of Israel'. Certain features of these monuments, such
as the existence of cupholes, are also found on similar structures in
Britain. The remains thus described are nearly identical in character
with those which are in England and Scotland.*

It appears that there are very good reasons to suspect that the strange rituals of Freemasonry have an origin back in prehistory at the megalithic sites of the British Isles and that the method of transmission was via the people of Israel.

The Jewish nation is said to have come into existence when Moses led 'his people' out of Egypt in search of the promised land. That promised land was Canaan and the traditional Jewish dating of the Exodus is 1447 BCE, which is long after the Grooved Ware People had disappeared from the British Isles. So if there is a connection between these two peoples, any beliefs and rituals would have had to be transmitted via an intermediary group. The two main candidates for such a linkage would be the ancient Egyptians or the Cannanites themselves, which includes the Jebusites who founded Jerusalem and the Phoenicians who occupied the coastal region.

We could see a chain forming. The Grooved Ware People appear to have founded these ideas centred on Venus, these ideas then moved to the eastern Mediterranean and were later taken up by the Jews before being recovered and 'resurrected' by the Knights Templar. The Templars were destroyed as an order at the beginning of the fourteenth century and Freemasonry formally emerged in the late sixteenth century, although there is good reason to believe that it was secretly functioning long before that date.

In *The Hiram Key* we established that the medieval warrior monks known as the 'The Poor Soldiers of Christ and the Temple of Solomon' were almost certainly the source of the rituals that became the basis of Freemasonry. The Knights Templar, to give them their shortened name, had been the richest and most powerful group in the known world from their formal establishment in 1128 until they were destroyed by the joint efforts of King Philip IV of France and Pope Clement V in 1307. Their demise came when the entire order was arrested on charges of heresy that included the accusation that they conducted strange rituals that were not Christian.

The order had been established by nine French knights who had been involved with the taking of Jerusalem during the First Crusade. Led by Hugues de Payen, the team set about secretly digging a network of tunnels beneath the ruins of the Jerusalem Temple that had been flattened over a thousand years earlier. The Muslims had built the magnificent 'Dome of the Rock' on the platform that once supported the Temple of the Jews, and the Knights Templar worked from the side in a section that was called Solomon's Stables.

In *The Hiram Key* we had speculated that there were links between the Knights Templar and the Freemasons, but at that time we did not have access to any early rituals which described this link. In 1999 we gave a talk about the origins of Freemasonry at the Assembly Rooms in Edinburgh. After the talk we were approached by an old gentleman, who introduced himself as a Mason. He carried with him an old, well polished, leather briefcase which he handled with great care.

'How much do you know about the early Masonic Templar rituals?' he asked.

We admitted we did not know very much, beyond the comments contained in the Masonic commentaries that we had found in the Mitrinovic Collection.

The old gentleman carefully opened his briefcase and took out two old and battered red-bound ritual books which he told us he had inherited from his grandfather, who had also been a Freemason.

'These are the rituals once worked by the Grand Mother Encampment of the High Knight Templars of Scotland' he said. 'They were once accepted by the Grand Council of Rites and the Sovereign Sanctuary of Scotland, but they've not been worked since the early nineteenth century. I've never worked them,' he added, with a tone of regret clear in his voice.

We were very interested to study the contents of these rituals and so we explained to this Brother how we were trying to reconstruct the whole story told by Masonic ritual in the form we have called *The Masonic Testament*. Once he knew what we were trying to do he allowed us to photocopy his treasured ritual books, and Robert immediately set about adding them to the *Web of Hiram*. We were interested to note that these books had been privately published by Hugh Murray, a printer whose shop was situated on the High Street of the town of Kilwinning in Ayrshire. This town we already knew was the home of one of the oldest lodges in Scotland, Lodge Mother Kilwinning.

As our database of rituals was growing, so was the detail in the story that we were reassembling.

It may be coincidence, but we found in the new sections of the *Masonic Testament* details that seemed to relate to the significance of the nine knights who founded the Templars. The ritual tells us that: [*Masonic Testament* 8:38]

> *King Solomon established the grade of Master Elect of Nine, and conferred it upon the nine companions.*

Did these nine Crusaders consider themselves to be the new 'Masters Elect of Nine'?

For nine years they lived in poverty, their only source of income the support they received from the new king of Jerusalem, Baldwin II. But as soon as their excavation ended they were suddenly massively rich, and very quickly the rumours of strange rituals started to circulate. We needed to find out what it was that they had found.

The answer came from one of the documents found at Qumran on the banks of the Dead Sea in 1947. The Copper Scroll is a long sheet of metal with stamped characters that was written some thirty years after the death of Jesus Christ. It lists sixty-one locations where precious items were buried at the outset of the Jewish war against the Romans. Dead Sea Scroll scholar John Allegro said of it:

> *The Copper Scroll and its copy (or copies) were intended to tell the Jewish survivors of the war then raging where this sacred material lay buried, so that if any should be found, it would never be desecrated by profane use. It would also act as a guide to the recovery of the treasure, should it be needed to carry on the war.*[1]

This scroll is a virtual treasure map and states that a second copy, with more details, was buried under the Jerusalem Temple. The passage concerned reads:

> *In the Pit (Shîth) adjoining on the north, in a hole opening northwards, and buried at its mouth: a copy of this document, with an explanation and their measurements, and an inventory of each thing, and other things.*

---

[1] Allegro, JM: *The Treasure of the Copper Scroll*, Routledge & Kegan Paul Ltd, 1960

THE LIGHT OF SECRET KNOWLEDGE

It then goes on to list huge amounts of gold, silver, precious objects and at least twenty-four other scrolls hidden below the Temple. Directions such as the following are provided to each cache:

> *In the inner chamber of the twin pillars supporting the arch of the double gate, facing east, in the entrance, buried at three cubits, hidden there is a pitcher, in it, one scroll, under it forty-two talents.*

> *In the cistern which is nineteen cubits in front of the eastern gateway, in it are vessels, and in the hollow that is in it: ten talents.*

> *In the mouth of the spring of the Temple: vessels of silver and vessels of gold for the tithe and money, the whole being six hundred talents.*

When a British army team excavated under the temple in the 1860s, with shafts that descended eighty feet down, all they found were artefacts left by the Knights Templar. It seems extremely probable that the wealth of the Templar order can be explained by the recovery of these huge amounts of treasure, and the rituals they practised may well have been recorded on the scrolls they also found.

We also found evidence that the founding members of the Knights Templar came from families descended from the Jewish priests who escaped to Europe after the destruction of Jerusalem in 70 CE. When we started to assemble the material that makes up *The Masonic Testament* we found that the higher rituals of Freemasonry confirm that these knights believed they could trace their lineage back to the time of the building of King Solomon's Temple two thousand years earlier and back again to the time of Moses. [*Masonic Testament* 6: 10–11]

> *Moses created Princes of the Tabernacle. The especial duties of a Prince of the Tabernacle were to labour incessantly for the glory of God, the honour of his country, and the happiness of his brethren; and to offer up thanks and prayers to the Deity in lieu of sacrifices of flesh and blood.*

It goes on to say that the High Priests were Eleazar and Isthamar, the sons of Aaron, and thereafter all Princes of the Tabernacle were Levites, the most senior form of Jewish priesthood. *The Masonic Testament* also tells us when the initiations took place: [*Masonic Testament* 6:12]

> *When the Pentagram, or Blazing star was to be seen in the east*
> *Moses called the Court together to initiate new Princes.*

A blazing star that is referred to as a pentagram can only be a reference to Venus, which has long been associated with the pentagram because of the planet's apparent movement around the Sun when observed from Earth.

We were also interested to read the Masonic material stating that Moses' brother Aaron died on the vernal equinox during the fortieth year of the wandering of the children of Israel. We doubt that any modern Freemason will be aware that Moses is claimed to have created his initiates when Venus was in the east, exactly as every Masonic Master Mason is raised today.

Early in the twentieth century, Masonic researcher JSM Ward noted that ritual records how these 'Princes of Jerusalem' were involved with building the next two temples in Jerusalem, and when the Romans destroyed Jerusalem and its Temple in 70 CE a number of them managed to escape to locations across Europe. It was from these families that the men who founded the Knights Templar came.[2] This was a period we needed to know more about, and fortunately more clues had come our way.

Towards the end of 1999 we gave a talk at Liverpool Masonic Hall and afterwards stayed for a meal, known as a 'Festive Board'. As we were leaving one brother came over to us, caught hold of Robert's arm, and drew him to one side.

'Here,' he said, 'take this. I think you'll find it useful.' He passed over a plain brown envelope which Robert could see contained a wad of photocopied sheets.

'What are these?' Robert asked.

'The rituals which were once used by a Masonic organisation known as the Royal and Select Masters of the Rite of Perfection,' came the reply. 'A group of us are trying to keep the traditions going, and we thought you would be interested in seeing the originals of the rituals you may have heard referred to as The Cryptic Rite.'

Robert thanked him, and afterwards in the car we looked through the

---

[2] Ward, JSM: *Freemasonry and the Ancient Gods*, Cassell & Co., 1928

papers we had been given. The rituals were said to have been worked at the Grand Lodge of Charleston, Virginia, in the eighteenth century. Rituals such as these were interesting to us for two reasons. First, as far as we know they are no longer in use, so the stories they tell are in danger of being lost; second, coming from an eighteenth-century American source, and one which is famous for its links with George Washington, the rituals could not have been censored by the Masons of contemporary London, who founded the United Grand Lodge of England. The rituals were soon scanned, and their stories fed into our fast-growing *Web of Hiram* and abstracted to add to *The Masonic Testament*.

The Masonic Testament now confirms that an order was formed by a Masonic group called the 'Princes of Jerusalem' in that city in the year 1118, and then tells us that at a later stage they took the name 'Princes of Jerusalem and Knights of the East and West' because their doctrines came from both directions.

In chapter 14 of *The Masonic Testament*, there is a ritual description that describes hereditary Mason-priests who were knights who marched into battle alongside the 'Christian princes' on the First Crusade: [*Masonic Testament* 15:3]

> *Finally, when the time arrived that the Christian Princes entered into a league to free the Holy Land from the oppression of the infidels, the good and virtuous Masons, anxious for so pious an undertaking, offered their services to the confederates, upon condition that they should have a chief of their own election, and whose name was only made known in the hour of battle; which being granted, they accepted their standard and departed.*

The fact that they allegedly had their own leader, whose identity would be secret until he was in the midst of battle, suggests that they were formed from the start as a self-contained group – an order. [*Masonic Testament* 15:6]

> *The valour and fortitude of these Elected Knights were such, that they were admired by, and took the lead of, all the Princes of Jerusalem, who, believing that their mysteries inspired them with courage and fidelity to the cause of virtue and religion, became desirous of being initiated. Upon being found worthy, their desires*

were complied with, and thus the Royal Art, meeting the approba-
tion of great and good men, became popular and honourable, and
was diffused to the worthy throughout these dominions, and thus
continued to spread, far and wide, through a succession of ages to
the present day.

The ritual here states that this previously unknown group of knights became
leaders of men, inspiring others to join them with their fighting ability and
their religion. This would certainly fit the description of the Knights Templar
who, from small beginnings as a band of nine middle-aged knights, became
an order of warrior monks who went on to become a living legend as the
mightiest, most influential and affluent group of their time.

JSM Ward also recorded how old Masonic rituals he had studied said
that certain documents were taken to Scotland by this group in 1140.
Because he lacked the advantage of knowing about the Dead Sea Scrolls,
he wrote:

One group came to Scotland and established a lodge at Kilwinning,
and there deposited the records of the Order in an abbey they built
there. At this point the first historical difficulty arose, for the abbey
was not built until about 1140, and the legend does not state
where they were during the period between AD *70 and* AD *1140.*

Ward knew that the scrolls concerned were supposed to have been held by
this Jewish Order prior to the destruction of the Jerusalem Temple, but he
could not tell what happened to them between that time and their arrival
in Scotland. Because of the discovery of the Dead Sea Scrolls we now know
that they were placed under the Temple in circa 68 CE and remained there
until they were removed again by the Order (now calling themselves the
Knights Templar) between 1118 and 1128 CE. That left a gap of just twelve
years when these ancient documents would have had to be stored before
they were shipped to the purpose-built abbey in western Scotland. The place
they were taken to was land that belonged to the St Clair family; the same
family who were to build Rosslyn almost exactly three hundred years later,
and who later still became the hereditary Grand Master Masons of Scotland.

We now needed to focus more attention on the artefact that we believe
is the link between the Templars and early Freemasonry. That link is the
building now called Rosslyn Chapel.

THE SECRETS OF ROSSLYN

Rosslyn Chapel is a tiny, heavily carved stone 'chapel' that lies in the Lothian Hills just a few miles south of Edinburgh. It sits just above Roslin Castle and overlooks the river valley where William Wallace's troops hid in a cave whilst resisting the English in the thirteenth century. Whilst the castle and the village are spelled 'Roslin', the name of the little chapel has been changed relatively recently to Rosslyn, because someone, quite erroneously, thought it sounded more Gaelic.

Our initial trawl of Rosslyn was not encouraging. The imagery we saw carved into every available bit of stonework was interesting but it was not particularly Masonic, although it was immediately evident that it was not a normal Christian church. However, as we looked further and absorbed the entire design rather than just studying points of decorative detail, we realised that this was a supremely important structure. We found that the whole idea of Rosslyn was to reconstruct the Temple of Jerusalem in Scotland right down to the only sentence inscribed onto the stonework, which was the riddle that the Persian king set the Jewish leader Zerubbabel before allowing him to rebuild the Temple in the sixth century BCE. The entire layout of the structure copied the ground plan of the Herodian Temple that had been destroyed in Jerusalem in 70 CE, and the western wall was of special interest.

The west side of Rosslyn is a large wall built on a different scale to the rest of the building. The ends of the wall are ragged and unfinished, as though the builders had suddenly stopped in their tracks. Indeed the assumption made in the guidebooks is that the main building was constructed as a 'lady chapel' and that the unfinished west wall was the start of a huge collegiate church that was never built. There is no record of any intention to build a great church, and there was no population for it to serve. The current village of Roslin only came into existence to house the many stone-masons brought from Europe to build the little chapel.

We came to the conclusion that the builders had completed their task exactly as intended, and that the west wall was a copy of the ruin of the Jerusalem Temple just as the crusading Knights Templar had found it at the beginning of the twelfth century. We were able to show that the Rosslyn ground plan was an accurate scaled-down copy of the last Jerusalem Temple, right down to the position of the pillars of Boaz and Jachin that stood at the entrance. The Knights Templar could not have known what the destroyed Temple had looked like above the ground but, thanks to their excavations, they had become experts on its subterranean layout.

The general arrangement of the remaining pillars formed a device known in Freemasonry as a Triple Tau, which is three 'T' shapes interlocked. Tau is the last letter of the Hebrew alphabet. According to the ritual of the Holy Royal Arch degree this signifies the following four things, which the ritual gives in Latin and then English:

Templum Hierosolyma	The Temple of Jerusalem
Clavis ad Thesaurum	A key to a treasure
Theca ubi res pretiosa deponitur	A place where a precious thing is concealed
Res ipsa pretiosa	The precious thing itself

This was an extremely exciting discovery, because the Masonic ritual that contained this otherwise meaningless definition had come from the keeping of the St Clair family when they were the Grand Master Masons. The keys to understanding the building appeared to be hidden in Masonic ritual.

We then realised that the design of the building was centred on a large six-sided star known as the Seal of Solomon. In the centre of this star shape is a huge engrailed cross on the roof which points down to the floor at the spot that corresponds to the place where the Ark of the Covenant was supposedly kept in King Solomon's Temple. The enigmatic words in the Holy Royal Arch degree associated with this symbol are:

Nil nisi clavis deest	Nothing is wanted but the key
Si talia jungere possis sit tibi scire posse	If thou canst comprehend these things, thou knowest enough

At this point we felt sure that Rosslyn had been built as a repository for the scrolls of the Princes of Jerusalem, and that it was considered by its builder, William St Clair, to be a 'New Jerusalem' built in Scotland's green and pleasant land.

At the launch of *The Hiram Key*, which took place inside Rosslyn, Baron St Clair Bonde, one of the Trustees of Rosslyn, stated that the Trust would support an archaeological excavation of the building on the condition that a world-class team of experts (including Scottish scholars) was put together to conduct it. Historic Scotland, the body responsible for all ancient monuments in the country, later stated that they too would be highly sympathetic to an application to investigate beneath the building.

The launch at Rosslyn was attended by biblical scholars Professor Philip Davies of Sheffield University and Professor Graham Auld from Edinburgh University. Both experts said how they were struck by the Herodian style of the west wall, which looked to them as though it was indeed based on the architecture of the Jerusalem Temple. Philip remarked how he could not believe it was designed as a church, saying that it seemed more likely that it was created to conceal some great medieval secret.

In August 1996 we met Dr Jack Miller and his colleague Edgar Harborne at Edinburgh airport and drove them to Rosslyn, where we all spent the weekend. Jack, who is a geologist and a Head of Studies at Cambridge University, was fascinated by the little building. He spent the Saturday examining the structure both inside and out. Over breakfast the next morning he told us that he had spotted some aspects of the building that would be very interesting to us, but he would not explain until we returned to Rosslyn. We ate quickly and then walked down the short lane from the Roslin Glen Hotel and entered the grounds of Rosslyn, where we looked expectantly at the distinguished geologist. Jack smiled and took us to the spot in the north where the main building met the oversized west wall. He pointed a finger at the meeting stonework as he spoke:

'This debate about whether the west wall is a replica of a ruin or an unfinished section of an intended bigger building. Well, there is only one possibility . . . and I can tell you are correct. That west wall is a folly.'

We were riveted to his every word as he continued:

'There are two reasons why I can be sure it is a folly. Firstly, whilst those buttresses have visual integrity, they have no structural integrity; the stonework is not tied into the main central section at all. Any attempt to build further would have resulted in a collapse . . . and the people who built this "chapel" were no fools. They simply never intended to go any further.'

Looking up, even our untrained eyes could see what he meant.

'Furthermore, come around here and look at the end stones.'

We followed him to the large stones at the end of the wall.

'If the builders had stopped work because they had run out of money or just got fed up, they would have left nice square-edged stonework, but these stones have been deliberately worked to appear damaged – like a ruin. These stones haven't weathered like that . . . they were cut to look like a ruined wall.'

Some months later we asked permission for Jack Miller to conduct a non-invasive ground scan outside the walls of Rosslyn. This was agreed and Jack arranged to hire the necessary equipment and for Dr Fernando Neeves to fly in from the Colorado School of Mines, the world's most famous institution for analysing below-ground structures. With just days to go we received a letter from the Trustees of Rosslyn telling us that permission had been withdrawn.

In late 1997 we saw a television programme about an American professor from Princeton University who was searching Israel for what he considered were missing documents that were contemporary with the Dead Sea Scrolls. We immediately thought that James Charlesworth should be made aware of Rosslyn and what we believed it contained. By amazing good fortune we found two direct routes to make contact.

A good friend of ours, a retired police officer called Tony Batters, worked at the time as security adviser to Xerox, a company which we knew was providing high-technology equipment to examine the multiple layers of ancient scrolls found by Professor Charlesworth. Tony was quickly able to make contact with him. At the same time Chris was at a Friday lunch meeting with Professor Philip Davies and he mentioned our desire to tell Professor Charlesworth about our case for ancient Jewish scrolls being hidden beneath Rosslyn. Much to Chris's surprise Philip responded by saying: 'Guess where I am for lunch on Sunday?' The answer came almost immediately: 'At Jim Charlesworth's house.'

Philip agreed to form a second line of attack on the scroll-hunting professor. The extremely encouraging reply came back through Tony Batters in the form of a fax:

From Prof. James H Charlesworth to Tony Batters – Feb 9th 1998

Dear Tony,
    Let me state how enthusiastic and supportive I am of the need to and opportunity to explore what may be in Rosslyn.

The Copper Scroll clearly refers to scrolls hidden under the Temple, and we must be open to the possibility that these were found during the First Crusade and taken back to Great Britain. Two reasons why this is more than just a guess: 1) the record that nine knights excavated under the Temple, and 2) the observation in 1895 that crusade relics were found under the Temple.

I am eager to work closely with you and your associates in seeking permission from Rosslyn to explore ways that we can discern, discover, recover and translate and publish what might be there.

Please forgive the delay in responding. I have been in confidential dialogue with several distinguished people about this enterprise. One of them is Mr Joe Peaples, president of the Jerusalem Historical Society. I understand he called and talked with you.

It might be possible to come and see you in early March.

Again, forgive my delay: I have been simply overwhelmed teaching classes, finalising work with the BBC on the film, directing the celebration of the 50th anniversary of the discovery of the Dead Sea Scrolls, excavating Zion (where Jesus' family is supposed to have lived after the crucifixion), and preparing my sabbatical plans to go to Germany as an Alexander von Humboldt scholar at the University of Tübingen, and then to go to Jerusalem in September to become Annual Professor of the Albright Institute (the archaeological research center).

> *Yours sincerely,*
> *James Hamilton Charlesworth*

We met up with Jim Charlesworth, Joe Peaples and Tony Batters in Manchester and drove northwards to Rosslyn the next day.

Jim, who is a clergyman as well as a professor, was fascinated by what he saw at Rosslyn. His immediate reaction was that the west wall was very Herodian and had been carefully modelled on stonework that can still be seen in Jerusalem. He pointed out the use of imitation 'robbed stones', where the stones built in to walled-up doorways will often have design features that belong to a previous usage. Because the Temple had been laid waste the local builders could find used stones in the rubble to meet their needs.

The poor condition of the building concerned Jim, who told us that an excavation should happen without delay, because anything that was underground would be suffering even more than the parts we could see. He was also sure in his own mind that Rosslyn is not a Christian building, and he cancelled his intention to attend the Sunday service on the basis that he felt it was an inappropriate venue.

We arranged a meeting with some of the Trustees and, over dinner, Jim suggested that he could put together a world-class team of scroll scholars and archaeologists. The requirement for this to include leading Scottish academics was no problem, because Jim had taken his PhD in Scotland and knew the people concerned. A full proposal was drawn up by Professor Charlesworth but, to the best of our knowledge, he has never received a response.

Currently there is a huge steel structure, like a Dutch barn, erected over Rosslyn to help the stonework dry out slowly, after mistakes by earlier restorers resulted in many years where the stonework absorbed too much water. The team of engineers involved with this ongoing restoration work cannot have failed to notice that the structure could not sustain further building and they must have reported the impossibility of the 'collegiate church' theory to the trustees. Yet at the time of writing this incorrect information is still fed to unsuspecting visitors.

PROVING THE MASONIC CONNECTIONS

We have recently been able to present new evidence that demonstrates a Masonic connection that cannot be reasonably denied by even the most doubting person.

On the south wall of the building, to the side of a window, is a small carving depicting two figures that have undergone amazingly rapid deterioration. When we first noticed the imagery in this piece of stonework back in 1997, it was in relatively good condition with defined features, but now some of the sandstone has crumbled across the surface. That a carving should last for more than five centuries and then start to return to sand in less than five years is worrying for the chapel as a whole. However, a stone carving showing a horned figure lifting a wrapped object from the ground, just inches away, has gone completely. It seems to us that the more that modern restorers interfere with this carefully constructed monument, the more it suffers.

Thankfully, all of the stonework was photographed some years ago and the imagery is recorded for posterity. The small sandstone scene that transfixed us when we first saw it contains a kneeling male figure with another man standing behind and slightly to the right of him. The circumstances shown demonstrate that the builders of this Jerusalem Temple in Scotland were acquainted with a ritual that Freemasons recognise as the degree of an Entered Apprentice, the rite that makes a man into a Freemason. Here for the first time we have evidence, carved in a tablet of stone, that Freemasonry started in fifteenth-century Scotland.

Today, when a candidate is initiated into the Craft he is prepared by being hoodwinked (blindfolded) and dressed in loose-fitting white trousers and top. One foot is in a simple slipper (so called slipshod), the right leg is exposed to the knee, and the left breast of the tunic is drawn aside so that the chest is bared on that side. He is also relieved of all metal objects, especially coins, before he is led into the temple with a noose called a 'cable tow' around his neck. There he will kneel in the east in front of the two pillars of Boaz and Jachin that once stood at the entrance to the Jerusalem Temple. As he kneels his feet are placed in the form of a square.

The front figure in the tableau on the south wall of Rosslyn appears as follows:

He is young and unbearded with short hair.
He is kneeling.
There are two pillars, one to each side of him.
He is wearing a blindfold.
He has a noose around his neck.
His feet are in the form of a square.
In his left hand he is holding a book-like object with a Cross engraved on it, which appears to be a Bible.

The man behind has shoulder-length hair, a full beard, and is holding the end of the noose. Looking closely at the statue in 1997 the faint outline of what appeared to be a cross was still visible on his chest. His presentation corresponds to that of a Knight Templar.

But our first concern was to investigate the apparent connection between this mid-fifteenth-century carving and modern Freemasonry. To do this we used statistical analysis, a subject that Robert teaches at Bradford University

School of Management, to test the suggestion that the appearance of this little statue was nothing more than coincidence.[3]

Robert's calculations showed that it is unscientific to accept a theory that assumes no connection between Rosslyn and modern Freemasonry, such as the view adopted by certain historians connected with the United Grand Lodge of England. Equally it has to be concluded that any theory that finds a connection between the two is at least entirely reasonable in this aspect. What this statistical calculation does not tell us, however, is what that connection might be.

CONCLUSIONS

Rosslyn Chapel lies a few miles to the south of Edinburgh. It was built between 1440 and 1490 by William St Clair of Roslin as a copy of the ruined Jerusalem Temple built by King Herod, using stone identical to the original Temple. The west wall is Herodian in its architectural style and its end stones are carved to look like broken parts of a ruin.

Our explanation of the purpose of the west wall is still being ignored, we believe because of a fear to publicly accept that our analysis of the building is correct, and hence to give credence to our further claim that the so-called chapel is a sanctuary for vitally important scrolls from Jerusalem at the time of Christ.

In 1997 we arranged for specialists in the field of non-invasive underground investigations to come to Rosslyn from Cambridge University and the Colorado School of Mines. With just a week to go to the agreed date the trustees cancelled the investigation and access was not allowed.

---

[3] The technique we used attempts to prove a null hypothesis, which means trying to demonstrate that there cannot be any link between the two subjects in question, which are this carving and the first degree ritual of modern Freemasonry.

We gave a weighting to all of the factors involved and assumed, in every case, the highest possible probability against any connection. For instance a probability needed to be placed on the likelihood of any statue of a person from this period including a blindfold. Cases of blindfolded figures in statues of the period are very rare indeed, and a figure of one in a thousand would have been reasonable. However, to give the maximum weight to the non-connection we gave this a rating of 50%. This is equivalent to assuming that every second medieval stone carving of a human being should show the person blindfolded. All of the other factors were given the maximum benefit of any doubt – i.e. this assumes that one in two statues have kneeling figures, nooses around their necks, twin pillars either side of them, and so on. In this way the null hypothesis, that there is no connection between the features of modern Freemasonic ritual and the statue at Rosslyn, chance is given the best possible chance of succeeding.

The results are conclusive. Even when we give the highest possible chance to the negative view, the calculation shows there is a 0.0078% chance that this carving at Rosslyn and the initiation degree of modern Freemasonry are unconnected. That is less than one chance in a thousand. The null hypothesis can be rejected with 99.9% confidence and so does not stand.

On the south wall of the building is a small carving which demonstrates that the builders of this 'Jerusalem Temple' in Scotland knew a ritual that modern Freemasons recognise as the rite that makes a man a Freemason. Rosslyn and Freemasonry are also linked via the heads of the St Clair family who became the hereditary Grand Master Masons of Scotland.

With proof of a Masonic connection we decided that our next task should be a more detailed investigation into the imagery in Rosslyn and the background of the family that created it – the St Clairs.

Chapter Four

THE NORSE
CONNECTION

THE HOLY SHINING LIGHT

The building now known as Rosslyn 'Chapel' was begun in 1441 and finished around 1490. The inspiration behind it was a powerful nobleman by the name of William St Clair of Roslin, whose family later became the hereditary Grand Master Masons of Scotland. The importance of William St Clair and his family is shown by the fact that even King James VI failed in his attempt in the year 1601 to take this title for himself.[1]

The building itself is covered with carvings which are a curious mixture of Old Testament, Celtic and Norse imagery. The 'green man' believed to be from Celtic tradition is manifested as a face, spouting vegetation from his open mouth, who peers out of the winding foliage that snakes around the interior. Moses appears holding the tablets of stone and sporting a wonderful pair of horns on his head. In the central section of the building, in the east there is a fantastically carved area with a ceiling that depicts medieval people playing instruments. Leading to each of these musicians is an arched string of individually designed cubes, which many people suspect are some kind of unknown musical notation. It seems that if only we could read them, we would be able to play the music of Rosslyn.

We had put forward the argument that the families that founded the order of the Knights Templar were themselves descendants of the high

---

[1] Stevenson, David: *The Origins of Freemasonry*, Cambridge University Press, 1988

priesthood of the Jews who left for Europe after the destruction of Jerusalem and its Temple in 70 CE. Indeed, as we have already mentioned, we were subsequently able to confirm that Masonic ritual states that the Knights Templar were descended from the builder-priests who constructed Solomon's Temple.

So we understood the motivation for Jewish imagery, but why, we wondered, did the builder also merge Celtic and Norse traditions with the Jewish, whilst virtually ignoring the Christian tradition which was the sole inspiration for all similar structures across Europe at the time? The answer was not far away.

We looked at the history of the family that produced William St Clair of Roslin and found that they appear to have merged the Jewish bloodlines with Norse bloodlines. On the male side they were descended from the Norse line of Rognvald, Earl of More (pronounced Moray), and from hereditary priests of the Jewish Temple via Gizelle, the daughter of the king of France, a matter we will return to.

Earl Rognvald ruled More, the part of Norway around the present city of Trondheim. The family was given Orkney and Shetland by King Harold, and Rognvald's brother Sigurd the Powerful ruled the Islands as Rognvald's regent.[2] Rognvald's son Hrolf invaded France and took control of Normandy early in the eighth century.[3] In 912 CE, at a village on the River Epte, he signed a peace treaty with King Charles the Simple of France that was later known as the Treaty of St-Clair-sur-Epte. It was at this time that Hrolf More and his cousins decided to take the name St Clair and established themselves as dukes of Normandy. To seal the bargain Hrolf married Gizelle, the daughter of King Charles.[4] The name St Clair can be traced back to a family member who called himself Guillermus de Santa Clair – which translated into English means 'William of the Holy Shining Light'.[5]

A member of this newly established French branch of the More family, William 'the Seemly' St Clair, left Normandy in 1057 to join the English court of Princess Margaret, granddaughter of Edmund Ironsides and a first cousin to Edward the Confessor. When his cousin, William of Normandy, conquered England in 1066 William the Seemly St Clair escorted Princess

[2] Palsson, H & Edwards, P (ed): *The Orkneyinga Saga*, Penguin Classics, 1981
[3] Thompson, WPL: *History of Orkney*, The Mercat Press, 1987
[4] Wallace-Murphy, T & Hopkins, M: *Rosslyn*, Element, 1999
[5] De St Clair, L: *Histoire Généalogique de la Famille de Saint Clair*, Paris, 1905

Margaret to exile in Hungary, where King Stephen of Hungary gave her a fragment of the 'True Cross' as part of her dowry for her marriage to King Malcolm Canmore of Scotland. When the bridal party finally arrived in Scotland King Malcolm gave William lands where the castle of Roslin now stands.

It was King Malcolm who later made William's son Henri the first Earl of Roslin when the younger St Clair returned from Jerusalem after taking part in the First Crusade with the nine knights who went on to found the Order of the Knights Templar.[6]

In *The Second Messiah* we pointed out that the name Roslin means in Scots Gaelic 'ancient knowledge passed down the generations'. This translation was kindly confirmed for us by Gaelic speakers from the Scottish Poetry Library. It follows that the full title of Henri de St Clair of Roslin would translate into English as:

Henry of the Holy Shining Light of Ancient Knowledge passed down the Generations.

At the time this seemed a very peculiar designation for anyone to choose, but it was soon to make perfect sense.

We recalled our meetings with one of the trustees of the Rosslyn Chapel Trust, Baron St Clair Bonde, who was a direct descendant of William Sinclair and a Scandinavian aristocrat. We had visited his beautiful stately home in Fife with Professor Philip Davies to discuss various aspects of our research around the time we published our first two books. Baron Bonde had shown us his family tree tracing his mother's line back to William, who built Rosslyn, and then he told us that through his father's line he was a descendant of the Norse god Thor. At first we did not think he was serious, but he insisted that that was genuinely what the ancient tradition said.

So our friend Sinclair Bonde was living confirmation of the merging of the Jewish and Norse traditions, both of which had been so elegantly woven together into the design of Rosslyn Chapel. Upon checking we found that it was traditional for Norse nobles to consider themselves descended from one or other of the main gods when they became Jarls (Norwegian lords). As rulers they were considered to be married to the goddess Freyja. A little

[6] De St Clair, L: *Histoire Généalogique de la Famille de Saint Clair*

digging into the history of the More region of Norway and its key city of Trondheim told us that there was a temple to Freyja in the city until around 1000 CE, when it was destroyed by Olaf Tryggvason as part of the series of battles that resulted in Rognvald becoming Jarl of Orkney.

This was of great interest because, according to Norse mythology, Freyja was the goddess of love, beauty and fertility, who was represented by the planet Venus. She was also closely associated with death and birth as well as gold and the rose flower. As we pointed out in *Uriel's Machine*, the five-petalled rose is an ancient symbol of Venus, as is the five-pointed star.

The possible connections to Grooved Ware belief and to Freemasonry were intriguing. Our next task was clear: we needed to check out Norse religious beliefs and see what, if anything, we could discover about the beliefs of Sir William's Norse ancestors in the late 900s CE.

THE NORSE QUEEN OF HEAVEN

An insight into the religion and culture of the Norsemen comes from the establishment of Iceland. The Vikings did not found many permanent settlements, but modern scholarship has learned a great deal thanks to the creation of an independent colony on the uninhabited island of Iceland, which lasted until the island came under direct Norwegian rule in the thirteenth century. When writing came in with Christianity in the eleventh century the Icelanders immediately recorded all they could about their settlement and early history. Those who set up the government and law system of Iceland were whole-hearted supporters of the old religion of the northern gods, and this has provided a unique opportunity to observe how they went about it and where their priorities lay.[7]

In 1178 CE a literary genius was born in Iceland. His name is Snorri Sturluson and he became concerned that the Christian innovation of writing was destroying the verbal poetic traditions of Iceland's Viking past. The Vikings loved puns and riddles, which they used in various formal forms of poetry, in particular in Eddic and Skaldic poetic forms and in a complex system of allegory known as kennings, which are metaphors that demand a great deal of background knowledge from the reader if they are to be understood. Many Viking poems seem to be in the form of a riddle or puzzle statement which the writers set, for the reader to solve. Snorri

---

[7] Ellis Davidson, HE: *The Lost Beliefs of Northern Europe*, Routledge, 1993

Sturluson wrote a handbook on how to use these Viking poetic structures and he called it *The Prose Edda*.[8]

Professor Hilda Ellis Davidson drew attention to one very important feature of Eddic poetry:

> *Eddic poems are not always narrative poems, since a number consist of questions and answers exchanged between two supernatural beings; such compositions must have been popular in the Viking Age among those skilled in lore about the gods and their world . . . The mythological poems of the Edda of the question and answer type name many places out of this world where cosmic events have taken place or will take place at the end of time, as well as obscure characters who may be minor gods or giants or supernatural animals who have played some part in these events or will do in the future.*[9]

This use of a catechism style of ritual was very familiar to us from the earliest Scottish rituals of Freemasonry (which can be seen on the *Web of Hiram*). It seemed to us that the source of inspiration when constructing his Masonic ritual could well be the poetic traditions of the Norse ancestors of the St Clair family who were the Jarls (or Earls) of Orkney. The very last Jarl of Orkney was William St Clair, the builder of Rosslyn.

Skaldic poems use syllibies, (a form of internally rhyming couplet or phrase), alliteration, internal rhyme and consonance, making it impossible to translate their complex form into other languages. The translator's choice is between keeping the sense or keeping the beauty of the original spoken language. Scholars have long recognised the difficulty of translating any poetic material with religious connotations, as Professor Evans-Pritchard, Professor of Social Anthropology at Oxford University, points out:

> *Statements about a people's religious beliefs must always be treated with the greatest caution, for we are dealing with what neither participant can directly observe, with conceptions, images, words which require for understanding a thorough knowledge of people's language and also an awareness of the entire system of ideas of*

---

[8] Sturluson, Snorri: *The Prose Edda*, translated Jean L Young, Cambridge Univ. Press, 1954
[9] Ellis Davidson, HE: *The Lost Beliefs of Northern Europe*

*which any particular belief is part, for it may be meaningless when
divorced from the set of beliefs and practices to which it belongs.*[10]

Language was an additional problem, as neither of us speaks Norse, so
we could not hope to read the originals, but we were fortunate to find
good translations, by Edward Turville-Petre.[11]

The use of kennings within the poems, hiding their meaning in a context of deep Norse myth, often made the writings obscure, until we gained
sufficient background knowledge to grasp their use of allegory. Kevin
Crossley-Holland, another translator of these myths into modern English,
said this about his approach to kennings:

> *The greatest pertinence of the scaldic poems lies in the countless
> kennings, or condensed metaphors, that comprise part of their dic-
> tion. Many of the kennings are rooted in myths with which the
> poem's original audience was clearly familiar. So, for instance, three
> of the kennings for gold are 'Freyja's tears', 'Sif's hair' and 'Aegir's
> fire'. This is because Freyja wept tears of gold; because when the
> goddess Sif's hair was cropped by Loki, it was replaced by spun
> gold; and because the sea god Aegir's hall was illuminated only by
> gold that shone like fire. Many of the kennings, then, endorse those
> that have survived and give us tantalising glimpses of those that
> have not.*[12]

We already knew, from research carried out for *Uriel's Machine*, that
the Roman historian Tacitus had written in the *Germania* that the tribes
of north Scandinavia chose their leaders for their valour and noble birth,
and added that any man who could claim divine descent made a powerful
contender. Armed with this knowledge, *Hyndla's Poem* made sense when
we read it.

In this story the goddess Freyja disguises Ottar, her human lover, as a
golden boar and takes him to meet the giantess Hyndla, who has drunk
the 'beer of memory' and so can remember the parentage of everyone in
the world. Hyndla recognises the boar as Ottar, son of Instein, and makes
sexual puns at Freyja's expense, accusing her of 'riding her lover on the

10 Evans-Pritchard EE: *Theories of Primitive Religion*, Oxford University Press, 1965
11 Turville-Petre, EOG: *Scaldic Poetry*, Oxford University Press, 1976
12 Crossley-Holland, K: *The Norse Myths, a Retelling*, André Deutsch, 1980

road to Valhalla'. Freyja denies that 'she has had her lover beneath her on the road', but Hyndla later taunts her again about her disguised lover, saying that 'many another has wormed his way under your apron. My noble goddess, you leap around at night like a she-goat cavorting with a herd of billy-goats.'[13]

The point of this story is that Ottar is in contention with another warrior, Angantyr, for leadership of his people. Freyja persuades Hyndla to recite Ottar's lineage, during which the giantess passes a comment about the child sacrifice, saying that long, long ago the young sons of Jormunrek were given to the gods in sacrifice.

Freyja tricks Hyndla into proving that Ottar is descended from the gods, by playing on the giantess's love of gossip and desire to show off her extensive knowledge of who has had children by whom. Once Hyndla has provided the information which shows Ottar is descended from the gods, Freyja admits that Ottar set out to become her lover as part of his quest to become leader of his people. She says that 'Ottar raised an altar to me. He built up stones and reddened the altar again and again with the blood of oxen.' She ends her speech by proudly asserting that Ottar, who has just been proved worthy of kingship because of his divine descent, always puts his faith in goddesses. The chief of the Norse gods is Odin, who is often called the Allfather. He lives in Asgard, the home of the gods. Sturluson says of him that he is the highest and oldest of the gods. He rules all things, and no matter how mighty the other gods may be they serve him as children do their father. He created heaven and earth and sky and all that is in them.[14]

Odin has but a single eye, and wears a wide-brimmed hat with a blue cloak to avoid being recognised, a description that seems to associate him with the characteristics of the Sun. He rules over the hall of Valhalla, where heroes, after a valiant death in battle, go to feast for ever and ever. Odin has children by various goddesses, but it is his coupling with the goddess who rules Earth that gave birth to the god Thor, from whom Baron St Clair Bonde claims symbolic descent as a Swedish noble. Excluding Odin, the Allfather, there are twelve other gods, who form a council beneath Odin, and each is paired at various times with one of thirteen goddesses, making sure that there is always a goddess left over to satisfy Odin. Odin

---

[13] Crossley-Holland, K: *The Norse Myths, a Retelling*
[14] Sturluson, Snorri: *Helmskringla*, Parts 1 & 2 translated by Samuel Laing, Everyman Library, 1961–4

with his single eye, blue cloak, and the cloud-like wide-brimmed hat he can pull down to hide his eye, is represented by the Sun.

One of Odin's other names is the Lord of the Gallows, a name he derives from his decision to experience death and learn the secrets of the grave. He has himself nailed to the great tree of Yggdrasil, saying:

I hung from the windswept tree, hung there nine long nights; I was pierced with a spear; I was an offering to Odin, myself to myself.[15]

The tale ends with this explanation:

These are the word of Odin before there were men. These were his words, after his death, when he rose again.[16]

We were struck by the obvious parallels to the myth of Jesus Christ. Crossley-Holland says of this story:

Odin learns from wise giants, he learns from seeresses whom he raises from the dead and from hanged men; and in this myth Odin makes the supreme sacrifice. He dies so as to win the occult wisdom possessed only by the dead, and rises again to use that wisdom in the world of the living . . . It is known that worship of Odin and other related gods involved human sacrifice. The eleventh-century historian Adam of Bremen records that he saw many human bodies hanging in the sacrificial grove at Uppsala near the temple that housed idols of Odin, Thor and Freyja . . . The parallels between Odin's death and Christ's crucifixion are striking: both die voluntarily; Odin is pierced with a spear and so is Christ; Odin alludes to the lack of a reviving drink, and Christ is given vinegar; Odin screeches or shrieks before he dies, and Christ cries out 'in a loud voice'.[17]

The obvious question is whether the Norse story of Odin was influenced by the Christian story. After much consideration Crossley-Holland dismisses the possibility of Christian influence. He points out that the Norse did not

[15] Crossley-Holland, K: *The Norse Myths, a Retelling*
[16] Crossley-Holland, K: *The Norse Myths, a Retelling*
[17] Crossley-Holland, K: *The Norse Myths, a Retelling*

convert to Christianity until 1000 CE and every element of the Norse myth can be explained as part of a pagan tradition that long pre-dates any possible Christian influence.

The mother of Thor is also known by other names, such as Freyja and Frigg. We were interested to see that Professor Ellis Davidson likened these aspects of the goddess to names we already recognised as representing Venus.

> The two main goddesses of Asgard indeed suggest two aspects of
> the same divinity; and this is paralleled by the two-fold aspect of
> the fertility goddess in the Near East, appearing as mother and as
> lover. Sometimes both roles may be combined in the person of one
> goddess, but it is more usual for the different aspects to be personi-
> fied under different names. It is even possible to recognise a triad
> of goddesses such as Asherah, Astarte and Anat.[18]

We knew these three names to be different aspects of the planet Venus from our study of Phoenician gods, which will be discussed in more detail later. Ellis Davidson goes even further in this linking, when she says:

> The literary sources also tend to give the impression of one
> supreme and powerful goddess who might be regarded as wife or
> mistress of her worshipper. If he were king, her cult would become
> part of the state religion, and she would receive official worship as
> part of the state religion along with the leading gods. In
> Scandinavian tradition the main goddess appears to be Freyja . . .
> but there is also Frigg, wife of Odin and therefore known as the
> Queen of Heaven . . . although sometimes it is Freyja who is
> paired off with Odin.[19]

So now we knew that the Norse worshipped a Queen of Heaven, who is linked with goddesses we also knew to be thought of as the planet Venus. We searched further to see if there were any more details about this Queen of Heaven and quickly found that there were. A kenning is included in *Hyndla's Poem* which gave a clear connection to the Venus goddess of the Phoenicians, Baalat-Gerbal. This goddess was often depicted wearing a

---

[18] Ellis Davidson, H: *The Lost Beliefs of Northern Europe*
[19] Ellis Davidson, H: *The Lost Beliefs of Northern Europe*

headdress of two horns, like those of a cow or sometimes as a stag. There is a very good reason for this, because the shape that the planet Venus sketches out in the sky around the rising and setting Sun, when plotted against the backdrop of the zodiac, is the shape of a pair of horns.[20]

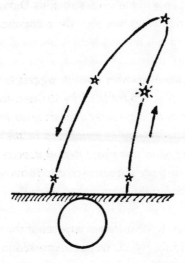

The Horns of Venus. The that Venus traces around the rising Sun when it is a morning star. When it moves to an evening star it traces the mirror image of this eastern path, in the west. It is this pattern which encouraged many ancient peoples to link Venus with horns.

Returning to *Hyndla's Poem,* as Freyja approaches the gate of Odin's hall she startles a horned stag which is grazing in the gateway. As the horned path of Venus disappears with the rising of the Sun, so does the horned stag flee from the place where Odin is to be found by the goddess. This is interesting but, as most kennings do, it leaves as much scope for misinterpretation as a broadsheet crossword puzzle clue. Then we found a very early myth that was much clearer.

Early in the history of the world, Odin fought a war with another group of gods and the walls of Asgard were destroyed. The story begins when a travelling mason arrives at Asgard and offers to rebuild its shattered walls, if the gods will give him three things in return. These are the Sun, the Moon and the goddess Freyja. Freyja is described as being clothed in raiment so bright that only Odin can look directly at her. The gods agree to the deal, but insist the work must be started on the day of the winter solstice and be

[20] Schultz, J: *Movements and Rhythms of the Stars,* Floris Books, 1987

complete by the day of the summer solstice (the two feast days of St John celebrated by Masonry and preserved in its ritual as the symbolic days for the initiation degree and the second degree of 'passing'). Three days before the summer solstice the mason has almost completed the circle of 'well cut and well laid stone, a sturdy wall high and strong enough to keep any unwelcome visitor at bay'. The gods despair that there will be no light left in the sky with the Sun, the Moon and the goddess Freyja, the three brightest objects in the heavens, all taken. But the day is saved when the god Loki tricks the mason into revealing that he is really a giant in disguise. Thor kills him with his hammer as the giant mason shouts 'Tricked by a gang of gods and a brothel of goddess!'[21] We well knew which are the three brightest objects in the heavens. In order of brightness they are the Sun, the Moon and the planet Venus, or the goddess Freyja as the planet was known to the Norse.

Next we found that the temples to Freyja were considered so important to the Jarls who built them that their political power could be destroyed by sacking these buildings. When Olaf Tryggvason wanted to overthrow Jarl Haakon of Heligoland, who was for a while the de facto king of Norway in the late tenth century CE, he did it by breaking down the image of Freyja from the temple, built by the More family to honour the goddess, where Haakon worshipped. This temple was near Trondheim, in the lands of the Jarls of More. And as we knew, Sir William's ancestors, from whom he inherited his Jarldom of Orkney, were Jarls of More.

We found one further detail about the Norse temples that struck us as very Masonic: they incorporated pillars. This was recorded in the excavation report of the eighth-century temple of Freyja, in Trondheim, when it was discovered under the floor of a medieval church dedicated to the virgin Mary.[22] A typical use of these temple pillars is described in the *Eyrbyggja Saga*, which tells how the Viking Thorolf decides to migrate to Iceland and needs to choose a landing place to come ashore. Kevin Crossley-Holland translates:

> *Thorolf threw over board the high-seat pillars from the temple –*
> *the figure of Thor was carved on one of them – and declared that*
> *he'd settle at any spot in Iceland where Thor chose to send the pillars ashore.*[23]

[21] Crossley-Holland, K: *The Norse Myths, a Retelling*
[22] Liden, K: 'From Pagan Sanctuary to Christian Church: the Excavation of Maere Church, Trondelag', *Norwegian Archeological Review*, 2, 23–32, Oslo, 1969
[23] Crossley-Holland, K: *The Norse Myths, a Retelling*

Could it be that the beliefs of the Grooved Ware People had survived in northwestern Europe through the periods ascribed to the Celts and on to the Norse people who have never lost their contact with northern Scotland? If we can sustain our belief that the Jews were also recipients of the same traditions, we were now looking at a reunification of two arms of the same original Venus cult that had broken apart more than four and a half thousand years ago and remerged some three and a half thousand years later under the guidance of the St Clairs – the family who called themselves *The Holy Shining Light*. Could this title be a reference to the planet Venus which was so important to both groups?

We were later to find that we were only partly right. The 'Holy Shining Light' was something even more remarkable.

Our investigation into the beliefs of William St Clair's Norse ancestors had uncovered several basic Norse beliefs. Here are the most important ones:

1   The sons of their kings claimed to be the sons of their gods.

2   When a man became king he also became the consort of the goddess.

3   There was a council of twelve god/goddess pairs who assisted an Allfather god/goddess to rule.

4   The three brightest objects in the sky, the Sun, the Moon and Venus, represented the three most important gods.

5   They believed in the power of sacred rocks and sacred trees.

6   They had a set of apocalyptic beliefs.

7   Their Venus goddess preserved youth.

8   Their Venus goddess encouraged sexual licence at her festivals.

9   They worshipped a promiscuous male god, famed for the size and power of his penis.

10 They had a father god who hung on a tree for eight days in order to

die so that he might know what death was like for ordinary mortals. Eight days after his death the Allfather resurrected himself.

As we will show, Norse theology has remarkable similarities to that of the Phoenicians, and the wearing of horns, long attributed to the Vikings, appears to have been derived from a symbol of a common backdrop of Venus worship to the Norse and to Old Testament prophets prior to the involvement of the Church. Only after the Middle Ages did horns become associated with evil in general and the Devil in particular.

FREEMASONRY'S FIRST TEMPLE

We have shown that the carving of the candidate at Rosslyn indicates a direct connection with modern Freemasonry. Sir William St Clair, the builder of Rosslyn, and his family had been aware of ancient rituals and, either immediately or over time, they must have begun to form the structure for the organisation we know as Freemasonry.

The year 1736 is important to Scottish Freemasonry because it was then that the Scottish lodges decided to elect a Grand Lodge to administer them. They decided that they would have to go back to their traditional loyalty, recorded in the St Clair charters of 1601 and 1628 which stated that the heads of the St Clair family were hereditary Grand Master Masons of Scotland from time immemorial.[24] The then head of the family was another Sir William Sinclair of Roslin who was automatically their Grand Master because he was a direct male-line descendant of the Sir William St Clair who had built Rosslyn Chapel.

The only snag with this plan of forming a Grand Lodge of Scotland under the hereditary mastership of this Sir William Sinclair was that he was not a Freemason. Before he could become Grand Master Mason of Scotland he had to be initiated and progressed through the minimum five degrees which are part of the Craft in Scotland. Once appointed, his very first act was to renounce and resign in writing his hereditary rights of patronage and institute the system of election of officers of the new Grand Lodge, which still protects the rights and privileges of Scottish Freemasons to this day.[25] The author of *Gould's History of Freemasonry* observed:

[24] Lomas, R: *The Invisible College*
[25] Knight, C & Lomas, R: *The Second Messiah*

*the opportune resignation of William St Clair was calculated to
give the whole affair a sort of legality which was wanting in the
institution of the Grand Lodge of England.*[26]

In building up our picture of the St Clair family and early Freemasonry
we have drawn on the earliest Masonic rituals of Scotland, collected over
a number of years spent visiting Scottish lodges and speaking to old Masons
who, as we have mentioned, often gave us copies of very early rituals
which are no longer in use. Using this knowledge of the whole sweep of
Freemasonic ritual, which we have incorporated into the document we call
The Masonic Testament, we were beginning to uncover a comprehensive
myth underlying the rituals. It tells a great sweeping story, which in many
places seems to be parallel to that told in the Bible, but doesn't stop at
the time of Jesus, continuing almost to the present day. It tells how Masons
were selected by God to share the knowledge of science and use it for
human good, how they were told the secrets of building a good society,
and how they used these secrets to create great Temples and Orders of
men devoted to the understanding of God, Tolerance and Science.

We now knew that the moral stories of the battles fought by the Masons
to promote Love, Charity and Truth despite persecution and hostility continue until the eighteenth century, when they culminate in the destruction
of the Order of the Knights of St John of Malta, under the Grand Mastership
of Ferdinand von Hompesch, by Napoleon, at which point the story ceases.

One of the key motifs of this story is the building of Solomon's Temple,
and it is this pivotal event we decided to look at next.

CONCLUSIONS

The founding of the St Clair family in France during the first half of the
eleventh century combined Jewish and Norse bloodlines. It is for this reason
that William St Clair later built Rosslyn with the imagery and motifs from
both traditions, which share a belief in the central importance of Venus.

We already suspected that Sir William St Clair had founded the organisation we now call Freemasonry using rituals that had come to him through
his family and from the scrolls found under the Jerusalem Temple. It now
seems that the Norse religion was an entirely complementary component
to the concepts that came from the Jewish sources.

[26] *Gould's History of Freemasonry*, Caxton, 1902

Chapter Five

THE TEMPLE OF SOLOMON

THE ENOCHIAN ARTEFACTS

There is no known archaeological evidence of King Solomon's Temple, which legend says was built in Jerusalem nearly three thousand years ago. Despite this, it remains a major icon in the minds of men, as it was the first stone temple built to the storm god Yahweh, who later became the one and only true God (with a capital 'G') for millions of people across the globe.

Both the Old Testament and the Masonic Testament tell us that Solomon was king of Israel in the tenth century BCE, born the second son of David to his wife Bathsheba. Jewish and Muslim literature later describe Solomon as the wisest of all sages, gifted with the power to control the spirits of the invisible world.[1] He is also traditionally regarded as a great author with a prodigious output, having many works ascribed to him. These are the biblical Proverbs, the Song of Solomon, Ecclesiastes, the Wisdom of Solomon, and the later Psalms of Solomon and Odes of Solomon. However, scholars now believe that several were written many centuries later, and the Odes are possibly over a thousand years more recent than the great king.

The Bible tells us that Solomon succeeded David (despite the claims of Adonijah, his older half-brother) and then divided Israel into twelve dis-

[1] Rappoport, AS: *Myths and Legends of Ancient Israel*, Senate, 1995

tricts for purposes of taxation and extended his territory from the river Euphrates to the land of the Philistines and on to the border of Egypt. He is said to have enslaved the Canaanites who remained in the land and formed an alliance with Hiram, king of Tyre, who effectively designed and built the Temple for Solomon. However, these alliances provoked discontent, since they led to the establishment of foreign religious cults in Jerusalem.

According to the biblical legend Solomon was forced to levy punitive taxes to pay Hiram's regular annual charges, and Israel's productivity was only just enough to pay for the king's ambitious building programme, which included a large palace and harem quarters as well as the much smaller Temple. According to Josephus, Hiram paid out over three tons of his own gold in advance for the building work but eventually wrote the debt off as unrecoverable.[2]

The Masonic Testament tells us a great deal more about the subject of Solomon and his Temple than the Bible. We are told that Hiram king of Tyre sent Hiram Abif as the chief architect of the Temple, and the main theme of the ritual is connected with the assassination of this master builder and the subsequent loss of secrets of initiation that he apparently possessed and died to protect. These secrets appear to have been something akin to a magical incantation, and their loss prevented some great process from ever happening again. In their place are substituted secrets which, presumably, would not have the occult effect of the originals.

The ritual states that Solomon first selected a place near Jerusalem for the proposed temple, but as the workmen cleared the ground they found the ruins of an ancient temple that Solomon assumed must have been to some unwanted god. Not wishing to use a desecrated spot, he changed the location of his new temple to Mount Moriah. Later he realised the site he had rejected was that of Enoch's temple.

Next we are told that Solomon king of Israel, Hiram king of Tyre and Hiram Abif were the three Grand Masters who understood that if Israel deviated from the laws of Moses and the Prophets their enemies would sack their cities and all of the sacred treasures contained in the Sanctum Sanctorum (or Holy of Holies) would be taken. To prevent this potential disaster they built a secret underground passageway that led from King Solomon's private apartment to a vault directly below the Sanctum

[2] Whiston, W (ed. and trans.): *The Works of Flavius Josephus*, William P Nimmo, 1895

Sanctorum. This Secret Vault was divided into nine arches or crypts, the last of which was used to hold all the holy vessels and sacred treasures that would eventually be placed in the Sanctum Sanctorum. This chamber was also used by the three Grand Masters to meet in secret and was the place where the ritual of the Degree of Master Mason was originally conducted. The passage concerned begins: [*Masonic Testament*: 7:4]

> *King Solomon builded a secret vault, the approach to which was*
> *through eight other vaults, all under ground, and to which a long*
> *and narrow passage led from the palace. The ninth arch or vault*
> *was immediately under the Holy of Holies of the Temple. In that*
> *apartment King Solomon held his private conferences with King*
> *Hiram and Hiram Abif.*

The murder of Hiram Abif must have been a major blow, because we are next told that the two kings stopped using the secret vault after the architect's death: [*Masonic Testament* 7:15]

> *After the death of Hiram Abif the two kings ceased to visit it,*
> *resolving not to do so until they should select one to fill his place;*
> *and that, until that time, they would make known the sacred name*
> *to no one.*

This was changed following a major discovery by three workmen. Solomon had decided to erect a Temple of Justice on the site where the ruins of Enoch's temple stood, the spot he previously rejected for the Temple of Yahweh. After the workmen removed the fallen columns and cleared away the rubbish, a survey of the ground was conducted prior to laying the foundations of the courthouse. At this point they discovered a hollow sound from a stone, and upon lifting it they could see a secret subterranean vault, which the ritual says was built by Enoch. When the men lowered themselves into the chamber they found treasures consisting of a golden delta inlaid in a cube of agate, a mysterious name and the fragments of a pillar containing the secrets of the arts and science of the world. These were taken to Solomon, who decided that they should be placed in the sacred vault of the ninth apartment of the secret chamber in his new Temple: [*Masonic Testament* 7:17]

After Adoniram, Joabert and Stolkin had discovered the cube of agate and the mysterious name, and had delivered it to King Solomon, the two kings determined to deposit it in the secret vault, permit the three Masters who discovered it to be present, make known to them the true pronunciation of the ineffable word, constitute the last degree of Ancient Craft Masonry, and term it Grand Elect Mason.

To us this sounds like a story that was invented in early Jewish history to post-rationalise how the Jews had become holders of secrets from extreme antiquity. They found the information that had once belonged to another people symbolised by the Enochian temple, and transferred it to the hub of their own culture – directly beneath the chamber containing their new God.

It is now widely accepted that the Old Testament was created around the sixth century BCE, when wise men and scribes combed through the vast amount of oral traditions to form a single story-line back to the Creation. This myth tells of a great transition from a period dominated by rural nomads through to a time of great cities and warrior princes. It seems to be trying to make sense of what folk memory preserved of the shift from the Old Stone Age culture of hunting and herding wanderers to the Bronze and Iron Ages when more powerful weapons of warfare became available. But could this story be an attempt to explain how the secrets of building and astronomy had been transmitted from the Grooved Ware People to their own culture? We knew from the evidence of the Book of Enoch that Enoch was believed to have travelled north to be trained in these subjects, and the secret knowledge he brought back was written down in that book around 250 BCE.

Freemasonic ritual claims that there was a secret and select group that maintained a secret knowledge of building and astronomy based on the knowledge of the movements of the bright morning star of Venus over the millennia. If the story was a complete fiction why should it fit the facts so well? How could the St Clairs, or anyone else, have dreamed up rituals that nobody understands but yet perfectly describe circumstances thousands of years ago?

The Book of Enoch was lost, and not recovered until the late eighteenth century – after these Masonic rituals were in circulation. So the ancient figure of Enoch is associated with the transmission of secret information from some time before history began to the new world being constructed in the Middle East. We were also interested to find out that the Arab people also remember Enoch in the Koran as a holder of great knowledge, calling him Idris, meaning teacher (from the root *drs*). They identify his last place on Earth as a village near Baghdad called 'Sayyid Idris', and today Muslims still pay homage to him on Sundays and particularly Easter Sunday.

THE VENUS ALIGNMENT OF SOLOMON'S TEMPLE

The earliest traces of human settlement of the city of Jerusalem, where Solomon built his Temple, are ascribed to the late Chalcolithic Period (when copper was first used) and the Early Bronze Age – which puts them at around 3000 BCE. The first known form of name for the city was Urushalim – 'uru', meaning 'founded by', and the suffix 'salem' or 'Shalem', which is the name of the Canaanite god of Venus in its evening setting. This evidence has been confirmed by archaeology, as tablets found in Elba, Syria, dating back to 3000 BCE make reference to the god Shalem, who was venerated in a city called Urushalim.

So the very name of Jerusalem effectively means the place dedicated to Venus in its evening setting – but Solomon's Temple was facing in the opposite direction, towards Venus rising in its role as Morning Star. Our researches had told us that the Grooved Ware People had viewed Venus at both ends of the day, and the association with horns appears to be a combination of the observation of both events. The Canaanite goddess Asherah (the Lady of the Sea) had twin sons: Shalim, who was Venus at dusk, and Shachar, who was Venus at dawn.

The original inhabitants of Jerusalem were Canaanites called Jebusites, and their city was tiny at the time even two thousand years after its earliest inhabitation. The Bible tells us how David seized it as his new capital, and archaeological evidence from that period suggests that it covered an area just 550 yards from north to south and 70 yards from east to west (see map). This small settlement was located outside and to the south of the present 'Old City Wall' on the western side of the Kidron Valley, and excavations have revealed a substantial town wall just above the Gihon Spring. The site that Solomon chose for the Temple was, at that time, some three hundred yards north of the city on a high point facing east across to the Mount of Olives.

According to Masonic ritual the finished temple has three special elements: a Porch, a Dormer, and a Square pavement. We were told that the Porch was the entrance to the Sanctum Sanctorum, the Holy of Holies where the Ark of the Covenant was kept; the dormer, or overhead window, allowed light to enter; and a square, or checkerboard pavement, was for the High Priest to walk upon.

What particularly caught our attention was the reference to a dormer, which we have also seen itemised in reconstructions of the building produced by scholars. In the strict sense of the word a dormer is a roof-light or other opening to allow light to enter a room where somebody sleeps. As only the high priest was ever allowed into the Holy of Holies, and then only once a year, the dormer in the eastern facing wall of King Solomon's Temple could have had only one objective: letting light into God, the only resident of the building.

In *The Hiram Key* we had reasoned that Jesus Christ had taken his followers to the Garden of Gethsemane for very good reason immediately before his arrest by the Romans:

> . . . *this was no arbitrary choice – Gethsemane was a deliberate and preordained place to change the course of history. The Garden of Gethsemane is just three hundred and fifty yards away from, and directly in front of, the eastern gate of the Temple – the 'righteous' gateway. As Jesus prayed he may have been high enough to see across the valley the two physical pillars that he represented in the building of the new Jerusalem and the coming 'kingdom of God'.*[3]

We had come to the view that Jesus had selected this particular spot opposite the Gate of Righteousness, which was the main gate, to launch his mission to establish himself as King of the Jews. And Venus was rising just before dawn on that day. We knew that the Book of Ezekiel (43:4) said of this location:

> *And the glory of the Lord came into the house by the way of the gate whose prospect is toward the east . . .*

Was the light of Venus considered to be the 'glory of God'?

But there was a problem of alignment. The Garden of Gethsemane is

[3] Knight, C & Lomas, R: *The Hiram Key*, Arrow, 1997

east of this gate on the Mount of Olives, but the Dome of the Rock, the Muslim building that now stands on what is thought to be the site of the Jewish Temple, is offset to the south. The alignment of the gate and the assumed position of the dormer window are not quite correct – unless the Temple was a little further north.

Because the Romans did such a good job of flattening the building, nothing is known about the exact location of Solomon's Temple and its two subsequent rebuilds under Zerubbabel and Herod. The third incarnation (which is often confusingly referred to as the Second Temple), built by Herod the Great two thousand years ago, totally reconstructed the site, although some of the underground cisterns may have been re-used. The ambitious King Herod more than doubled the size of Temple Mount to approximately thirty-six acres.

The only surviving part of the Temple complex from Herod's period which experts claim to be certain about is the partial line of the enclosure wall which is reasonably preserved on the south, west and east sides, although the eastern wall appears to have survived holding its original line. Most people assume that the 'Dome of the Rock' was built over the exact site of the 'holy of holies' in the seventh century CE. Jews and Christians alike take it that the centre of Solomon's Temple is beneath that dome. But as we revisited what we knew about Solomon's Temple we found that there are three different theories about where the Temple stood on Jerusalem's Temple Mount. And one of these theories particularly excited us.

Dr Asher Kaufman, a Hebrew University physicist, who has spent years studying Temple Mount, places the Temple site some 280 feet northwest of the generally assumed position. He first published his theory in the early 1970s after studying every scrap of the available evidence, including the records of the British army team, under Lieutenant Warren, who conducted extensive excavations in the 1860s. Kaufman concluded that the site of the Temple was at the northwest corner of the Mount. For reasons totally unconnected to our thesis he determined that the east–west line aligned the Mount of Olives with the Eastern Gate and the Temple!

This line exactly bisects at the site of a small cupola which has bedrock inside. This is the only bedrock to break the surface on the entire Temple Mount, and the rest of the area around the Dome of the Rock is paved. He believes that this ignored lump of rock jutting out of the flat surface is none other than the foundation stone of the world, called by the Jews 'Even Shetiyyah'. This famous stone was said to protrude inside the ancient Holy of Holies, the most sacred place on Earth for Jews.

The *Mishneh Torah* by Maimonides quotes Jewish Talmudic writings from the times before the Temple was destroyed in 70 CE. Eyewitnesses declare that 'the Temple Courtyard was not situated directly in the centre of the Mount. Rather, it was set off farther from the southern wall of the Temple Mount than from the wall of any other direction. The reason for this was said to give worshippers room to gather after they entered from the southern gate. Maimonides continues to quote sources insisting that the Temple was situated directly opposite the Eastern Gate, placing it in the northern part of the Mount:

'These five gates were placed in a straight line' from the Eastern Gate into the entrance hall of the Holy of Holies. These gates were as follows 'the Eastern gate, the gate of Chayl, the gate of the Women's Courtyard, the gate of Nicanor and the gate of the entrance hall. So if the temple was built on flat ground, one would have been able to see through all the gates at once'.[4]

If you were to stand on the hillside across the valley to the east (placing you in the Garden of Gethsemane lower down or on the Mount of Olives if higher up), your view as you look due west gives a straight line over the Eastern Gate into the area north of the Dome of the Rock. If you projected a laser beam forward it would cut right through the Eastern Gate (if it was not now walled up) and travel on through the centre of the cupola known as the 'Dome of the Spirits' or the 'Dome of the Tablets'. Arabic titles often preserve original place names, and we thought these titles seem highly reminiscent of the Divine Presence that accompanied the Ark and the tablets of the law stored within it which once rested inside the Holy of Holies. We felt that the presence of this line makes a compelling argument to confirm the importance of an astronomical alignment for the siting of all three Temples. As we will show, this insight turned out to be of vital importance later in our quest.

We only recently became aware of Dr Kaufman's work and, as far as we know, he is unaware of our claim that the orientation of the Temple was directly linked to the rising of Venus in the east.

In *Uriel's Machine* we showed how the modern Masonic temple is

[4] *Mishneh Torah*, Commentary Halachah 5 and 6

designed along the same astronomical lines as the Jerusalem Temple, with the free-standing eastward pillars of Boaz and Jachin marking the extremities of the rising Sun at the summer solstice in the north and the winter solstice in the south. On the equinoxes the Sun rose between the two in a position due east, and on certain dates the planet Venus rose as a bright star ahead of the Sun to shine directly through the dormer of the Temple. The layout of every Masonic Temple is said to be a model of Solomon's Temple, and today every Master Mason is raised from his temporary 'death' by the pre-dawn light of the rising Venus at a symbolic equinox.

We also noted that the New Testament places Jesus' arrest, crucifixion and claimed resurrection around the Jewish festival of the Passover, which commemorates Moses leading the exodus of the Israelites from Egypt and their safe flight across the Red Sea. The celebration of the feast begins after sunset on the 14th day of Nisan, the first month of the Jewish ecclesiastical year, which is the time of the vernal equinox. So, according to tradition, Jesus was conceived and resurrected at the equinox that falls in spring.

The tradition of this Jewish festival has been carried on in the dating of the Christian moveable feast of Easter, whose date is defined as the first Sunday following the first full moon after the vernal equinox.

The dormer in Solomon's Temple appeared to us to operate exactly like the lightbox at Newgrange. It allows the Sun in, but actually its more important role was to admit the light of Venus.

To try to understand the Solomonic tradition better we decided to investigate the Phoenicians.

HIRAM THE MASTER BUILDER

The so-called 'promised land' that Moses and Joshua led the Hebrews into was the land of Canaan, which means the stretch of land some three hundred miles long and fifty miles wide that spans from south of the Dead Sea up to the southern parts of the country that is now Lebanon. The inhabitants of this region were generically known as Canaanites, but their land was made up of a whole series of city states. Their cities were somewhat similar in organisation to the later Greek city states whose citizens considered themselves to be Athenians, Trojans, Spartans or Corinthians.

The people of the more prosperous Canaanite seafaring city states on the more northerly Mediterranean coast became known to the outside world as Phoenicians. The word is Greek and alludes to the Tyrian purple dye that these Eastern Canaanites extracted from molluscs and supplied for use in the manufacture of regal robes. These Phoenicians, literally meaning 'purple people', came to see themselves as different, and superior to other Canaanites. But they had the same early influences and held broadly similar theological beliefs to the people of the inland city states such as the Jebusites (the original inhabitants of Jerusalem). All of the population of this land were therefore Canaanites, but other terms such as Jebusite or Phoenician described more clearly which part of Canaan the individual was from.

The Phoenician locality of Canaan was a narrow strip of territory about two hundred miles long that reached inland between five to fifteen miles and was bounded to the east by the Lebanon Mountains. Although they considered themselves a single nation the Phoenicians were not a unified state but a group of city-kingdoms where one usually dominated the others. The principal cities were Simyra, Zarephath (Sarafand), Byblos, Jubeil, Arwad (Rouad), Acco (Akko), Sidon (ªaydâ), Tripolis (Tripoli), Tyre (ªúr), and Berytus (Beirut). The cities of Tyre and Sidon tended to alternate as the ruling power. From about 1800 BCE, when Egypt was beginning to build an empire in the Middle East, the Egyptians invaded and took control of Phoenicia for around four hundred years. The raids of the Hittites against Egypt gave the Phoenician cities an opportunity to rebel, and by 1100 BCE they became free once more.

Like all Canaanites, each Phoenician city worshipped a favourite deity, usually known as Baal (meaning 'lord'). But the most important Phoenician deity was Astarte or Ashtar, the goddess associated directly with Venus.

According to both the Old Testament and Freemasonic ritual, Solomon was unable to build his Temple with his own designers and so enlisted the help of Hiram, the Phoenician king of Tyre, and his master builder, also called Hiram. The ritual says that the arches leading under the 'Holy of Holies' were constructed by twenty-two men, skilled in the arts and sciences, who came from the northern Phoenician city of Byblos. So we can be certain that King Solomon's Temple was built by Canaanites who were known to worship Venus.

We decided we needed to find out more about this Phoenician king and the cities his people lived in.

The Book of Samuel (2 Sam. 5: 11) explains how Hiram, king of Tyre, offered to supply Solomon's father, King David, with cedar wood, carpenters and stonemasons, and even built him a house as a sample of the type of workmanship the Phoenicians could offer for hire. David must have been grateful for the help, as he was hoping to turn his small, newly conquered Jebusite town into a fit home for Yahweh, his new God. But he never got around to building the Temple, leaving the task to Solomon.

According to 1 Kings 5:2–6, the first thing Solomon did after he became king was to write to King Hiram requesting that the Phoenician should prepare a workforce. The next verse suggests that Hiram was an astute businessman who knew how to make his customers feel good about placing an order with him. The Phoenician responded by saying: 'Blessed is the Lord this day, which hath given unto David a wise son.' He thanked the Jewish Baal (Yahweh) and flattered Solomon for having the wisdom to give Hiram the business, for the entire planned building programme was a seriously sizeable contract.

In an unusual way of handling a major contract, Solomon seems to have given Hiram an open cheque and no upper limit on price. Hiram wrote back by return messenger, asking for large quantities of wheat and olive oil for each year the contract was to run, apparently omitting to mention a completion date.

Archaeological work at Gebal shows that the Phoenicians built large stone houses in the Bronze Age and later developed a model for public buildings, in a style known as Bit-hileni. A characteristic of this type of building is a large outer courtyard surrounded on three sides by rooms which are entered through a central audience hall. But if the style was used to build a temple the outer courtyard would have a purely decorative function. It did, however, lead to a single central door that opened into a holy place. As one expert comments:

> 'There was another detail of the great building [Solomon's Temple] which, like the division of the rooms, was typical of Phoenician architecture: the pillars of Boaz and Jachin, which towered sky-wards in the outer courtyard on the left and right of the entrance to the temple. Similar designs were found in Canaanitish temples. Herodotus tells us, for instance, that the temple of Melqart at Tyre also had two pillars of the same kind, 'one of pure gold, the other of emerald which shone brilliantly at night'. Besides which, bases of similar pillars have been found in a temple of Baal in Cyprus and in various Palestinian towns such as Samaria, Megiddo and Hazor.[5]

[5] Herm, Gerhard: *The Phoenicians*, Victor Gollancz, 1975

The Phoenicians were famous businessmen, exporting and trading in anything that would make them a profit, and they had a colony for mining copper on Cyprus, where a two-pillared temple of Baal was excavated. The Bible is full of praise for Hiram's builders, who prepared timber and stones in advance before assembling Solomon's building on site without using any iron tool.[6] The implication is that the Phoenicians were skilled at making precise measurements and prefabricating large elements of buildings. The first-century historian Josephus was obviously aware of a tradition of impressive standards of workmanship, as he wrote that slabs had been cut so smoothly that 'the onlooker could see no trace of hammer or other tools'.

We were surprised when we learned more about the achievements of Hiram of Tyre. The Masonic ritual tells us very little about him, and to most modern Masons Hiram king of Tyre is only thought of as a supporting player in the ritual performances. But as we researched the archaeological literature about Phoenicia we began to realise that Hiram was a builder of huge historical importance.

It was a Roman Catholic priest, Father Antoine Poidebard, who first located the now sunken remains of Hiram's amazing harbour when he carried out an aerial survey of Lebanon by hot air balloon in 1925.[7] Hiram's brilliant idea was to transfer the core of his city from the coast out into the sea, which was an immense and inspired undertaking, using all the experience of his engineers.

At the beginning of Hiram's reign the main port of Tyre stood on the mainland, but this builder king realised that an island lying six hundred metres from the shore would form a highly defensible stronghold and also provide a fully integrated docking system for his fleet. The site he chose was composed of two flat, partly submerged rocky ledges. According to historian Gerhard Herm, construction must have kept thousands of men busy for years, since the rubble and boulders used as filling material were brought over from the mainland. Herm describes the structure further:

The whole enterprise was based on an extensive, carefully worked out plan. To the north of the man-made island the so-called inner or Sidonian harbour was made, by filling in and excavation, and to the south the outer or Egyptian harbour, by building quays and

[6] 1 Kings 5 and 6
[7] Renfrew, Colin: *Archaeology: Theories, Methods and Practice*, Thames and Hudson, 1996

jetties. Over the smaller, newly won island – it lay to the east of the larger reef and therefore nearer to the coast – Hiram had a vast and handsome civic building erected, which was later called by the Greek name Eugehoros. The determined ruler seems to have pulled down most of the older buildings and re-used the material for this. The Jewish historian Flavius Josephus says: 'He [Hiram] also went and felled timber in the mountains which are called Lebanon for the roofs of the temple, and tore down the old temples and erected new ones to Heracles [Melqart] and Astarte [Venus].'

Tyre's reputation for being not only one of the strongest but also one of the most beautiful metropolises of the ancient world dated back to this time. It was hardly surprising, since Hiram employed descendants of the architects who had once built Mycenaean royal castles and the Cretan villa palaces. The then inhabitants of Tyre called their town Sor, which means 'rocks' in the Phoenician language. The present-day inhabitants also call it by the same name in Arabic: Sur. Both are right: Tyre was a town on the cliff, an artificially made stronghold in the sea.

If one is looking for a symbol of what Phoenicia would be from now on, one might well choose the town built by Hiram.[8]

The problem of supplying the man-made island with water was also solved with breathtaking ingenuity. There were no springs to spurt fresh water from the rock that Hiram chose for his foundations, and when the site was excavated the archaeologists assumed that the city must have depended on rainwater cisterns to supply drinking water for the city, if ever it was under siege. But they were wrong: Hiram was a far more sophisticated engineer than that. Using breath-holding divers, the Phoenicians located freshwater springs gushing out of the seabed and affixed funnels where they entered the salt water. The drinking water was driven upwards by the pressure of the outflowing spring and the water fed through a network of leather pipes to where it was needed. Amazingly, the Greek geographer Strabo recorded how the system continued to work almost nine hundred years later. Hiram's civil engineering projects were built to last.

So now we knew that Hiram, king of Tyre, was a serious builder and a superb engineer. We felt that his important place in Masonic ritual is well

[8] Herm, Gerhard: *The Phoenicians*

earned. But what could we discover about the religious beliefs he held, beliefs that Masonic ritual told us persuaded him to worship a different god to Solomon?

HIRAM, THE SON OF VENUS

The finding of inscriptions on the coffins of King Ahiram of Byblos and his royal descendants opened a new window into the nature of kingship in the Phoenician sea towns of 3,000 years ago. The royal tombs, excavated by Pierre Montet, all contained detailed inscriptions, written in the Canaanite linear alphabet.[9] These finds prompted further searches, and in 1923 a French expedition discovered the stone coffin of Hiram, king of Tyre. The huge sarcophagus contained a Phoenician inscription around the edge of the lid written in a linear alphabet, revealing another line of development from the earlier Canaanite Semitic alphabet used at Ras Shamra.[10]

When the Phoenician royal tomb inscriptions were deciphered they told the story, previously unknown, of a line of kings who regarded themselves as the earthly representatives of gods. These kings took names which reflected their relationship to the gods. Ithobaal, Abibaal, Yehimilk, Elibaal and Shipitbaal all left their last messages to posterity couched in pharaoh-like terms. The inscriptions also tell of their close relationship with Baalat-Gebal, who, as we now knew, was the goddess who manifested as the planet Venus.

This is the temple wall which Shipitbaal, King of Byblos, son of Abibaal, King of Byblos, son of Yehimilk, King of Byblos, had built for Baalat-Gebal, his lady.

This is typical of the tone of the inscriptions which describe the king as the consort of Baalat-Gebal (Venus). The Phoenicians of Tyre, Sidon, Aradus, Byblos and Ugarit worshipped a trinity of gods consisting of El, the father god, his wife Baalat (also known as Asherat and Astarte [or Venus]) and their son Baal, the Lord (also known as Adon, Adoni – Graecized as Adonis – Melqart or Eshmun).

El was the mightiest of the three gods, and he was represented by the

[9] Montet, P: *Byblos et l'Egypte*, Paris, 1928
[10] Hackwell, W John: *Signs, Letters, Words. Archaeology Discovers Writing*, Charles Scribner's Sons, New York, 1987

Sun and its light. He would see and punish all evil deeds. His only human attribute was his infidelity to his wife, Venus. He was fond of impregnating any human female who took his fancy, and to do so he would disguise himself as a passing stranger. In order to make sure he was able to satisfy his desires El imposed a religious duty on all Phoenician woman to make themselves sexually available to passing strangers at his wife's temples during certain periods of the year, particularly around the spring and autumn equinoxes. This aspect of Phoenician belief was no doubt a boost for their tourist trade, but it has always troubled judgmental Christian theologians, as the following quote shows:

> There is a still graver charge to be brought against the religion of ancient Palestine. It was not merely indifferent to the claims of simple ethics, it even condoned and authorised direct violations of the moral law. Sexual irregularity was condemned by the common feeling of the western Semites, but sacramental fornication was a regular feature of the religious life, clearly appearing at other times as well as the spring and autumn festivals. Indeed, it may well have been that this vice was practically confined to the 'high places'. And the great festivals, especially that of the autumn, seem to have been times of riotous licence, when free rein was given to human passions.[11]

This was an ongoing tradition. The Greek satirist Lucian, writing in around 120 BCE, tells how the women of Byblos carried out 'secret rites' in the Temple of Baalat:

> The women of Byblos beat their breasts, cried and wailed, and then when they have finished wailing and weeping, sacrifice to Adonis, as to one who has departed this life. Then they announce that he lives again, set up his image in the open air. They then begin to shave their heads, like the Egyptians when they mourned the death of Apis. Those women, however, who refuse to have their heads shaved have to undergo the following punishment: for a whole day they have to be prepared to sell their bodies. Only

[11] Oesterley, WOE & Robinson, TH: *Hebrew Religion, Its Origin and Development*, SPCK, 1952

strangers are allowed access to the place where this takes place. An
offering to Baalat is bought with the money derived from the
traffic with these women.[12]

Baalat was the long-suffering wife of El and the mother of Baal.[13]
Herodotus, writing in 460 BCE, also tells of a similar practice carried out
in the Temple of Astarte in Babylon:

The following is the most shameful practice in Babylon. Every
woman born in the country must sit in the temple of Astarte and
associate once in her life with a strange man . . . They sit with a
wreath of braids round their head in the holy precinct. There are
many women, some coming, some going away. Straight paths are
made between them in every direction, along which the strangers
can walk to make their choice. When a woman sits there, she may
not go home until one of the strangers has thrown money in her
lap and associated with her outside the holy place . . . But when
she has given herself, she has fulfilled her holy duty to the goddess
and returns home, and however much she is offered thereafter, she
is not to be won. All those who are beautiful and well-made
quickly return home, but the ugly ones have to wait a long time,
until they can satisfy the custom, many having to wait for three to
four years.[14]

These temple prostitutes were called Hierodules, meaning the holy servants who worked in the temples. Gerhard Herm says of these practices:

We have no way to conceive of liturgies which pertained to sex;
which saw the working of godly powers in generation and concep-
tion. We know too much about the pure mechanics of sexual inter-
course to be able to see the process of copulation as a mystery. Yet
the ancients seem to have been in complete control of this act. 'If it
has such importance in the life of individuals, why should it not be
declared a sacred public institution?' they may have argued. And in

[12] Lucian: *Dialogues of the Gods*, Penguin Classics, 1960
[13] When Lucian uses the term Adonis, a Greek word meaning 'Lord', he is referring to the
Phoenician word *adôn* which means Baal.
[14] Herodotus: *Histories,* Wordsworth Classics of World Literature, 1996

*so doing they must have avoided and forestalled much difficulty
and misplaced prudery and spared themselves at any rate the elaborate uncertainty which can give rise, as in our case, to a whole literature.*

*It remains to say that temple prostitution and the public offering
of virginity occurred in all eastern temples between the
Mediterranean and the Indus valley. Hierodules even worked in the
older Jewish churches, where they were called Kedeshim, consecrated ones.*[15]

It seems honour was satisfied all around. El indulged his wicked ways
with all the women of the lands he ruled, so he got to know all his womenfolk, but they charged him for his pleasure, donating the money earned
to placate his deceived wife. The symbol of the phallus certainly figured
large in the Phoenician religion, as this poem to El tells:

> *El's penis grew as long as the sea,*
> *Yea, El's penis as the ocean.*
> *El took the two inflamed ones.*
> *And lo, the two wives cried out*
> *'O husband! Husband! Lowered is your staff,*
> *Drooping the rod in your hand!'*
> *He stooped: their lips he kissed.*
> *Oh, how sweet were their lips,*
> *As sweet as pomegranate;*
> *From kissing came conception,*
> *From embracing, impregnation.*

We couldn't help remembering the Norse god Odin, who was also promiscuous and famed for the potency of his penis. There seemed to be many
similarities with the Norse belief that the son of a king was born a descendant of the goddess and when he became king he also became the consort
of the goddess. Could these two concepts of kingship have a common
origin? How much similarity was there between the Phoenician and Norse
pantheons? We made a mental note to return to this question when we had
researched the Phoenician gods more fully.

[15] Herm, Gerhard: *The Phoenicians*

The poem that prompted this thought was found as part of the Phoenician literature discovered at the ancient city of Ugarit.[16] Of particular interest to us were the references to the two wives of El, referring to the morning and evening appearances of Venus, and also the allusions to pomegranates. We knew that these fruits were closely associated with lovemaking at the time, and we were beginning to suspect that it is no coincidence that Solomon's Temple was liberally decorated with images of this sexual fruit.

El's wife Baalat, the 'Queen of Heaven' and 'Queen of the Sea', was an adviser at the council of the gods. Like her husband El, she could only be approached via lesser gods, and the most suitable lesser god was the king, the earthly consort of Baalat. As her consort he was able to intercede with her on behalf of his people and through her gain the ear of the Almighty El. People would pray to Baalat, who was referred to as 'our dear lady', to ensure good harvests, the safe birth of children and long life for themselves. She was the mother of the heavens and also the earth-mother who could satisfy people's need for security and warmth.

Baalat had a son, Baal-Adon-Eshmun-Melqart, who is perhaps the most interesting figure in ancient Phoenician mythology, because he alone amongst the gods is not immortal. Once every year at the autumn equinox he dies and is resurrected at the following vernal equinox. This is obviously a manifestation of the yearly fertility cycle celebrated by many early cultures, yet there was an added strangeness about his destiny. In the late summer, when the harvest was collected, the young god died so that he could return to life on Earth with the new sprouting seeds the following spring. But although this idea started with something primitive and earthy, Baal's story led to a rich development and later to abstraction, which finally left nothing but the idea of a god who suffered death as a sacrifice for mankind. Gerhard observes:

> It was probably the most influential of all non-Jewish mythological concepts in the east and doubtless also prepared the ground for the later flowering of the story of Christ's death and resurrection.

To follow this analogy through, we can see how great the similarity is between the Venus goddess, Baalat, and the virgin Mary, as both are hailed as the mother of a resurrected saviour god.

16 Man, John: *Alpha Beta, How Our Alphabet Shaped the Western World*, Headline, 2000

By the time the Phoenician city states flowered again after their period of Egyptian dominance, Baal was their special favourite. His image was developed with the most fantastic features, including the physical endowments of a great and potent lover, and he came to be represented in many other guises. Indeed, he finally almost entirely superseded his father El – who is sometimes fused into one being with him.[17] He was worshipped as Baal-Shamim, the lord of the heavens, Baal-Lebanon, the lord of the mountain, Cul Baal-Rosh, the lord of the promontory, and as Melqart in Tyre, where he also gradually took on the status of a Sun god.

This mortal son of Venus was represented on Earth by the Phoenician kings. And when a king was made he was promoted from 'Son of Venus' to earthly 'consort of our lady'. Inscriptions in the royal tombs of Byblos and Tyre speak of this sacred relationship:

> *This is the statue which Abibaal, King of Byblos, son of Yehimilk, King of Byblos, had brought from Egypt for Baalat, his lady.*

> *This is the temple, which Yehimilk, King of Byblos, built for his lady. May Baalat-Gebal and may the whole council of gods prolong his life.*

Hiram was a strong king of Tyre, and like every other Canaanite king, he was a living but mortal god. But this knowledge made us pose another question. How did Solomon hope to become a king/god without the established theological structure of Temples and High Priests/Priestesses that the Canaanite kings enjoyed? After a detailed discussion we were forced to the conclusion that Solomon was probably not just buying buildings from Hiram, king of Tyre, when he commissioned the Temple of Yahweh, but he was also trying to buy the means of making himself a king of great standing who would match in stature the Canaanite rulers with their link to their gods. We believe he wanted to become the divinely appointed earthly representative of his new God, Yahweh.

We can understand that Solomon had no tradition of his own to give him the knowledge of how to build a temple that was properly constructed

---

[17] This is highly reminiscent of the way Christians fuse the resurrected Jesus with God, and dissolve the two into a single entity, presumably to maintain the deification of the man who was Jesus Christ whilst still satisfying the later Jewish tradition that there is only one god.

to interface with the heavens and the gods therein. However, we were perplexed that these Venus-worshipping Phoenicians were allowed to build God's house when we knew that only priests of Yahweh were ever allowed to even touch the stones that were destined for the Temple. According to Jewish tradition the priests of Yahweh had existed from the time of Moses, several hundred years earlier. Why, we wondered, were they not the builders?

Perhaps, we thought, the official history of the Jews as recorded in the Old Testament has been constructed to inflate the role of Yahweh and post-rationalise the idea of their monotheism. Could it be that Solomon was himself involved in rituals concerning Venus, and his relationship with the cult of Yahweh was not as strong as we are led to believe?

CONCLUSIONS

Our database of Freemasonic ritual describes in detail a series of tunnels and chambers secretly constructed under King Solomon's Temple which have no counterpart in the Bible. The ritual claims to know a great deal about the subterranean layout of the Jerusalem Temple which may be meaningless invention, but some of these inventions we found to be remarkably accurate.

Masonic tradition credits important sacred knowledge to the Jews, as their property, inherited from the Patriarch Enoch rather than simply bought from the Jebusites or the Phoenicians. All this ancient lost knowledge is stored directly under the chamber where God resides, making Yahweh the guardian of the knowledge of the ancients. We believe this idea to have an authentic ancient Judaic feel to it.

Archaeology tells us that the City of Jerusalem, its Jebusite name meaning 'Foundation of Venus in its evening setting', was established *circa* 3000 BCE, which is contemporary with the Hebrew dating of Enoch. The ritual claims that Solomon discovered the ruins of an Enochian temple dating from the foundation of Jerusalem.

We discovered that Hiram, king of Tyre, was far better suited than King Solomon to be an early Grand Master of Freemasonry, and his engineering and building skills earned him his key place in Masonic ritual.

Hiram, like previous kings of Tyre, practised a form of Venus worship, which involved sexual rituals at solstices and equinoxes, particularly when Venus rose before the Sun. As king he was considered to be a living but mortal god. We concluded that Solomon was not just buying buildings from the king of Tyre, but really buying the secrets and apparatus for making himself a king in the manner of the Phoenicians.

Chapter Six

THE MARITIME
CONNECTIONS

WHATEVER HAPPENED TO THE GROOVED WARE PEOPLE?

All of the evidence we had was pointing to some kind of connection between the beliefs of the early Canaanites (the forerunners of the Phoenicians and the Jebusites) three thousand years ago and the Grooved Ware People some five thousand years ago. These Solar- and Venusian-based beliefs were then passed onto the Jews. We decided that we needed to investigate the possibility in more detail by studying what is known of the origins of the Canaanites and of their seafaring coastal-dwelling cities whose inhabitants history has named the Phoenicians. But first we needed to consider the relatively sudden ending of the Grooved Ware culture in and around the British Isles.

The people who built the megalithic structures of the British Isles suddenly abandoned their sacred places and just seemed to disappear during the first half of the third millennium BCE. The archaeology of their sites shows periods of hundreds of years before the then derelict sites were reoccupied by a culture known as the Beaker Folk, again because of their distinctive pottery.[1]

Unless the Grooved Ware People were completely wiped out by some disaster or disease, we have to assume that they took their culture to some other location where it could have continued to develop. There are no

[1] Eogan, G: *Knowth and the Passage Tombs of Ireland*, Thames and Hudson, 1986

101

remains of their sailing vessels, but from the wide extent of their trading of distinctive stone tools and pottery which has survived in the archaeological record, many prehistorians have commented on their obvious skills as sailors. We can be confident that they travelled large distances, probably by sticking close to the coastline.[2] The thought that they might be connected to other civilisations who possessed building skills caused us to reconsider the Sumerian people who are said to have suddenly appeared as a fully formed civilisation in what is now Iraq at a similar time to the building of Newgrange and Enoch's visit.

Sir Leonard Woolley, the archaeologist who excavated the site of the city of Ur, where according to biblical legend Abraham was born, wrote a book detailing his findings entitled *Ur of the Chaldees, Seven Years of Excavation*, in which he said:

> *The history of Ur goes back far beyond the Flood into those dim days when the Euphrates Valley, at least at its lower end, was still a great marsh through which the waters of the two rivers made their sluggish way to the sea. Gradually, as the streams brought down more and more silt from the north, the marsh land began to shrink, 'the waters were gathered together into one place, and the dry land appeared,' and from the uplands of Arabia or from the higher reaches of the middle Euphrates settlers drifted down to occupy such islands as gave a chance for men to live and cultivate the earth, that rich alluvial soil which as soon as it was free from the water would 'bring forth grass, the herb yielding seed, and the fruit tree yielding fruit after his kind, whose seed is in itself.*[3]

Woolley was the first archaeologist to comment on the abrupt changes that occurred in Mesopotamia during the fourth millennium BCE. He wrote about excavating layers of crude and frail mud huts which comprised the solid mud mound, but he goes on to talk about the new people that arrived:

> *People of a new race made their way into the valley, coming whence we do not know, and settled down side by side with the old inhabitants. These were the Sumerians.*

[2] Wickham-Jones, CR: *Scotland's First Settlers*
[3] Woolley, Sir Leonard: *Ur of the Chaldees*, Pelican, 1929

The Sumerians believed that they came into the country with their civilisation already formed, bringing with them the knowledge of agriculture, of working in metal, of the art of writing – 'since then,' said they, 'no new inventions have been made' – and if, as our excavations seem to show, there is a good deal of truth in that tradition, then it was not in the Euphrates valley that the arts were born, and though it is not likely to have been the Indus valley either, later research may well discover some site where the ancestors of our Sumerians developed the first real civilisation of which we have any knowledge.[4]

It is accepted by mainstream archaeology that the Sumerians arrived as a fully formed civilisation from somewhere distant. The question is from where did they come?

Lord Renfrew, the distinguished professor of archaeology from Cambridge, has dated their arrival as occurring between 3500 and 3000 BCE.[5] This is precisely the time when the Grooved Ware culture was at its height and major sites such as Newgrange and Maes Howe were being constructed. It has often been the case throughout history that cultures that are at their zenith travel, trade and colonise new lands. Could that have happened here?

As we have already mentioned, the Grooved Ware civilisation developed a wide-ranging trade in stone tools. They had at least three major factories involved in the mass production of stone axes which were then traded over most of the British Isles and the coastal areas of nearby Europe. The factories were at Mount's Bay, Cornwall, Penmaenmawr, North Wales, and Great Langdale in Cumbria. The woodcutter's axes that these people mass-manufactured, which have survived in large enough quantities for their distribution to be plotted in the archaeological record, were an essential tool which made possible the spread of farming and a resultant increase in food surpluses and economic wealth.[6]

This wealth in turn led to a vast building programme of ritual and astronomically aligned buildings around the coasts of Britain, involving such magnificent structures as Maes Howe in Orkney, Newgrange in Ireland, and Bryn Celli Ddu in North Wales.

[4] Woolley, Sir Leonard: *Ur of the Chaldees*
[5] Renfrew, Colin: *Before Civilisation*
[6] Dyer, J: *Ancient Britain*, Routledge, 1997

Archaeologist Dr Euan Mackie considered what was happening in this society and talked in terms of applying an evolutionary understanding of how this society developed. He said:

> Not least of the advantages of this Darwinian approach to prehistoric cultural revolution is that it specifies what is likely to have happened in terms familiar to students of living societies. Instead of undefined cultural processes or influences, or open-ended assumptions about local inventiveness or capacities for exchanging ideas, we have a picture of an evolution of a specific institution – professional priesthood in this case – and of the physical movement of some of its members to new territories together with their special knowledge and skills. These energetic newcomers and their hybrid descendants would create out of local resources and imported ideas a vigorous new theocratical culture, which in favourable circumstances, would develop from small beginnings to something quite elaborate.[7]

In *Uriel's Machine* we drew attention to the construction of an early megalithic stone circle at Nabta, in southern Egypt, at a latitude where the sun stands directly overhead at the summer solstice, a location which could have been religiously significant for this 'professional priesthood'.[8] The timing of this does not only coincide with the establishment of a small Mediterranean-side trading village at Byblos, on the Canaan coast; it also occurred when the manufacture and trade of stone tools on the west coasts of Europe was growing rapidly, suggesting it was a period when trading was seen as a very useful and desirable activity.

A later influx of newcomers, whom we will discuss more fully later in the book, came from the North Sea coast, to the area which would eventually become Canaan. This wave of trading influence coincided with a surge in copper production, based around one of the old axe factories in North Wales. Between 2400 and 500 BCE the copper mine at Great Orme Head, Llandudno, produced many thousands of tonnes of copper, making it one of the major sources of copper metal, throughout the British Bronze Age.[9] The copper produced was widely traded.

[7] Mackie, E: *The Megalithic Builders*
[8] Knight, C & Lomas, R: *Uriel's Machine, The Ancient Origins of Science*
[9] O'Brien, W: *Bronze Age Copper Mining in Britain and Ireland*, Shire Archaeology, 1996

The people who dug the copper were trading over great distances, and on long voyages they would set up temporary sites in order to grow crops and replenish their supplies. These settlements sometimes grew into villages and ports in their own right. In this way we suspected they had come to influence the developing cultures of the Middle East. We do not think that vast numbers of people migrated from western Europe to the Middle East, but to create influences would have only required relatively small numbers of skilled traders and their astronomer priests. After all, a lot of the British cultural heritage of the United States grew from the ideas of the Pilgrim Fathers, who sailed on the *Mayflower*. They formed a small part of the population of Britain, but their influence on US culture has been immense over time. We envisaged a similar type of trading process, setting up small trading villages and promoting Grooved Ware ideas as a mechanism for seeding some of the changes that occurred in Sumer and Egypt.

The Norwegian historian and explorer Thor Heyerdahl was fascinated by the possible origins for an influx of innovative people who came from a mysterious land they called 'Dilmun' to sail up the Persian Gulf and found the Sumerian civilisation. In *The Ra Expeditions* he said about the event:

The Sumerians do not have to come back to give witness to their origins. Their words are still with us. They left their written testimony. Their tablets record how they came and from where. It was not by spacecraft. They came by ship. They came sailing in through the gulf, and in their earliest works of art they illustrated the kind of water-craft that brought them. They came as mariners to the coast of the twin river valley where they founded the civilisation which during the ensuing millennia was to affect in one way or another every corner of our world. The real puzzle was that human history has no known beginning. As it stands it begins with civilised mariners coming in by sea. This is no real beginning. This is the continuation of something lost somewhere in the mist.

If we are to believe the Sumerians, who ought to know, their merchant mariners returned to Dilmun many times. In their own days, at least, their ancestral land was neither sunk in the sea nor buried by volcanic ash. It was within reach of Sumerian ships from Sumerian ports. One little piece missing from the big puzzle is that nobody knows the range of a Sumerian ship. Their seagoing qualities were forgotten with the men who built them and sailed them, their range lost with their wakes.

The sea roads between them were in use before the Sumerians came to settle in Sumer. Their tablets speak of navigating kings and merchant mariners coming from or going to lands overseas, and they give long lists of cargo imported from or exported to foreign ports. A few even speak of shipwrecks and maritime disasters. Such records reflect the hazards always involved in a marine enterprise even when the vessel is built with the experience of a whole nation and manned by a crew at home with the craft. In reading the tablets such dramas come to life.

Sir Leonard Woolley, who excavated the city of Ur, says that Sumerian civilisation arrived fully developed with the influx of a new race, Lord Renfrew tells us it happened between 3500 and 3000 BCE, and Thor Heyerdahl refers to Sumerian records saying that they sailed to the mouth of the two rivers, the Tigris and the Euphrates, from a land that was already civilised. Once again we knew of only one contemporary civilisation with the skills and the ability to navigate long distances: the Grooved Ware People of Western Europe. But to arrive at the valley of the two rivers by sea they must have sailed to the Persian Gulf from the Atlantic, and a coast-hugging voyage from the British Isles to modern Kuwait involves no less than a staggering thirty thousand miles of sea. Could such a journey be possible, on a repeated basis, over five thousand years ago?

In *Uriel's Machine* we argued that they reached an isolated spot on the Tropic of Cancer called Nabta in southern Egypt, where there is the remains of a stone circle, by sailing down the Nile. This in itself would have been a major expedition, but to sail the length of the Atlantic and round the infamous Cape of Good Hope into the Indian Ocean does seem incredible. However, we have to remember that the late Thor Heyerdahl repeatedly crossed open ocean in his rudely made balsa and reed craft to bravely, and successfully, demonstrate that our estimation of ancient people is limited only by our unfounded conviction that we must be smarter than they were.

In *Uriel's Machine* we have already drawn attention to the similarity between the early Elamite script of the Sumerians and the symbolic inscriptions of the Grooved Ware People. We also drew attention to the meanings of some of the Grooved Ware symbols. A single spiral represented a quarter of a year, and a triple spiral the gestation period of a woman. The

Saltair cross, used above the light-box at Newgrange, represented a full year, whilst the diamond or lozenge shape could be used as a sort of post code to show the latitude of a place, by encoding the angles between the summer and winter solstice sunrises.[10]

This similarity in proto-writing symbols seemed to be more than simple coincidence. We wondered if the influx of newcomers who brought civilisation to Sumer could have been Grooved Ware traders who settled in an environment they found attractive, whilst still keeping links with other groups, possibly in places like Gebal in Lebanon or the newly founded cities of Egypt. To check out this idea we decided to look more closely at the start of the Egyptian civilisation.

THE BEGINNINGS OF EGYPT

The official history of civilised Egypt starts with the reign of Menes in 2920 BCE, and the time before the arrival of the pyramid builders is known to historians as the pre-dynastic period. So once more we noticed that there was an historical discontinuity in Egypt, resulting in a sudden upsurge in technology, building and astronomy. The basis of this framework is the work of an Egyptian priest of *circa* 250 BCE by the name of Manetho. He recorded a list of the kings of Egypt, starting with Menes and ending with the Meroitic kingdom. In all Manetho listed the details of 30 dynasties in his king lists. Mark Lehner, writing in 1997, said of him:

> Our framework for ancient Egyptian history is still based on
> Manetho's king list, grouped into 30 dynasties, and he is the first
> source to organise the kings from Menes to Unas into five dynas-
> ties.[11]

The reason Manetho is still used is that he proves to be consistently accurate when cross-checked against other sources. Egyptologist Michael Hoffman says of him:

> Archaeologists and Egyptologists have discovered five other king
> lists, which despite some discrepancies, support Manetho in general.[12]

[10] Knight, C & Lomas, R: *Uriel's Machine, The Ancient Origins of Science*
[11] Lehner, Mark: *The Complete Pyramids*, Thames and Hudson, 1997
[12] Hoffman, Michael A: *Egypt before the Pharaohs*, Michael O'Mara Books, 1991

But Manetho makes claims for the pre-dynastic period which are not so widely accepted. He splits the history of Egypt into three eras. In the first era, Egypt was ruled by the gods; in the second era the 'Followers of Horus' arrived in Egypt and established the conditions which eventually led to the third era, that of the dynastic kings, starting with Menes.

Professor Frankfort of the University of London wrote about this aspect of Manetho's work:

> It appears that 'Followers of Horus' is a vague designation for the kings of a distant past, but it would be unwise to treat the term primarily as being of an historical nature. For each king became at death one of the corporation of 'transfigured spirits' and merged with that nebulous spiritual form which had supported the living ruler and descendants of the Throne of Horus since time immemorial.[13]

Plato wisely said that 'we Greeks are children compared with these people with traditions ten times older than ourselves'. He also noted that the walls of the Egyptian temples were covered with inscriptions which recorded their early history. One of the most complete 'building texts' of the type Plato refers to was found at the temple of Edfu. According to Professor Raymond of Manchester University, who has transcribed and translated the Edfu Texts, said the story they tell concerns:

> the foundation, building and bringing to life of the historical temple during a mythical age. The historical temple is interpreted as the work of the gods themselves, and as an entity of a mythical nature.[14]

In Raymond's interpretation of these Edfu Texts the builders of the Temple came originally from an island known as the 'Homeland of the Primeval Ones', from which they fled when it was threatened by destruction. These incomers who arrived in Egypt became 'the Builder Gods', who were also known as the 'Lords of Light'. These primeval ones were not immortal: after they completed their tasks they died, and their roles were taken over by their children.

[13] Frankfort, Henri: *Kingship and the Gods,* University of Chicago Press, 1978
[14] Raymond, EAE: *The Mythical Origin of the Egyptian Temple,* Manchester Univ. Press, 1969

So Egyptian texts all seem to be telling of a sudden influx of skilled individuals that led to the founding of the united kingdom of Egypt in around 3150 BCE. This is exactly the time that we believe Enoch was in Britain receiving instruction, and we also believe it is the time that the Grooved Ware People were expecting a disastrous comet impact, which actually missed their land but hit the Mediterranean, causing considerable damage.[15]

Whoever arrived in Egypt at this time brought with them the skills of building, navigation and astronomy that kick-started one of the greatest civilisations of all time. It is interesting to note that the main feature of Newgrange is its spectacular white quartz wall that dominates the valley of the river Boyne. It may be coincidence, but the first city of ancient Egypt was called Memphis, which means 'White Wall'.

We also knew of another thread that supports our Grooved Ware theory. Analysis of DNA of the indigenous people of the British Isles shows a close relationship to the people of North Africa. This has led some of the researchers concerned to assume that North Africans (once thought to be the older civilisation) travelled to Britain.[16] Perhaps they have the direction wrong.

THE PHOENICIANS

The people we remember as the Phoenicians lived on the coastal areas of the eastern Mediterranean Sea between the Gulf of Alexandretta and the headland of Carmel. They called their homeland Kinahna, and that is the root of the name Canaan, which extends over a far greater area than the thirty-mile coastal strip associated with the Phoenicians.[17]

It is to the insecurity of the emperor of France, Napoleon III, that we owe the beginnings of our understanding of ancient Canaan. The younger Napoleon lived in the shadow of the exploits of his more famous uncle, Napoleon Bonaparte, but when an Islamic sect called the Druze massacred 30,000 Christians in Syria he saw an opportunity to follow in the footsteps of his famous predecessor.

Napoleon Bonaparte had invaded Egypt in 1796. As well as an army and a fleet (which Nelson destroyed at the Battle of the Nile in 1803), he also sent an enormous entourage of scholars to study ancient Egypt, and

[15] Knight, C & Lomas, R: *Uriel's Machine, The Ancient Origins of Science*
[16] Sykes, B: *The Seven Daughters of Eve*, Corgi, 2001
[17] Gray, J: 'Israel's Neighbours', *Peake's Commentary on the Bible*

so effectively founded the academic discipline of Egyptology. Keen to establish his own credentials as a leader in the heroic mould, in 1860 Napoleon III sent an expeditionary force to assist the sultan of Constantinople, who was already engaged in trying to suppress the religiously inspired killings. With his battalions of French troops, Napoleon III sent a lapsed Roman Catholic priest, Father Ernest Renan, with instructions to study the history of Phoenicia.

Father Renan, an expert on Semitic languages, was working on a history of early Christianity when he was given the opportunity to investigate the site of the Phoenician town of Byblos. It is from Byblos that the Greeks take their name for papyrus, or writing material, and from this comes the later word Biblion, meaning book, which gives the word 'Bible'. What better place to study for a biblical scholar than the town that gave its name to the Bible?

Renan also knew the site by its Semitic name of Gebal, and was aware from his biblical studies that the town was a centre for seafaring traders. The prophet Ezekiel said that 'the ancients of Gebal possessed great skill in shipbuilding and carried much of the volume of trade goods of Tyre in the ships they built'.[18]

When Renan travelled the forty kilometres from Beirut to Gebal in the mid-nineteenth century, he described the town as a 'wretched Arab dump'. Here amongst the squalor he saw a ruined Crusader's castle brooding over the remains of a once fine oval harbour.[19] He did not carry out any excavations, but within the Crusaders' castle he found granite columns carved by the Phoenicians, which were re-used to build the fortress. Searching further he discovered that many of the houses of the town incorporated stone panels carved with Egyptian hieroglyphs in their construction. His most important find was a bas-relief, which he took back to France.

The carving shows a goddess with curved horns and a Sun disk behind her head. Renan assumed this was Hathor, the Egyptian goddess of the sky, who was the daughter of Ra and the wife of Horus. But he was wrong. Later research discovered that the goddess, whose image is still on display in the Louvre, is Baalat-Gebal, the Phoenician queen of heaven, and the local Baalat or patron goddess of Gebal. The heavenly luminary which represented this goddess would later be known by the Roman name of

[18] Ezekiel 27
[19] Renan, E: *Mission de Phénicie*, Paris, 1864

Venus, and her horns, as we have already mentioned, are the shape that the planet Venus traces out in the sky around the rising and setting Sun.

Renan did not manage to discover much more about ancient Gebal, as the building materials of the Phoenician town had been recycled and buried beneath modern Gebeil. It was more than fifty years before any scholar followed up his pioneering work. Just after the end of the First World War, the French Egyptologist Pierre Montet travelled to Gebeil in search of the hieroglyphic inscriptions Renan had recorded. He found most of them still in situ, and became so interested in what he translated that two years later, in 1921, he led an expedition to dig in search of Byblos. Montet and his assistants spent the next three years digging trenches through all the open ground around the houses of Gebeil, where they found the seals of pharaohs from various Egyptian dynasties, showing that this really was the site of an ancient trading centre. As Montet records in the account of this expedition that he gave in his book *Byblos et l'Egypte*, published in 1928, he then experienced an enormous stroke of luck.

The spring of 1922 was a particularly wet one in the Lebanon, and the heavy rain caused a landslip of part of the cliffs to the south of Gebeil. A large chunk of the cliff face dropped some twelve metres and revealed a tunnel leading into a man-made cave, a burial chamber which had lain untouched since the reign of Ithobaal, king of Byblos, during the eleventh century BCE. Ithobaal dug the tomb to house the sarcophagus of his father Ahiram. The inscriptions in the tomb tell us that Ithobaal was not only 'beloved of Baal' but also a highly confident ruler. His warning to would-be tomb raiders was spelt out clearly in the alphabet the Phoenicians invented:

This coffin was made by Ithobaal, the son of Ahiram, King of Byblos, as the eternal resting place for his father. If any ruler or governor or general attacks Byblos and touches this coffin, his sceptre will be broken, his throne overthrown, and peace will forsake Byblos. And as for himself: may vandals look upon his epigraph.[20]

Of course, these finds encouraged the French colonial government to support further excavations. In 1930 the French placed compulsory purchase

[20] Montet, P: Byblos et l'Egypte, Paris, 1928

111

orders on the houses which impeded the progress of the archaeologists, demolished them and so cleared the ground for more extensive investigations. This major dig revealed that the site of Gebeil dated right back to the Old Stone Age, which at the time made it one of the oldest known permanently occupied settlements in the world.

The earliest habitations showed that around 4500 BCE a large village was established consisting of circular huts with wood, pebble and mud walls and floors of limestone grit.[21] By 2900 BCE Gebal/Byblos became a much larger complex of stone buildings. Archaeologist Michel Dunand, who excavated the site, wrote that by this time 'Byblos had become a town'.[22] It was a significant site protected by a wall with only two entrances: one to the land and the other to the sea. At its centre stood a temple dedicated to Baalat-Gebal, the 'Queen of Heaven'. The streets of the town were laid out in concentric circles about the temple and a canal system carried rain and drainage water away. Dunand comments that the level of amenity and the rich funerary offerings showed that the inhabitants of the town were prosperous and well prepared to defend their wealth if they needed to.

We reminded ourselves that this temple in Byblos was two millennia older than Solomon's Temple, and whilst there is considerable archaeological evidence for the existence of this Phoenician structure, no remains on the site of the Temple in Jerusalem have ever been identified as being from Solomon's Temple. Every part of the ruin that is now still standing dates from the Temple built by King Herod at the time of Christ, almost 1,000 years after Solomon. So our knowledge of the layout of Solomon's Temple relies on the descriptions in the Bible.

But around 2300 BCE the six-hundred-year-old temple of Baalat-Gebal was destroyed by fire, which Dunand suggests was due to the city being ransacked by nomad hordes who descended on the coastal plain from the desert of the Sinai. These Semitic Amorite Bedouins merged with the people who established and developed Gebal in the previous thousand years, and formed a new tribal group, which would eventually develop into the people known as the Phoenicians.[23]

But who were the people who had developed Gebal into such a major port? Dunand calls them Giblites, and in the absence of any evidence he assumes that they must have 'fashioned their own culture from fragments

---

[21] Dunand, M: *De l'Amanus and Sinai*, Beirut, 1953
[22] Dunand, M: *De l'Amanus and Sinai*
[23] Dunand, M: *De l'Amanus and Sinai*

of the civilisations of other ancient races.'[24] We knew the Giblites became seafarers and traders who were extremely successful in their navigating and trading, and that at some early date they had dedicated their town to the worship of the goddess who manifested herself as the planet Venus. Our next task was to see what else we could find out about Byblos, and in particular its fame as a world centre of shipping and international trade.

One clue to this tradition was found in 1954, when archaeologist Ahmed Youssef excavated two complete cedarwood boats from diggings just to the south of the Great Pyramid of Khufu, near Cairo. The boats were buried in sections as a kit of parts, but when they were reassembled the larger one was 142 feet long and of a design capable of ocean-going.[25]

Thor Heyerdahl investigated the origins of Egyptian shipbuilding skills whilst preparing for his Ra Expeditions, and he said of these boats:

There are only two possibilities. Either this sea-going, streamlined shape had been developed by Egyptian seafarers of the same brilliant generations which had already evolved writing and pyramid building, mummies, brain surgery and astronomy; or the pharaoh's shipwrights had been trained abroad. There are facts which point to the latter. No cedars grow in Egypt; the material of which Cheops's ship was built came from the cedar forests of Lebanon. The Lebanon was the home of the Phoenicians, experienced shipbuilders who sailed the whole of the Mediterranean, and part of the Atlantic with their ships. Their principal port, Byblos, the oldest known city in the world, imported papyrus from Egypt because Byblos was a centre of book production in ancient times, hence the word Byblos or Bible, which means book. There were lively trade relations between Egypt and Byblos at the time when the Pyramid of Cheops was built, so Cheops' shipbuilders might have copied their specialised design here.[26]

He went on to add some fascinating detail about megalithic structures at an ancient city called Maqom Semes, 'the City of the Sun' that once stood on the Atlantic coast of North Africa, close to present-day Larache:

[24] Dunand, M: *De l'Amanus and Sinai*
[25] Lehner, Mark: *The Complete Pyramids*
[26] Heyerdahl, Thor: *The Ra Expeditions*, George Allen & Unwin Ltd, 1971

On a desolate beach just south of our starting place, an angled mole [an ancient type of jetty] made of thousands of tons of megalithic stone blocks still projects towards the reefs and provides a magnificent harbour. Fantastic quantities of gigantic quarried stones have been dragged out into the sea by experienced marine architects. Who built such a lasting bulwark that the Atlantic waves have not succeeded in washing it away after thousands of years? Who needed such a big harbour on that desolate sandy point before the Arabs and Portuguese had begun to sail down the Atlantic coast of Africa?

On a height where the broad Lucus River flows into the Atlantic on the north-west coast of Morocco stand the gigantic ruins of one of the mightiest towns of antiquity, with a past disappearing into the darkness of pre-history. Huge megalithic blocks weighing many tons were transported up the cliffs and lifted on top of one another in giant walls several metres high which can be seen from the sea. The blocks are cut and polished, the joints accurate to a millimetre. The oldest known name of the megalithic town is Maqom Setmes, 'City of the Sun'. When the Romans found it they wrote that fantastic legends were associated with its earliest history. They called the town Lixus, the Eternal City, and built their own temples on top of the ancient ruins.

At this point Heyerdahl considers who might have made these megalithic structures at this ocean seaport:

The very few archaeologists who have embarked on small test digs have found that the Phoenicians used 'Sun City' long before the Romans. But who founded it? Perhaps the Phoenicians. If so, Phoenician stonemasonry was equal to the best on both sides of the Atlantic. The Phoenicians' home was in the distant eastern Mediterranean, the present Lebanon. 'Sun City' was no Mediterranean port, but a true Atlantic harbour established at the very edge of the powerful current which swings westward through the Canary Islands and ends in Mexico. How old are the walls? No one knows. They are covered to a depth of fifteen feet by the detritus of Phoenicians, Romans, Berbers and Arabs. The Romans believed in Hercules and Neptune, but not in the Sun-god, and the Roman ruins lying uppermost are therefore not solar-oriented. But recent test digs down to the very bottom have shown that the lowest and largest of the giant blocks, those which were already covered with detritus when the Romans came, and which the Romans therefore failed to demolish or rebuild into their temples, provide the foundations for extensive buildings which were carefully oriented according to the Sun.[27]

This solar-oriented city was certainly used by the Phoenicians as an Atlantic trading base for dealing with Spain and Britain, but the magnificent stonework was already there when they made use of it. We knew of a civilisation much older than the Phoenicians who were capable of this standard of stoneworking, who were expert navigators, traders and astronomers, and whose civilisation established outposts in the Mediterranean. We wondered if Lixus, the city of the Sun, was built by the same group of megalithic craftsmen who constructed structures such as Newgrange and Maes Howe.

As the Phoenician civilisation developed it drew on the expertise of what Dr Dimitri Baramki, curator of the Museum of the American College in Beirut, described as the 'North Sea Peoples' – people who came from the lands that the Norse seafarers had inherited from the Grooved Ware culture. As we read Dr Baramki's work we were reminded of Thor Heyerdahl's description of the people from 'Dilmun' who established Sumer, which we discussed earlier in this chapter. Could these expert seafarers be the source of the legend of the mysterious Sumerians? Baramki wrote about how these intruders from the northwestern Atlantic coast of Europe migrated into the Lebanon bringing with them absolute supremacy at sea, superb navigational skills and traditions of shipbuilding in both war and trading vessels. Although the Canaanite Proto-Phoenicians were a people who possessed all the qualities necessary to open up the Mediterranean to navigation and trade, they did not show much evidence of a developing tradition of nautical and technical knowledge. This knowledge came from the invasion of the group known as the 'Sea Peoples' or Thekel. What the Canaanites added to the strength of the Phoenician culture was a long-established 'astral based religion which involved a knowledge of astronomy and astral navigation'.[28]

[27] Heyerdahl, Thor: *The Ra Expeditions*
[28] Baramki, D: *Phoenicia and the Phoenicians*, American College Press, Beirut, 1961

Baramki's hypothesis suggested to us a simple explanation for the previously puzzling origins of the Phoenicians. The original Canaanite settlement, with its ancient traditions of astronomically aligned temple building, developed from a group of coastal sailors into international navigators when they fused with a new wave of proto-Norse invaders from the area we knew as the homelands of the Grooved Ware People. From what we already knew about the Grooved Ware People we believe it might have been they who set up the original settlement and then lost touch with it.

Some people may find it hard to believe that people could sail large distances so far back in time, but history is littered with examples of early people travelling great distance. Among these there are records of Phoenicians travelling right around the continent of Africa on a number of occasions – perhaps regularly using Lixus as a major staging post to the Gulf of Aqaba at the northeastern tip of the Red Sea. The Greek historian Herodotus tells how King Necho II of Egypt ordered 'Phoenician men to sail home through the Pillars of Hercules [the Strait of Gibraltar] into the northern sea [the Mediterranean] to get to Egypt'. This can only mean he instructed them to sail around Africa.

The Phoenicians carried out his orders, as Herodotus adds that they

Sunrise over Africa. To see the sunrise over land these ancient sailors must have been circumnavigating the entire continent from the Red Sea to the Mediterranean.

sailed from 'the Red Sea and sailed across the southern sea'. When autumn came round, they landed and sowed their crops, finding themselves in Libya each time, and there they waited for the harvest. After harvesting the grain, they sailed on, so that in the third year they came through the Pillars of Hercules and back to Egypt again. They said, so Herodotus doubtingly reports, that on the voyage around Libya they had the rising Sun over the land as they sailed along the coast. It is this simple fact of astral navigation which confirms the truth of the story. To have observed this accurately the Phoenicians must have sailed down one side of Africa and back up the other.[29]

If we are right when we suggest that both the Sumerians and the Phoenicians were a subset of the Grooved Ware People, then these two groups should show some similarities above and beyond a Venus-based theology. But we found that others have already linked these two groups. Nearly two and a half thousand years ago Herodotus said that the Phoenicians came from Sumer:

> The Phoenicians, who had formerly dwelt on the shores of the
> Persian Gulf, having migrated to the Mediterranean and settled in
> the parts which they now inhabit, began at once, they say, to
> adventure on long voyages, freighting their vessels with the wares
> of Egypt and Assyria.[30]

If a substantial group of people from the British Isles and Brittany had arrived in the Persian Gulf with their pre-existent civilisation and sailing skills – calling themselves 'Sumerians' – it would make sense for them to eventually move northwest to the Mediterranean coast to afford themselves a short-cut route back to the old land that their forebears had abandoned.

THE PRIEST-KINGS OF THE PHOENICIANS

We decided that we now needed to construct as good a picture as we could of the rituals used by the Phoenician people, particularly their kings.

The earliest Canaanite to rate a full description in the Bible is Melchizedek. He is a figure closely associated with Abraham, the father of the Jewish nation. The New Testament tells us that Jesus was a priest of the Order of Melchizedek,[31] and we were aware of a Masonic organisation based upon

[29] Herodotus, *The History*, trans. George Rawlinson, New York, Dutton & Co., 1862
[30] Herodotus, *The History*, trans. George Rawlinson
[31] Hebrews 5: 6

this ancient priesthood called The Holy Order of the Grand High Priest.

Abraham is often taken as being the first person mentioned in the Bible who just might have been an actual person rather than a symbolic character from ancient myth.[32] The preceding figures referred to in the Book of Genesis, such as Adam, Eve, Cain, Abel, Noah and Enoch, are often considered to be types rather than historical individuals. Abraham is usually dated between 1800 and 1600 BCE, but some sources put him as far back as the twentieth century BCE. We think it is almost certain that Abraham is entirely mythical and was invented, possibly based on some inspiration from old oral traditions, to explain how the new Jewish religion carried the weight of some far older authority. Our researches and conversations with biblical scholars have convinced us that it is extremely likely that the stories of Abraham, Moses and David are mainly composite inventions. Nevertheless, in our own discussions we found it simpler to speak about them as if they were real people, so in this vein, as we tell his story we will continue to treat Abraham as a single individual.

In Genesis 14 the story is told of how four kings from the north of the land of Canaan raided the five kings of the cities of the Dead Sea plain, which is the lowest land on Earth. The kingdoms were taken, and among the captives from the city of Sodom was Abraham's nephew, Lot. When Abraham heard of this he led his clan of 318 men along with his Hittite and Amorite allies to attack the invaders and free Lot. As was the usual custom of the time, Abraham plundered his defeated enemies.

On his return from battle Abraham met with Melchizedek, the Jebusite/Canaanite king of Salem, who was also the high priest of a god called El Elyon, which meant 'the Most High'. The place called Salem is synonymous with Jerusalem, as Psalm 76: 2 makes clear. What happened next has not just puzzled us but is a rich source of debate for many biblical scholars, because the story is not what anybody would expect the scribes of the Bible to say.

Despite the high authority attributed to Abraham the writers of the Old Testament are not shy of reporting his open subservience to both this priest-king of ancient Jerusalem, and the god he represented. Abraham paid tithes to Melchizedek, which meant that he handed over a tenth of his war spoils. In return Melchizedek then blessed Abraham in the name of the god El

---

[32] Hook, SH: Genesis – *Peakes Commentary on the Bible*

Elyon and conducted a ritual whereby Abraham received bread and wine; an act that several biblical experts see as a direct precursor to the Christian Eucharist.

This suggests that Abraham was showing great respect to the Cannanite god, and the entire episode of preparing to sacrifice his son Isaac may have been an attempt to gain favour with this new god. It is recorded that in early biblical times travelling people considered that their own gods were left behind in their own city and they came under the power of new deities once they were in a new country.

Psalm 110 also describes King David as a priest of the Order of Melchizedek, in a manner which certainly was adopted for Jesus Christ:

The LORD said unto my Lord, Sit thou at my right hand, until I make thine enemies thy footstool.

The LORD shall send the rod of thy strength out of Zion: rule thou in the midst of thine enemies.

Thy people shall be willing in the day of thy power, in the beauties of holiness from the womb of the morning: thou hast the dew of thy youth.

The LORD hath sworn, and will not repent, Thou art a priest for ever after the order of Melchizedek.

The Lord at thy right hand shall strike through kings in the day of his wrath.

He shall judge among the heathen, he shall fill the places with the dead bodies; he shall wound the heads over many countries.

He shall drink of the brook in the way: therefore shall he lift up the head.

Whilst this passage relates Yahweh to the priesthood of Melchizedek, it is widely accepted that this order was a Canaanite cult that long pre-dated the arrival of the Israelites and El Shaddai (the mountain god), who later became 'Yahweh', the God of the Jews.[33] The term Zion is a reference to Jerusalem, which was said to be captured by David. The '*rod of strength*' or power held by a king or a leader such as Moses developed from the Asherah, the fundamental astronomical instrument used as a marking pole to measure movements of the Sun's shadow.

Like many passages in the Old Testament this one appears to indicate the absorption of some truly ancient Canaanite ritual into early Judaism. Biblical scholars have long been aware that such rituals must have existed, and one leading scholar said of this psalm:

> *The reference to Melchizedek implies an appropriation of the pre-Davidic religious traditions of the city; and there seem to be allusions to a wider background of myth and ritual . . . The priestly functions of the king are here associated with Melchizedek. This doubtless indicates a fusion of Hebraic usage with ancient cultic traditions of Jerusalem.*[34]

The exact content of the ritual of the Order of Melchizedek may not have ever been written down. There are other ancient concepts whose meaning has been lost, such as the nature and purpose of the Urim and the Thummim[35] which were carried in the priest's breastplate. All that is now known of these objects is that they were used for guidance in decision-making by casting a sacred lot.

When something is not written down it tends to be for one of two reasons: either it is of no particular importance or it is secret. The Order of Melchizedek was certainly important, so we tend to consider that its adherents conducted their rituals in private and kept the entire procedure restricted to an oral tradition. Certainly the *Masonic* Order that follows Melchizedek states that it is a secret Order. As the ritual tells the candidates for priesthood, they are required to 'take a solemn Obligation to keep inviolate the secrets of this Holy Order'.

We thought it reasonable to speculate that anyone who is King and the High Priest of Israel might be made Master of the Order automatically at their coronation, just as the king or queen of England also becomes head of the Church of England at the moment of enthronement. We also found

[33] Oesterley, WOE & Robinson, TH: Hebrew Religion, Its Origin and Development
[34] Anderson, GW: Psalms – *Peakes Commentary on the Bible*
[35] Exodus 28: 30

evidence, in the research of the Reverend Professor SH Hooke, which showed that the enthronement was renewed every autumn equinox during a new year ritual.

Twentieth-century archaeological discoveries such as the Ras Sharma tablets[36] mean that there is now much more known about ancient Canaanite rituals, and we noted interesting parallels with the central, third degree of Freemasonry that causes the candidate to be symbolically killed before being resurrected. Professor Hooke put Melchizedek into a context that we recognised as having definite Masonic resonances:

At the beginning of the second millennium B.C. we find that the king, representing both the god and the people, is the centre of great emotional religious activities whose object is to secure for the community those material benefits upon whose continuance the well-being of the community depends. These activities had assumed what we might almost call a stereotyped form, and involved the existence of an organised body of people possessing the knowledge of the right way in which the ritual must be performed and of the myth which embodied the situation enacted in the ritual.

It is possible that in the beginning a single individual possessed the knowledge and the magical powers in virtue of which he became the focus of the religious activities of the community, and that with the increasing complexity of urban life a devolution took place. The god became the embodiment of the mysterious powers whose control had been the original purpose of the ritual while the priest became the depository of the sacred knowledge necessary for the right performance of the ritual; while the king, still representing the god in the great annual rituals, came to be the centre of the secular activities of the communities, the head of the state for the purposes of war, politics, and justice, and, as representing the god, the owner of the land.

Early Mesopotamian sources point to the existence of 'priest-kings', of whom the mysterious figure of Melchizedek may have been a representative surviving in Canaan in the time of Abraham.

[36] The Ras Shamra tablets, found on the site of the ancient seaport of Ugarit, contain a large number of poems of ritual and religious importance from the second millennium BC. They have enormously enlarged our understanding of early beliefs and practices in Canaan.

The general pattern of the annual ritual . . . consisted of the preparation of the sacred buildings by purificatory rites, some of them symbolic of elements in the myth. Then the king went through a ceremony in which he divested himself of his regalia at the door of the shrine, made a confession to the priest, who struck him on both cheeks and then restored to him the emblems of his kingship. This part of the ritual probably represents an earlier ritual killing of the king when his strength showed signs of waning. Then came the central and probably secret part of the ritual, the dramatic representation of the death of the god, followed by his resurrection . . . A memory of this element of the ritual survives in Hebrew poetry in the myth of the fight between Jahweh and the dragon. [37]

We decided to summarise the main points of this description of the early Canaanite priest-king (Melchizedek) ritual:

1   There was an organised body of people possessing the knowledge of the right way in which the ritual must be performed.

2   There was a myth enacted in the ritual which embodied the message.

3   Originally a single priest-king alone possessed the knowledge and the magical powers.

4   Only later did the priest become the depository of the sacred knowledge necessary for the right performance of the ritual and the king represented the god in the great annual ritual.

5   The annual ritual included the preparation of the sacred buildings.

6   The king divests himself of his regalia at the door of the shrine.

7   The king is struck on both cheeks before being restored, perhaps in imitation of an earlier ritual when the king is killed.

[37] *A Companion to the Bible,* published by T & T Clark, Edinburgh, 1939. Quote from section three, 'The Early Background of Hebrew Religion', by SH Hooke.

8   Then came the secret ritual concerning a dramatic representation of the death of the god followed by his resurrection.

9   This ritual was conducted at the autumn equinox.

Next we listed the attributes of the third degree of Freemasonry:

1   The third degree ritual was originally secret and known only to Master Masons.

2   The myth of the killing of Hiram Abif is enacted in the modern ritual.

3   In the story only Hiram Abif knew the secret words.

4   Only later did more people learn the substituted secrets.

5   The setting of the ritual is the making of the sacred temple.

6   The candidate for the ritual is divested of his regalia at the door of the lodge.

7   The candidate is struck a blow to each side of the head before being 'killed' in imitation of the original victim by a final blow in the centre of the forehead.

8   The candidate is then figuratively resurrected.

9   The ritual is symbolically enacted at the equinox (when Venus is rising in the east).

We already knew that the rising of Venus was central to Canaanite theology and was associated with resurrection, as it is in Freemasonry. The parallels were truly impressive.

If the priest-king Melchizedek of Salem is a historical figure, we can be reasonably sure that this type of annual ritual would have been conducted by him, perhaps with all the central secrets known to him alone. There are major similarities to the ritual of the Masonic Third Degree, despite the fact that no one knew anything about the Canaanite practices until about seventy years ago. The number of points of correspondence is considerable, and we thought it extremely likely that there is some connection between the two.

We decided to look at what is known of Melchizedek himself before looking further into the ancient Canaanite practices.

As we have seen, the Old Testament tells us that even Abraham was subordinate to Melchizedek, the priest/king of Jerusalem. Abraham, the progenitor of all Jews, was happy to pay tribute to the Canaanite creator deity El Elyon (the Most High). Hundreds of years later, the Bible says that the Hebrews arrived from Egypt and seized most of the land of Canaan. Eventually King David took the city of Jerusalem by force and effectively installed himself as the successor of Melchizedek.

The name Melchizedek is said by the Masonic Order to mean 'King of righteousness', and Salem, of which he was King, means 'peace'. These translations may be correct in their later use, but they originally held much more specific meaning. The Hebrew word 'zedek' or 'tsedeq' which makes up the final part of Melchizedek's name is indeed normally translated into English as 'righteousness', but it carried deeper overtones than simply 'not doing wrong'. It stood for the founding principle underlying the divinely appointed order of the universe and derived its origin from an ancient god. But just as few people today think about the Norse god Woden when they speak about Wednesday (Woden's-day) or the Venus goddess Freyja when they say Friday, most Jews at the time of Christ would be unaware that zedek was once the divine essence of a Canaanite god.

Zedek for the Canaanites was the beneficent manifestation of the Sun god, its bright light revealing hidden crimes and righting wrongs done to the innocent. When the Canaanite gods were eventually merged into Yahweh, 'zedek' became his attribute.[38] In reality the single God concept has come into existence, not because there necessarily is only one super-entity, but because all positive attributes of the old gods have been transferred into one deity and all negative attributes to a second entity we call 'the Devil'.

The first half of the priest-king's name is universally accepted as meaning 'king' or 'the king is', which is based on the Canaanite root word 'malak' – meaning councillor,[39] or more specifically 'member of God's council'. So

---

[38] Cohn, Norman: *Cosmos, Chaos and the World to Come*, Yale University Press, 1993
[39] Hook SH: in *Myth, Ritual and Kingship*, Oxford at the Clarendon Press, 1958. See section 'Hebrew Conceptions of Kingship' by AR Johnson.

the Masonic translation of Melchizedek as 'king of righteousness' certainly holds good for its usage in the first and second centuries BCE, but its original usage in the first half of the second millennium BCE was much more specific, and must have carried an import something like this:

> *The living man who is a member of God's council representing his people in heaven and carrying responsibility on Earth for the upholding of the cosmic order defined and delivered by the Sun.*

This suggests that Melchizedek, the civil and religious head of Jerusalem, was so mighty that he sat on God's council. We soon found that this definition made even more sense when we looked deeper into Masonic ritual.

Melchizedek is recorded as being a priest of the Canaanite god El Elyon, who was associated with the city of Jerusalem. The association of the Sun with El Elyon is consistent with the name, which means 'Most High' – it could simply be a literal description of the Sun's perceived position in relation to the world. And, of course, the city itself was named after Venus, a planet that never moves far from the Sun in our skies. With such high-flying authority supporting Melchizedek, it is little wonder that Abraham was in awe of him.

The Masonic organisation known as The Holy Order of the Grand High Priest makes reference to the unique circumstances of Melchizedek:[40]

> *The tradition of his priesthood must therefore have continued for nearly nine hundred years, until the reign of David. His importance is that, unlike the other local kings who had warred and carried off Abram's nephew, he was also a priest. Nevertheless it is surprising that Abram, the Mesopotamian, recognised by the payment of tithes the authenticity and authority of a Canaanite Priest-King.*

It further describes aspects of ritual associated with the degree:

> *In former times it was customary for some of the companions to form two sides of an equilateral triangle and to kneel during prayer in the Opening and Closing of a Convention. In most Councils this is no longer practised.*

[40] Web of Hiram http://www.brad.ac.uk/webofhiram

We note that the term 'council' is used here to describe the gathering.

> . . . the ritual makes reference to the presence of the 'indispensable number of three'. Should nine Anointed High Priests be present, then traditionally it is said that the Ceremony is performed in 'due and ample form'.
>
> . . . A Tabernacle of the Order represents the encampment of Melchizedek in the valley of Shaveh (the King's dale). The room is divided by curtains which must be capable of being opened and closed. The Eastern part represents the royal tent of Melchizedek. These curtains are open during the Opening of the Convention: they are closed for Part I of the Ceremony of Reception and for the first portion of Part II, until the Candidate is invited to enter the Tent: thereafter they remain open. During Part II, if there is room, all the companions move inside the Tent and stand in the North and South in order to partake of bread and wine.
>
> . . . an equilateral Triangle is placed in the centre of the floor outside the Tent: three candles on tall candlesticks form a further equilateral Triangle outside the former: the apex of each Triangle points towards the East.
>
> During Part 1 there is a pedestal in the centre of the inner Triangle on which is placed a Volume of the Sacred Law, [the name Volume of the Sacred Law used by Masons to refer to the Scriptures accepted by the Masons present. In an English lodge it will be the Christian Bible but in addition there could also be open the Torah, the Koran, the Book of Mormon, or Hindu writings] opened at Genesis, chapter 14. For Part II both pedestal and Volume of the Sacred Law are moved inside the Tent and placed in front of the President's chair: a small kneeling stool or cushion is then placed in the centre of the inner Triangle.
>
> . . . The President wears a white robe, with a breastplate over it, and a mitre. The Vice-President wears a scarlet robe and the Chaplain a light blue robe.

The manner of the investing of candidates into the Order is described on the assumption that there will be more than one being anointed at the same time:

When the Representative Candidate is invited to enter the Tent, he will be placed on the extreme right of the opening formed by the curtains: the other candidates will then be led up to stand in line with him, in order that they may all partake of bread and wine which must be offered to each candidate in the traditional manner by the President.

During the partaking of wine, the sword may be passed along the line, handed from one candidate to the next, for each in turn to hold horizontally in front of him: alternatively the M. of C. from behind may hold the sword horizontally in front of each candidate in turn.

When the Conductor is directed to place the Representative Candidate in the centre of anointing, the other candidates will be formed behind him in the West. After the Representative Candidate has been anointed and raised, he will be temporarily led aside: each other candidate in turn will then kneel in the centre of the Triangle, be anointed, raised and conducted back to his place. After all anointing has been completed, the Representative Candidate alone will be entrusted and invested in the centre of the Triangle by the President.

A candidate in this Order is said to be 'admitted and anointed, consecrated and set apart to the Holy Office of Grand High Priest'.

The Regalia traditionally worn in this Order consists only of a Jewel in the form of a mitre on an equilateral triangle, both in gold, suspended by a red ribbon: the apex of the triangle points upwards.

A prayer is said before opening the ceremony:

May the Supreme High Priest of Heaven and Earth enlighten us with the knowledge of His truth, and grant that the members of this Convention may be endued with wisdom to understand and explain the mysteries of our Holy Order. May He be with us in all our assemblies, guide us in the paths of rectitude, enable us to keep all His statutes while life shall last, and finally bring us to the perfect knowledge of His holy Name.

The candidate is then advanced to the pedestal in the east and addressed by the President:

> *Companion you have duly presented yourself to be Anointed,*
> *Consecrated and Set Apart to the Holy Office of High Priest. The*
> *members of this Convention, yielding a ready response to your*
> *wishes, are now prepared to confer on you that exalted honour.*

The ritual then tells the story of Abraham and Melchizedek. Before continuing, the pedestal is moved from the centre of the triangle and placed within the tent in front of the president's chair. All the companions then move inside the tent and stand to form the two sides of an equilateral triangle to the north and south in order to partake of bread and wine. Outside the door the candidate is armed with a sword unsheathed, which he holds at the carry, and he is instructed how to parry a blow with his sword by sinking on one knee and holding the sword horizontally above his head by the hilt in his right hand and by the point in his left hand.

The candidate is then advanced slowly via the north towards the east, when suddenly the President appears through the curtains with a sword raised in his right hand which he brings down in a sweeping blow towards the candidate's head. The candidate drops to one knee and parries the blow in the manner he has just been taught.

The ceremony continues until the president places a piece of bread on the blade of his sword, breaks off a small piece and eats it. He then takes the sword in his right hand and presents it vertically to each Companion in turn within the tent, who breaks off a small piece of bread from the point of the sword using his own right hand and eats it.

Then Psalm 133, which the Bible tells us is 'a song of degrees of David,' is read aloud:

> *Behold, how good and how pleasant it is for brethren to dwell*
> *together in unity! It is like the precious ointment upon the head,*
> *that ran down upon the beard, even Aaron's beard: that went*
> *down to the skirts of his garments; As the dew of Hermon, and as*
> *the dew that descended upon the mountains of Zion: for there the*
> *Lord commanded the blessing, even life for evermore.*

This is an interesting choice of passage from the Old Testament. It has a distinctly Masonic character to it, referring to 'degrees of David' and using the phrase about 'brethren' dwelling together in unity, but it is not these that most interested us. The precious ointment upon the head is a reference to the messiah, as the word 'messiah' means 'anointed one' or more specifically 'the one smeared with holy oil'.

It is considered likely that this psalm was once a song used for cultic purposes by a covenant community at a Canaanite sanctuary (possibly the one later used by the priesthood of Dan) in celebration of one of the great festivals of the pre-Hebrew period.[41] So once again we see Canaanite priestly traditions associated with the Order.

We believe that there has been no one who has used this degree over the last few hundred years who understands what it all means. The use of an equilateral triangle facing east is important to this degree although it is an apparently meaningless device, but because of the astronomical focus of Freemasonry we suspect that it is likely to have its origin in the astral religion of the Canaanites. In Craft Freemasonry we can be certain that the rods (also called wands) carried by the two deacons are Asherah, the marker poles for gauging the movements of the Sun.[42] These took their name from the Canaanite goddess who was mother of the twins of Venus at dawn and dusk. Such an Asherah placed in the ground in front of a tent (remembering that gods including Yahweh and his ark were originally kept in a tent) would cast a shadow at daybreak towards the southwest at the summer solstice and the northwest at the winter solstice, thereby creating a delta shape against a baseline running north to south.

The angle of these shadows created by the maximum seasonal excursions of the Sun varies considerably according to latitude. We have already mentioned how this fact was used by the Grooved Ware People to create diamond shapes which encoded the latitude of the site they were drawn at, forming a sort of Neolithic symbolic postcode. At the Equator the angle is extremely narrow and at the Arctic Circle it is incredibly wide. In southern Scotland, where modern Freemasonry first developed, the solstice angle is a perfect 90 degrees, producing a square lozenge when mirrored with the sunset shadows.

The inner angles of the equilateral triangle used in this Melchizedek degree are all 60 degrees, which, if we are right about the meaning of this

[41] Anderson. GW: Psalms – *Peakes Commentary on the Bible*
[42] Knight, C & Lomas, R: *Uriel's Machine, The Ancient Origins of Science*

geometric shape used throughout the ritual of The Holy Order of the Grand High Priest, should correspond with a latitude in the northern hemisphere. And it does:

Jerusalem!

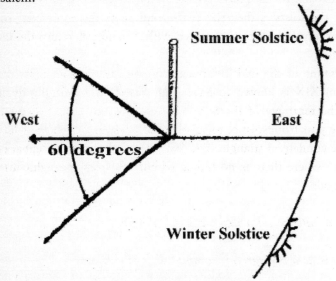

A stick placed in the ground at Jerusalem will cast a shadow that moves through sixty degrees between the winter and summer solstices.

An Asherah placed in the ground in the ancient city that Melchizedek knew as Salem produces an equilateral triangle when the shadows of the solstices are marked out. In this way the shadows from the free-standing pillars of Boaz and Jachin that stood in the porchway of King Solomon's Temple would have pointed into the Holy of Holies at exactly 60 degrees. At no other latitude in either hemisphere does this happen. However, everywhere on the planet at this exact latitude, either north or south, will produce this result. For example Shanghai in China fits, as does Marrakech in Morocco and Wollongong in Australia; but these sites did seem significant in the story of Melchizedek.

The chances of the angles occurring in the ritual by coincidence are vanishingly small given the way we now know the Canaanite mind worked. It seems likely that this ritual is ancient but that the meaning was lost long, long before Freemasonry came into existence. This is yet another example of how ancient oral traditions and ritual postures can carry information over a huge period of time without the people involved in the transmission having a clue about the meaning of the content.

The members of the Order stand along the two edges of the triangle that was formed by the solstice shadows. The candidate is made to kneel in the centre of the Triangle, where he is anointed, then raised before being conducted back to his place. As the outer edges of the triangle or delta represent the solstices then the centre represents the equinoxes, so, symbolically, every candidate is anointed with oil and taken into the Order at the equinox.

The Psalms of the Old Testament contain ancient Canaanite material, and Psalm XIX is known to have been based on a morning hymn concerning the marriage of the Sun.[43] It describes the transit of the sunrise across the year from solstice to solstice and back again, which at Jerusalem forms the equilateral triangle. The last line alludes to the original concept of 'zedek', where there is no hiding of untruth from the righteous eye of the Sun god:

In them hath he set a tabernacle for the Sun,

Which is as a bridegroom coming out of his chamber . . .

His going forth is from the end of the heaven, and his circuit unto the ends of it; and there is nothing hid from the heat thereof.

The experts tell us that the Sun god is getting married in this pre-Hebrew myth, married to Anat (also known as Astart), which we know as the planet Venus.[44]

The old legend behind Psalm XIX is that the bridegroom is the Sun and the bright morning star of Venus his bride.[45] Biblical scholars have noted from passages such as 1 Kings 11:5 that Venus was worshipped by Solomon in her special form as the deity of the Phoenicians.[46] The official worship of Venus as 'The Queen of Heaven' (Astart) continued in the kingdom of Judah until *circa* 600 BCE.[47]

---

[43] Hooke, SH: *Myth, Ritual and Kingship*, Oxford at the Clarendon Press, 1958. See 'Early Hebrew Myths and Their Interpretation'.
[44] *Myth, Ritual and Kingship*, Oxford at the Clarendon Press, 1958. See 'Early Hebrew Myths and Their Interpretation'.
[45] Engnell, J: *Studies in Divine Kingship*, SPCK, 1962
[46] Mauchline, J: 1+11 Kings – Peakes Commentary on the Bible.
[47] *Myth Ritual and Kingship*, Oxford at the Clarendon Press, 1958. See 'Early Hebrew Myths and Their Interpretation'.

So here, described in the Psalms of the Bible, we have a marriage of the two principal astral deities, the Sun and its partner who dances around the god of zedek with delicate precision over forty years – and around the zodiac in 1440 years. These attributes were continued in the name of Yahweh, the God of the Jews . . . and therefore of Christians. The story becomes even more interesting as we look at the outcome of this marriage. Here is one expert's view:

That the sacred marriage should bring as its fruit the birth of the Saviour-King is in accordance with the general myth and ritual pattern . . . Here the pre-natal history of Isaac comes to the fore. The traditions in question are now scattered over the chapters Genesis xvii–xviii . . . In the Isaac-oracles we assume a Canaanite mystical motif and it can easily be demonstrated that the very literary category of the oracle about the birth of the divine-royal child goes back to a Canaanite pattern.[48]

With Yahweh now the only God, in Genesis 21: 1–3 He is said to have 'visited' the wife of Abraham, who was at this stage an old man:

And the Lord visited Sarah as he had said, and the Lord did unto Sarah as he had spoken.

For Sarah conceived and bare Abraham a son in his old age, at the set time, of which God had spoken to him.

And Abraham called the name of his son, that was born to him, whom Sarah bare him, Isaac.

But the verb used for visit is *pâqad*, which means to visit a woman in a sexual sense of having intercourse, rather than just going innocently to say hello.[49] So Sarah appears to be a much earlier Mary – the mother of a divinely conceived child of God. Abraham was of a remarkably old age for procreation: according to Archbishop Ussher's calculations he was exactly

---

[48] *Myth, Ritual and Kingship*, Oxford at the Clarendon Press, 1958. See 'Early Hebrew Myths and Their Interpretation'.
[49] *Myth, Ritual and Kingship*, Oxford at the Clarendon Press, 1958. See 'Early Hebrew Myths and Their Interpretation'.

one hundred when Isaac was born, so the visitation of a god to Sarah was much more likely to produce offspring.

Given that the Sun or any other astral deity is unlikely to produce pregnancy in a young woman, we can start to suspect that the man-god Melchizedek might have been somehow involved. So it seems that whilst the aged Abraham was paying tithes to the priest-king his host was 'visiting' his wife.

We marvelled at the ancient nature of the eternal (if not equilateral) triangle.

Sarah means 'queen' or 'princess' and it has been established that the name Isaac (Yishâq) is derived from the Canaanite word for 'he laughs' – which appears to be a play on the statement in Genesis that Sarah 'laughed within herself' when God gave her a child. Furthermore, 'he laughs' is a trait closely associated with the god El in Ugaritic mythical literature. It is also highly relevant that the child suckled on the breasts of the virgin, Anat (Venus).[50] So we can conclude that this story of Abraham, Sarah and God is an adaptation of an ancient Canaanite tradition of the 'visit' of a deity to the queen to enter into a sacred marriage leading to the birth of the royal and divine child.

In studying what is known about the influence of Canaanite ritual on Judaism we were intrigued to find that many scholars find a great deal more of the feminine side of God than is obvious in the Bible. One such scholar summed up the situation as follows:

From the Old Testament alone we should never have guessed that Israel associated a goddess with Yahweh, even popularly, but the conclusion is irresistible, and we are justified in assuming that she played her part in the mythology and ritual of Israel. It is difficult to avoid the conclusion that rites, similar to those found elsewhere, were observed in pre-exilic Israel, and that these included a recital or a representation of the annual marriage of Yahweh and Anath.[51]

[50] *Myth, Ritual and Kingship*, Oxford at the Clarendon Press, 1958. See 'Early Hebrew Myths and Their Interpretation'.
[51] *Myth, Ritual and Kingship*, Oxford at the Clarendon Press, 1958. See 'Early Hebrew Myths and Their Interpretation'.

CONCLUSIONS

We began to believe that the influx of newcomers who brought civilisation to Sumer might have been Grooved Ware traders who settled in an environment they found attractive, whilst still keeping links with other groups, possibly in places like Gebal in Lebanon.

We believe that the Sumerians and the 'incomers' to the Levant were Grooved Ware migrants, and both groups show similarities beyond their Venus-based theology.

Sun worship is central to many ancient religions, but Venus is also important to the cultures that we believe are connected to the Grooved Ware People. Venus was highly important to megalithic Britons, and it is the light of the rising Venus that illuminates 'the darkness of death' for a third degree Masonic candidate. We discovered Venus associations amongst the Sumerians, the Canaanites, the Egyptians and the Jews.

The founders of Egypt at this time also brought with them the skills of building, navigation and astronomy that kick-started one of the greatest civilisations of all time. We noted that the main feature of Newgrange is its spectacular white quartz wall; and the first city of ancient Egypt was called Memphis, meaning White Wall.

We now believe that there is a strong case to be made that the dispersion of the Grooved Ware People seeded the later civilisations of the Middle East.

The Ras Shamra tablets tell much about ancient Canaanite rituals, and these have parallels with The Third Degree of Freemasonry when the candidate is symbolically killed and resurrected. Recent Old Testament studies put Melchizedek, the Canaanite astral priest-king, into a context with definite Masonic connotations.

An Asherah or shadow rod placed in the ground at the latitude of Jerusalem creates an equilateral triangle when the shadows of the solstices are plotted out. This ancient ritual is still alluded to in modern Freemasonic ritual, but the meaning has been lost. The members of the Masonic Order of The Grand High Priest stand along two edges of the triangle that forms from the solstice shadows. The candidate kneels in the centre of the Triangle, where he is anointed and raised. As the outer edges of the triangle or delta represent the solstices, then the centre is the equinox. This means that every candidate is anointed with oil and taken into the Order at the equinox.

There was a continuation of the Canaanite priesthood after David took the kingship for himself. So King David carried on the tradition which Abraham started with Melchizedek, of recognising the validity of the Canaanite High-Priest and King of Jerusalem. This began the Jewish belief in distinct kingly and priestly messiahs.

Chapter Seven

THE TWIN CULTS OF JUDAISM

THE NEW NATION

The Old Testament claims that the Israelites gradually subjugated the Canaanite cities during the latter half of the second millennium BCE, when the Hebrews had left Egypt under Moses and Joshua intent upon taking the land of Canaan for themselves. Nobody knows exactly when this happened, but Jewish tradition puts Moses' Red Sea crossing in the year 1447 BCE and the King James Bible dates it just a few years earlier in 1491 BCE.

By the end of Solomon's reign, over five hundred years later, it appears that the eastern Canaanites had been assimilated into the Jewish nation and the western Canaanites had become Phoenicians, and were thereafter viewed as a separate people. However, it would seem that the Hebrews and the Canaanites were not as different as the Old Testament would suggest. Biblical scholars now believe that the Hebrew language was derived from Canaanite sources and that the Phoenician language itself was the same as early forms of Hebrew.[1]

The Jewish scribes who first recorded the Bible painted a picture of a long chain of events, from the time Adam was thrown out of the Garden of Eden, via the Covenant of Abraham and the Exodus of Moses, down to King David's conquest of Jerusalem, that was predestined to establish the Creator God's seat of power administered by His Chosen People. But

[1] 'Canaanites', *Microsoft® Encarta® Encyclopedia 2001*. © 1993–2000 Microsoft Corporation. All rights reserved.

that, we believe, is simple post-rationalisation to justify their world-view.

The historical evidence says that during the period when the Hebrews were supposedly taking the land of Canaan at the close of the late Bronze Age, the entire area was in disarray. The whole region in the twelfth century BCE experienced a sudden cultural collapse and widespread population shifts.[2] This was due, claims Professor William Stiebling, to a marked climatic shift that a wide variety of evidence shows to have occurred at that time. It began with a global warming from around 1300 BCE that lasted over two hundred years, resulting in the desert areas of the land of Canaan going into rapid decline because of lack of rain. According to the wide-ranging evidence put forward by Stiebling, most villages in inland Canaan were abandoned, and occupation only resumed after 1000 BCE.

This later date coincides with David's taking of Jerusalem, and this whole period of arid conditions coincides with the general settlement of the Hebrew people in Canaan. The question this raised for us is, did the Hebrews occupy abandoned land because others were driven out by lack of water and food?

Stiebling explains how, at this time, there are records of internal rebellions in Babylon coinciding with a population drop of up to 75 per cent. In Egypt there were major grain shortages, and constant trouble with marauding tribes looting and killing as they pillaged the remaining food stocks. The facts support a thesis of a Hebrew migration into vacated lands.

Putting aside the scientific argument, such as tree-ring analysis and the changes that occurred in water tables and native flora, we can see how the pattern of human settlement did indeed change. Whilst the coastal-living Canaanites (i.e. those who became the Phoenicians) coped well with the heat problem, the people to the east, living in higher and more remote areas, suffered badly.

A survey of settlement sites in the area of Israel supposedly allotted to the Jewish tribe of Manasseh shows there was a pattern that fits the effects we would expect if a climatic problem arose. Manasseh is hill country with desert fringes that covers an area some ten or fifteen miles inland of the coast, stretching to the River Jordan, and is centrally placed between the Sea of Galilee and the Dead Sea. The author of this analysis, Dr Adam Zertal, is an agricultural economist turned archaeologist, which makes him splendidly qualified to undertake such a study. He has shown how the number of sites of occupation varied over the period we are interested in.

---

[2] Stiebling, WH: 'Did the Weather Make Israel's Emergence Possible?', *Biblical Review*, vol. X, no. 4, August 1994

In the Middle Bronze Age (1750–1550 BCE) there were 116 settlements, but by the Late Bronze Age (1550–1200 BCE) this dropped to just 39. This is the sort of decline we would expect during Stiebling's claimed period of dry, inhospitable climatic conditions. Then in Iron Age 1 (1200–1000 BCE) the number of settlements jumps past the original level to 136. Zertal comments:

> This dramatic increase in settlements suggests the entry of a new population into the area during Iron Age 1. This correlates with the Biblical account of Israel's entry into Canaan during the same period.[3]

In addition, Zertal's team noted that whereas the previous population were more likely to have settled in valleys rather than on hills (at a ratio of three to one), the population that arrived later settled on mountains in preference (at a measured ratio of two to one). These data tend to suggest that the new population were indeed different people with fresh ideas of where to site their settlements.

We found that there are three principal theories about the Hebrews arriving in Canaan. The first, William Albright's 'conquest model',[4] accepts the battles described in the Old Testament as an historical reality. The second, Albrecht Alt's, is a 'peaceful infiltration' model. The third is George Mendenhall's 'peasant revolt or social revolution' model.

Albright appears to have been looking for evidence to support the story told in the Bible, but archaeological discoveries since he first published his theory have not supported him. Our view, arrived at after checking substantial amounts of information, is that Mendenhall's theory (particularly as developed by Norman Gottwald) is likely to be closer to historical reality.

Mendenhall, and later Gottwald, drew on modern anthropological and sociological concepts to propose that most of the early Israelites were not outsiders who arrived in the land, but were Canaanite renegades who revolted against their feudal urban oppressors. This Canaanite underclass fled east and south to the central hills, abandoning the western part of the country. Put simply, Israel emerged from within Canaan rather than invading

[3] Zertal, A: 'Israel Enters Canaan', *Biblical Archaeology Review*, vol: XVII, no: 5, Sept./Oct. 1991

[4] Albright, WF: *From the Stone Age to Christianity*, The Johns Hopkins Press, 1940

it from outside. If this model is accepted, and we do accept it, then the Hebrews are simply Canaanite peasant stock.

This explanation fits with the Old Testament 'Period of the Judges', which occurred at the time of Iron Age 1 with its influx of population into the hill country. Before the introduction of Hebrew kingship, the various tribes were led by chiefs who are remembered in the Bible as 'the Judges'. The later writers of the Book of Deuteronomy tried to list these men as though they held power sequentially, but modern biblical studies suggests that many might have been contemporary competitors with each other.

Gideon, one of the later judges who changed his name from the Canaanite Jerubbaal, seems to have surpassed the standing of other judges. He kept and serviced a harem, having seventy sons. In his spare time he established a religious centre at Ophrah, where he created a cult object called an ephod. This was a divination instrument which was comparable in religious significance to Moses' Ark of the Covenant (not to be confused with the upper part of a priest's clothing of the same name). At Ophrah he formally named one of his sons Abimelech, a name which honoured God as Father and King, and by doing so took the first steps towards the development of Jewish kingship.

The peasant Canaanites became known as Hebrews from the word 'Apiru.[5] More than three hundred cuneiform tablets have been found at Tell el-Amarna, capital of the Egyptian Pharaoh Akhenaten (1353–1335 BCE). Many contain correspondence between Akhenaten and his vassal kings in Canaan which reveals that Egypt was losing control of its subject states, including those in Canaan, itself beset by problems inflicted by these mysterious 'Apiru. From the descriptions given it is clear that the 'Apiru came from outside the ranks of normal Canaanite society and acted as hired agricultural workers, mercenaries or even outlaws. One letter tells how a group of 'Apiru, led by someone called Lab'ayyu, took control of the city of Shechem in the central hill country of Canaan.

We felt we could see a clear picture emerging.

The aristocracy and middle classes of coastal Canaan became too successful. They controlled virtually all international trade, becoming rich and prosperous merchants. The well-to-do of the coastal cities no longer needed a large labour force because they made their money abroad and imported

---

[5] *Peake's Commentary on the Bible*, Thomas Nelson and Sons, 1962

all of the exotic foods and goods they could consume. They progressively lost contact with their own, almost unemployable, peasant stock and these disenfranchised and demoralised 'Apiru became an unwanted underclass who took to travelling the countryside desperately searching for employment and food.

No doubt some went down to Egypt to act as agricultural workers, labourers and mercenaries – perhaps the story of Moses being a Hebrew ('Apiru) is based on the memory of a highly successful mercenary who held the rank of general in the Egyptian army. Under this scenario the account of the Hebrews' exodus from Egypt makes sense, as they escaped eastwards and northwards in search of their promised land – their own land promised to them by birthright. When they arrived back in the Canaan that their ancestors had abandoned generations earlier, they discovered they were now just one group amongst many almost stateless 'Apiru.

Perhaps these refugees from Egypt were more sophisticated than the run-of-the-mill peasants they found living in their promised land. They started to organise them into a new kind of social order – led by the men who, the Bible tells us, called themselves 'the Judges'. The Canaanite city kings must have been worried when they saw the country dwellers motivated to demand a better lot for themselves, and perhaps there were battles, with peasant uprisings led by ex-mercenaries with sufficient military skills to topple a minor city or two. But we found that our studies kept bringing us back to the stories of King David.

The earliest stories of the creation of a true Jewish state concern King David, from whose line Jesus claimed descent. The Old Testament says that as soon as David took Jerusalem the process of centralising the priesthood in the city began, creating an increasingly elaborate organisation with practices that separated it from the religious rites of the surrounding country. In the rural areas the priests at local shrines known as 'the high places' carried on a form of Yahwistic cult which was more or less the same as the old Canaanite practices, but now authorised by the name of a new god. Biblical scholar Professor Samuel Hook has said:

> The next change from the introduction of (Hebrew) kingship was
> the separation between the religious practice of the capital and that
> of the country. From the evidence of the Deuteronomic editors of
> the book of Kings and from the Prophets we know that in the
> country the local shrines, 'the high places', with their local priests

*carried on a form of Yahwistic cult which was strongly influenced
by Canaanite practice. Hosea shows to what extent Yahweh and
Baal had become confused in the minds of Israelite worshippers.
This state of things persisted, in spite of prophetic denunciations
and the efforts of reforming kings, until the fall of Jerusalem in
586 B.C.*[6]

The Jews, however, introduced a concept of kingship with a special
quality into the lands they controlled. Their first king, Saul, is portrayed
as being a type of the old judge who receives a divine appointment for
mainly military purposes. King David's authority is different: it is based on
a covenant. This is a mutual agreement between three parties: the king, the
people, and Yahweh. David's right to kingship was supported by his special relationship with God.

David was considered to be the first messiah, and his claim was based
on his special relationship to Yahweh, through this convenant.[7] The agreement included terms and conditions on two sides: the monarch's and the
nation's. Yahweh's role was that of an enforcer, to ensure that the bargain
was duly kept by both sides. This set-up was a remarkably democratic concept that was original and unique. It was effectively a charter and a coronation oath with inbuilt limitations to the royal prerogative, and a divine
guarantee of extensive rights and liberties for the subject.

In every other surrounding country at that time the king was an absolute
autocrat whose subjects had no rights whatsoever. Whilst previously the
court language of Israel had sometimes adopted a terminology whereby the
ordinary citizen was called the 'slave' of the king, under David's regime a
new conception of social organisation was put in place where the subject
was considered to be a 'brother' (Deuteronomy 17: 20) or a 'neighbour'
(Jeremiah 22:13) of the king. This was a revolutionary theory of the relationship between the government and the governed – but it was to be short-
lived.

As time went on, more and more territory fell under the control of the
rural people – even southern ports such as Ashkelon were taken – but the
northern coastal cities of the Phoenicians remained unassailable. The Jews
took Jerusalem late in the day, and it may well have been a political victory rather than a bloody military one.

[6] Hooke, SH: 'The Religious Institutions of Israel', *Peake's Commentary on the Bible*, 1962
[7] Hertzberg, Arthur: *Judaism*, George Braziller, New York, 1962

According to the Old Testament, King Solomon's Temple for Yahweh was eventually built on land that David bought for six hundred shekels of gold from a Jebusite[8] called Araunah (also known as Ornan). He had previously used it as a place for threshing wheat.[9] Six hundred shekels was a substantial sum of money, and the inclusion of this payment in the story is probably meant to indicate that David was behaving in a proper manner towards the indigenous population. The Book of Samuel tells how David bought this high place on the advice of the prophet Gad. He saw a need to placate God, who was annoyed because David had conducted a census within his new kingdom to assist in the collection of taxes. The Book of Samuel says God sent an angel to slaughter a large number of David's subjects, but the king was given the choice of the means of destruction. On behalf of Yahweh, Gad offered David three options of different calamities as punishment. These were famine for seven years, disastrous war for three months, or pestilence for three days. Not surprisingly, David opted for the last. Accordingly, at the time of the wheat harvest a plague began among the people, killing seventy thousand people. Then, just as this virulence was about to reach Jerusalem, David prayed to Yahweh and the plague was stayed.[10] The story seems improbable for several reasons, not least the number of people allegedly killed by disease in just three days.

Given that the Old Testament was written down several hundred years after the events described, was David a living, historical figure or just a composite myth? Some people claim he was real because the 'House of David' seems to be referred to in the ninth-century Tel Dan stela and the stela of a Moabite king called Mesha who reigned *circa* 849–820 BCE. But even this claimed evidence is from two hundred years after the supposed event.

We asked our friend Professor Philip Davies for an authoritative opinion. Philip replied:

The Tel Dan stela does have one word that can be translated as 'House of David' but can also mean other things. Even if it means 'House of David' it would not mean that the 'David' is the character depicted in the Bible. Even the most enthusiastic of experts

[8] The Jebusites were the Canaanite inhabitants of Jerusalem prior to the arrival of the Hebrew people.
[9] 1 Chronicles 21: 15–26
[10] 2 Samuel 24: 13–16

*admit that there never was a big Davidic empire, that Jerusalem
was a piddly little village and that the legends about David are
probably huge exaggerations. At best we are talking about a historical core to a legend, and even that I'm not too sure about. I'll
stick with an analogy of King Arthur; possibly some historical core
but not the man of the legends.*

So we probably are dealing with a Jewish myth, constructed much later,
to explain why certain beliefs exist and certain places are venerated. When
the later Old Testament writers were trying to prove that the nation of
Jews had a history, it would never have been acceptable to say their beliefs
were simply aspects of Canaanite theology. So they personified a process
in the legendary person of King David. To simplify our discussions, however, we accepted their convention and continued to refer to David as a
single person.

Young King Hiram had not been long on the throne of Tyre when the
'Apiru warlord David took control of Jerusalem from the Jebusites, turning
the city of the Venus-priesthood of Melchizedek into a city of David. The
Old Testament states that David, the ambitious king of the 'Apiru, persuaded the Jebusite aristocracy of Jerusalem to hand over control to him.
Josephus tells us that the leaders of the city insulted David by using all the
maimed, the lame and the beggars of Jerusalem to bar his way, saying that
even the lame were enough to stop him taking the city.[11] David promptly
besieged the city until its leaders were forced to deal with him. He took
the city but retained the services of the priesthood of Melchizedek,
appointing Zadok as his high priest.

Hiram, realising that his vulnerable and wealthy port of Tyre, complete
with a full set of king-making temples, might be next on David's list of
cities to acquire, decided to win himself some time. He made friends with
David; offered him support and technical skills; built him a palace in
Jerusalem to consolidate his power; and kept the Jewish warlord in
Jerusalem and away from Tyre. Josephus said of these events:

*Hiram, also king of the Tyrians, sent ambassadors to him [David]
and made a league of mutual friendship and assistance with him.
He also sent him presents, cedar trees, and mechanics, and men*

11 Whiston, W (ed. and trans.): Josephus, *Antiquities*, vii, iii, 1

skilful in architecture, that they might build him a Royal Palace in Jerusalem.[12]

This ploy worked and won Hiram enough time to rebuild his city of Tyre on the artificial rocky island he constructed out to sea. Hiram was careful to make sure that all his sources of Royal power were removed to his new island fortress. He built new Temples to his gods, who guaranteed his Royal power, and then demolished the older, more vulnerable, onshore ones.

The requirement for David to be recorded as establishing a new line of kings was, in our opinion, the reason the 'Apiru are described as taking Jerusalem at a given point in time, and why later scribes made so much of the fact that David was anointed. Anointing was a part of the process of Phoenician king-making in a special ritual carried out in an east-facing Temple with two pillars at its entrance.

The claim that Samuel anointed first Saul and then David appears to be an attempt to copy the Canaanite rituals, but the scribes knew that more was needed in order to claim to have a 'real' king. The Jebusites knew that real Canaanite kings were consorts of Venus: the name of their city, Jerusalem, reflected this. To match a Canaanite king's level of Divine authority David needed an east-facing Temple of his own, preferably dedicated to his new Ark-dwelling God, Yahweh, where he could carry out king-making rituals and marry the goddess Venus in the cold glow of early dawn.

Josephus tells of the decision but not the motive:

Now when the king [David] saw that his affairs grew better almost every day, by the will of God, he thought he should offend Him, if while he himself continued in houses made of cedar, such as were of a great height, and had the most curious works of architecture in them, he should overlook the ark while it was laid in the tabernacle and was desirous to build a temple to God, as Moses had predicted such a temple should be built.[13]

The house with the most curious works of architecture was the gift of Hiram, king of Tyre. The claim that Moses predicted the building of a

[12] Josephus, *Antiquities*, vii, iii, 2
[13] Josephus, *Antiquities*, vii, iii, 4

144

Temple to Yahweh is not to be found in any present versions of the Pentateuch, but we knew it was included in *The Masonic Testament*, where Moses says that the Tabernacle is the model for the Temple, which will one day be built of stone, when he instructs Bezaleel to make it. [*Masonic Testament* 6:7] We found it interesting that Josephus adds a detail which is in the Masonic record and nowhere else.

We found support for this view of what was happening from Professor Jagersma, who holds the chair of Hebrew and Old Testament Studies at Brussels University. He observes about the Bible stories of David and the Ark:

In the stories which follow his anointing by Samuel, David is constantly referred to as a mighty warrior and an able general . . . [David's] capture of Jerusalem put paid to the key position which the Philistines had occupied in this area for some time . . . Another important fact which favoured this change of power was the weakening of the power of the [Phoenician] old city states. This is clearly connected to the economic sphere. Whereas earlier the economic focus was to be found principally in the coastal plain, there was an increasing shift eastwards, towards the hill country . . . the incorporation of the inhabitants of Jerusalem and other Canaanite cities into the kingdom of David had far-reaching consequences not only for religious but also social and economic affairs. David probably understood all too well that Jerusalem could only function properly as a political centre if it also attained the status of a religious centre in his kingdom . . . for David the Ark was clearly of great significance . . . The result of bringing the Ark to Jerusalem was that the city increasingly became the focal point of the cult [of Yahweh].[14]

The city of Jerusalem was tiny but well fortified, and taking it must have been the ultimate victory for David, the peasant king of myth and legend. The Bible tells us that he immediately took an army of thirty thousand picked men to bring the Ark of the Covenant from Kiriath-jearim (Baalah) to his new capital – dancing in front of it as it went. On route, the driver of the cart carrying the Ark was struck dead for accidentally touching the home of Yahweh, so to avoid further problems David sacrificed an ox and a buffalo every six paces.

It must have been a slow and bloody journey.

[14] Jagersma, H: *A History of Israel to Bar Kochba*, SCM Press, 1985

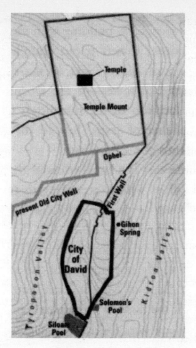

The City of David was a tiny settlement with the later temple being built on the high ground to the north.

RICH MAN, POOR MAN

In our researches so far we had identified two different strata of Canaanite society: the wealthy and sophisticated city dwellers, personified by the inhabitants of Byblos and Tyre, and the peasants who occupied the outer rural areas. The urban people not only differed in the quality of their clothes and their food, they were also better educated in matters of science, philosophy and theology. They enjoyed culture and tradition based around their temples, whilst the 'Apiru could boast only a jumble of old myths identified with sacred sanctuaries marked with stones.

However, the 'Apiru set about organising their myths and developing a new heritage with such determination and vigour that they eventually eclipsed all the rest. Their success is today's religious heritage of monotheism – a feat that must be greatly admired. But this legitimising process was not easy. We were finding more and more evidence to confirm the hints we had found in Masonic ritual, that conflicts surfaced as two different religions were welded, unhappily and temporally, together.

146

As the 'Apiru began to organise they gave themselves a first semblance of heritage by dividing into four tribes named after the wives of Jacob and his maidservants: Leah, Zilpah, Rachael and Bilhah. Once the population stabilised each person became associated with a tribe by virtue of the region they lived in, rather than their ancestry.[15]

The priest-kings of the great cities, such as Melchizedek in early Jerusalem and Hiram in contemporary Tyre, worshipped the Sun and Venus, understood astronomy and practised secret rituals for king-making. The commoners of the surrounding countryside followed a typical peasant religion based on the age-old simple theme of the god or his son dying each season and being resurrected the following spring. We have come to this view after considering the views of many leading biblical scholars and archaeologists. Whilst both the urban and rural peoples had similar beliefs involving the ancient concepts of death and resurrection, and both had an astrological content, the differences are very significant.

The kings and their aristocratic followers considered the resurrection to be for themselves, and Venus, in its role as the Bright Morning Star, appears to have been central to this concept. The country folk saw the death and resurrection concept as an event that happened yearly to a king, or to a god, one that marked the seasons in order to ensure that they had the food stocks that they needed. For these commoners, it was usually the Sun that drove the resurrection of the land.

One biblical scholar, the Rev. Professor William Irwin, says of this simple resurrection imagery:

> The cultis of the dying god must be recognised as nothing less than the profound sacrament of the ancient world: a god laid down his life that through death life might be triumphant, and suffering and sorrow give place to joy.[16]

This theme continued across thousands of years – for instance the god Mithra was said to have been born in a stable on the winter solstice some six hundred years before Christ, and his resurrection was celebrated at Easter. But none of these cults had an obvious Venus component. This, it seems, was reserved for the rites and rituals of kings and senior members of their mighty city states.

---

[15] Fohrer, G: History of Israelite Religion, S.P.C.K., London, 1973
[16] Irwin, WA: 'Job', Peake's Commentary on the Bible

The key differentiation between these two aspects of Canaanite/Jewish theology that we wish to stress here is one of time-frame. The king-making Venus ritual associated with the aristocratic groups is concerned with long-term issues – the belief that individuals can be personally resurrected from one lifetime to a series of others. Biblical heroes such as Enoch (and apparently Melchizedek) lived for hundreds of years, and when kings did move on to the life beyond, they joined the gods in heaven because of their belief that they were at one with the workings of the stars and planets. The commoners, on the other hand, had a short-term view that caused them to think season to season. Their primary concern was that their crops did not fail and they could feed themselves for another year. 'The dying god has risen' was their cry each Easter. What might happen at the next Venus cycle forty years later was wildly beyond the limits of their theology and even their imagination.

The term 'Canaanites' appears to us to generally refer to the city dwellers of places such as Hiram's Tyre and Melchizedek's Jerusalem. The 'Apiru were originally the peasant stock who were, by necessity of survival, a wandering people who moved according to climatic conditions and the availability of work as labourers or as mercenaries. It is known, for example, that the ancient Egyptians would freely allow these nomadic people to camp on the Nile when drought drove them south in a desperate search for water. The Egyptians also gave them work, and many fought in the Egyptian army. This may explain why an 'Apiru like Moses became a general in the Egyptian army before he was accused of committing a murder and had to escape northwards back to Canaan. Another expert explains how, over time, the 'Apiru or Israelites came to settle in fixed locations:

> At first most of the Israelites were peasants living in closed communities; a portion of them finally arrived at a truly urban economy. This is one of the reasons for the later enmity between city and countryside, to this extent that it was not rooted, like the antipathy of the rural population of Judah towards Jerusalem, in the fact that the majority of the city-dwellers were Canaanites . . . Israelites gained admittance to some Canaanite sanctuaries. The clan gods were soon linked to these sanctuaries rather than to the clan, which now settled permanently; deities of the road became deities of specific places.[17]

[17] Fohrer, G: *History of Israelite Religion*

From a very early date there had been a linkage between Venus worship and the concept of a dying and rising nature god, and it is possible that such an association goes back deep into prehistory. The Phoenicians knew Venus in the form of Ashtoreth, whose consort was Tammuz, the god of plant and animal fertility. In public rituals these deities would be represented by the king and high priestess.

This theme of a god dying for the good of the world and being subsequently resurrected must have been very easy for the common people to buy into. It has a primordial charm and is an obvious reflection of the patterns of the seasons. But the king-making rituals, which remained so secret, were clearly very different. This was part of a personal resurrection plan similar to that used by the ancient kings of Egypt, whereby the Horus travelled to the 'Duat' – the land of the dead – to be crowned by the gods themselves.

By the time that the 'Apiru had become the Jewish nation and the Greek civilisation was in full swing, the astral cult appears to have declined and Venus had become solely a feature of dying and rising vegetation cults. The king-making Venus cult died away with the broadening of city states into something more nationalistic and inclusive of people at all levels of society. But the early Jewish kings must have known that they really needed to have access to the higher aspects of Venus ritual if they were to become divine themselves, and therefore qualified to lead the vegetation aspects of their nation's needs.

Saul was made the first king of these wandering 'Apiru when they started to become urbanised. But he was advanced to the rank of king, not by divine right, but by three steps:

First, he was elected king by an assembly of tribesmen at the town of Mizpah.

Next he was anointed by the prophet Samuel at Ephraim.

Finally he was acclaimed king at Gilgal.

Gilgal (meaning 'stone circle'[18]) held an important place in the developing Jewish myth as the place where the 'Apiru army were circumcised en masse after they first carried their Ark of the Covenant across the Jordan

[18] *Peake's Commentary on the Bible*, Thomas Nelson and Sons Ltd, 1962

into the promised land. As we talked through this material we asked the question: How did these peasants know the accepted method of turning a commoner into a king?

It seemed to us that they would not have access to the rituals that the city dwellers believed could make a man into a king. These rituals were closely guarded secrets that the Jebusite kings of Jerusalem and their high priests had used from the time of Abraham and Melchizedek, which explains why the 'Apiru were so keen to take Jerusalem, known later as 'the city of the great King'. But it seems unlikely that any Jebusite king would step down and simply hand over the secrets of political power.

As we have already noted, David's rule, for all its unpleasantness, was totally unlike any other before it in that it treated citizens as equals, not possessions. Perhaps the equality that he extended to his subjects was due to the fact that he was still only a 'super-judge – he did not have the divine status that only the ritual of true, sacred kingship could confer. Here, we believed was a possible explanation for Solomon's need to establish himself as a sacred king, after the manner of the ancient Canaanites.

Solomon was born in the latter part of David's life, when Jerusalem was a well organised city, and by the time he became king he believed that he was definitely superior to his subjects. He demonstrated no sympathy with the conceptions of society introduced by his father, and his very accession has been described as a triumph of the principles of autocracy over those of democracy.[19] King David is portrayed as an ordinary person who was chosen to lead his people – like a modern president. But King Solomon was something quite different. His behaviour does not denote equality with his people, it belongs to a man with a divine right to rule. How did he acquire this divine right?

CONCLUSIONS

The aristocracy and middle classes of coastal Canaan controlled a profitable international trade. These well-to-do seaside cities didn't need a large labour force; they made their money abroad and imported all the goods they needed. They lost contact with their unemployable peasant stock, and these demoralised 'Apiru became an underclass who travelled the countryside looking for employment and food. Some must have gone to Egypt to

---

[19] Robinson, TH: *The History of Israel (A Companion to the Bible)*, T & T Clark, 1939

work, so the story of Moses being a Hebrew ('Apiru) could be based on the actions of a successful mercenary general in the Egyptian army. The account of the Hebrews' exodus from Egypt now makes sense, as they escaped eastwards and northwards in search of their own land promised to them by birth.

On their return these 'Apiru organised the underclass into a new social order led by the Judges. The Canaanite city kings became worried when they saw the country dwellers demanding a better lot for themselves, and there were uprisings by ex-mercenaries having enough military skill to win a city or two. More cities fell to the rural people – even Ashkelon succumbed – but the northern coastal cities of the Phoenicians remained secure.

By now two different strata of Canaanite society had developed: the city dwellers, typically Byblos and Tyre, and the rural unwashed. The urban people were better educated in science, philosophy and theology. They enjoyed culture and tradition, whilst the 'Apiru could boast only a jumble of old myths, but the 'Apiru organised their myths into our religious heritage of monotheism.

The Canaanite city dwellers ruled by Melchizedek in Jerusalem and Hiram in Tyre worshipped the Sun and Venus, understood astronomy and practised secret rituals for king-making. The 'Apiru followed a less complex peasant religion where the god or his son died each season to be reborn next spring.

This Canaanite astral religion grew from a race of extremely successful seafarers and traders who worshipped a goddess who manifested herself as the planet Venus. The original Canaanite settlements with their traditions of astronomically aligned temple building fused with a new wave of invaders who sailed in from the homelands of the Grooved Ware People.

David, an ambitious leader of the 'Apiru, persuaded the Jebusite aristocracy of Jerusalem to hand over control of the city to him, but they did so only after insulting David's kingly credentials. David immediately set about creating a shrine to the God he had inherited from Moses, and brought the Ark of the Covenant to Jerusalem. Hiram of Tyre was worried by these developments and instituted a two-pronged political solution. He made friends with David by building him a palace in Jerusalem, whilst also moving his city and its king-making temples to safety on an artificial island he built in the sea.

Chapter Eight

REAL KINGS, HUMAN SACRIFICE AND RAINMAKING

THE FAILURE OF THE FINAL INSTALMENT

In the minds of many, Solomon's rule was the moment of triumph for the Jewish people, but the reality was different. His building work was impressive but it was also extravagant and wasteful, way beyond any realistic financial means of his fledgling nation. The Bible tells us that even the treasures accumulated by David were not enough to pay the costs of Solomon's desire to prove himself a king amongst kings. Because of his buildings, including the Jerusalem Temple, he ended up subjecting his people to forced labour to grow the crops to pay Hiram, King of Tyre. For this purpose Solomon divided the country into twelve districts that shared out his labour demands. These included everyone in the kingdom except those from Judah, which understandably aggravated the growing discontent felt over the rest of the land. Revolts ensued both in Edom and among the Aramaean tribes to the northeast, leading to a loss of labour and revenue and putting more strain on the rest of Solomon's suffering subjects.

We believe that Solomon wanted to be a real king in the Canaanite tradition. The only person willing and able to sell the rituals of king-making to him was Hiram, King of Tyre. But if we are right and Hiram did indeed do a trading deal to sell Solomon suitable apparatus and rituals for king-making, what might the deliverables of this contract have been? We knew about the hardware – the detail of the Temple in the Bible and *The Masonic Testament* is comprehensive – but what of the software? What rituals married a son of El (Baal) to the goddess Baalat and so made him a member of the council of God?

Applying what we knew about Sir William St Clair's riddling Viking heritage, we decided to look again at Masonic ritual. As we have seen, Viking poetry abounds in a device known as a kenning, a form of allegorical reference which can only be understood by applying a lot of background knowledge of the subject. We asked ourselves, might the method of Jewish king-making that Hiram sold to Solomon be hidden in a Masonic 'kenning'? We decided to piece together what we now knew into a sensible hypothesis, to assemble a picture from our jigsaw of evidence.

We saw in Chapter 5 how from earliest times the Phoenician king was the earthly representative of El, the great Sun-god, and husband of the queen of the heavens (Baalat). The vernal equinox festivals of fertility, held at the Temple of Baalat, involved ritual prostitution as a religious duty, imposed on all the fertile women of the kingdom. They must give themselves in uninhibited sexual congress to any passing stranger who wishes to take them. It was believed that El would come in disguise as a stranger, and so the women must give themselves to all strangers in case one of them might be El. To appease El's wife, Baalat, they donated the fee they took from their 'customers' to her Temple as a charge for providing the necessary brothel facilities.

Perhaps the king, in his role as earthly representative of El, opened the proceedings by a public copulation with the High Priestess of Baalat. Nine months later, the fruit of such unions would be born around the winter solstice. Sometimes the Goddess would smile on these births. She would appear close to her husband in the morning sky and her pleasure would be evident from the brightness of her glory, clearly visible in the lightening sky of the dawn. Who could doubt her pleasure as they watched her dance around the bright glory of her husband, following the ritual path which traces out the symbolic horns of the headdress of Venus around the Sun's risings and settings?

Such favoured births, sired by the king in his role as earthly representative of El, and birthed by the High Priestess of Baalat as the earthly representative of the goddess, at a moment when her bright star could be seen embracing the Sun during his morning rising, must have truly been regarded as favoured Sons of Venus.

We reconstructed the chronology of the reigns of the kings of Tyre from the information in Josephus and found that King Hiram was born at a part of the eight-year Venus cycle when the planet was close to the Sun in a morning star rising. So he fulfils all necessary conditions to be seen as the son of Venus (Baalat) and the Sun (El). This son is normally known as Baal, the god who dies in the autumn and is reborn in the spring.

But what of the tomb inscriptions which describe kings of Tyre as married to the Goddess Baalat?

This seems to be the key to a ritual which takes a Son of Venus and turns him into a Royal consort of the Goddess and the earthly embodiment of the Most High (El). We cannot be sure how this ritual was carried out, but the archaeological remains of the Phoenician temples have all suggested that it involved an east-facing Temple with two pillars at the entrance; a dormer about the doorway to let in the pre-dawn light of Venus, and a pavement for the High Priest to walk on and carry out his rituals.

But we had an additional clue to help our understanding of this ceremony from Masonic ritual.

When Chris was giving a public talk in Dallas he was given a small package by a woman who had been in the audience but had left when the talk ended and questions began. When he opened the brown envelope he found a handwritten note which read:

> Thank you both so much for all of your good work, may God bless you. I have some old papers for you that belonged to my father who was a life-long Freemason. I hope they are of use to your endeavors.

The enclosures were typed sheets of Masonic ritual which did indeed prove to be helpful, as they covered a set of degrees known as the Rite of Perfection, whose details concerned just what was supposed to have happened when Masons carried out the very first raising ceremony for the body of Hiram Abif.

These rituals were reported to have been taken to America by travelling Scottish military lodges in the seventeenth century and eventually adopted by the Grand Lodge of Charleston, Virginia, from where this set of degrees came. As they pre-dated the censorship which followed the formation of the United Grand Lodge of England, we looked at them with great interest. The detail of their contents can be found in *The Masonic Testament* [8:11–13], which says what happened when a travelling lodge of Masons found the body of Hiram Abif in a shallow grave. It was this ritual which eventually helped us understand the Phoenician king-making ceremony and see how a son of Venus could become the earthly consort of the mother Goddess. Although the significance of the ritual was not immediately clear to us.

11. *They performed their task with the utmost fidelity, and on reopening the ground one of the Brethren looking round observed some of his companions in a position expressive of the horror of the afflicting sight, and others viewing the ghastly wounds still visible on his forehead smote their own in sympathy with his sufferings: two of the Brethren then descended the grave; one of them endeavoured to raise our Master by the Entered Apprentice grip, which proved a slip; the other tried the Fellow Craft's grip, which proved a slip likewise; having both failed in their attempts, a more zealous and expert Brother descended, and, using the strong or lion grip of a Master Mason, with their assistance raised him on the Five Points of Fellowship, while others, still more animated, exclaimed words having a nearly similar import; King Solomon ordered that these casual signs, tokens, and words should designate all Master Masons throughout the Universe, until time or circumstances should restore the genuine ones.*

12. *The body of our Master was ordered to be re-interred as near to the Sanctum Sanctorum as the Israelitish laws would permit. There in a grave from the centre three feet East, three feet West, three feet between North and South and five feet or more perpendicular.*

13. *He was not buried in the Sanctum Sanctorum, because nothing common or unclean was allowed to enter there, not even the High Priest except once a year and not even then until after many washings and purifications, against the great day of expiations of sins, for by the Israelitish law all dead bodies are deemed unclean.*

The key factor in this passage is that Hiram Abif (whose name, as we noted in *The Hiram Key*, means the lord or Baal who has been lost) is raised on the Five Points of Fellowship. This is a strange five-point embrace which takes place in the centre of the Temple, between the Candidate and the Worshipful Master, who is in charge of the ritual for the ceremony. Just before this ceremony is carried out this prayer is recited in the Freemasonic Temple:

> *Almighty and Eternal God, Architect and Ruler of the Universe, at whose creative fiat all things first were made, we, the frail creatures of Thy providence, humbly implore Thee to pour down on this convocation assembled in Thy Holy Name the continual dew of Thy blessing. Especially we beseech Thee to impart Thy grace to this Thy servant, who offers himself a candidate to partake with us the mysterious Secrets of a Master Mason. Endue him with such fortitude that in the hour of trial he fail not, but that passing safely under Thy protection, through the valley of the shadow of death, he may finally rise from the tomb of transgression, to shine with the stars for ever and ever.*

Now, with our increased knowledge of the basic principles underlying Phoenician kingship, and knowing that Solomon bought these secrets to add to the existing traditions of Abraham and Moses that David capitalised on when he established Jerusalem as the home of Moses' Ark of the Covenant, a possible interpretation of this strange embrace came to us.

At the moment of raising, whilst the candidate is still embraced at five points of contact, this is said to him by the Master who has just raised him:

> *Let me now beg you to observe, that the light of a Master Mason is darkness visible, serving only to express that gloom which rests on the prospect of futurity; it is that mysterious veil which the eye of human reason cannot penetrate, unless assisted by that light which is from above; yet, even by this glimmering ray, you may perceive that you stand on the very brink of the grave into which you have just figuratively descended, and which, when this transitory life shall have passed away, will again receive you into its cold bosom. Let the emblems of mortality which lie before you, lead you to contemplate on your inevitable destiny, and guide your reflections to that most interesting of all human studies, the knowledge of yourself. Be careful to perform your allotted task while it is yet day; continue to listen to the voice of nature, which bears*

witness, that even in this perishable frame, resides a vital and immortal principle, which inspires a holy confidence that the Lord of life will enable us to trample the king of terrors beneath our feet, and lift our eyes to that bright morning star, whose rising brings peace and salvation to the faithful and obedient of the human race.

We now knew that our Grand Master Hiram, King of Tyre, held the following religious belief. Every year Baal, the son of Baalat and El, dies at the autumn equinox and is reborn at the vernal equinox. Checking out the dates given by Josephus, we know that Hiram of Tyre was conceived at the vernal equinox and born at the winter solstice, when Venus rose close before the Sun. This made him a son of Venus. When his father died, Hiram had to change from being the Son of the Goddess to embracing her in marriage. This raised him from a Prince to a King.

As Baal, he entered the Temple of Venus on the eve of the autumnal equinox and ritually but only symbolically died, acting out his role as Baal. He was laid to rest, his feet pointing East and his head West. Could this be connected to a five-pointed embrace of resurrection under the light of Venus at dawn?

The planet Venus, as she moves around the sky, touches the path of the Sun (the zodiac) in just five places. So the High Priestess of Baalat personifies the Goddess as she comes to her husband at dawn, just as he rises from the grave of the dark earth. First she reaches down to take his hand, then she places her right foot against his. Two priests of El, who celebrate the Sun at his zenith and setting, assist her to pivot the king forward out of the cold embrace of his grave into the warm embrace of the Goddess. As Hiram is lifted by the priests of El the High Priestess presses her right knee against his, pulls him tightly to her breast and completely embraces him, throwing her arm across his shoulders to reach down his back as she breathes the secret words of kingship into his ear.

It seems to us that the whole ancient precept that underpins the concept of the Divine right to rule is that the candidate for kingship must die to attend the council of the gods in heaven and return to life as one accepted by the spirits of his forebears. We have already mentioned that Melchizedek was considered to be a member of the council of the gods, and the inscriptions on the tombs of the Phoenician kings also assigned them a role as mediators or Meleks on El's council. We had also formed a similar opinion when we wrote about the ritual in Ancient Egypt of turning the Horus, the son of the Goddess Isis, into the King, and now we feel very confident we were right. The light of Venus is considered to be the light of the returning soul of the resurrected or reincarnated king – the councillor who represents his people at the council of the gods.

So the new king embraces the Goddess in the five-pointed embrace, which can be seen each generation in the higher reaches of heaven, and his power is established. This is the secret knowledge that Solomon attempted to buy from Hiram, King of Tyre, and the detail has been preserved in the weird and ancient rituals of Freemasonry.

But did Hiram sell all his secrets to Solomon? *The Masonic Testament* says not. Chapter 8 verse 10 says this about what happened when the grave of Hiram Abif was discovered by one of the searching Masons:

On a closer examination he found that the earth had been recently disturbed; he therefore hailed his Brethren, and, with their united efforts, succeeded in reopening it and there found the body of our Master Hiram very indecently interred. They covered it again with all respect and reverence, and in order to distinguish the spot stuck a sprig of Acacia at the head of the Grave; they then hastened to Jerusalem, to impart the afflicting intelligence to King Solomon, who, when the first emotions of his grief had subsided, ordered them to return and raise the body of our Master to such a sepulchre as became his rank and exalted talents; at the same time informing them that by his untimely death the genuine Secrets of a Master Mason were lost; he therefore charged them to be particularly careful in observing whatever casual signs, tokens or words that might occur among them while paying this last sad tribute of respect to departed merit.

At the present time all candidates are told that the secrets of a Master Mason are substituted secrets, the real word has been lost and another one has to be whispered. The substituted word, as we suggested in *The Hiram Key*, is Egyptian, which came from the traditions of Moses. But the postures, embraces and temple ritual appear to be pure Phoenician, suggesting that Freemasonry does well to remember Hiram, King of Tyre, as one of the two living holders of the true secrets.

The Masonic ritual says this about the nature of the secret word, apparently assuming, as we do, that the Master Mason has been raised to the role of the Phoenician Sun god, El. During the ceremony the newly made Master Mason is resurrected from his grave, which is along the line of the equinox, and once he has been restored to life, under the rays of the Bright Morning Star he is told that he is now authorised to travel along the path of the Sun. The ritual says:

Q: As a Master Mason whence come you?

A: The East.

Q: Whither directing your course?

A: The West.

Q: What inducement have you to leave the East and go to the West?

A: To seek for that which was lost, which, by your instruction and our own industry, we hope to find.

Q: What is that which was lost?

A: The genuine secrets of a M. M.

Q: How came they lost?

A: By the untimely death of our Master Hiram Abif.

The ritual goes on to add more information about who knows what:

Our Master [Hiram Abif], true to his Obligation, answered that those secrets were known to but three in the world, and that, without the consent and co-operation of the other two he neither could, nor would, divulge them.

Those other two were Hiram, King of Tyre, and Solomon, King of Israel. And it seems most likely that the reason Solomon was forced to substitute an Egyptian secret word was because Hiram, the husband of Venus, was not prepared to compromise the Goddess by repeating the pillow talk she used on the morning of her wedding to him. The five-pointed nature of the embrace was not a secret between king and Goddess, as it could be observed by the witnesses in the Temple and also be seen happening in the sky. Hiram, it would seem, gave Solomon as little as he could get away with, as long as Solomon continued to pay his contractual charges. Perhaps if Solomon had paid for the extra palace he ordered, then we might have had a different Mason's Word.

Down to the present day, candidates for Freemasonry are raised in this same secret five-pointed embrace, known as the Five Points of Fellowship. The two wardens, whose role in the lodge is to mark the Sun at its zenith and at its setting, assist the Master, whose role is to mark the rising Sun, and during the raising ceremony to sit under the helical rising star of Venus. (See Plate 3 of *The Hiram Key*, which shows the five-pointed star illuminated above the Master's chair.)

The ritual describes the duties which become incumbent on the candidate once he has been embraced at the five points of contact between the Goddess and her Consort.

Q: *Name the Five Points of Fellowship.*

A: *Hand to Hand, Foot to Foot, Knee to Knee, Breast to Breast, and Hand over Back.*

Q: *Explain them briefly.*

A: *Hand to hand, I greet you as a Brother. Foot to foot, I will support you in all your laudable undertakings. Knee to knee, the posture of my daily supplications shall remind me of your wants. Breast to breast, your lawful secrets, when intrusted to me as such, I will keep as my own. And Hand over back, I will support your character in your absence as in your presence.*

Q: *Explain them at length.*

A: *Hand to hand, when the necessities of a Brother call for aid, we should not be backward in stretching forth the hand, to render the assistance which might save him from sinking, knowing him to be worthy, and that not being detrimental to ourselves or connections. Foot to foot, indolence should not cause our feet to halt, nor wrath turn our steps aside, but forgetting every selfish consideration, and remembering that man was not born for his own enjoyment alone, but for the assistance of his generation, we should be swift of foot to help, aid, and execute benevolence to a fellow-creature, particularly a Brother Mason. Knee to knee, when we offer up our ejaculations to the Most High a Brother's welfare we should remember as our own, for as the voice of babes and sucklings are heard at the throne of grace, so most assuredly will the breathings of a fervent and contrite heart reach the dominions of bliss; our prayers being reciprocally required for each other's welfare. Breast to breast, a Brother's lawful secrets, when intrusted to us as such, we should keep as our own; for to betray the trust which one Brother reposes in another, might be to do him the greatest injury he could possibly receive in this life; nay, it would be like the villainy of the assassin who, lurking in darkness, stabs his adversary to the heart when unarmed and in all probability least suspicious of danger. Hand over back, a Brother's character we should support absent or present; we should not revile him ourselves, or knowingly suffer it to be done by others. Thus, Brethren by the Five Points of Fellowship ought we to be united in one sincere bond of fraternal affection, which will sufficiently serve to distinguish us from those who are strangers to our Masonic Order and may demonstrate to the world, in general, that the word Brother among Masons is something more than a name.*

The story of the building of Solomon's Temple, told in *The Masonic Testament*, is a story of failure, not success. Everything is going to plan, and the Temple is almost complete, when somebody tries to extract the secret incantation used for king-making from the Phoenician, Hiram. Unfortunately they kill him, and the magic words are lost to the Jews, not to be found again until the restoration of the Temple by Zerubbabel.

If this myth has some basis in reality it would mean that Solomon never did get to be made a 'real' king in Canaanite fashion in his new temple.

To put it in modern terms, he had the hardware for kingmaking in the Temple itself, but he never got the software to run the program. We know that Solomon failed to make his payments to Hiram, King of Tyre. So, we speculated, did the Phoenician ruler recall his high priest and architect, refusing to give Solomon the required software because he had not kept up the instalments? Masonic ritual insists that the two kings remained the very best of friends, but might this be an attempt to show Solomon in the best possible historic light?

The Old Testament and *The Masonic Testament* both tell us that Solomon suddenly turned away from his new god Yahweh towards strange gods and child sacrifice. Does this mean that he did not have the ritual to cement a relationship with his own, new God and was trying to make himself a 'true' king by relating to the old gods?

Solomon seized the throne during a palace revolution, and once he had control he appears to have been bound by no restrictions whatever. His reign was that of the typical Eastern despot. His death, however, gave a new opportunity for the revival of the national claims already emphasised from the critical point of view of the prophets of Yahweh.

Solomon's son, Rehoboam, was asked to grant a new charter and to enter into a new covenant, whereby the freedom of the subjects from oppressive forced labour would be assured. This, with his father's example before him, he refused to do. The tribes at Shechem repudiated him and decided to make Jeroboam their new king. Judah, with less ground for dissatisfaction and probably more easily overawed by the royal bodyguard, cut the nation politically in two by staying loyal to Rehoboam. According to 1 Kings, Rehoboam was restrained from making any immediate attack on Jeroboam by a message from the prophet Shemaiah, but we hear of continual war between the two kingdoms.

Rehoboam met with much success, and left to himself he might have recovered the whole kingdom, but we gather that Jeroboam appealed to his former protector, Pharaoh Sheshonk, and the latter was only too glad of an opportunity to assert once more the ancient claim of the pharaohs to an empire in Palestine. Certainly the Egyptian king invaded the country in or about 928 BCE, and left us a record of his triumphs. The places he mentions include cities as far north as the plain of Esdraelon, which leads us to suspect that by this time they were in the hands of Rehoboam.

Neither the Israelite nor the Egyptian records state that Sheshonk actually captured Jerusalem, though both mention an enormous spoil taken from the city. We must suppose that Rehoboam, finding his situation hopeless, consented to hand over his treasures, and that Sheshonk accepted his submission rather than undertake the difficult task of taking Jerusalem by force.

The political separation of the two kingdoms was now complete, and was emphasised by Jeroboam's religious policy. In the north of Israel there were many ancient Canaanite sanctuaries that still followed a fertility cult based around a pagan bull fertility-cult. Jeroboam took over these sanctuaries, and whilst continuing the sexual practices of the bull-cult renamed them to honour the God of the Jews, Yahweh – a matter we will return to later. Two of the old sanctuaries, those of Bethel and Dan, were raised to special eminence.

Dynastically there is a striking difference between the twin countries of Israel and Judah which split away after Solomon's death. Except for a short period in the latter half of the ninth century, Judah maintained its unbroken fidelity to the house of David; Israel did not, and the first fifty years after the disruption saw no fewer than three families of kings on the throne.

King Ahab, who succeeded Jeroboam, married Jezebel, a High Priestess of Baalat and daughter of King Ithobaal of Tyre, formerly the high priest of Baalat. She brought with her the religious and sexual practices of the Phoenicians, which caused trouble with the prophets of Yahweh because she persuaded her husband to build a temple to Baalat. She and her astral priests of Venus were destroyed by the efforts of the nature-worshipping Yahwehists, in the form of Elijah and his successor Elisha. We will return to them later.

Jezebel's daughter, Athaliah, followed in her mother's footsteps but failed in her attempt to wipe out the line of David and replace it with the line of Ithobaal when she provoked a revolution from the rural Israelites, who saw her favouring the seafaring city states of the coast. They revolted against her and caused a complete break between the Israelites and the Phoenicians.

During this period of frequent outbreaks of petty local struggles, border warfare and plundering raids the wonderful dream of creating a powerful new state under David and Solomon apparently disappeared for ever. Why, we asked ourselves, did it all go so wrong? Was it Solomon's expensive attempts to turn himself into a real king and a Divine representative of God that lay behind his destructive legacy?

SUFFER LITTLE CHILDREN

Anyone who watches the heavens closely for a long period will appreciate that the Sun and Venus have a special relationship and the mythical marriage of the two makes sense astronomically. The question that we now confronted was, why is there not more astronomical-based myth in Jewish theology?

Our core hypothesis is that the Grooved Ware beliefs survive in Freemasonry today because they were inherited from the Jews, so we need to understand what Grooved Ware rituals were passed from the Canaanites to the Jews, and how they were transmitted through the thousand years between Solomon and the turbulent period that surrounded the death of Jesus Christ. We looked at several possible entry points to tackling this issue, and soon found that the 'wise king' – Solomon himself – offered a surprising starting point.

In Masonic ritual there is a passage in the fourteenth degree of the Ancient and Accepted Scottish Rite that almost certainly goes unconsidered by the few people who are even aware of its existence. It says about King Solomon:

> . . . *much intoxicated with his great power, he plunged into all manner of licentiousness and debauchery, and profaned the Temple by offering incense to the idol Moloch . . .*

The ritual confirms the biblical account that King Solomon turned away from Yahweh to favour older gods. But who or what was Moloch?

We were interested to know what sort of idol had turned Solomon's head away from the new god of the Jews, which for Jews, Christians and Muslims today is God Himself.

We found that Moloch was more than an idol. Many scholars believe that he was a Canaanite god of the Sun whose name came to represent the practice of 'child sacrifice' amongst the Jewish people. His name derives from, and is synonymous with, the word Malak,[1] meaning 'king', as we knew from the name 'Melchizedek'. Moloch began in the distant past as a Canaanite Sun god; a king who reigned from the heavens through his 'son' – the king on earth. However, we discovered that the writers of the Old Testament used the term Moloch to describe a form of sacrifice rather

---

[1] *Cassell's Concise Bible Dictionary,* Cassell and Company Limited, 1998

than the name of a god. The sacrifice in question was the burning alive of the king's own children, to persuade the gods to be kind.

Surely, this could not be true of King Solomon?

Then we recalled how ancient kings such as David and particularly Solomon had huge harems and therefore probably countless children – so they could afford to lose a few that were born to less favoured wives or concubines. They may not have even known the children that they offered up as a 'sacrifice'.

Early depictions of Moloch show him as a man with a bull's head. The central feature of his worship was the ritual burning of children in 'the fire of Moloch' (Milton described this ancient god in *Paradise Lost* as 'Moloch, horried king'). This practice of committing living children to scream slowly to death in the remorseless heat of the god's fire began at an early period and retained such power over parental compassion that Mosaic law stated that if any man made or permitted his children to 'pass through the fire of Moloch' he was to be put to death.[2] The Bible calls this child sacrifice 'the abomination of the Ammonites', but we have to accept that this horrific ritual was still being conducted at the time the Jewish Law was written down, else why was it necessary to have rules against it?

Encyclopedia Mythica claims that a statue of Moloch acted as a horrific child incinerator:

Moloch was represented as a huge bronze statue with the head of a bull. The statue was hollow, and inside there burned a fire which coloured the Moloch a glowing red. Children were placed on the hands of the statue. Through an ingenious system the hands were raised to the mouth (as if Moloch were eating) and the children fell into the fire where they were consumed by the flames. The people gathered before the Moloch were dancing to the sounds of flutes and tambourines to drown out the screams of the victims.

This is a fanciful account, to be found at www.pantheon.org/articles/m/moloch.html, which possibly owes far more to later French novelistic invention than biblical authority, but we think it captures the horror of child sacrifice.

We could not help but notice that the story of Moloch seems to have

2 Lev. 18: 21 and 20: 1–5

similarities with the myth of the Minotaur, the creature with his bull's head and man's body that lived in the labyrinth of Minos on the island of Crete. The Minotaur (in Greek the name simply means 'bull of Minos') was the offspring of Pasiphaë, wife of Minos, and a snow-white bull that the god Poseidon sent to the king. The bull was so handsome that Minos refused to sacrifice it, as Poseidon intended. When Minos disobeyed him, Poseidon became angry at this show of disrespect. He took revenge on Minos by using his divine powers to make Minos's wife Pasiphaë fall in love with the bull. Her infatuation was so intense that she was impregnated by the handsome white bull.

We decided not to enquire too closely into the exact mechanics of this liaison, feeling the detail must be a divine mystery beyond the understanding of all except the most innovative pornographers.

When Pasiphaë gave birth to the bull-headed half-man, Minos did not rush to embrace his new stepson. Instead he ordered the architect and inventor Daedalus to build a labyrinth so intricate that escape from it, without assistance, would be impossible. In the centre of this intricate maze the king hid the evidence of his wife's beastly liaison.

Minos did not dare kill Poseidon's contrived bastard, for fear of even worse reprisals, and he couldn't just leave the monster to starve, so he needed to feed the brute. The Minotaur liked children, so much he could eat up to fourteen whole ones at a sitting. Fortunately he only dined once a year.

Confined to the labyrinth, the Minotaur was fed with seven young girls and seven young boys every year. Minos exacted a supply of suitable children as an annual tribute from Athens.

There is every reason to suspect a link between this Minoan legend and the Canaanite Moloch because the Philistines, who were a subgroup of the Canaanites, originally came from Crete. This is an accepted fact for most authorities. Professor Philip Hyatt of Vanderbilt University in Nashville, Tennessee says of the Philistines: 'These people lived in south-western Palestine, originally in a confederation of five cities.'[3] He goes on to observe that the ancient historian Herodotus visited the temple of Venus at Ashkelon, one of these five Philistine cities, before saying: 'The Philistines came from the Aegean region, including the Island of Crete.'[4]

[3] Hyatt, JP: 'Zephaniah', *Peake's Commentary on the Bible*
[4] Hyatt, JP: 'Zephaniah'

The story of the Minotaur is probably based on a memory of a time when child sacrifice existed on Crete, which was interesting to us because it does suggest that this murderous procedure may have had a connection with the Grooved Ware People. The reason we suspect this is because ancient Crete has a provable link with the Megalithic Yard, the unit of measurement used by the Grooved Ware People. The palaces of the Minoan culture on Crete were surveyed in the 1960s by architect and stonemason Professor J. Walter Graham, who found that they used a standard measurement that he called the Minoan Foot. The unit he detected was equal to 30.36 cm, which has been accepted as a reality by most archaeologists. The length of this unit had no special significance to him, although it was obvious that it only deviated from the modern foot by 1.2 mm (0.4%). However, the writer Alan Butler recognised the length of 30.36 cm as derived from the Megalithic system of measurement, being exactly 1,000[th] of a Megalithic second of arc at the Equator (366 Megalithic Yards).[5]

The fact that the people of Crete were using a 'Megalithicly' derived unit of measurement four thousand years ago strongly suggests a link to the Grooved Ware People, and it is a reasonable extension to believe that they would have also inherited ritual practices as well. The Phoenicians are known to have had strong links with the Minoan culture, and a connection between their belief systems is not an unreasonable thing to expect.

ABRAHAM AND CHILD SACRIFICE

The Canaanite shrine that became the location for Solomon's Temple predates even the mythical David by the best part of a thousand years. In the Masonic material we have already referred to, Solomon is reported to have first chosen the site of a ruined Enochian temple and then changed his mind and selected Mount Moriah to the north of the early city.

Now, according to the tradition recorded in chapter 22 of Genesis, Mount Moriah was the spot where Abraham began preparations for the sacrifice of Isaac, his eldest child.[6] It was on this spot that the remote founding father of Judaism built a wooden pyre to destroy his first-born in the searing flames of Moloch. The story in Genesis 22: 4–10 tells how Abraham was to set fire to young Isaac before drawing on all the strength of his religious

---

[5] Butler, A: *The Bronze Age Computer Disc*, W Fulsham & Co. 1999
[6] Hooke, SH: 'Genesis', *Peake's Commentary on the Bible*

superstition to ignore his son's tortured cries while he slowly roasted towards the release of death, in order to ensure his father's good fortune:

Then on the third day Abraham lifted up his eyes, and saw the place afar off.

And Abraham said unto his young men, Abide ye here with the ass; and I and the lad will go yonder and worship, and come again to you.

And Abraham took the wood of the burnt offering, and laid it upon Isaac his son; and he took the fire in his hand, and a knife; and they went both of them together.

And Isaac spake unto Abraham his father, and said, My father: and he said, Here am I, my son. And he said, Behold the fire and the wood: but where is the lamb for a burnt offering? And Abraham said, My son, God will provide himself a lamb for a burnt offering: so they went both of them together.

And they came to the place which God had told him of; and Abraham built an altar there, and laid the wood in order, and bound Isaac his son, and laid him on the altar upon the wood.

Of course, the writers of the Old Testament have to show how Abraham did not carry out the 'Moloching' of his first-born son. They explain that God let him off – but only after Abraham demonstrated his committed intent to murder his son in honour of the Sun god El Elyon, 'the Most High'.

We are told that Abraham saw the site of the proposed sacrifice in the distance, which fits with the view one would get of this high ground north of the Jebusite city at that time. He was clearly travelling with other people and he did not want them, or his son, to guess what he was about to do in the name of El Elyon, for the god he was sacrificing his son to was certainly not Yahweh at such an early date (generally held to be *circa* 1900 BCE, but never considered to be more recent than 1700 BCE.

It is widely accepted that the location was Melchizedek's kingdom of Jerusalem, and that the site of the intended immolation was the same place that would become the location of Solomon's Temple many centuries later.[7] Professor Hooke has observed:

> *From the anthropological point of view it may be regarded as evidence for the existence of child sacrifice amongst the Hebrews . . .*[8]

Once this episode is complete the Old Testament tells us that Abraham and his party travelled to Beersheba, only fifty miles south of Jerusalem, again confirming the location.

CHILD SACRIFICE AND YAHWEH

Somehow it seemed imaginable that the Grooved Ware People, the Minoans, the Canaanites and even Solomon might well have sacrificed children, but surely such practices must have died out as Israel and Judah developed their relationship with their God during the first millennium before Christ? The idea that such barbaric practices could have continued into the established period of Yahweh's rule over his Chosen People struck us as quite alarming, and alien to the modern concept of the Jewish-Christian God of love and forgiveness.

Startlingly, chapter 16 of the Second Book of Kings, verses 1–5, gives us information that demonstrates that Ahaz, king of Judah,[9] worshipped Moloch well over two hundred years after the reign of Solomon and his temple of Yahweh.

> *In the seventeenth year of Pekah the son of Remaliah, Ahaz the son of Jotham king of Judah began to reign.*

> *Twenty years old was Ahaz when he began to reign, and reigned sixteen years in Jerusalem, and did not that which was right in the sight of the Lord his God, like David his father.*

> *But he walked in the way of the kings of Israel, yea, and made his son to pass through the fire, according to the abominations of the*

---

[7] Hooke, SH: 'Genesis'
[8] Hooke, SH: 'Genesis'
[9] The Annals of the Assyrian king Tiglath Pileser III yield an accurate date for Ahaz's (Ia-u-ha-zi) reign as 740–725 BC.

heathen, whom the Lord cast out from before the children of Israel.

And he sacrificed and burnt incense in the high places, and on the hills, and under every green tree.

Then Rezin king of Syria and Pekah son of Remaliah king of Israel came up to Jerusalem to war: and they besieged Ahaz, but could not overcome him.

Here we are told how this king caused his son to 'pass throught the fire', which may well mean that the child died in 'the fire of Moloch'. Furthermore, we are told that this is the 'way of the kings of Israel', the Northern Kingdom of the two Jewish states. So the practice of burning children alive was customary even at this late date.

Ahaz caused worship to take place at the old Canaanite sanctuaries on the high places and under sacred trees around Judah (the Southern Kingdom). If anyone is in doubt about the meaning of the previous passage, 2 Chronicles 28: 2–3 explicitly states that King Ahaz did indeed sacrifice his children and worship old gods:

For he walked in the ways of the kings of Israel, and made also molten images for Baalim [other gods]. Moreover he burnt incense in the valley of the son of Hinnom, and burnt his children in the fire, after the abominations of the heathen whom the Lord had cast out before the children of Israel.

The valley of Hinnom, to the southwest of Jerusalem's city wall, is where the child sacrifices to Moloch took place. Later, the city's rubbish was burned there. This association with consuming children in flames gave this valley its name of Gehenna, the place of torment for the wicked that was the original inspiration for the concept of the eternal fires of 'hell'.

We knew from our previous research that discussions about heaven and hell are particularly characteristic of Enochian literature, which is filled with the idea of heavenly abodes for the righteous after death and places where the wicked are held until the Judgement comes and they are punished in Gehenna.[10] The abode of the righteous is known as Paradise, a Persian word for a park or garden, and the picture of heaven is filled out by descriptions of a restored Eden. The opposite of Paradise is Gehenna – defined as the Valley of Hinnom for its association with Moloch sacrifices.[11]

Further investigation into child sacrifice showed that it was connected with sacred oak trees, ritual sex and a cult of the dead – all strange ideas that seem a long way from what most people associate with the Jews and their chosen God. Drs Oesterley and Robinson in their definitive study of the origins of the Hebrew religion discuss the influence of these three concepts, and we decided to review their main findings.

Trees were thought to be sacred because they were regarded as living beings or the homes of gods. They swayed and murmured in the wind and so were thought to be inhabited by minor gods.

Cause and effect, as we understand them, not being recognised, the idea that the branches of a tree moved through the force of the wind did not occur. It was a spirit which occasioned this; but here it must be remembered that the distinction between matter and spirit which is so obvious to us was unknown to man in undeveloped stages of culture.[12]

The Roman historian Pliny the Elder mentioned this practice in Palestine in Roman times saying:

With ancient ritual the simple country folk dedicate a lofty tree to a god. Not more do we adore images that shine with gold and ivory than they do groves and the very silence in them.

In the early Hebrew religion Oesterley and Robinson also point out that standing stones were believed to represent sexual functions of local gods:

The Semitic mazzeboth (pillars or standing stones) are regarded as males and the flat tablestones as females.[13]

The standing stones formed the basis of sanctuaries and were very common

[10] 1 Enoch 27: 61
[11] Black, M: 'The Development of Judaism in the Greek and Roman Periods', *Peake's Commentary on the Bible*
[12] Oesterley, WOE & Robinson, TH: *Hebrew Religion, Its Origins and Development*
[13] Oesterley, WOE & Robinson, TH: *Hebrew Religion, Its Origins and Development*

in northern Canaan. Oesterley and Robinson go on to comment on how the cult of Yahweh was incorporated into later sexual practices of these sanctuaries, saying:

> In the eight century [BCE] we hear of complaints made by Amos and suggested by Hosea, of inequities associated with the northern sanctuaries. Yahweh was worshipped as a fertility God under the form of a bull, and this in itself would seem to imply a sexual element in the cult.[14]

Bull worship among the Hebrews is first mentioned in Exodus 22, which tells how the people grew anxious at the prolonged absence of Moses on the mountain and so they melted down their golden jewels and made a golden calf to worship. Oesterley and Robinson comment that this story was used to justify the continuation of ritual sex carried out at bull-cult sanctuaries in places like Bethel and Dan:

> Possibly we have a relic of the bull cult connected with Horeb and transferred to northern Israel. It is significant that Elijah, for whom Yahweh's dwelling was in Horeb, made no protest, as far as we know, against the cult of the bull.[15]

Also there is clear evidence for an early Hebrew belief in the power of some holy men to speak with the dead and learn their secrets. Again Oesterley and Robinson observe:

> Elisha is also represented as being able to raise the dead by means of a somewhat elaborate ritual (2 Kings 4: 32–35). This should perhaps come under the head of imitative magic; this at any rate is suggested by the ritual; for Elisha, the living, lays himself upon the dead boy and puts mouth on mouth, eyes on eyes, and hands on hands; just as Elisha is alive, so the dead boy must become living.[16]

Most of the references in the Old Testament consist of prohibitions on the

[14] Oesterley, WOE & Robinson, TH: *Hebrew Religion, Its Origins and Development*
[15] Oesterley, WOE & Robinson, TH: *Hebrew Religion, Its Origins and Development*
[16] Oesterley, WOE & Robinson, TH: *Hebrew Religion, Its Origins and Development*

practice of consulting the dead. But why prohibit something unless it is being carried out?

There is a very early reference to asking the dead for advice to be found in I Samuel 28: 3–25. This story occurs after the death of Samuel, when King Saul is worried that he will not be able to defeat the Philistines. Saul decides to ask advice from Samuel, and to do this goes to the witch of Endor in order to speak, through her magical intervention, with the dead prophet. Oesterley and Robinson comment on the significance of this story:

> *Nobody will deny that this narrative is an important illustration of the belief of the early Israelites concerning the departed. They continue to live, they remember, they foresee; they can leave whatever place it is in which they abide; and they can return to the world, in a certain sense.*[17]

These traits, which are not often mentioned about the early Israelities, were, however, well known to the Celts, the inheritors of Grooved Ware thinking in the British Isles. They too used oak groves in their worship, had involvement with their dead ancestors and practised ritual sex.

There is a poem in Isaiah 57: 3–13, written after the Exile and around the time of the second Jerusalem Temple, which complains about these practices. It has been translated from the Hebrew by Susan Ackerman, a professor of Far Eastern and Judaic studies, who has highlighted the clever use of puns in the text which appear to have been lost in earlier translations:[18]

> *But you, draw near, you sons of a sorceress, seed of an adulterer and of her who plays the harlot, at whom do you jeer, at whom do you open your mouth, do you stick out your tongue?*

> *Are you not children of transgression, offspring of deceit, who burn with lust among the terebinths [sacred oak trees], under every green tree, who slaughter children in the wadis, among the clefts of the rocks?*

[17] Oesterley, WOE & Robinson, TH: *Hebrew Religion, Its Origins and Development*
[18] Ackerman, Susan: 'Sacred Sex, Sacrifice and Death', *Bible Review*, vol. vi, no. 1, February 1990

With the perished of the wadi is your portion, they, they are your lot.

Even to them you have poured out a libation, you have offered up an offering,

Shall I be appeased for these things.

On a mountain high and lofty, you have set your bed.

There you went up to offer sacrifice, and behind the door and the doorpost you set up your symbol.

For a hundred times you stripped and you mounted and spread upon your bed.

You . . . yourself from them the love of their bedding, the phallus which you envisioned.

You anointed the mulk-sacrifice with oil, you multiplied your perfume oils.

You sent them down even to Sheol.

In the length of the way you wearied, but you did not say, 'There is no hope'.

You found revivification for your strength, therefore you did not weaken.

Whom did you dread and fear that you lied, that you did not remember me, that you did not give me a thought?

Have I not kept silent even from old?

But me you did not fear.

I, I will declare you righteous, and also your deeds, but they will

*not help you when you cry out, they will not save you those
deceased spirits of yours.*

The wind will carry all of them off, a breath will take them away.

*But whoever takes refuge in me will possess the land, and will
inherit my holy mountain.*

Here Professor Ackerman finds references to sexual intercourse being
performed under terebinth (oak) trees as well as on the Temple Mount in
Jerusalem. This corresponds to everything we know of the Grooved Ware
People and the later Celts of the British Isles.

Ackerman confirms that this poem is explicit about where sexual activity
is taking place: 'On a mountain high and lofty, you have set your bed.'
The terminology 'high and lofty mountain' in the Hebrew Bible, she comments, only ever refers to Mount Zion, the mount on which the Jerusalem
Temple stands.[19]

Thus the sacred sexual activity described in certain verses of this passage must have occurred on Temple Mount itself. This she confirms by reference to a clever wordplay, using the Hebrew word for bed, 'mishkab',
which deviates by only one letter from the word for shrine, which is
'mishkan'. Ackerman believes that the description of offering sacrifice at
the 'bed' confirms that the bed/shrine pun is intentional.

She goes on to list the long line of Jewish kings who killed their own
children as ritual sacrifices right down to the sixth century BCE:

*Child sacrifice to appease some deity was well known in Israel
before the Exile. The Book of Judges describes the sacrifice of
Jephthah's daughter as payment for Jephthah's rash and irrespon-
sible vow to sacrifice to God the first thing he saw on his return
home from battle (Judges 11: 29–40). King Ahaz of Judah
(734–715 C.E.) burned his own son as an offering (2 Kings 16: 3).
Ahaz's contemporary in Israel, King Hoshea (732–722 B.C.E.),
allowed the cult of child sacrifice to flourish among his subjects (2
Kings 17: 16–17). In seventh-century Judah, after the destruction of
the northern kingdom of Israel in 722 B.C.E., child sacrifice*

[19] See Isaiah 2: 2, 40: 9; Ezekiel 17: 22, 40: 2; Micah 4: 1.

continued; King Manasseh (687–642 B.C.E.), like Ahaz before him, sacrificed his own son (2 Chronicles 33: 6). Jeremiah (Jeremiah 7: 30–32, 19: 5, 32: 35) and Ezekiel (Ezekiel 16: 21, 20: 31, 23: 39) both condemn the practice of child sacrifice in the early sixth century B.C.E. Our poem indicates child sacrifice continued even after the Israelites returned from Exile. In verse 5, the prophet asks if these are not the people 'who slaughter children in the wadis, among the clefts of the rocks.'

According to the Revised Standard Version (RSV) of the Bible, the first half of Isaiah 57: 9 reads 'You journeyed to Moloch with oil and multiplied your perfumes.' Ackerman says that this is a description of the ritualistic preparation of a child ready for immolation in the flames.

We found this idea that the Jews might have sacrificed children to Yahweh – to God – to be strange indeed, and something that is not discussed in polite company today. We asked our good friend Professor Philip Davies for his expert opinion on this issue, and he replied: 'I see no reason why child sacrifice would be absent even from among the Israelites.'

Ackerman's article shows a photograph of the ashes of a child, sacrificed

The ashes of a sacrificed child rest in an urn beneath a stone bearing a depiction of the goddess Tanit.

to appease a god.[20] They are in the urn below the large stone that depicts the goddess Tanit standing in the portal of a temple with a tambourine in her hand. Could there be, we wondered, similar items buried deep below Temple Mount in Jerusalem from the time when Solomon embraced the principle of Moloch worship?

In our researches for *The Hiram Key* we found strong links in early Jewish belief to those found in Egypt. This seemed entirely reasonable, as the Old Testament legend of Moses tells us that he was an adopted member of the Egyptian royal family and a general in their army. If he was going to lead a group of immigrant workers out of that country in search of a 'promised land', then he, and they, would have spoken Egyptian and thought like Egyptians. As this was the first time that any of Moses' followers would have left the country, it seems hard to imagine how any new religion could be more than a variation on their existing belief system.

We had read the stories of how Moses and Joshua murdered and plundered their way across the land of Canaan at the behest of their new-found god, Yahweh. According to the biblical account city after city was destroyed and their populations massacred. However, we now knew that such archaeological evidence as there is suggests that most of these events did not happen, and the story of the Hebrews' invasion, like the story of King David, is almost entirely fictitious.

If it were not for the fact that the Christian Bible concerns itself with the history of the Jewish people and their adopted God, the archaeology of this insignificant desert region at the eastern end of the Mediterranean would be the preserve of a few obscure scholars. As it is, most people know something about the so-called 'Holy Land' and its inhabitants two and three thousand years ago. The biblical tradition, repeatedly taught in the Western world, says the Jewish people are an ancient race with a clear-cut religion that also provided the God of Christianity and Islam. However, in relative terms the Jews are not particularly ancient, they are not racially different to other groups in the region, and we now knew that they certainly did not embrace monotheism for hundreds of years after the time of David and Solomon.

From the time of Moses through to the almost total destruction of Jerusalem in 70 CE the religion of the Jews was a melting pot for ideas absorbed from everywhere around them. Their struggle to make sense of

[20] Ackerman, S: 'Sacred Sex, Sacrifice and Death', *Biblical Review*, vol. vi, no. 1, February 1990 – Photograph Asor Punic Project/ James Whitred

colliding oral traditions whilst adopting new concepts led to a wide range of interpretations of what Judaism stood for.

The standard Christian interpretation of the Old Testament creates a picture of a people founded by Abraham, Isaac and Jacob and brought to Israel by Moses and Joshua before being led to an expected greatness by a line of priests and kings. The impression is that the law of God was given directly by Him to the Jews and that their beliefs therefore stand apart as authentic and unique against a backdrop of pagan idolatry practised by the superstitious peoples of other countries. For Christianity the usefulness of the Jews ends abruptly with the birth and subsequent murder of the promised Messiah who, as their version of the timeless concept of 'the son of God', brought everlasting redemption to all mankind.

When one examines what is now known about the Old Testament the most surprising aspect is how relatively recent these 'ancient' books are in relation to the events they describe. Even the account of the Creation, the description of the beginning of time, in the first chapter of Genesis is believed to have been written down in the sixth century BCE.[21] At first view such a date does sound pretty ancient, but to put it in perspective we reminded ourselves that it was four hundred years after the time of King Solomon and almost three thousand years after the building of some of the great megalithic structures in the British Isles. To put this fact into perspective, the writers of the book of Genesis are as close to us, in the twenty-first century, as they were to the men who built advanced astronomical structures such as Newgrange in Ireland, Maes Howe in Scotland or Bryn Celli Ddu in Wales.

We also could not help observing that the ritual sacrifice of the children of Jewish kings was still happening when the Bible was being written.

Although the Bible is a great deal younger than most people imagine, many of the stories contained within it are ancient, having been passed down the generations as oral traditions before scribes first put pen to papyrus. It seems highly likely that it was during the Babylonian Captivity that the Old Testament was put together as an attempt to meld jumbled traditions into a coherent story. Whilst the scribes had the intention of putting Yahweh at the centre of their belief system, they cannot help but reveal the popularity of the astral cult.

[21] Cohn, Norman: *Cosmic Chaos and the World to Come*

THE RAINMAKERS

There is a story in the Old Testament (1 Kings 18: 17–40) that tells of the point in history when the astral Venus cult, inherited from the Canaanites, was first subjugated to the Yahweh cult. The prophet Elijah had a conversation with the king about a dispute amongst the people as to which religion they should follow.

King Ahab, king of Judah and husband of Jezebel, priestess of Baalat, was more concerned with matters of state than religion and obviously thought Elijah and his fanatical support for Yahweh was the real problem, particularly when it manifested itself as hatred for his queen Jezebel. But the prophet was certain that it was the king who was backing the wrong gods (Baalim) and suspected him of being too strongly influenced by the religious and sexual practices of his wife Jezebel the Phoenician princess, who is remembered elsewhere in the Bible as the whore of Tyre. The scribes of the Book of Kings tell the story:

And it came to pass, when Ahab saw Elijah, that Ahab said unto him, Art thou he that troubleth Israel?

And he answered, I have not troubled Israel; but thou, and thy father's house, in that ye have forsaken the commandments of the LORD, and thou hast followed Baalim.

Now therefore send, and gather to me all Israel unto mount Carmel, and the prophets of Baal four hundred and fifty, and the prophets of the groves four hundred, which eat at Jezebel's table.

So Ahab sent unto all the children of Israel, and gathered the prophets together unto mount Carmel.

Next Elijah admitted that the country was split, and showed how the Yahweh party was on its knees when he claimed to be the only prophet of Yahweh left to face the eight hundred and fifty yelling, screaming priests of Baal and of Asherah, the Venus cult:[22]

---

[22] The King James Bible refers only to these prophets belonging to Baal, whereas up-to-date translations such as the New English Bible connect them to Asherah too.

And Elijah came unto all the people, and said, How long halt ye between two opinions? if the LORD be God, follow him: but if Baal, then follow him. And the people answered him not a word.

Then said Elijah unto the people, I, even I only, remain a prophet of the LORD; but Baal's prophets are four hundred and fifty men.

To decide the issue of whose god was the best, Elijah engineered a competition at the sacred Canaanite site of Mount Carmel. Two altars were set up, each containing sacrifices for burning, and he challenged the opposing horde of prophets to ignite Baal's pyre through their prayers. Then this anti-Canaanite prophet employed the megalithic principles of the Venus cult to undermine them.

The Old Testament describes how Elijah goes to an old broken-down sanctuary and erects twelve stones and then digs a trench around them which he then proceeds to fill with water.

And Elijah took twelve stones, according to the number of the tribes of the sons of Jacob, unto whom the word of the LORD came, saying, Israel shall be thy name:

And with the stones he built an altar in the name of the LORD: and he made a trench about the altar, as great as would contain two measures of seed.

And he put the wood in order, and cut the bullock in pieces, and laid him on the wood, and said, Fill four barrels with water, and pour it on the burnt sacrifice, and on the wood.

And he said, Do it the second time. And they did it the second time. And he said, Do it the third time. And they did it the third time.

And the water ran round about the altar; and he filled the trench also with water.[23]

---

[23] 1 Kings 18: 31–35

This description is typical of a Canaanite sanctuary, and corresponds to the stone circle at Gilgal where the Israelite army was circumcised after Joshua had first led his people into the promised land. As we have already mentioned, the word Gilgal means 'stone circle', it was a common form of structure for the Canaanites and early Jews, and they were all known as Gilgal. Professor Fohrer says of the first Gilgal taken as the people of the Exodus first arrived:

> Gilga . . . was likewise a pre-Israelite sanctuary . . . The name of the cultic site derives from the 'circle' of stones that delimited it.[24]

We can be confident that Elijah's twelve stones were also in a circle and the trench around them was also circular – to fill it with water from the pyre in the centre it had to be a continuous ring around the site.

Circles of standing stone with trenches around them were a standard feature of the Grooved Ware culture of the British Isles three thousand years before Elijah's time. So was he deliberately constructing a megalithic-style stone structure complete with a surrounding henge according to an ancient tradition?

Elijah then has the henge filled with 'water', which is known to have happened at Grooved Ware sites in the British Isles, especially Ireland. But Elijah had a different motive for surrounding his altar with liquid. His 'water' proved to be highly inflammable. This description of the construction of a traditional Canaanite structure built by a prophet of Yahweh demonstrates how confused everything was at this time. It seems that no one really understood where these ideas came from, but they did not hesitate to use the most powerful 'magic' and the most potent public symbols to promote their god.

The plan worked. When the Canaanite prophets could not persuade their deity to ignite their pyre Elijah teased them, suggesting that their god might be talking, or perhaps he was out for the day, or maybe asleep. Naturally, they failed to draw down heavenly fire, but somehow Elijah succeeded. He then took full advantage of the situation by telling the assembled crowd to seize his opponents and drag them to a nearby stream. There he stood, so the Bible tells us, and personally dispatched his unarmed religious rivals as the crowd forced the defeated prophets of Venus, one by one, onto his sword blade:

[24] Fohrer, G: *History of Israelite Religion*

And Elijah said unto them, Take the prophets of Baal; let not one of them escape. And they took them: and Elijah brought them down to the brook Kishon, and slew them there.

And Elijah said unto Ahab, Get thee up, eat and drink; for there is a sound of abundance of rain.

Elijah proved himself to be important because he delivered an 'abundance of rain'. The exchange between Elijah and Ahab took place after a long drought, and the idea of the coming of rain was a symbol of God's goodness falling upon the Earth.

Rainmaking appears to have been an ancient Canaanite practice which was adopted from the earliest times of the development of the Jewish nation. The Bible tells how Joshua, the leader of the 'Apiru people, first led his army into the Promised Land by crossing the river Jordan from the east to the west bank. This story tells how the 'Apiru troops are taken to the Canaanite sanctuary at Gilgal (about five miles north of Qumran), and here amongst the circle of megalithic standing stones they conducted an ancient ritual. This involved every man being circumcised with a flint blade. There is no explanation as to why they used flint and not metal knives.

Here we have an army of men being led into a circle of standing stones to have their foreskins cut off with a piece of stone. It is hard to imagine that this was anything else but a ritualistic throwback to the Neolithic Age.

There is no explanation either for the fact that these Hebrew men had not been circumcised at birth in the manner supposedly adopted since the time of Abraham. The whole story is odd, and whilst we were discussing what this mass circumcision ritual may have been about we remembered a comment made by Professor Richard Dawkins linking Australian Aboriginal rituals for rainmaking to foreskins:

As an added precaution, the Great Council of the Dieri would also keep a stockpile of boys' foreskins in continual readiness, because of their homeopathic power to produce rain (do penises not 'rain' urine – surely eloquent evidence of their power?).[25]

[25] Dawkins, R: *Unweaving the Rainbow*, Penguin, 1998

Here was the first time we had seen an anthropological reason advanced to explain the Covenant of Abraham, and as we discussed it we soon realised that this explanation also made sense of a story which had puzzled us for a long time. The promised land that the 'Apiru had just entered was arid from the long drought, and rain was essential if they were to settle in their new homeland. The circumcision ceremony just had to be part of an ancient method of making rain, but there is a further reason to believe that this entire episode is about rainmaking.

More than a thousand years after the Gilgal ritual, John the Baptist was considered by many to be the new Elijah. Professor John Marsh says of this:

The description of John is in terms which once had been sufficient for Ahaziah to recognise as a description of the prophet Elijah.[26]

Professor Robert Eisenman also comments:

John the Baptist plays a role in the Transfiguration scene too, since in all the Synoptics (the first three Gospels), he is identified with Elijah.[27]

This connection between Elijah and John the Baptist is important because it shows how a theme of circle construction and rainmaking continued right to the time of Christ. Eisenman believes that the Dead Sea Scrolls have opened up our understanding of the role of such ideas in connection to leading figures in the New Testament:

Themes develop, when pursued, that provide new clues for ideas and motifs hitherto unsuspected or previously unknown. One of these themes is 'rain' and eschatological 'rain' imagery . . . There are in the literature of this period several such primordial rainmakers. The first immediately recognizable is Elijah, which links the rain-maker concept to redivivus notions centering about his person, thereby tying the tradition to activities related to John the Baptist.[28]

[26] Marsh, J: 'The Theology of the New Testament', *Peake's Commentary on the Bible*
[27] Eisenman, R: *James the Brother of Jesus*, Faber and Faber, 1997
[28] Eisenman, R: *The Dead Sea Scrolls and the First Christians*, Element, 1996

In his footnotes Eisenman confirms the role of constructing circles:

'Circle-drawing' is the mechanism for rainmaking.

John the Baptist was a second cousin to Jesus, and this ability to create rain from a Joshua/ Elijah style circle appears to have been a family tradition. Eisenman believes that Jesus' brother James also performed these feats, which were associated with Messiahship and the Star Prophecy. Before the time of John there came a man who was possibly a member of Jesus and John's family and who was a particularly famous rainmaker. He was known as 'Honi the Circle Drawer', but was also called Onias, which is a derivative of the title Oblias, meaning stone pillar[29] – a term that also became associated with James. Furthermore, Eisenman believes that this Honi was the grandfather of John, James and Jesus. He states:

That James, too, functioned as a rain-maker is confirmed by Epiphanius in 'Haeres'.

'Circle-drawing' and 'rainmaking' skills are directly associated with the Star Prophecy that foretells the coming messiah. They are also linked directly to the family of Jesus and to the practices of the Essenes who created the Dead Sea Scrolls. Professor Eisenman says on this subject:

We hear about similar circles being drawn by (in the writings of) Josephus' and Hippolytus' 'Essenes', who in their observation of the Sabbath would not step out of a certain radius even to relieve themselves.[30]

This whole area of circle-drawing and rainmaking is associated with a hidden tradition that centres on the coming of the promised messiah. Elijah is the role model and the early influences are clearly Enoch and Noah. The family of Jesus, John and James are, it seems, the last known practitioners in a rite that must be of extreme antiquity. The subject is fascinating but highly complex, too complex for us to do justice to the emerging thesis in this book. For readers who wish to know more we strongly recommend the writings of Robert Eisenman and also those of Michael Wise.

[29] Eisenman, R: *James the Brother of Jesus*
[30] Eisenman, R: *James the Brother of Jesus*

CONCLUSIONS

Our investigations into Jewish child sacrifice shows that it was connected with sacred sex, sacred oak trees, bull worship and a cult of the dead. These ideas are very different from what people usually associate with the Jews and Yahweh, their God. But we concluded that it is very likely that the Jews once sacrificed children to Yahweh.

We believe that child sacrifice originated with Sun worship and that El Elyon, the Sun-god, was worshipped at Jerusalem for at least a thousand years before the time of Solomon. Sun worship amongst the Jewish people did not disappear as quickly as the Bible would like us to believe.

David, the first Jewish messiah, established his kingship on the basis of a covenant with Yahweh, but Solomon, his son, was a typical Eastern despot and wanted a more absolute form of control. This, we believe, is why Solomon approached Hiram, king of Tyre, to buy the secrets of astral kingship and the absolute power this conferred. His extravagance and oppression split the kingdoms of Israel and Judah after his death.

The beliefs seemed to be connected with circumcision, the building of stone circles and rainmaking, with clear evidence emerging that the ruling classes kept these ideas alive.

The picture that was emerging was that the Jewish kings either had a religion of their own or some very different version of the Yahweh cult than the one that the Old Testament principally engages with. We were seeing a two-tier belief system, with early Canaanite solar and Venus ideas attached to the concept of kingship whilst something much more ordinary was believed by the peasant population.

Chapter Nine

THE SONS OF DAWN

THE DIAL OF AHAZ

A few years ago a 'bulla', or clay impression seal, that once belonged to King Ahaz of Judah was found.[1] On its back the impression of the strings that tied the roll and of the fabric of the papyrus are still visible. The seal, inscribed in Old Hebrew letters, reads simply: *l'hz y hwtm mlk yhdh*, which translates to 'Belonging to Ahaz (son of) Yehotam, King of Judah'. Whilst confirming the existence of this contemporary of the prophet Elijah, there was nothing particularly surprising about finding a 2,800-year-old relic of this ancient king of Judah.

Recently, however, another far more astonishing bulla came to light. This seal had been used by Ahaz's son, Hezekiah, who lived *circa* 715 to 687 BCE. The bulla of Hezekiah is tiny, measuring only about 0.4 inches in diameter and a little less than 0.08 inches in thickness. Its inscription reads: *Ihzqyhw 'hdz mlk yhdh*, 'Belonging to Hezekiah, (son of) Ahaz, king of Judah'. But what amazed us is the emblem etched into it. It shows a two-winged beetle pushing a circular ball of dung, a symbol of the rising Sun.[2]

The meaning of the symbol is clear from Malachi 4: 2:

[1] Deutsch, R: 'First Impression – What We Learn from King Ahaz's Seal'. *Biblical Archaeology Review*, May/June 1998

[2] Bonnet, H: 'Skarabaeus', in *Reallexikon der ägyptischen Religionsgeschichte*, Berlin, DeGruyter, 1952

For you who revere my Name, the Sun of righteousness [tsedeq]
shall rise with healing in its wings.

Such imagery would hardly be surprising if found amongst any of the countries surrounding Israel, but until recently it was thought that Yahweh worship was not linked to the Sun. In the context of our investigation of the solar aspects of post-Solomon Judaism, it becomes clear that the use of this symbol has nothing to do with Yahweh. But it has everything to do with the old Canaanite Sun-god, possibly even the child-hungry Moloch.

Two- and four-winged Sun discs appear on other artefacts belonging to Hezekiah, for example on the handles of a *l'melekh* he once owned, so the two-winged scarab with the Sun disc is not the only occurrence of solar symbolism on the king's property. This evidence suggested to us that there was an intent to make Yahweh a solar deity in Judah. It seems that Sun worship with its solar deity was a strong contender to unseat Yahweh as principal God.

In 2 Kings 20: 8 we noticed a statement saying that the shadow viewed on something called the 'dial of Ahaz' should go forward ten steps or degrees, meaning that the shade of the declining Sun would be lengthened unnaturally quickly, or that it should go back that amount, a phenomenon reversing the order of nature. Sundials were known at this time in Babylonia, but the description used in this biblical quote refers to a series of aligned steps which Ahaz constructed so that the shadow cast by the Sun would read out the time of day.

And Hezekiah said unto Isaiah, What shall be the sign that the
Lord will heal me, and that I shall go up into the house of the
Lord the third day?

And Isaiah said, This sign shalt thou have of the Lord, that the
Lord will do the thing that he hath spoken: shall the shadow go
forward ten degrees, or go back ten degrees?

And Hezekiah answered, It is a light thing for the shadow to go
down ten degrees: nay, but let the shadow return backward ten
degrees.

And Isaiah the prophet cried unto the Lord: and he brought the

shadow ten degrees backward, by which it had gone down in the
dial of Ahaz.

In Isaiah 38:8 we are told specifically that the device is a sundial:

Behold, I will bring again the shadow of the degrees, which is gone
down in the sun dial of Ahaz, ten degrees backward. So the sun
returned ten degrees, by which degrees it was gone down.

This whole idea of a supreme god being connected to the Sun was so deep-seated that hundreds of years later the Sun became the distinguishing mark of the new deity – whom Christians now call God. We note that the Christian Sabbath is now Sun-day, and all heavenly beings have a Sun shining behind their head. The concept of 'God on high' appears to be a memory of the Sun-god El Elyon – meaning the 'Most High' – the shining light of goodness above our heads. The whole idea of holiness is rooted in the Jewish concept of 'righteousness' known as Zedek, which, as we have shown, had its origins in Canaanite Sun worship, where the Sun's rays seek out evil and corruption. The concepts of light and darkness, good and evil, are wrapped up in a primordial awareness that the benign energy radiated from the Sun brings warmth and succour to the Earth. And what could be more natural? Nothing in the human experience can possibly have a more central and visible role than the giant star that rises each morning to chase away the fears of the darkness of night. This god leaves us but always returns, he brings the promise of a new day and nourishes the crops that provide our daily bread. The evildoers that hide in the shadows of night have to run for cover to hide their shame from the inescapable light of goodness.

For many later Israelites God had become a concept apart from the Sun, but the available evidence strongly suggests that these astral worshippers continued their practices and beliefs right through to the time when the Babylonians destroyed Jerusalem and its Temple in 596 BCE, the time when the city's leading figures were taken into exile. As late as the beginning of the Babylonian Captivity the prophet Ezekiel refers to a vision that reveals his horror of those who continue to worship the dawn:

And he brought me into the inner court of the LORD's house,
and, behold, at the door of the temple of the LORD, between the

porch and the altar, were about five and twenty men, with their
backs toward the temple of the LORD, and their faces toward the
east; and they worshipped the sun toward the east.[3]

In this verse Ezekiel berates the Enochian Jews for turning their backs to God and worshipping the Sun. He goes on to blame their astral activities for the fall of Jerusalem.

We now knew that Jewish kings had followed in Solomon's footsteps for hundreds of years, worshipping Sun-gods and conducting ritualistic destruction of their own children in their pursuit of divine power. This kingly cult appears to have had a low level of connection to the God of the Jews originally, but we suspect that after the return from the Babylonian Captivity, the child sacrifice disappeared and Yahweh gained predominance.

Our next question was to unravel how the royal line protected their ancient astral beliefs whilst coexisting with the peasant theology.

RETURN FROM EXILE

The Jews who were seized and taken into the cities of the Babylonians had mourned the loss of their city and its temple, but they quickly acclimatised to their new circumstances in various cities, and they prospered as part of a successful empire. They must have identified with their new masters, because they too aspired to understand the heavens and their meaning for mortal man.

It has always struck us as strange that after three generations the Babylonians suddenly let the Jews return to their home city.

There was a lot of political turbulence after the death of Cyrus the Great and only when Darius came to the throne were 42,462 people sent back to Jerusalem.

Writing of this event six hundred years later, Josephus felt that he understood Darius' motivation. He describes it as follows:

Now he, while he was a private man, had made a vow to God,
that if he came to be king, he would send all the vessels of God
that were in Babylon to the temple at Jerusalem.

[3] Ezekiel 8: 16

Darius was a Zoroastrian, and his God was Ahura Mazda (the Sun-god and Lord of Wisdom), not Yahweh, the local god of Jerusalem.

Josephus is a wonderful, if occasionally biased historian, but his view here has been moulded by his own belief in a single God. It is certain that the Jews who were taken into captivity believed that many gods existed, and that Yahweh was in control in Israel but not in other places such as Babylon. When they were in other lands the Jews would pay their respects to the local god. By the time they were released they had acquired the idea of a single, all-powerful God from the Zoroastrians who were themselves monotheists, believing in a cosmic dualism of Truth (Asha) being opposed by the Lie across the entire universe.

According to the record left by Josephus, Darius set a riddle, the correct answer to which would permit the rebuilding of the holy Temple of the Jews. The question was about the relative strengths of four possible contenders; kings, truth, women and wine. The correct answer was given and, interestingly, those few words are the only written inscription in the entire structure of Rosslyn, built by William St Clair as a final manifestation of the Jerusalem Temple. They appear on a cross lintel in the south of the building in medieval Latin:

WINE IS STRONG, A KING IS STRONGER, WOMEN ARE EVEN STRONGER BUT TRUTH CONQUERS ALL

This classic Zoroastrian sentiment gave new life to the Jerusalem Temple.

As the Jews returned from their captivity in Babylonia, only a few of the most elderly would have ever set sight on the city of Jerusalem before. Even the people taken in the second-wave exile were forty-eight years older than when they left. A new generation of city rulers must have welcomed them with caution and, no doubt, distrust. Were these sons and grandsons of the old power base seeking to resume life where their forebears had left off? Did they want their family land returning from its new owners, and, most importantly, did they want to try and take high office in the running of the city and its ruined Temple?

Josephus tells us that no fewer than 42,462 people followed Zerubbabel back to Jerusalem, expecting to continue where their forebears had left off. We have concluded that it was at this point that the divide between 'nature' and the 'astral' became a polarised issue. The followers of the peasant 'nature' principles were focused on the tradition associated with Moses, while the returning elite astral cult was dedicated to the astral teachings laid down by Enoch.

For the royal Enochian line the astral aspects were central to achieving the greatness of their nation through their long-term plans, which would be fulfilled by the leadership of their promised messiah who would arise at a preordained moment in the future. And they knew that the moment would be marked by the appearance of the Divine Shekinah, the light that shows the presence of God.

Zerubbabel is said to have built his new Temple on top of the ruins of the old one, and life in Jerusalem returned to normal. The Bible does not tell us as much about the next period, during which the astral ideas were being merged into the cult of Yahweh. However, whilst this was happening another great influence appeared, and that was the culture of the Greeks.

The serious intrusions of Greek culture (Hellenism) begin with the conquests of Alexander the Great in 331 BCE, which put the Jews on the defensive. A civil war broke out in Israel in 165 BCE between Jewish Hellenisers and resistant Israelites. The Maccabean revolt began as a civil war; it ended as a successful war for Judaean political independence from Syrian occupying forces led by Antiochus Epiphanes.

Members of the Hasmonaean priestly family who led the revolt proclaimed themselves hereditary kings and high priests despite the fact that they were not of the ancient high priestly lineage. This caused outrage amongst the true priesthood, who set up their own community at Qumran at the lowest place on the surface of the Earth in an attempt to maintain the purity of their own traditions. The Qumran community was originally a difficult alliance of Zadokite and Enochian priests formed in the aftermath of a shared disillusion with the Maccabean authority in Jerusalem.[4]

One clear implication of our findings is that a previously unidentified Enochian group also continued in its pure form, as well as the hybrid form centred on Qumran.

Pliny, the Roman historian, wrote of the people of the Qumran community:

On the west coast of Lake Asphaltitis [the Dead Sea] are settled [a number of] the Essenes, at some distance from the noisome odours that are experienced on the shore itself. They are a lonely people,

[4] Boccaccini, G: *Beyond the Essenes*, Eerdmans (Grand Rapids), 1998

the most extraordinary in the world, who live without women, without love, without money, with the palm trees for their only companions.[5]

Like the Order of the Knights Templar, these priests of Qumran held ritual initiations, wore only white linen and held all things in common. And like original Freemasonry the initiation period for membership took three years to become a full member of the sect. We also recalled how we were both clothed in white linen for each of the three rituals of Craft Masonry and how we were asked to hand over our money during the First Degree, although we were prompted to reply 'Nothing have I, or freely would I give.'

It is known that the Essenes retained elements of Sun worship, as they sang hymns at dawn in praise of the 'Sun of Righteousness'. They too would have been subject to the wrath of Ezekiel, who had criticised their practice of turning 'their backs toward the temple of the LORD, and their faces toward the east; as they worshipped the sun toward the east'.[6] The Jerusalem authorities did not like their traditions either, because they eventually passed a law forbidding the Essene practice of kneeling towards the rising Sun at dawn, on pain of death.[7]

Biblical scholar Morton Smith has interpreted a golden staircase described in one of the Dead Sea Scrolls as a device built to worship the Sun, 'beseeching him to rise'. That the Sun, Moon and stars were revered as angels is evident from the text of Psalm 148: 1–4:

Praise the Lord out of heaven; praise him in the heights. Praise him, all his angels; praise him, all his host. Praise him, sun and moon; praise him, all you shining stars; praise him, heaven of heavens.

But that staircase, Morton Smith mentions, may well have really existed, as the remains of a spiral staircase were found during the excavation of the Qumran site.[8] Is it just coincidence that the Second Degree of Freemasonry describes just such a staircase as the route to follow in order to discover the hidden mysteries of nature and science?

[5] Pliny, *Natural History*, 5:73
[6] Ezekiel 8: 16
[7] Graves, R: *The White Goddess*, Faber and Faber, 1948
[8] Vermes, G: *The Dead Sea Scrolls in English*, Penguin, 1995

ASTROLOGY AND SUN WORSHIP

Many Christians today vehemently detest astrology, believing it to be a pagan abomination, a superstition that courts the Devil and opposes the teachings of Jesus. But we were finding that knowledge of the movements of the heavens and a belief in the effect of helically rising stars on the affairs of mankind was central to the beliefs of the Jewish group that gave rise to Christianity.

Historically, astrology was a problem for early rabbinic Jews, who also denied its role in their religion. The Babylonian Talmud (Shabbat 156b) records a debate about the validity of astrology where Rabbi Hanina, a Babylonian who came to Palestine around AD 200 to study with Judah ha-Nasi, a compiler of the Mishnah, said:

The planetary influence gives wisdom, the planetary influence gives wealth and Israel stands under planetary influence.

However, the influence of astrology had been fiercely opposed by Rabbi Johanan, who stated:

There are no constellations for Israel.

Surprisingly, in the light of his statement in support of planetary influence, Judah ha-Nasi's Mishnah (a book which codifies the Jewish law) spoke against some aspects of astrology, stating that anyone who finds an object with representations of the Sun, the Moon or a serpent must cast it into the Dead Sea. This instruction indicates that such images must have been common and that there was a major tension between those who supported the Sun and astral imagery and those who did not.

The fascination with Sun worship amongst the Jewish people did not go away as quickly as the Bible would like us to believe. A mosaic recently uncovered at a synagogue in ancient Sepphoris shows a zodiac with an abstract depiction of a Sun-god riding in his quadriga – a four-horse chariot. Other synagogues show the Sun-god in human form, rather than as simply an abstract Sun disc.

We had noticed that many Masonic lodges are decorated with the signs of the zodiac, but we also found that there was a much stronger astrological influence in Freemasonry, once we started to look for it. On a visit to the library of the Grand Lodge of Scotland with biblical scholar Professor Philip Davies, whilst inspecting the uncatalogued Morrison collection of Masonic works that date from before the French Revolution, this influence became very clear.

Philip was attracted by a large leather-bound volume. Taking it down from the shelf he placed it on the desk and opened it. The book was hand-written in a precise but faded copperplate. As he leafed carefully through the rustling pages he came to a folded pull-out section in the centre of the book. He carefully teased it open to reveal a wheel-like diagram showing the tribes of Israel and indicating which sign of the zodiac and which gem-stone was associated with each. The early Freemason who wrote this book was clearly concerned to record a close link he had identified between astrology and Jewish beliefs.

The twelve signs of the zodiac in a radial arrangement around the Sun chariot of Helios can be found in at least seven ancient synagogues in Israel, but such images were not seen in early Christian buildings, and only in three synagogues outside Israel. A poem found in the genizah (a store of worn-out documents) of a synagogue in Cairo states that:

> *There arose a dispute among the months, when the August one sent to the land of Egypt. Come let us cast lots on the zodiac, that we might know in which of us Israel is to be redeemed.*

As we searched for more information about Sun worship in early Israel we found a reference to an object found amongst the stones from the ruins of Herod's Temple that had no explanation. But to us it looked exactly like a device for monitoring the position of the Sun as it rises each morning on its constant swing across the horizon from solstice to solstice. As we pored over the picture of the strange object we realised that if a gnomon was placed at the back of the central groove it would cast a shadow down the curved section of the stone in the same manner as the marked lines.

Our hypothesis was borne out when we checked the angles formed by the outer lines. These we found to correspond with the angles of the extreme solstice sunrise shadows (60 degrees) as they would be cast at the latitude of Jerusalem. The variations in the spacing of the lines would be due to the hills across the valley from the Temple, which have a dip in them that would affect the elevation of the Sun at first light. The line that runs left to right could have been used to mark the Sun's elevation at a

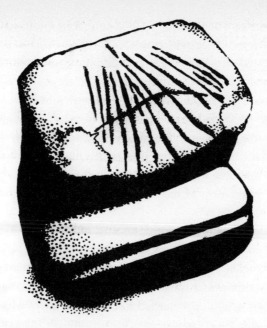

*This strange stone was found in the ruins of Herod's Temple. No explana-
tion for it exists but we believe it is likely to have been a sunrise marker
used by the priests from Qumran who seized the Temple shortly before the
entire city was destroyed by Titus in 70 CE. It is known that the Essenes
would bow to the rising sun at the Temple and it seems that the hurriedly
cut lines may have been created over approximately nine months to mark
the angle of the sunrise.*

given time shortly after sunrise – perhaps the limitation of time when the
official period of 'dawn' is deemed to be over. The shadow of the gnomon
would be at its longest when first light broke and it would shorten as the
Sun rose. When the shadow no longer crossed the horizontal line, dawn
would be over. The shadow would be at the centre during the equinoxes
and at the outer edges for the solstices. The right-hand side of the object
would be the summer solstice, when the Sun would gain elevation quickly,
whilst at the opposite side the Sun would rise slowly and move more horizontally. This means that we should expect to see a sunrise marker stone
having its horizontal line higher on the right than the left if it was to indicate a constant period of dawn throughout the year.

That is just what we could see on this stone.

The cut-out curve of the device compensates for the speed of the Sun's
apparent movement along the horizon. There are six segments between the
lines, and each of these represents a two-week period. The workmanship

of this important but puzzling relic is poor, suggesting that it was not part of the officially constructed temple.

We discussed the importance of finding a crudely made dawn timer in the stones which had once made up Herod's Temple. We felt that our theory of the function of this device makes especial sense for a number of reasons. As we knew, it is said that the Essenes were in the habit of worshipping at the Jerusalem Temple by kneeling towards the rising Sun at dawn.[9] We also knew that the priests of Qumran are considered to have been Essenes, and at some point between the start of the Jewish War in 66 CE and the destruction of the Temple, four years later, they gained control of the Temple.

This group called themselves 'The Sons of Dawn', and as such, we argue, they would surely have reintroduced their practice of bowing to the rising Sun. The Temple was still not complete, but Herod's architects had no reason to incorporate a dawn-measuring device in the stonework, so the Sons of Dawn would have needed to create a new 'sunrise stone' for themselves.

A magi priest needed nine months to calibrate this stone, which thereafter gave anyone the ability to tell the faithful when dawn was officially over and the period of bowing could end.

We also came across another strange artefact from this period which makes no sense to archaeologists but does to us. It was unearthed at Qumran and was first reported as a sundial, which it simply cannot be. We believe it measures solar movements across the year. This 'sundial' was found some forty-five years ago by Father Roland de Vaux at Qumran. Father de Vaux described the three concentric circles within the disc as a unique system for telling time: the inner circle measured daylight hours during winter, the middle circle during spring and autumn, and the outer circle during summer.

In antiquity the period from sunrise to sunset was usually divided into twelve equal hours, and since the period between sunrise and sunset varies from season to season, the length of each of the twelve hourly subdivisions also varied. The length of daylight varies with location, as well as season, so the length of an hour is location-specific. This means that we can be sure that this object found at Qumran cannot be a sundial. The lines on it are not equally spaced all the way around, and there is no way that the unequally spaced lines within each circle on this roundel can measure seasonally

[9] Graves, R: *The White Goddess*

adjusted hours. Additionally, shadows are shortest in summer and longest in winter, so the inner and outer circle seasonal designations which are claimed to identify it as a sundial cannot be correct.

Several real sundials have been found in Jerusalem as well as at other sites around Israel.[10] An important small white limestone sundial was discovered in Jerusalem in 1972 during a massive excavation south of the Temple Mount. It is a mere 2 inches wide and 2 inches tall, but the hour and seasonal lines on the dial are carefully computed for use in Jerusalem. It was found in the debris from the destruction of the Jerusalem Temple and it belonged to the Temple priests, as a seven-branched menorah is engraved on its back (before the destruction of the Temple, the menorah as a symbol was restricted exclusively to the Temple priests).[11]

Father Vaux's 'sundial' has been likened to an ancient board game called Mehen, which means 'to coil' or 'Coiled One' – because the board resembles a coiled serpent.[12] This game is known in Egypt from as early as the Pre-dynastic period (fourth millennium BCE), and is also found in Lebanon, Syria, Cyprus, Crete and on other Aegean islands.[13] We came to the conclusion that this is no game, and we doubt that the early similar artefacts were games either. Maybe they were used as games in more recent times, but originally we think these items were Sun trackers, devices to measure the seasons of the year, similar but slightly different in operation to the sunrise stone already mentioned.

Whilst the sunrise stone marked the movements of the rising Sun across the horizon from solstice to solstice, the Mehen coil measures the Sun at midday between the solstices and equinoxes. We were aware of the shape the Sun's shadow casts over seasonal periods, and we described this spiralling effect of the Sun's movement in *Uriel's Machine*, based on work done by American artist Charles Ross.

Ross showed how tracking the shadow of the midday Sun over the seasons produced a spiral for each quadrant between solstices and equinoxes. The spiral he produced shows the coiling line of the shadow in towards the summer solstice from the spring equinox and a second one out again towards the autumn equinox. In each case there are four coils to this particular serpent, corresponding with the structure of the disc found at Qumran.

10 Layish, Dov Ben: *A Survey of Sundials in Israel*, 1969
11 Levy, A: 'Bad Timing', *Biblical Archaeological Review*, July/August 1998
12 Levy, A: Bad Timing
13 Bellesort, Marie-Noel: 'Le Jeu de Serpent: Jeux et Jouets dans l'Antiquité et le Moyen Age', *Dossiers d'Archéologie*, 1992

We believe that it is the four grooves that are important in the disc, rather than the three raised sections. A bead could have been placed in the slot corresponding to the top edge of the shadow from the gnomon when the Sun was at its zenith each day which would mark the Sun's spiralling path through the year. Once calibrated it would give warning, for instance, that the next day was a feast day – information given directly by the infallible Sun rather than by the 'spurious' calendar calculations used by all other Jews.

It is well known that the people of the Qumran community used a solar calendar, not a lunar one like other Jews. It was based entirely on the movements of the Sun, in contrast to the Pharisees' calendar which was highly lunar-oriented. According to the solar calendar of Qumran there were 364 days to a year consisting of twelve months, each with thirty days plus an additional day which was inserted after each three months between each quarter.

The device found at Qumran would have given the people of this solar cult a date reminder delivered daily by the finger of the Sun; a fool-proof method of ensuring that they were celebrating exactly the right festival on precisely the right day.

The Qumranians considered that other Jews had gone astray from the calendar of the Sun and were consequently celebrating their festivals on the wrong days. The Dead Sea Scrolls tell how their authors railed against the other sects of Jews for their inability to understand when holy days should be observed, because their calendars were hopelessly wrong. So different was the outlook of the people of Qumran that one leading present-day scholar posed the question: 'Can we call them Jews at all?'[14]

Where evidence of Sun worship exists after the time of David and Solomon it tends to be dismissed as an influence of the Egyptians, Greeks or Persians, or seen as assimilated aspects of Sun-gods like Ra, Helios or Mithra. We cannot deny that these factors must have been influences, because no religion is entirely self-contained, but such thinking distorts the true nature of the solar beliefs of the Jews. It certainly has to be said that Sun worship is an obvious concept that was invented in cultures across the globe. But we have become sure in our own minds that the Canaanite concept of the Sun deity was the principal inspiration of this recurring and somehow 'underground' version of Judaism that was interesting us. And it

[14] Davies, Professor Philip: private communication

seemed to us that the beliefs of the Essenes were key to understanding this philosophy.

Josephus explained how extraordinary these Essenes were – a group with a single-minded focus who were a powder keg waiting its moment to explode:

> . . . *They have an inviolable attachment to liberty; and say that God is their only Ruler and Lord. They also do not value dying any kind of death, nor indeed do they heed the deaths of their relations and friends, nor can any such fear make them call any man Lord.* [15]

They also spread their beliefs by taking in children to teach them:

> . . . *They neglect wedlock, but choose out other persons' children, while they are pliable, and fit for learning; and they esteem them to be of their kindred, and form them according to their own manners.*[16]

Hippolytus in the *Refutation of all Heresies*, tells us more specifically what these children were taught:

> . . . *And they lead [these adopted children] into observance of their own peculiar customs, and in this way bring them up and impel them to learn science.*

We were reminded of what a candidate for Freemasonry is told on the completion of the Second Degree:

> . . . *you are permitted to extend your researches into the more hidden mysteries of nature and science.*

We have already shown that the study of science in Freemasonry refers mainly to the science of astronomy. Could this also have been a principal science of the Essenes; particularly an understanding of the movements of the Sun and Venus?

[15] Josephus: *Antiquities*, 18:1:6
[16] Josephus: *Jewish War*, 2:8:2

Josephus recorded the Essenes' worship of the Sun at dawn – an action that he, as a Jew, found hard to understand:

> . . . *And as for their piety towards God, it is very extraordinary;*
> *for before sunrise they speak not a word about profane matters,*
> *but put up certain prayers which they have received from their*
> *forefathers, as if they make a supplication for its rising.*[17]

If they regularly observed the sunrise, they couldn't avoid seeing the pattern of the appearances of the Morning Star.

Josephus records how the Essenes owned no personal possessions and lived a totally austere life, owning just a simple white garment and one pair of sandals that they wore to destruction. They were also known as people having an ancient knowledge of healing:

> . . . *They also take great pains in studying the writings of the*
> *ancients, and choose out of them what is most for the advantage of*
> *their soul and body; and they inquire after such roots and medical*
> *stones as may cure their distempers.*[18]

Their curative skills were linked to the usage of stones. Hippolytus referred to the Essenes as 'busying themselves as regards the operative powers of these [stones]'. If the record left by Josephus is accurate they must have possessed some tremendous knowledge affecting the preservation of health, for he states:

> *They are long-lived also; insomuch that many of them live above a*
> *hundred years.*[19]

There would seem to be little reason not to believe Josephus on this matter, and such a lifespan must have been truly remarkable two thousand years ago for any one individual, let alone 'many' of these Essenes.

Also, according to Josephus, gaining membership of this order was no simple matter. First the candidate was given a loin girdle, a white tunic and a small hatchet, and he was required to live in the style of an Essene for one year, although not permitted to live with the Order. If he passed this

[17] Josephus: *Jewish War*, 2:8:5
[18] Josephus: *Jewish War*, 2:8:6
[19] Josephus: *Jewish War*, 2:8:10

stage he was kept as a novice for two more years, after which time, if he proved worthy, he was admitted into the society. This same term, 'worthy', is used in the ritual of the first degree of Freemasonry as the new candidate is about to be admitted a member of the Order:

It is my duty to inform you that Masonry is free and requires a perfect freedom of inclination on the part of every candidate for its mysteries. It is founded upon the purest principles of morality and virtue. It possesses many and invaluable privileges to worthy men, and I trust to worthy men alone.

The similarity to Freemasonry is more than superficial, because the candidate for the Essene order undertook an obligation to help his fellow man. Josephus describes it:

And before he is allowed to touch their common food, he is obliged to take tremendous oaths; that, in the first place, he will exercise piety towards God; and then, he will observe justice towards men; and that he will do no harm to any one, either of his own accord, or by the command of others; that he will always hate the wicked, and be assistant to the righteous; that he will ever show fidelity to all men, and especially to those in authority, because no one obtains the government without God's assistance; and that he be in authority, he will at no time whatever abuse his authority, nor endeavour to outshine his subjects, either in garments, or any other finery; that he will be perpetually a lover of truth, and propose to himself to reprove those that tell lies; that he will keep his hands clear from theft, and his soul from unlawful gains; and that he will neither conceal anything from those of his own sect, nor reveal any of their doctrines to others, no, not though any one should compel him so to do at the hazard of his life. Moreover, he swears to communicate their doctrines to no one any otherwise than as he received them himself; that he will equally preserve the books belonging to the sect, and the means of the messengers [the names of the angels].

This obligation strongly resembles that taken by a new Freemason just before he is admitted to share his first meal with the brethren. Whilst

Josephus could not have known the exact words used by the Essenes, he knew the general content. Anyone would draw similar conclusions from Freemasonry today if they heard the ritual.

We decided to draw up a list of the comparisons between the two Orders:

Essene: And before he is allowed to touch their common food, he is obliged to take tremendous oaths.

Masonic: . . . keep me steadfast and firm in this my first, great and solemn oath.

Essene: . . . he will exercise piety towards God.

Masonic: To God, by never mentioning His Name but with that awe and reverence which are due from the creature to his Creator; by imploring His aid on all your lawful undertakings and by looking up to Him, in every emergency, for comfort and support.

Essene: he will observe justice towards men . . . will ever show fidelity to all men.

Masonic: To your neighbour, by acting with him upon the square; by rendering him every kind of office, which justice or mercy may require; by relieving his distresses and soothing his afflictions, and by doing to him as, in similar cases, you would wish he should do to you.

Essene: he will ever show fidelity to all men, and especially to those in authority.

Masonic: . . . you are always to recommend kindness and condescension to inferiors, courtesy and affability to equals; obedience and submission; to superiors.

Essene: . . . he will be perpetually a lover of truth.

Masonic: . . . imprint indelibly on your mind the sacred dictates of Truth, of Honour, and of Virtue.

Essene: . . . nor reveal any of their doctrines to others.

Masonic: . . . do hereby and hereon, of my own free will and accord, most solemnly promise, vow and swear that I will forever hele, keep, conceal, and never reveal, any point or points, secret or secrets, mystery or mysteries of, or at all belonging to this the 1st degree in Freemasonry.

The Essenes were centre stage when the Jewish War broke out against the Romans. Their bravery, even in defeat, was remarkable. Josephus, who started the war as a Jewish officer and (rather wisely) ended it as a Roman one, said of the Essenes:

And as for death, if it will be for their glory, they esteem it better than living always; and indeed our war with the Romans gave abundant evidence what great souls they had in their trials, wherein, although they were tortured and distorted, burnt and torn to pieces, and went through all kinds of instruments of torment, that they might be forced either to blaspheme their legislator, or to eat what was forbidden them, yet could they not be made to do either of them, no, nor even once to flatter their tormentors, or to shed a tear; but they smiled in their very pains, and laughed those to scorn who inflicted the torments upon them, and resigned up their souls with great alacrity, as expecting to receive themselves again.

The Essenes who left us their documents at Qumran show us how they sometimes used cryptic devices when copying their sacred books. Dead Sea Scrolls scholar JT Milik refers to the use of two different alphabets with arbitrarily chosen signs which replace the normal Hebrew characters, or to documents where the writing even runs from left to right, instead of the normal right to left. Occasionally, Greek or Phoenician letters appear in place of their Hebrew equivalents. These sacred documents were prepared in readiness for the day when Yahweh would arise in the last times.

The Enochian tradition is at the heart of these secret texts not only in the Book of Enoch but also in the Book of Jubilees, which is widely thought to be just part of a far bigger collection of texts that existed at the time.[20]

[20] Russell, DS: *The Method and Message of Jewish Apocalyptic 200 BC – AD100*, SCM Press Ltd, 1960

In Jubilees Enoch is depicted as a mystery figure conversant with both esoteric and scientific knowledge, the latter being the ability to measure the
movements of the heavenly bodies and understand their meaning. The Book
of Jubilees also lays out the solar calendar system used by the Qumran
group. It has been said by Christian scholars that Jesus Christ may well
have followed this Enochian calendar himself – suggesting that he was
indeed associated with this group of hereditary priests that shunned the
'misguided' Jerusalem establishment. The Reverend Professor Harold
Rowley has said of the solar calendar described in the book:

> We need not ascribe the authorship of Jubilees to a member of the
> [Qumran] sect, and this calendar, which was older than the book of
> Jubilees, may have been followed by others besides the sectaries,
> including our Lord, who then would celebrate Passover on the
> Tuesday night. This date is not contradicted by synoptic evidence.[21]

There were secret Enochian traditions connected to Moses and Ezra, to
Enoch and Noah, and to Daniel. There is little doubt that these traditions
are the oldest in which Enoch represents the survival of Divine Secrets from
extreme antiquity which are passed on to subsequent generations.

The Book of Jubilees, so important to the people of Qumran, says of
Enoch:

> He was the first among men that are born on earth to learn
> writing and knowledge and wisdom and who wrote down the signs
> of heaven according to the number of their months in a book.[22]

The legends of Noah and Enoch appear to be essentially similar, and it is
believed by biblical scholars that the Noah legend is older than that of
Enoch, and that the latter reconstructs the remnants of the former.[23]

We now needed to understand how the Venus worship had survived
along with Sun worship. If we are right in our belief that the idea of Venus
ritual came from the Grooved Ware People through the Canaanites and
early Jews, it must have existed right through to the time of Christ and the

[21] Rowley, HH (ed.): Apocalyptic Literature, *Peake's Commentary on the Bible*, Thomas
Nelson and Sons, 1962
[22] Book of Jubilees 4: 17
[23] Charles, RH: *The Book of Jubilees*, OUP, 1902

fall of the Temple. Our task now was to find hard evidence of its existence. Without this vital link our hypothesis could never be proven.

CONCLUSIONS

We found that Canaanite ideas about a Sun-god and a religion based on the appearance and movement of the stars persisted in Israel until the time of the Babylonian Captivity (*circa* 596 BCE) and have been carried through into modern Christianity in the image of the halo.

During the period of the rebuilding of the Temple under Zerubbabel the newly emerging Greek culture began to influence Israel. Certain groups did not approve of adopting Greek ideas, and a set of Zadokite and Enochian priests formed the Qumran community in the aftermath of a shared disillusionment with the Maccabean authority in Jerusalem. This group used ancient astronomical techniques to create their own solar calendar, distinct from the lunar calendar used by the Maccabean priesthood, who controlled the Temple at Jerusalem.

Chapter Ten

THE HOLY SHEKINAH

THE VENUS CYCLE IN JUDAISM

The meaning of the ancient name of Jerusalem tells us unequivocally that it was founded with Venus in mind. According to tradition its high sanctuary was the spot where Abraham prepared to sacrifice his son, and where Solomon built the Temple that is aligned to the pre-dawn rising of that planet. We also knew from our study of Grooved Ware structures of the British Isles that the period of the Venus cycle is forty years – a number which we now noticed seemed to be of great importance in the Bible.

To check out if our assessment of the biblical use of forty was more than wishful thinking, we pulled out as many references as we could find to forty-day or forty-year periods in the Bible. Here are just a sample of forty mentions of forty we extracted from the Old and the New Testaments:

1   The Flood was associated with rains that fell for 40 days and nights. (Gen. 7: 4)

2   The Flood was on the earth for 40 days. (Gen. 7: 17)

3   Isaac was 40 years old when he took his wife. (Gen. 25: 20)

4   Esau was 40 years old when he took his wife. (Gen. 26: 34)

5 Israel ate manna for 40 years. (Exodus 16: 35)

6 God said that at the end of 40 years He would end the captivity of the Jews amongst the Egyptians. (Ezekiel 29: 13)

7 Moses was with God on the mount for 40 days and nights. (Ex. 24: 18)

8 Moses was again with God for a further 40 days and 40 nights. (Ex. 34: 28)

9 Moses led Israel out of Egypt aged 80 (2 x 40), and after 40 years in the wilderness he died aged 120 (3 x 40). (Deut. 34: 7)

10 Spies searched in the land of Canaan for 40 days. (Num. 13: 25)

11 God made Israel wander for 40 years. (Num. 14: 33–34)

12 40 stripes was the maximum whipping penalty. (Deut. 25: 3)

13 God allowed the land to rest for 40 years. (Judges 3: 11)

14 God again allowed the land to rest for 40 years. (Judges 5: 31)

15 God again allowed the land to rest for 40 years. (Judges 8: 28)

16 Abdon (one of the Judges in Israel) had 40 sons. (Judges 12: 14)

17 Israel did evil and God gave them to an enemy for 40 years. (Judges 13: 1)

18 Eli judged Israel for 40 years. (1 Samuel 4: 18)

19 Goliath presented himself to Israel for 40 days. (1 Sam. 17: 16)

20 Saul, the first Jewish king, reigned for 40 years. (Acts 13: 21)

21 Saul was 40 years old when he became king. (Acts 13: 21)

22 Ishbosheth (Saul's son) was 40 when his reign began. (2 Sam. 2: 10)

23 David reigned for 40 years. (2 Sam. 5: 4, 1 Kings 2: 11)

24 Solomon reigned for 40 years. (1 Kings 11: 42)

25 The holy place of the Temple was 40 cubits long. (1 Kings 6: 17)

26 40 baths (measurement) was the size of lavers in the Temple. (1 Kings 7: 38)

27 The sockets of silver were in groups of 40. (Ex. 26: 19 & 21)

28 King Ahaz arose, and did eat and drink with an angel, and went in the strength of that meat forty days and forty nights unto Horeb the mount of God. (1 Kings 19: 8)

29 Elijah had one meal that gave him strength for 40 days. (1 Kings 19: 8)

30 Ezekiel bore the iniquity of the house of Judah for 40 days. (Ezekiel 4: 6)

31 Jehoash reigned for 40 years in Jerusalem. (2 Kings 12: 1)

32 Egypt was to be laid desolate for 40 years. (Ezek. 29: 11–12)

33 Ezekiel's vision of the new Temple is 40 cubits long. (Ezek. 41: 2)

34 The courts in Ezekiel's temple were 40 cubits long. (Ez. 46: 22)

35 God gave Nineveh 40 days to repent. (Jonah 3: 4)

36 Forty years God grieved for generation of people. (Psalms 95: 10)

37 Jesus fasted 40 days and nights. (Matthew 4: 2)

38 Jesus was tempted for 40 days. (Luke 4: 2)

39 Jesus was ministered to by angels in the wilderness for 40 days. (Mark 1: 13)

40 Jesus remained on Earth for 40 days after his resurrection. (Acts 1: 3)

Having found 101 examples, we went along to ask Professor Philip Davies if there was any standard explanation for the biblical fascination with this particular number. Philip replied that the only suggestion that he knew was the idea that forty years represented a generation, but he felt that this was unlikely, as it is closer to two generations.

Clearly, forty years is more than a human generation but less than a lifespan in a healthy society (a biblical lifespan being described as three score years and ten). So why does the Bible discuss periods of length forty so much? Could it be because of the length of the Venus cycle, given the planet's fundamental role in Canaanite theology and the establishment of Jerusalem itself?

We found it particularly interesting that the first three kings of Israel, Saul, David and Solomon, all reigned for exactly forty years. Were they allotted precisely one Venus period or was this a post-rationalisation of later scribes who believed in the importance of the Venus cycle as some divine period? The chances of it being coincidence are very low indeed.

We detected two much longer periods that were also of significance, both of which are multiples of forty years. No biblical scholar has ever been able to explain satisfactorily the forty-year cycle that is used throughout the Old and New Testaments – the span of a human generation is the only attempt. Additionally, several of the experts of the last century also mention two, much longer, periods almost in passing. They describe them as rather inexplicable and unimportant; however, once the significance of the Venus cycle is known the pattern is striking and, we think, of pivotal importance.

With careful scrutiny we found that these two longer periods had been carefully described but never explained. We have named the periods found in the Old Testament as follows:

Venusian Generation = 40 years (one Venus cycle)

Venusian Epoch = 480 years (12 x one Venus cycle)

Venusian Aeon = 1,440 years (12 x 3 x one Venus cycle).

We called the forty-year period a 'Venusian generation' because it was a period of rule for the early kings rather than because of any connection to parent/ child relationships of time. In the dictionary the word is defined as 'any of a number of stages, levels or series'.[1]

The term 'Venusian epoch' seemed entirely suitable because an epoch is defined as 'a point in time fixed or made remarkable by some great event from which dates are reckoned – a precise date from which a new state of things dates'.[2]

Finally we selected 'Venusian aeon' for the longest period because an aeon is defined as 'a vast age. It is also known that in Gnosticism it was considered to be a power emanating from the supreme deity associated with the government of the universe'.[3] This sounds like a very good way of describing long-term Venus cycles – and we recalled that Gnosticism was directly connected to Judaism at the time of Christ.

The periods we found are directly connected to major events. In the First Book of Kings 6: 1 we read about an important Venusian epoch of 480 years:

> *And it came to pass in the four hundred and eightieth year after the children of Israel were come out of the land of Egypt, in the fourth year of Solomon's reign over Israel, in the month Zif, which is the second month, that he began to build the house of the Lord.*

So the building of the great Temple of Jerusalem is said to have commenced exactly twelve Venus cycles after Moses and his 'Apiru band travelled across the parted Red Sea. The 'Apiru or Hebrew group wandered in the wilderness for exactly the duration of the first of these cycles, and then at the end of that cycle Moses died.

The question here is whether the period of 480 years claimed in 1 Kings is an attempt at recording a true date for this event or whether it was a 'sacred' period of time allocated to the gap between the two important events by some later writers. If the Exodus had happened at that time the

---

[1] *Chambers Dictionary*
[2] *Chambers Dictionary*
[3] *Chambers Dictionary*

pharaoh concerned in the Moses story would have been Thutmose III (1479–1425), which brings two problems. First, Thutmose III was a great builder but his construction work was in upper Egypt, not the Nile delta from where the Hebrew workers are said to have escaped. Second, this pharaoh conducted many successful military campaigns all across the land of Canaan and his troops would have quickly overrun the band of plague-bringing renegades led by Moses and Joshua.

Many biblical scholars believe that the 480-year gap is an artificial construct and that a more probable dating for the Exodus (if it happened at all) is *circa* 1250 BCE.[4] So, the next question is – why did someone feel the need to attribute this precise gap?

It is fully accepted that the Old Testament was a careful working of several oral traditions, and this element appears to belong to a strand that generally faded from view. The sacred 480-year period remained, but the reason for its existence became forgotten. Our feeling is that this number may well be from an older Enochian tradition that was adopted to the Moses tradition to give authority to the much newer story of the Exodus.

The 480-year period was also applied to the second arrival of the Hebrews in their Promised Land – the return from Babylonian Captivity. This has been identified by the Reverend Frederick Foakes-Jackson, a professor of Christian Studies who believes that the same timespan could have also been intended between Solomon's Temple and the ending of the Babylonian Captivity. He says:

The foundations of the Temple were laid in the four hundred and eightieth year after the Exodus . . . a similar period might be said to intervene between Solomon and the Captivity (430 years to the time of the last king, Zedekiah, and 50 years for the captivity).[5]

This is not an invention, as the dating of these events falls within recorded history, but it seems that the people concerned would have appreciated the importance of the 480-year period even if they did not understand its meaning.

The forty-year cycles are often associated with an individual's life and the two longer periods are said to separate major events in Jewish history.

[4] Stalker, DMG: 'Exodus', *Peake's Commentary on the Bible*
[5] Foakes-Jackson, FJ: *Peake's Commentary on the Bible*, T.C. & E.C. Jack Ltd, London, 1920

These points in time may not be historically accurate, but what matters is that the ancient priests imposed this pattern believing it to be true.

The longest period, which we have called a Venusian aeon, is described by Josephus, the first-century historian of the Jews:

> *Solomon began to build his temple . . . after the deluge one thousand four hundred and forty years.*[6]

Josephus recorded this as a fact that he had come across, but it meant nothing to him. He does not tell us which tradition gave this information but, as we will see later, there had been a resurgence of Enochian thinking prior to the time of Josephus' writings in the second half of the first century.

For us, a big picture was forming in front of our eyes. Solomon's Temple was started exactly 480 years after Moses led the Exodus out of Egypt (to wander for 40 years in the wilderness) and 1,440 years after the Flood (which lasted 40 days). There is a clear belief that God works to a mechanism that can lead to prediction. Biblical scholars have repeatedly noted the existence of this number sequence but they have never suggested any reason for it. We were fast becoming convinced that it relates to the appearances of Venus in the dawn sky.

We had definitely found a usage of the Venus cycle by the Jews that corresponded to our findings at Grooved Ware sites in the British Isles – but we still needed to find reference to the appearance of Venus at propitious moments. We were quickly amazed by what we found both in our assembled *Masonic Testament* and in the Bible itself.

The Old Testament tells us that something called 'the Divine Shekinah' shone at the time of Moses' birth, and as we already knew that Moses was supposed to have been born at the start of a Venus cycle it seemed that this must be the term used for Venus rising at its forty-year return point. But then we also read that the innermost sanctuary of King Solomon's Temple was considered to be the dwelling place of this Shekinah, which the Bible describes as 'the Divine Presence Himself'.

This seemed to suggest that the light from Venus, which we knew entered the megalithic building at Newgrange, was considered to be a manifestation of God. We remembered the dormer window in Solomon's Temple and

---

[6] Josephus, *Antiquities* 8:3:1

how the Holy of Holies could be entered only by the High Priest and only on the Jewish New Year's Day.

When scanning through Masonic rituals we found that one of the old historical lectures of the Royal Arch said the following:

The First or Holy Masonic Lodge was opened after the Exodus of the Israelites from the Egyptian bondage, by Moses, Aholiab, and Bezaleel, on consecrated ground at the foot of Mount Horeb, in the Wilderness of Sinai. Here the host of Israel had assembled and pitched their tents to offer up prayers and thanks-givings for their signal deliverance from the hands of the Egyptians. In this place the Almighty had thought fit to reveal Himself to his faithful servant Moses. Here the Most High delivered the forms of those mysterious prototypes, the Tabernacle, and the Ark of the Covenant; here was delivered the Sacred Law, engraven by the hand of the Most High, with those sublime and comprehensive precepts of civil and religious policy which by separating His favoured people from all other nations he consecrated them a chosen vessel to His service. For these reasons this is denominated the First or Holy Lodge.

There is nothing too startling here, but the ritual goes on to connect the Shekinah both to Moses' experiences in the wilderness of Sinai and to Solomon's Temple:

Bezaleel was the inspired workman of the Holy Tabernacle which he built to house the Ark of the Covenant and to allow the light of the Divine Shekinah to shine upon it. His design afterwards became the model of King Solomon's Temple, and conforms to a pattern delivered on Mount Horeb by God to Moses, who afterwards became the Grand Master of the Lodge of Israel.

This passage specifically states that King Solomon's Temple was designed to allow this external light to enter. But the ritual continues to give even more detail about where the Shekinah appeared and when:

This favour was signalled to the brethren by the appearance in the East of the Divine Shekinah which represents the Glory of God

213

appearing on Mount Sinai at the deliverance of the Sacred Law.

So we had a clue that the Shekinah is an external light which is in some way a facet of God, and it appears in the East and shines onto the Ark at special times. We also knew that it was distinct and different from the light of the rising Sun, which has always been important to Freemasonry. Later in the same lecture mention is made of the fact that the shining of the Shekinah is not necessarily a regular or predictable event. The ritual warns that God can remove this sign of His favour, if He chooses:

At the consecreation of the Holy Tabernacle, and afterwards at the dedication of the Temple of the Lord by King Solomon, the Divine Shekinah descended so its light shone upon the Ark or Mercy seat as it stood in the Holy of Holies, covered by the wings of the Cherubim, where it appeared for several generations, until the Israelites proved unfaithful to the Most High. And so may the light of Masonry be removed from all who prove unfaithful to their God!

This statement that the appearances of the Shekinah were irregular was unexpected. We knew that the whole point of studying the movements of Venus is the regularity of the cycle – the very predictability of its reappearance. Unless this was an error of some kind the Shekinah could not be Venus, despite the description of the Shekinah light entering through the dormer of the Jerusalem Temple. This was certainly an unanticipated item of information, but the conclusion to this puzzle was not far away.

Next we found a reference, in the ritual of the Ancient and Accepted Scottish Rite, which describes the scene as the seven candidates for the degree of Secret Master assemble outside Solomon's Temple in preparation for their Initiation. As they enter the inner chamber of the Temple, before the rising of the Sun, they are exposed to a sacred light that is beautifully described:

In the grey dawn of morning, even before the Sun rising over Mount Olivet flushed with crimson the walls of the Temple, the chosen few, awe-stricken and grave, had assembled. The light from the seven-branch candlestick in the East was reflected back from the golden floor, from the brazen laver of water, with hyssop and napkins, but fell sombrely on the heavy drapings of the sack-cloth on the walls. Amidst the prayers and exhortations, and the solemn chanting of the Levites, the seven entered into a mystic bond, and the duty of secrecy and silence was laid upon them. And then the doors of cedar and olivewood heavily carved and gilded were opened, the veils of blue, and purple, and scarlet, and richly embroidered white linen were drawn aside, and the mysteries of the Holy of Holies revealed to them.

None but the Priests and Levites had entered the Sanctum Sanctorum since the Sacred Ark had been brought thither, and now as the Seven Secret Sentinels put off their shoes and washed their feet, and stepped over the golden threshold, they stood in silence blinded with the light that burst upon them. The spreading wings of the Cherubim covered the Ark of the Covenant, but from all sides the walls glittered with gold and precious stones.

Here we had found a description of how, in the pre-dawn darkness of the inner sanctum of Solomon's Temple, a light burst in that blinded them. The first lecture of the Craft degrees confirms that Moses' tent was orientated in the same easterly direction and became the model for the Temple of Solomon, to allow the Shekinah to enter:

And for the better solemnisation of Divine worship, as well as a receptacle for the Books and Tables of the Law, Moses caused a Tent or Tabernacle to be erected in the wilderness, which by God's especial command was situated due East and West, for Moses did everything according to a pattern shown him by the Lord on Mount Sinai. This Tent or Tabernacle proved afterwards to be the ground-plan, in respect to situation, of that most magnificent Temple built at Jerusalem by that wise and mighty Prince, King Solomon, whose regal splendour and unparalleled lustre far transcend our ideas. This is the third, last, and grand reason I as a Freemason give, why all places of Divine worship, as well as Masons' regular, well-formed, constituted Lodges are or ought to be so situated.

In the summing-up of this lecture, when a series of questions is put to the candidate for Secret Master, the situation starts to become clearer.

What is the hour?

*The morning star has driven away the shades of night, and the
great light begins to gladden our Lodge.*

*As the morning star is the forerunner of the great light which
begins to shine on our Lodge, and we are all Secret Masters, it is
time to commence our labours.*

The 'morning star' is Venus, so the question remained, was the Shekinah
something different?

The Royal Order of Scotland is a Jacobite invention, but it claims within
its ritual to have been established originally 'on the holy Mount Moriah
in the Kingdom of Judea' and later re-established, 'at Icolmkill, and afterwards at Kilwinning, where the King of Scotland first sat as Grand Master'.
The reason for this re-establishment by the Jacobite Kings of Scotland is
given as 'to correct the errors and reform the abuses which had crept in
among the three degrees of St John's Masonry' – a reference to English
Freemasonry. The Royal Order makes a specific reference to the Shekinah
and links it to the First or Holy Lodge held by Moses on Mount Horeb.
The ritual asks and answers the following two questions:

*What does the Blazing Star represent? – Answer: The Glory of
God appearing on Mount Sinai at the deliverance of the Law.*

*Why do the Star and circling G appear? – Answer: The Star and
circling G declare, The Shekinah, wherever it appear. Whether on
Sinai, Salem or the place where the Eastern Magi saw the blessed
face.*

They are mentioned again when the ritual says:

*Whom did you meet in the Middle Chamber? – Answer: Three
wise men.*

*How did they dispose of you? – Answer: They led me to the
Cabinet of Wisdom.*

*How were you conducted? – Answer: By a Blazing Star appearing
in the East.*

The ritual obviously considers the appearance of the Shekinah to be
extremely important in the history of Freemasonry, as this spectacular event
is described in detail:

*I desire to know what was the first and highest honour ever con-
ferred on Freemasons.*

*The descent of the Divine Shekinah, first at the consecration of
the Holy Tabernacle, and afterwards at the dedication of the
Temple of the Lord by King Solomon, placing itself on the Ark or
Mercy-seat of the Holy of Holies, covered by the wings of the
Cherubim, where it continued to deliver its oracular responses for
several generations.*

How many?

Fourteen.

Was the Shekinah ever removed?

It was.

Why so?

*Because the Israelites proved unfaithful to their God. And so may
the light of Masonry be removed from all who prove unfaithful to
their God.*

So again we read that the Shekinah failed to appear which was considered to be due to the poor behaviour of the Jews. We were still quite
puzzled about the way that the Shekinah sometimes fits the Venus pattern
and yet it has periods when it goes away. We decided to look for any further information on the subject, and then we came across some interesting
work produced by the early twentieth-century Masonic researcher, AE
Waite.

METATRON, SHEKINAH AND THE KABBALAH

Waite, writing about the Kabbalah, refers to the celestial nature of the Shekinah as a recurrent theme and describes a sexual dimension associated with it where God in heaven directly has a relationship with Mother Earth. But the genders are not fixed and the Godhead and the world are both male and female, interacting in a supreme love-play of melded sexual identity.

The Kabbalah tells us a great deal about the subject of the female aspects of God, which is claimed to be a system of belief based on a secret tradition of astral Judaism that was unknown to the outside world before the first century CE. The following quotations from AE Waite's famous book, *The Holy Kabbalah*, deal with the Shekinah as described in the Kabbalah:

> *Now, it is in this manner that I open the high conference respecting the Mystery of Shekinah, which is a Mystery of man and God, of man in the likeness of the Elohim [gods], of the relation between things above and things below, of intercourse for union upon earth performed in the spirit of celestial union, and the transmutation of one by the other for the work of God in the world.*

Immediately the tradition in the lore of the Kabbalah appears to agree with our deduction from the Grooved Ware sites of the British Isles, that the light of Venus was directly connected with sexual intercourse, birthing and resurrection – linking heaven to Earth.

Waite continues:

> *She is now the Daughter of the King; she is now the Betrothed, the Bride and the Mother, and again she is sister in relation to the world of man at large. There is a sense also in which this Daughter of God is – or becomes – the Mother of man. In respect of the manifest universe, she is the architect of worlds.*

> *She is Matrona who unites with the King, for the perfection of the Divine Male is in the Divine Female.*

The picture was building of an ancient belief in the absolute importance of the female on her own terms and as an essential ingredient in fulfilled man.

> She is that Divine Presence which walked in the Garden of Eden in the cool of the evening.

This strongly suggests Venus in its role as evening star.

> Of her it is said: 'Behold, I send an angel before thee, to keep thee in the way, and to bring thee into the place which I have prepared.' But it is stated that this Liberating Angel manifests as male and female, being male when it dispenses the celestial benedictions on the world below, because it then resembles a male nourishing the female; but when charged with offices of judgment it is called female, as a woman who carries her child in the womb of her.

> In her office as architect of the world, the Word was uttered to her, was by her conceived and brought or begotten into execution. We have seen that Shekinah below concurred with the architect above and was also a builder.

> Though it is forbidden to separate the Heavenly Bride and Bridegroom, even in thought, it is this which has come to pass by reason of the sufferings of Israel, with whom Shekinah was destined as we have seen to endure even from the beginning. 'When Israel is in exile the Shekinah is also in exile. It is for this reason that the Holy One will remember Israel, meaning that He remembers His covenant, which is Shekinah.'

Here the Shekinah is absolutely associated with the central role of kingship – the successful protecting of the country from its enemies. When the country is unworthy Shekinah goes away, and its return has to mark a change in fortunes just as expected within the Messianic expectation.

> . . . in respect of all other lights of creation is that which soul is to body, though in relation to the Holy One she is as the body to the soul, notwithstanding that she and God are one. She is the Mistress of the Celestial School, called the Abode of the Shepherds, and this

219

is a school of METATRON, understood as a vesture or form assumed by Shekinah.

Here we have more associations with astral events and a combining of genders within the godhead. Again we see Metatron being described as having responsibility for the running of the heavens under the higher authority of the Shekinah. Next Waite detects how the Kabbalah makes direct reference to Abraham:

It was after his circumcision that the letter HE was added to the name of Abram and it was also thereafter that he was united with Shekinah. Most of the divine visions beheld by Abraham were visions and manifestations of Shekinah, who dwelt constantly in the tent of Sarah . . .

The all-important covenant of circumcision that defines male Judaism stems from Abraham and Isaac – this is here directly connected to the Shekinah. We can only assume that God in the form of the Shekinah was in its male mode when it lingered in the tent with Abraham's young and beautiful wife.

. . . on leaving his house, Abraham beheld Shekinah lighting the way before him and encompassed by many celestial legions. She was present when Isaac 'blessed' Jacob; it was she who conferred upon Jacob the name of Israel, and she was with him when he set up the mystic stone as a pillar. When seeking a wife it was with Shekinah that Jacob uttered his intention that when he married Rachel he united heaven and earth. Shekinah, however, did not ignore or forget Leah but – as the Holy Spirit – inspired her, so that she knew respecting her part in the bearing of the twelve tribes.

Here we have a description of the Shekinah as a bright object in the night sky. As we have seen, only the Moon and Venus can produce enough light to cast a shadow on the ground, and it is evidently not the Moon that is being described here. We find it of great importance that this ancient Jewish legend says that the Shekinah was present when the mystic stone pillar was erected. (The name Jacob means 'pillar'.)

The exodus brought about by Moses occasioned, moreover, the manifestation of Shekinah before the people of Israel, she being the pillar of fire by night, as Jehovah was that of cloud by day.

This confirms what we already know, that Venus was said to be rising in the east at the moment in time attributed to the Exodus. She was indeed a bright pillar at night.

Moses caused Shekinah to manifest in the Ark of the Covenant over the Mercy-Seat, between the figures of the Kerubim. The Tabernacle was erected to serve as her residence; and at the moment when it was set up by Moses, there was another erected in the world above. What seems to have happened, however, was that the Mosaic Tabernacle became the residence of METATRON, who connects so curiously with Shekinah.

    The male principle or Jehovah is said further to have spoken from the Tabernacle by the intermediation of Shekinah, who is the female principle . . . She is described as resident throughout the Holy of Holies, yet is connected in an especial manner with the western wall of the temple. The Holy of Holies was guarded moreover by METATRON.

The original tabernacle was a double tent established by Moses, and the Temple in Jerusalem was a stone version of the same. The downfall of the Second Temple is attributed to the failure of the light of the Shekinah; the divine radiance was withheld. However, it is here directly related to Venus:

. . . it is Shekinah who presides over birth, seeming to be in analogy with the chaste and conjugal Venus.

Here we have a confirmation drawn from the Kabbalah of our view that the Shekinah is connected to Venus and to important births, such as Moses himself. Whatever the source of the information within the Kabbalah, its parallel associations of the Shekinah to our own separate investigations tell us that our investigation might be heading in the right direction.

Waite also mentions a character already familiar to us from Jewish legend:

> *So also METATRON, who is an aspect of Shekinah, is indifferently*
> *male and female, changing incessantly according to the vibrations*
> *of the union. Now, it is said that Shekinah is to METATRON*
> *what the Sabbath is to the weekdays. In other words, she is rest*
> *and the rapture of rest, yet it is that rest in which there is the*
> *intercourse of spiritual union.*

Suddenly, and fascinatingly, we found Metatron closely connected to the Shekinah. Metatron is the name given to Enoch after God 'translated' him into heaven without experiencing death. In the Book of Enoch (first written down from oral tradition at Qumran) he is the man who was given instructions by Uriel on how to build a megalithic circle by recording the movements of the Sun at dawn and dusk throughout the year.[7]

The name 'Metatron' appears to be Greek and, if so, 'meta' has a meaning that implies change and 'tron' is an agent or instrument. Put together we could reasonably say that the name carries an import something like 'measurer of change'. This really seems to imply that the man who was Enoch took his astral knowledge to heaven when he took on his new name, just as the Book of Jubilees states.

The analogy of the week to the Sabbath could be taken as meaning that Metatron is the measurer of normal times but it is the Shekinah that defines special moments. In other words Metatron is responsible for the mechanisms of the the Sun through its daily and annual cycles, but the Shekinah is concerned with the divine, long-term Venus cycle.

Interestingly, it seems that the Kabbalah itself was based on remnants of Enochian Judaism that were in circulation in the first century CE. Whilst the Kabbalah – meaning 'received tradition' – only surfaced to the world in general during the medieval period it is undoubtedly much older. It dates from the first centuries AD, and is the earliest known form of Jewish mysticism in which the adept, through meditation and the use of magic formulae, journeys ecstatically through and beyond the seven astral spheres.[8] The fact that Enochian literature was lost to the public world from early in the second century CE shows how this secret tradition must have been known to some select people, or just possibly it was discovered amongst the scrolls that we believe the Knights Templar

---

[7] Knight, C & Lomas, R: *Uriel's Machine, The Ancient Origins of Science*
[8] 'Kabbalah', *Microsoft ® Encarta® Encyclopedia 2001*. © 1993–2000 Microsoft Corporation. All rights reserved.

recovered from deep beneath the ruins of the Jerusalem Temple in the twelfth century.

THE STAR OF BETHLEHEM

One evening we were reviewing biblical sources to see if we had missed some further clue to the meaning of the Shekinah patterns. Then the following comment by Professor Foakes-Jackson triggered an interesting thought:

> *The numerical date of the Exodus, 480 (12 x 40) years before the*
> *foundation of the Temple in the fourth year of Solomon's reign in*
> *967, is obviously the artificial reconstruction of some pious antiquary.*

The date 967 BCE suddenly jumped off the page – because it is so remarkably close to being two Venusian epochs (480 x 2 years = 960 years). The foundation stone of Solomon's Temple was said to be laid as the Shekinah rose in 967 BCE – so two Venusian epochs later leads to the very interesting date of 7 BCE. The modern calendar system is based on the number of years since the birth of Christ, which is represented as the year 1 CE. But we were well aware that modern scholarship recognises that the assumed year of the Christian messiah's birth is wrong. A quick look at the Encarta DVD Encyclopedia confirmed this:

> *Jesus Christ (between 8 and 4 BC–c. AD 29), the central figure of*
> *Christianity, born in Bethlehem in Judaea. The chronology of the*
> *Christian era is reckoned from a 6th-century dating of the year of*
> *his birth, which is now recognized as being from four to eight*
> *years in error.*[9]

If Jesus was born in 7 BCE it is entirely possible that he, the acclaimed messiah, could have been born under the shining Shekinah exactly two Venusian epochs after the consecration of Solomon's Temple. Whatever the Shekinah was, it should have returned in that year according to the 480-year rule. Another thought struck us – the first-century historian of the Jews, Josephus, recorded that Solomon's Temple was begun exactly one

[9] 'Jesus Christ', *Microsoft® Encarta® Encyclopedia 2001.* © 1993–2000 Microsoft Corporation.

thousand four hundred and forty years after the Flood, and now there was the tantalising possibility that Jesus might have been born exactly one thousand four hundred and forty years after the time the scribes had determined to be that moment when Moses had led his people through the Red Sea.

Could there be something in this? The pattern of dates of 480 years and its multiples for major events described in the Bible is fully accepted by biblical scholars, but because they are not explained they are almost entirely ignored. We concluded that these periods must have been sacred to a very early tradition, almost certainly Enochian, and they continued to be used for one of two reasons: either the meaning had become forgotten and their use was purely ritualistic, or there was a priesthood in the background who did understand it, but who chose to not reveal its meaning to the world in general.

We needed to understand more ourselves before we could resolve this problem.

The so-called Shekinah was a mystery. It came and went, so the Bible told us, at the whim of God. But we knew that the beautiful megalithic observatory at Newgrange in Ireland allowed the pre-dawn light of Venus to its inner chamber on the winter solstice once every eight years, and therefore five times per forty-year Venus cycle. We had previously calculated the Venus pattern at Newgrange and, remembering that Venus was sometimes bright enough to cast a shadow at night, we wondered if something similar might have been happening at the time of Christ's birth.

According to tradition, Jesus' birth is celebrated on 25 December, which is the first day on which it is clearly possible to see, by measuring the movement of shadows cast by Asherah, that the Sun has begun to move northwards again, after the winter solstice. Could it be that Jesus really was born under the helically rising Venus on 'Christmas Day'?

The modern celebration of Christ's birth is usually taken as a symbolic date borrowed from a Yuletide pagan festival that originally marked midwinter. All ancient peoples appreciated that the winter solstice is the day on which the sunrise reaches its maximum excursion southwards on the horizon. For three months they had witnessed the sunrise move from its easterly, equinoctial position, slowing its daily rate of movement across the horizon, until it seemed to stand still before swinging backwards again in a northerly direction.

Although it is taken as entirely symbolic by biblical scholars, Christian tradition tells us that Jesus was conceived at the vernal equinox and born at the winter solstice, to the light of a brilliant star in the east. But could it be a literal truth? Could the Star of Bethlehem be Venus? We decided to check out what was in the sky that morning, so Robert moved to the computer keyboard and opened an astronomical simulation program.

The program took a few minutes before it was ready to go.

'I'm ready now,' Robert called across. 'Give me the time and place details slowly.'

'Twenty-fifth of December, 7 BCE, shortly before dawn, looking around east-southeast,' Chris said, adding the latitude and longitude of Jerusalem from the atlas he held on lap.

Robert entered the data and fiddled with the mouse.

'Do you see anything interesting?'

'Hang on, hang on, nearly there,' replied Robert.

He went quiet for a minute or so, then, 'Wow!' he exclaimed, before pausing for several more seconds. 'There's a really massive object blazing, like really blazing, in the east but it's far too big and bright, even for Venus at maximum magnitude.'

Chris moved over to look at the screen. Robert continued. 'Yes, it's Venus all right, but it's in conjunction with something else. Mercury I think.' He manipulated the program to identify the components of the bright object. 'Yes it's definitely Mercury. Both it and Venus are at a high magnitude and the effect before dawn must have been unbelievable, truly dazzling.'

'A blazing star in the east on what is possibly the original Christmas Day! Is this the answer to the myth of the Star of Bethlehem?' asked Chris.

'It certainly looks that way. Astronomical programs are pretty reliable these days. And I agree with you that 7 BCE is certainly a top contender for the true year of Christ's birth,' said Robert as he rechecked all of his coordinates.

The impact of this find was quite stunning. Many people in the past have tried to explain the myth of the Star of Bethlehem, by thinking of all kinds of potential bright objects that might have been in the sky – but we know of no one before us who has tried to deduce what should be there using the expectations of early Jewish theology.

'Can you wind your program back and check the same early morning sky on that date of 967 BCE whilst we're at it please?' Chris asked.

'OK. Give me a moment or two. It would be a massive coincidence if there was another conjunction at the dedication of Solomon's Temple too.'

Some minutes later Robert had the new time entered into the program. He gave a low whistle.

'Just look at that – it's the same again. A brilliant blaze in the East. The myth of the Shekinah looks like it's describing a real, genuine historical event.'

We seemed to have found an explanation of why the Shekinah came and went. Whilst Venus moves with the precision of a metronome, its conjunctions with Mercury or other planets happen at complex and irregular intervals, but we could clearly see that they appeared to resynchronise every 480 years.

We now had a tentative explanation for the Jewish Shekinah and the Christian Star of Bethlehem, and the more we looked again at descriptions of both of these biblical phenomena the better the solution seemed.

Masonic ritual clearly states that the Shekinah and the Star of Bethlehem are the same thing:

Reflecting but a faint and glimmering ray, the star and circling
glory declare the Shekinah, wherever it appear. Whether on Sinai,
Salem or the place where the Eastern Magi saw the blessed face of
the Redeemer in the Ox's stall.

Biblical scholars have also linked the two, as the following quotation (taken from his commentary on Luke in Peakes), by the Reverend AJ Grieve, one-time Professor of Systematic Theology at Edinburgh, says:

. . . the shepherds in the district are startled by seeing an angel and
the Shekinah radiance, but are reassured and told the Messiah has
been born in the village.

What we had found is an ancient Jewish belief that major events happen within a preordained pattern that we now knew was linked not only to Venus, but to that planet's conjunctions with Mercury. Not only that, but we now had the intriguing possibility that Jesus himself was a part of some grand plan based on astronomical calculations.

We just had to have a closer look to see whether there was an equivalent of the Star of Bethlehem reported at other major events, and we soon found that there was.

THE PATTERN OF THE SHEKINAH

We could find no references within our ritual database of Freemasonry which specifically named the periods of forty, four hundred and eighty, or one thousand four hundred and forty years, but a search of the Bible had thrown up plenty, so we could confirm the importance of the time periods. The Masonic rituals suggest that the Shekinah was a periodic arrival of a bright light that would appear a number of times at important occasions and then disappear for many years. These periods without the Shekinah were attributed to God's displeasure due to a failure of his Chosen People to be worthy of His presence.

We now knew that Venus appeared in conjunction with Mercury at dawn around the winter solstice in 7 BCE to produce a blazing red glow that would have quickly turned a steely white as the object rose higher in the pre-dawn sky. We needed to understand whether this was a coincidence or part of a pattern that would begin to explain the Shekinah and the fascination with the periods we were now calling Venusian generations, Venusian epochs and Venusian aeons.

Robert set about the task of calculating what was on the eastern horizon prior to dawn in Jerusalem at a variety of dates, and he found that the Shekinah conjunction happened in 'packets'. Around the four-hundred-and-eighty-year reappearance there would be other conjunctions because the planets were suitably aligned, but they would pop up repeatedly for some time and then go away for many generations.

We found that there were many interesting and spectacular astral events occurring every 480 years, just before and just after the historical events described in the Bible. In all these conjunctions planets were close to each other (within a degree or so), so causing them to appear as single, incredibly bright stars.

- 7 BCE 25 December. Mercury/Venus. Venus phase 99.3% – Mercury phase 97.8%. Eight degrees away from the Sun and rising 22 minutes before the Sun.

- 8 BCE 18 May. Mercury/Venus. Venus phase 99.2% – Mercury phase 95.2. Eight degrees away from the Sun and rising 25 minutes before the Sun.

- 8 BCE 26 January. Jupiter/Venus. Venus phase 81.9% – Jupiter phase

99.7. Thirty-five degrees away from the Sun and rising almost two hours before the Sun. This would have been easy to see even in daylight.

- 487 BCE 30 December. Venus/Saturn. Venus phase 75.1% – Saturn phase 99.9%. Thirty-eight degrees away from the Sun and rising about two and half hours before the Sun in a dark sky, making it a bright red rising event that would have been easy to see in daylight as a bright white point in the blue sky.

- 488 BCE 15 August. Venus/Jupiter/Mercury. Venus phase 94.2% – Mercury phase 59.6% – Jupiter phase 99.9%. Eighteen degrees away from the the Sun and rising about 1 hour 40 mins before the Sun.

- 489 BCE 4 February. Venus/Mercury. Venus phase 90.3% – Mercury phase 90.3%. Fifteen degrees away from the Sun and rising 27 minutes before the Sun.

- 966 BCE 13 May. Jupiter/Venus. Venus phase 71% – Jupiter phase 99.6%. Forty degrees away from the Sun and rising just about an hour before the Sun. Easy to see in daylight.

- 967 BCE 22 February. Jupiter/Venus. Venus phase 98.7% – Jupiter 100%. Ten degrees away from the Sun and rising 10 minutes before the Sun.

- 967 BCE 3 March. Venus/Mercury. Venus 99.2% – Mercury 21%. Eight degrees away from the Sun and rising 15 minutes before the Sun.

- 1447 BCE 21 March. Venus/Mercury. Venus phase 80% – Mercury phase 50%. Twenty-eight degrees away from the Sun and rising about one and half hours before it.

- 1447 BCE 3 May. Venus/Saturn. Venus phase 90% – Saturn phase 99%. Twenty-seven degrees away from the Sun and rising an hour before it. This would be visible in daylight.

- 1447 BCE 8 July. Venus/Mercury. Venus phase 98.7% – Mercury phase 50%. Ten degrees away from the Sun and rising 45 minutes before it.

There were many conjunctions of these bright planets around the dates we were interested in, but otherwise they are rather rare.

Having found this interesting pattern we decided to share it with Alan Butler, the expert in megalithic mathematics who had worked with us unravelling the mystery of the Megalithic Yard. Alan is an amateur astronomer and it seemed sensible to ask him to check the results independently. He came back with great excitement having also calculated Venus/Mercury conjunctions that corresponded with the sequence Robert had found. These 'Shekinah' conjunctions occurred in packets every forty years after 1447 BCE for four more visits, but it had then failed to appear in 1207 BCE and had not arrived in the dawn sky again until 967 BCE.

Now we were certain that the Shekinah appears every Venusian epoch and for some time around it, but then it seems to go away. This seems to explain why the Jews considered the Shekinah to be a regular event at Venusian epochs but not predictable in between. The conjunction might have been predictable to skilled astrologers, like the magi, who were better at maths and astronomy, but the Jews might not have had many people who understood how to do the calculations.

Alan had been amazed at the pattern of conjunctions we asked him to check out. He commented that whilst Venus was always easily predictable, Mercury was not, and conjunctions of the two planets would occur regularly for a period of time and then stop happening until the next 480-year cycle began. Alan felt that the best way to calculate the Venus/Mercury conjunction repetition cycle, using the integer mathematics of the Grooved Ware People, was to use a megalithic year of 366 days and multiply by forty, then subtract forty days. He also added that as the megalithic people and the Jews seemed to hold the Sun and Venus in great esteem, as respectively the male and female aspects of God, and Mercury was adopted by the Greeks as 'the messenger', he could imagine that they would have considered these events especially meaningful.

So it appeared that the Jews knew that the Venus cycle, the 'Venusian generation', was a completely predictable cycle of forty years, but they also expected that the Shekinah would appear in the same position on a clutch of occasions that were spaced out a Venusian epoch (480 years) apart. Could they not calculate exactly when Venus would rise as the blazing Shekinah – the glory of God that entered the dormer window of the Temple, creating an all-enveloping red glow in the incense-filled chamber around the Ark of the Covenant?

229

This implied that the conjunction of Venus and Mercury that rose shortly before the dawn in the star-spangled sky that Moses saw above the Sinai as he led his people towards the Promised Land was the same heavenly event that Solomon saw as he laid the foundation stone of his Temple and that the magi witnessed as they were led to the promised messiah. History was repeating itself in heaven and upon Earth. But did this mean that the builder of the Temple expected the Shekinah to appear?

Our generation learned the words of the Lord's prayer so thoroughly at school that we can say it almost without hearing the meaning of the words, but as we sat discussing the previous paragraph, we both suddenly found ourselves repeating the familiar words:

Our Father, which art in heaven, hallowed be thy name. Thy kingdom come, Thy will be done on earth as it is in heaven.

Most people are vaguely aware that the Christian tradition places heaven in the sky and hell somewhere underground. We still refer to the night sky as 'the heavens', and the Lord's prayer tells us in the first words that God resides there – amongst the stars. The priests who wrote down the Old Testament were driven by a belief that the heavens ruled events upon Earth. Past events were post-rationalised as having occurred at these astronomically auspicious moments, and expected great events of the future would be anticipated to conform to the same pattern system.

Whilst we can be sure that the authors of the Old Testament believed that the great events of their history happened in Venusian epochs and Venusian aeons, they could have known nothing of future events. Of course, some Christians claim that various passages from the Old Testament were prophetic references to Jesus, but it seems much more likely that Jesus and his followers did their best to ensure that he appeared to conform to messianic expectation.

CONCLUSIONS

No biblical scholar satisfactorily explains the forty-year cycle used throughout the Old and New Testaments, but once the significance of the Venus cycle is known the pattern becomes strikingly important.

We have rediscovered an ancient Jewish belief that major astral events happen within a pattern linked not only to Venus, but to that planet's more random conjunctions with Mercury. These extremely bright but irregular astral events were called the Shekinah and were taken as a sign of God's favour. The pattern we found underlying these conjunctions fitted perfectly the Jewish chronology of key events in their history.

The writers of the Old Testament were driven by a belief that events in the heavens ruled the Earth. Previous events were post-rationalised as occurring at astronomically auspicious times and great events of the future were expected to fit the pattern. We believe that the authors of the Old Testament thought the great events of their history occurred in Venusian epochs and Venusian aeons, but they had no way to foretell the future. It is claimed that some passages from the Old Testament are prophecies of Jesus, but it seems more likely that Jesus and his followers were trying to conform to the Jews' messianic expectancy that these passages had aroused.

Chapter Eleven

THE COMING OF THE MESSIAH

THE RISING OF THE STAR

The Christmas myth holds that the magi followed the star in the east and were led to a stable in the town of Bethlehem, the town where King David was born a millennium earlier. However, it would take a low-flying helicopter with a powerful searchlight to spotlight an individual building. It was obviously impossible for the magi to literally follow a star to anywhere, because starlight is non-directional. However, 'following' the star could mean that they were seeking the messiah because they were 'following' the rules that allowed them to understand the star's meaning.

The words of Matthew's Gospel have the magi saying 'we have seen his star in the east', and modern techniques of coordinate geometry show that a Venus/Mercury conjunction rose in the east on the morning of 25 December that year. So we asked ourselves, is there any evidence that a prophecy had been in existence at that time – a prophecy that a king of the Jews would be born when a special star appeared in the pre-dawn sky?

We soon found that there was. The so-called Star Prophecy is recorded in Numbers 24: 17, where it states:

I shall see him, but not now: I shall behold him, but not nigh: there shall come a Star out of Jacob, and a Sceptre shall rise out of Israel, and shall smite the corners of Moab, and destroy all the children of Sheth.

Here we see an ancient prediction by the prophet Balaam which he says was revealed to him by God. He concludes his oracle by foreseeing the future glory of Israel. His prophecy claims that at some point in the future a kingly messiah will arise whose birth will be marked by a star. The sceptre he mentions is a well established symbol of kingship, referred to many times in the Bible – for example Hebrews 1: 8 says:

> Thy throne, O God, is for ever and ever: a sceptre of righteousness is the sceptre of thy kingdom.

Our study of Jewish texts has established that their writers believed that cycles of 40, 480 and 1,440 years were of fundamental importance. We have calculated that this is because these were the patterns that Venus provided for them as the bright planet danced its horn-shaped pattern in and out of the Sun.

We also knew that the magi, seeking out the messiah, believed that exactly 1,440 years (3 x 480) had elapsed since Moses led the Hebrew people out of Egypt, that 2,400 years (5 x 480) had passed since the Flood, and that it was 960 years (2 x 480) since the foundation of Solomon's Temple.

So around that winter solstice of 25 December 7 BCE these astronomer priests waited for the Shekinah to rise in the east, exactly as they believed it had done at the moment the Red Sea parted and the Hebrew people walked to a new-found freedom. As prophesied centuries before, the bright morning star did arrive and it rose in red brilliance a few minutes before dawn. They then believed that this was a sign from God of the arrival of the messiah of Israel, and their task was to find him. This methodology seems remarkably similar to the way that Tibetan priests still find a new leader when their old one dies. They cover the country in a mission to seek out the newborn infant Dalai Lama using their knowledge of specific signs to identify the true reincarnation of their spiritual leader.

Remarkably, we found that there are contemporary documents, from the time of Christ, that state that the first part of the Star Prophecy was fulfilled. And the source of those records is none other than the Dead Sea Scrolls. The War Scroll of Qumran unambiguously records that when this long-predicted star appeared in the pre-dawn sky the kingly messiah arrived – but his work of defeating Israel's enemies was yet to be done. The words speak for themselves when compared to the Star Prophecy:

> A *star* has *marched forth from Jacob, A sceptre* has *arisen from Israel, And he will shatter the temples of Moab, And destroy the sons of Seth.*[1]

The use of the past tense in the first two lines proclaims that the expected kingly messiah has arrived because the star appeared – but another of the Dead Sea Scrolls, the Damascus Document, states:

> And the star is the Seeker of the Law who is coming to Damascus; as is written. 'A star has marched forth from Jacob and a sceptre has arisen from Israel.'

> The sceptre is the Prince of all the Congregations and when he arises he will destroy all of the sons of Seth.[2]

The words recorded by the people of the Qumran community could not be clearer. The messiah had arrived and he was expected to come to Damascus. (There was a large Essene group in Damascus and 'Damascus' is also thought to have been a term used to describe Qumran itself.) They believed that after his arrival at 'Damascus' the messiah would rise up and destroy their enemies. These brief descriptions of the messiah's role show how he is going to be a king who will lead his army in a war to result in the victory of the Jewish nation.

We also checked what the historian Josephus had to say about the Star Prophecy. We found that he says it was the motivating force behind the uprising against Rome. He describes a star that looked like a sword, with a light so great that it shone round the altar in the temple, making it appear to be as bright as daytime for a full half an hour.[3] The description of looking like a sword is consistent with the elongation of the conjunction which would be seen in the sky as Venus and Mercury overlapped.

So, we asked ourselves, was Jesus the Christ, who the Bible says was born at the time of the appearance of the 'Bethlehem' star, the person spoken of in these Qumran scrolls?

As far as his birth is concerned it seems likely that either Jesus or his followers would have claimed this Divine moment of genesis whether it was true or not. It is impossible to know for sure who the Qumran scrolls

[1] IQM 11: 16
[2] CD 7: 18–21
[3] Josephus: *Jewish War*, 6: 290

were referring to, especially as there were many people suspected of being the messiah – including John the Baptist. But we can reasonably conclude that both Jesus and the person described in the Qumran scrolls were attempting to fulfil the same role through adherence to the ritualistic demands of ancient prophecy.

Our next question had to be, could the Qumran community have been writing about the same Jewish champion as the one described in the Gospels of the New Testament?

First we needed to consider the idea that Jesus was born to high station, as described by the magi in the Gospel of Matthew when it says:

> . . . *where is he that is born King of the Jews?*

The Bible claims that Jesus' paternal lineage goes back to Abraham, the founding father of the Jewish people. He is also described in chapters 5 and 6 of Hebrews as 'a priest for ever after the order of Melchisedek' an Order more ancient and with more authority than the Levites. We found this highly significant when we considered that only a Levite was considered holy enough to enter the Holy of Holies in the presence of God on one day each year.

The ancient prophet Isaiah wrote of the future messiah in terms that appear to be based upon the Shekinah, and he introduced the gifts that should be given to this newly arrived king:

> *Arise, shine; for your light has come, and the glory of the Lord has risen upon you . . . And nations shall come to your light and kings to the brightness of your rising . . . For they shall bring gold and frankincense, and shall proclaim the praise of the Lord.*[4]

The fact that the developing myth of Jesus incorporated the presentation of such gifts shows how early Christians were seeking to make their Messiah conform to the prophecies within Judaism.

A Qumran text (4Q521) describes a messiah that is more usually found in Jewish texts of this period but that also appears to connect directly with the ideology attributed to Jesus Christ:

[4] Isaiah 60: 1,3, 6

[. . . The hea] vens and the earth will hearken to His Messiah, [The sea and all th] at is in them. He will not turn aside from the commandment of Holy Ones.

Take courage all of you, all you who seek the Lord and his work.

Will you not thus find the Lord, all you who bear hope in your hearts? Surely the Lord will seek out the pious, and will call the righteous by name. Over the poor will His spirit hover; faithful ones will He restore by His might. He will honour pious ones on the throne of the eternal kingdom,

Release the captives, make the blind to see, raise up th[ose bent low]. For[ev]er will I cling [to Him aga]inst the [po]werful, and [trust] in His loving kindness,

A[nd His] go[odness (will be) forever. His] holy [Messiah] will not be slow [in coming.]

As for the wonders that have not (henceforth) been, the Lord will do (them), when he [i.e., the Messiah] [come]s; then will he heal the sick and resurrect the dead; to the oppressed will he announce glad tidings,

. . . he will lead the [ho]ly ones, he will shepherd [th] em . . .

Even the few Qumran texts that we have quoted in this section show that the expected messiah would be known by his ability to perform various tasks. The messiah expected by the priests at Qumran would be known because he would do the following:

1 He will have his birth marked by the appearance of a star.

2 He will be a 'son of God'.

3 He will command heaven and Earth as his eternal kingdom.

4 His spirit will be over the poor.

5 He will restore those with faith.

6 He will restore sight to the blind.

7 He will raise up those bent low (by lowly station in life).

8 He will show loving kindness.

9 He will heal the sick.

10 He will resurrect the dead.

11 He will bring 'glad tidings' to the oppressed.

12 He will be 'a shepherd' to his flock of holy followers.

These are also the claimed hallmarks of the ministry of Jesus Christ.

Could it be that the person who is remembered as the Christ was not trying to satisfy the Sadducees or even the Pharisees, he was specifically presenting himself as the 'promised one' expected by the priesthood of Qumran?

When the Dead Sea Scrolls were discovered in 1947 the Roman Catholic scholars who were in charge of the excavations played down any similarities to the New Testament. They chose to emphasise the differences. There was a clear intent to put as much space as possible between the existing myth of Jesus and any potential new evidence that might emerge from these unwelcome Jewish documents. But the parallels have now become impossible to deny.

One scroll section from Qumran (4Q246) is actually known as 'The Son of God' text. It is written in Aramaic and it is highly messianic, referring to someone it calls 'the Son of God' and 'the Son of the Most High' who is going to establish an eternal kingdom that will make previous kingdoms seem like 'shooting stars'.[5]

Throughout the Qumran texts 'the Righteous' are described as 'the sons of God'. They are also in line with Christian thinking because they are highly eschatological in nature, with an emphasis on 'judging' or 'the Last Judgement'.

[5] Eisenman, R & Wise, M: *The Dead Sea Scrolls Uncovered*, Element, 1992

Prior to the publication of the Dead Sea Scrolls, the idea of the messiah as God's son was not known in pre-Christian Jewish texts. Expert opinion was that this idea arose exclusively within Christianity and could not be Jewish. The announcement of the content of one particular scroll changed everything, as it provided a Jewish antecedent to the concept of a messiah who commands 'heaven and earth'. As Professor Norman Golb put it, 'a far more exalted picture of an idea once thought to be a Hellenistic-Christian innovation'.[6]

As we discussed in chapter 9, the community at Qumran was originally an alliance of Zadokite and Enochian priests. We also believe that a previously unidentified Enochian group continued to exist in a pure form as well as the hybrid survival at Qumran.

Could it be that Jesus was a representative of this entirely Enochian group, and that Christianity itself has picked up elements of this antediluvian cult?

We also note that the curious figure of Melchizedek appears in both Christian and Qumranic texts. A scroll fragment from Cave 11, known as the 'Melchizedek text', tells how the ancient priest-king of Jerusalem was then viewed as a heavenly spirit responsible for the judgement of the angels. He is expected to exact vengeance for the people of God in the great battle that will be fought against Satan and the spirits under his command.[7] And we must remember that the Bible describes Jesus as a priest of the Order of Melchizedek.

FORTY DAYS IN THE WILDERNESS

We have detected the Venus cycle of forty years throughout the Bible, but there are also many mentions of a period of forty days. These range from the length of the Flood to the time of Jesus' stay in the wilderness. We believe we can now explain these periods, which are also directly linked to Venus.

Cyclical appearances of the planet Venus, in a pre-dawn rising against a particular part of the sky, were clearly of great importance in the early period of Jewish kings, as the Bible tells us. For example the Judge Eli ruled for exactly forty years, as did the kings Saul, David and Solomon. It seems probable that the allotted period for an elected individual to reign was one

[6] Golb, N: *Who Wrote the Dead Sea Scrolls?* BCA, 1995
[7] Golb, N: *Who Wrote the Dead Sea Scrolls?*

Venus cycle, and preparation for new kingship required an interregnum of forty days to carefully select the new king.

This makes perfect sense if the people concerned were using the year of 366 days that we have already described as being the basis of calculations used at megalithic sites in the British Isles. The technique of predicting the next Venus arrival in its forty cycle was to count forty years of 366 days and then subtract forty days. This is far more logical than it first sounds, because it is actually the precise difference between two kinds of year: first, the solar year of 365 days; second, the stellar year of 366 days, which is the actual number of revolutions of the planet Earth in a year. The difference arises because the Earth's orbit around the Sun causes sunrise each day to be late by 236 seconds, which adds up to exactly one day over a year. Tracking Venus through one cycle involved forty solar years followed by a 'fallow' forty days to wait for the stellar year.

There is one passage in the Old Testament that tells us that this was the method of calculation used. In Numbers 14: 33–34 it says:

And your children shall wander in the wilderness forty years, and bear your whoredoms, until your carcases be wasted in the wilderness.

After the number of the days in which ye searched the land, even forty days, each day for a year, shall ye bear your iniquities, even forty years, and ye shall know my breach of promise.

This clearly states that the forty days exists because it is 'each day for a year' over forty years. We also knew that the Essenes bowed towards the rising Sun, which strongly suggests they understood the dawn Sun's role in defining the mechanism for kingly rule.

Our next questions were unavoidable and extremely interesting.

Did Jesus spend forty days in the wilderness because a new Venus cycle was about to commence?

And, if so, did he do this because he believed the moment of his own kingship was about to begin?

There can be no doubt that Jesus would have been aware of the importance of playing out the Divinely ordered plan, and the import of Numbers 14: 33–34 would not have been lost upon him. Jesus would have needed to prepare for his next forty years by reflecting on the iniquities of the last, and by facing temptation like the Hebrews led by Moses though the wilderness.

In this forty-day period at the beginning of his active phase (his ministry) he tested himself with Old Testament quotations, starting with Exodus 34: 38 – 'And he was there with the Lord forty days and forty nights; he did neither eat bread, nor drink water.' We can imagine how Jesus faced out the Devil in his forty days in the wilderness and psychologically prepared himself for the 'mother of all battles' that lay ahead of him.

These thoughts raised another important issue. Jesus was born when the Shekinah was in the heavens; if he waited a full Venus cycle to fulfil the prophecy of leadership that means he must have been over forty when he was crucified. Tradition, however, tells us that he was in his early thirties when he was crucified. So if we were to accept this explanation of Jesus' actions we realised that we would have to look more closely at evidence about his age. Is there any shred of substantiation that points to Jesus' age at his death?

As we looked at the small amount of information regarding Jesus' age we quickly discovered that there are good reasons to believe that he was over forty years old at the time he was crucified. In verse 57 of chapter 8 of the Gospel of John the following words are spoken to Jesus:

Thou are not yet fifty years old.

Surely this would be a very strange expression to choose if the person concerned was still in his early thirties. It strongly suggests that Jesus was by then in his fifth decade.

And then we read that the early Church Father Irenaeus firmly believed that Jesus was in his forties at the time of his crucifixion.

The Romans kept good records, and we know that Pilate, the man who sentenced Jesus to death, was Procurator of Judea for the ten years between 26 and 36 CE. Given that Jesus was born in 7 BCE and that there was no year zero, he must have turned forty at the end of the year 34 CE. We calculated that the maximum age that Jesus could have reached was forty-two; which would certainly fit with the comment that he was not yet fifty.

Another strand of evidence comes from the dating of the death of John the Baptist. John was murdered just before Jesus started what is described in Christian circles as 'his ministry'. Professor Robert Eisenman believes that the date of the death of John is clear from Josephus.[8]

[8] Josephus *Antiquities*, 18:5:2

Josephus' reference to John the Baptist is perhaps the most com-
plete and provides valuable new data that helps place John in a
real historical framework, as opposed to the quasi-mythological one
encountered in the Gospels. One of the things the notice clears up
is the year of John's death, approximately 35–36 CE, which is, of
course, totally at odds with how it is presented in the Gospels.[9]

If John died in 35–36 CE that means that Jesus must have died later in 36 CE, just as our research suggested to us. This would confirm that Jesus' death occurred when he was past the age of forty, probably only months after he began his mission, in support of his own messianic claims.

We could find no counter-evidence to support the traditional idea that Jesus died aged thirty-three, and we conclude from our own findings and documentary support that he was forty-two.

As we have seen, the time period of forty years is of huge importance to a would-be king of the Jews. Moses lived a life that was made up of three forty-year phases, David and Solomon ruled for forty years, and anything that Jesus did would carry greater weight if it followed the same pattern. Indeed, Jesus would have believed that God would require these holy patterns to be kept to, and his whole mission would have to be constructed around the demands of God's holy cycle.

Having passed his test in the wilderness he was now into his second 40-year period, ready to assume the role of King of the Jews and to lead God's Chosen People against the Roman occupiers.

THE MAN WHO WOULD BE KING

John the Baptist, Jesus and his brother James all came from the agricultural region of Lower Galilee around Lake Gennesaret; otherwise known as the Sea of Galilee. The people of Galilee had a clear sense of their own identity and were intensely proud of their Jewishness, but they were considered country bumpkins by the Judeans, although their reputation for being brave and tough is made clear by Josephus, who describes them as 'from infancy inured to war'.[10] They spent most of the hundred years before the Jewish War in an almost permanent state of rebellion against anyone who tried to rule them, whether Hasmonean,

---

[9] Eisenman, R: *James the Brother of Jesus*
[10] Josephus: *Jewish War*, 3:41

Herodian or Roman. In rabbinic parlance they were known as 'Gelili shoteh', which means 'stupid Galilean', for they were considered to be religiously uneducated.

It seems strange, therefore, that John, Jesus and James should have made such an impact when they arrived in Judea. According to the Gospels Jesus became a famous healer and exorcist throughout his native Galilee. At that time, and for hundreds of years afterwards, sickness and sin were directly related, and healing was believed to come as a result of God's forgiveness of sins, rather than of any physical treatment. The healing gifts claimed for Jesus are never attributed to the study of disease or any acquired knowledge of treatments such as the Essenes possessed. Whether or not Jesus also used the plants and stones of the Essenes, he is described in the Gospels as having the power to cure by touch or by command alone.

There are mixed messages in the New Testament as to whether Jesus was a peaceful man or the leader of a group intent upon armed revolt. His 'loving' message is in line with Essene thinking, but there are passages that paint a rather different picture, more in line with the warlike content of the Dead Sea Scrolls. He appointed five principal 'minders': two Simons, a Judas, and James and John, whom he described as 'sons of thunder'. One of the Simons is called a Zealot, which is the name given to a member of a revolutionary movement founded in Galilee, whilst Judas was described as a Sicarius, meaning 'knifeman'. In Luke 22: 35–38 we read how Jesus tells his followers to sell their clothes to buy weapons.

In the medieval Hebrew document known as *The Josippon* there are several important references to the revolutionary activity of the followers of Jesus. Slavonic scholar Dr Eisler believed that this is a Latin translation of Josephus made about 370 CE by Gaudentius, and then some centuries later someone unknown made a Hebrew translation. In the ninth century this Hebrew translation was 'improved' by some Jews in the interests of Judaism. In this revision they used the Greek version of Josephus, which escaped the reworkings conducted by Christian censorship; thus *The Josippon* is far nearer the unexpurgated original. However, the various medieval versions of this revised *Josippon* were sought out by the ecclesiastical censors and their offending passages deleted to varying degrees. But all censors fail to be absolutely thorough, and the survival of three different manuscripts has permitted the reconstruction of original passages, including the one in which the followers of Jesus are described by Josephus as 'robbers of our people' and as fighting against the Pharisees during the time of the Emperor Caligula.

Dead Sea Scroll experts Professor Robert Eisenman and Dr Michael Wise have pointed to the similarity of the warlike nature of the Qumran and Christian mindsets, where the expected king creates peace on earth – but only through the terrible destruction of enemies. They quote some key examples:

> *That the concepts incorporated in words of this kind have gone directly into Christian presentations of its Messiah and his activities is hardly to be doubted. See, for instance, Line 4 in Column 2 and Matt. 10: 34: 'I came not to send peace, but a sword.' This kind of 'sword' allusion is also found in Column xix of the War Scroll, 'the sword of God', used in the war against 'the Kittim' . . .*
>
> *One point, however, should be emphasised: the Messianic figure envisaged in texts like the Son of God, War Scroll, etc., whether taken figuratively or otherwise, is extremely war-like. This is in line with the general uncompromising, militant and nationalist ethos of the Qumran corpus; the Messianic figure was to be a triumphant, quasi-nationalist king figure. One should also note that the peace envisaged in this text will only come after the cataclysmic Messianic war. As in the War Scroll, God will assist in this enter-prise with His Heavenly Host. For the War Scroll, this is the point of the extreme purity.*[11]

We believe that this is a crucial point. If Jesus was acting out a role-play with himself as the promised messiah, he will have truly believed that he was the King of the Jews whose destiny was to wage war on Israel's enemies and destroy them. God would ensure success. All he had to do was follow the preordained requirements and he would sweep to an inevitable victory, even over the unimaginable might of the Roman Empire. The evidence suggests that Jesus believed in his mission yet still had moments of fear, because he fully understood the scale of the war that was about to take place. Was he concerned that the right moment, astrologically speaking, was chosen?

Further information about the actions of the would-be messiah have been found in another early version of Josephus, known as *The Slavonic Halosis*, of which specialist scholar Dr SGF Brandon said:

---

[11] Eisenman, R & Wise, M: *The Dead Sea Scrolls Uncovered*

Jesus is referred to as 'a man' and 'a wonder-worker'; he uses his miraculous power to perform many healings, and is briefly condemned for breaking the Law and violating the Sabbath, but it is expressly stated that he did nothing shameful. His influence stirs many Jews to hope that he might be instrumental in freeing them from the Roman domination.

He is consequently invited to lead an insurrection in Jerusalem to exterminate the Romans there. What was the nature of his response is not clearly stated; however, before any effective action is attempted, the Jewish (sacerdotal) leaders take alarm and warn Pilate, who takes strong repressive action, as a result of which the wonder-worker is captured and finally condemned by the procurator as a rebel, desirous of kingship.[12]

If Jesus' followers were indeed pressing him to murder the Roman garrison at Jerusalem it would not take long for such an idea to filter through to the authorities. The concern of the Jewish leaders that this would-be king was a threat to the stability of the whole nation is described in an account given in John 11: 47–51, where a council of Pharisees is worried about this 'wonder-worker'. They had sympathy for the nationalist cause, but their concern was that if they left him to continue, his following would increase and the Romans would inevitably move against the entire country when they suspected serious insurrection. The council therefore decided that Jesus would have to die rather than put the whole nation at risk of a heavy-handed Roman response to terrorist attack. The outcome was that Pilate was alerted and he ordered the arrest of this 'terrorist', who was subsequently put to death on a charge of insurrection.

There is little doubt that nobody thought that Jesus was a god or some earthly aspect of Yahweh Himself prior to his crucifixion. To some Jews he was the expected messiah, who would be their king to rule on Earth as a regent for Yahweh, and who, with God's help, would drive the Kittim (all invaders) out of the Jewish homeland; to other Jews he was a threat to national stability; and to the Romans he was simply a troublemaker they needed to remove before he did anything seriously damaging.

Early Christian writers were looking for quite a different person. They wanted a man who was God Incarnate and would suffer to save all of

---

[12] Brandon, SGF: *The Fall of Jerusalem and the Christian Church*, SPCK, London, 1951

mankind (even the Romans) from the consequences of their own sins. They needed to deal with information that collided with their preferred account, and many of them changed written texts to 'correct' the obvious errors of earlier writers.

A few enlightened scholars, such as Origen, were too honest for this type of behaviour and tried to make sense of the evidence they found. Origen states that the versions of Josephus' *Antiquities* that he possessed say that Josephus definitely repudiates the messiahship of Jesus. He goes on to say that the historian states that the overthrow and virtual annihilation of the Jewish nation by the Romans between 66 and 70 CE is God's vengeance for the murder of James, Jesus' younger brother. Furthermore, Origen adds that the first-century Jewish writer praised James and recognised him as righteous whilst dismissing the importance of Jesus to the point of condemnation.[13]

The consequences of this denial are important: if the original works of Josephus did specifically deny that Jesus was the messiah, it necessarily follows that Josephus was aware that Jesus was a claimant to messiahship (in its normal political meaning rather than in the later Christian sense of a 'deity' that was created around the alien Greek concept of 'Christos').

In his work *The Jewish War* Josephus says that the Jews were led to their fatal resistance against Rome by a belief in an ambiguous oracle taken from their sacred scriptures which foretold that at a specific time a man from Palestine would become ruler of the world. He went on to say that the Jews interpreted this prophecy as meaning that a member of their own race would gain this supreme position, and many of their wise men were deceived by this oracle. The paper trail we were uncovering in dusty academic texts, archaeological reports and computer simulations of the morning sky was telling us that this 'oracle' is a reference to the Star Prophecy and the anticipated return of the Shekinah to herald the new messiah.

THE GREAT FAILURE

We cannot be sure if the Jesus of Christian myth is the individual referred to in the Dead Sea Scrolls as the expected messiah who arrived. However, we feel sure that Jesus and his followers were doing their best to ensure that his life and actions conformed to the expectations associated with this messiah.

[13] Brandon SGF: *The Fall of Jerusalem and the Christian Church*

The Jesus who was the elder brother of James the Just and whom Josephus described as 'a rebel desirous of kingship' certainly existed and had a high profile. He was invited to become king, and it seems to us that he got the support of the Essenes of Qumran. On the balance of probabilities we would put our money on the Jesus of the New Testament being the same person as the one described in the Dead Sea Scrolls.

In our view Jesus believed he was working his 'grand plan' around the guidance of Yahweh and His Spirit, as exemplified by the light of the Shekinah. Jesus' ministry, or period of political activity, could not begin until a full Venus cycle was complete and he reached his fortieth year. At first he would have been able to pass himself off as nothing more than a harmless 'wonder-worker', but as he gained followers they expected to hear of the delivery of the 'kingdom of heaven'. And they expected actions, not just words.

Jesus gave them action when, with his minders, he entered the Temple in Jerusalem to smash up the trading that was the norm there. All Essenes despised trade, and to trade inside the bounds of God's house was, to them, an abomination. His action took place right in the face of the Sadducees and just in front of the Roman fortress of Antonia, so any pretence of peacefulness was now gone for ever.

Jesus went public in a big way. He started by making a dramatic entry into Jerusalem to the sound of an apparently spontaneous outburst of acclaim. This applause can only have been the response to a statement of messiahship, whereby Jesus, by his choice of transport, said: 'I am the one who has been prophesied . . . I am your king.' He was acting in fulfilment of the prophecy in Zechariah 9: 9:

> *Rejoice greatly, O daughter of Zion; shout, O daughter of*
> *Jerusalem; behold, thy King cometh unto thee: he is just, and*
> *having salvation; lowly, and riding upon an ass, and upon a colt*
> *the foal of an ass.*

This was just the beginning of his launch programme for full messiahship, as the Bible tells us that most people did not know who Jesus was when he made this triumphant entry into the city. Matthew 21: 10 admits as much when it says:

> *And when he was come into Jerusalem, all the city was moved,*
> *saying, Who is this?*

So here was a man, unknown to the people of Jerusalem, claiming to be their messiah – their king. In making this claim he publicly affirmed his intent to remove the Romans from the Jewish land and build a powerful kingdom to dominate the world. His actions left the authorities no option but to arrest him. Smashing up the stalls in the Temple was a crime, but the threat to overthrow Roman rule was serious enough to warrant this rebel's death. Jesus and his team beat a fast retreat before the Roman guard could turn out. They headed five miles exactly due east to the village of Bethany, but returned the next day.

Jesus must have known that he needed speed and overwhelming public support to achieve his mission to be installed as the messiah king. He knew what could happen to failed claimants because, all too recently, John the Baptist had died when Herod became suspicious that John was the messiah.

In Luke 3:15 we read how there was a general expectation of the Messiah's arrival and John the Baptist was the likely candidate:

And as the people were in expectation, and all men mused in their hearts of John, whether he were the Christ, or not;

As we know that Jesus only became active after the death of John, it appears he was reticent to take the lead role. The words of the Gospel of John (6: 15) now take on a clearer meaning:

When Jesus therefore perceived that they would come and take him by force, to make him a king, he departed again into a mountain himself alone.

The end was getting nearer. There was no groundswell of support to overthrow the Romans and Jesus' small group of immediate supporters were not strong enough to launch an attack on the enemy. It was only a matter of time before they would be arrested, and even his disciples were looking for ways out. According to the Gospel of Mark the whole drama that began with his supposedly triumphant entry into Jerusalem, continued with the crowds calling against him at his trial, and ended with his subsequent crucifixion, all took place in a single week. The betrayal of Jesus is key to understanding these events.

Mark 14: 16 –18 tells us:

And his disciples went forth, and came into the city, and found as
he had said unto them: and they made ready the passover. And in
the evening he cometh with the twelve. And as they sat and did
eat, Jesus said, Verily I say unto you, One of you which eateth
with me shall betray me.

This can be read two ways. The first option is to take the traditional interpretation that it was preordained that Jesus would fail and be horribly tortured and die. He would do so in order that this suffering would transfer the
responsibility for the sins of believers – past, present and future – back onto
his own, i.e. God's shoulders. If this interpretation is true then if follows that
if Judas had not betrayed Jesus, there would have been no suffering, no death,
no resurrection and no salvation. So if we accept this reading we have to conclude that Judas must be considered the greatest hero in the history of mankind.

Alternatively, it could be that Jesus knew that his entire plan was failing
and thought it extremely likely that one or more of his followers would
try to save their own skins by turning him in to the authorities.

The words spoken by Jesus on the cross suggest that the second interpretation is more likely to be correct. This failed revolutionary hangs dying,
nailed beneath a titulus that reads 'Jesus of Nazareth, king of the Jews',
and he pushes down against the agony of his nailed feet trying to take in
enough breath to speak. The physical effort and pain involved in strug-
gling to force enough air into his cramped lungs to be able to shout is
unimaginable. But according to the Gospels he did manage it, and what
did he choose to say after this agonising struggle?

Mark tells us he cries out in a loud voice:

'Eloi eloi lama sabachthani?' My God, my God, why hast thou for-
saken me?[14]

Now if Jesus is God, why did he talk to himself and so undermine his
own credibility at this critical juncture? These seem to be the despairing words
of a man who fervently believed he was carefully acting out actions prophesied long ago that would give him the power to overthrow the Romans. He
feels utterly betrayed – not so much by Judas as by Yahweh Himself.

[14] Mark 15: 34

THE ENOCHIAN JESUS

All of the evidence was pointing towards Jesus being associated with the messianic expectations of the Qumran community and the continuing Enochian priesthood. The claim that Jesus was a priest of the Order of Melchizedek is a direct statement of his association with an early Canaanite belief that long pre-dates Moses and his new god, Yahweh. We have already noted that rainmaking was a sacred art that was still practised at the time of Jesus, but it is also given an additional layer of symbolism in the War Scroll at Qumran, where heavy rain is equated to the pouring down of eschatological Judgement and the final Judgement Day.

We have already mentioned, in chapter 8, that Jesus' cousin, John the Baptist, was considered by many to be the new Elijah and John also created stone circles. Likewise another member of Jesus and John's family was the second rainmaker, 'Honi the Circle Drawer',[15] who Professor Robert Eisenman suspects is really James, the brother of Jesus.

We have already discussed many references around the time of Jesus' birth to this hidden tradition, including that the first 'Honi the Circle Drawer' fathered a son called 'Hanan the Hidden', who was also a sacred rainmaker and was close to John the Baptist. We believe this practice of stone circle making was thriving at the time of Jesus but its associated 'magic' practices were known only to the select few – all of whom appear to be connected to the family of Jesus.

Now we found additional evidence that a magical belief had been passed down from the time that the original Star Prophecy was made, all the way to Jesus and his family. It was the Canaanite magic of 'lachash', which translates to 'whisper' or to 'mutter'. The technique is a form of incantation used to resurrect the dead, a magical practice biblical experts have already identified:

In Isa. iii. 3 the rendering 'skilful enchanter' means in Hebrew literally, 'experienced (in composing) an incantation,' i.e. in writing magical formulas.

This term is used only in connection with magic, and when, as we shall see, the idea of raising the dead by means of magic was not unknown to the ancient Hebrews, it is possible there is in

[15] Eisenman, R: *James the Brother of Jesus*

reality a reference to an attempt to resuscitate David's child by means of a whispered incantation.[16]

So the old Canaanite blend of magic and religion still seemed to continue when the Star Prophecy was made.

We found this idea of muttering secret words as a way to resurrect an individual highly reminiscent of the third degree ritual of Freemasonry. In this ritual the 'magic' words are whispered into the candidate's ear at the instant he is hinged out of his grave under the pre-dawn light of Venus shining from its helical rising in the east. This form of magic is also closely connected to Jesus, as the Bible claims he resurrected the dead before ultimately being resurrected himself.

The subject of necromancy (the magic of foretelling future events by consulting the dead, which we have noted was part of Norse belief) also appears to have been a hidden tradition amongst a section of the Jewish people. It is referred to in Isaiah 8: 19 in a passage which is strangely out of context with the rest of this book:

And when they shall say unto you, seek unto them that have familiar spirits, and unto wizards that peep, and that mutter: should not a people seek unto their God? For the living to the dead?

In this verse Isaiah appears to be telling people that anyone who uses the dead in this way will have 'no dawn' themselves. When viewed with another verse from the same book, it would seem to be a reference to resurrection under the light of the Shekinah. The illuminating verse from Isaiah is popular in churches today and is extensively quoted during Christmas carol services. It deals with the expected coming of the Jewish Messiah, and is often mistaken for some divinely inspired reference to the Christian Messiah. The key verses are 9: 2 and 9: 6–7:

The people that walked in darkness have seen a great light: they that dwell in the land of the shadow of death, upon them hath the light shined . . . For unto us a child is born, unto us a son is given: and the government shall be upon his shoulder: and his name shall

[16] Oesterley, WOE & Robinson, TH: *Hebrew Religion, Its Origin and Development*

be called Wonderful, Counsellor, The mighty God, The everlasting Father, The Prince of Peace.

Of the increase of his government and peace there shall be no end, upon the throne of David, and upon his kingdom, to order it, and to establish it with judgment and with justice from henceforth even for ever. The zeal of the Lord of hosts will perform this.

Christians believe this section of Isaiah to be the beginning of an understanding of messianic hope in Israel when, as one theological scholar put it, 'a bright light shines in the darkness and the oppressor's yoke is broken as in Gideon's day'.[17] To us, however, it seems to be a reference to the promise of the returning light of the Shekinah and the political dominance this return will herald for Israel when the new king leads the way. A Shekinah made an appearance at the vernal equinox in the year 740 BCE, which is exactly the time that Isaiah began to prophesy the coming of the messiah. How could such a dramatic heavenly event fail to inspire Isaiah?

For Christians this passage is interpreted as a prophecy of their strange interpretation of the word 'messiah' as the figure of the mythical Christ. But this cannot be so, because Jesus did not succeed in becoming the king of the Jews and his appearance marked the beginning of the most disastrous period of Jewish history ever. None of the Jewish messianic promises were met, although subsequently every attempt was made to suggest that they were.

But Christianity was about to take a totally different track when the rural nature myth of the dying and resurrecting god almost totally ousted the Canaanite astral secrets of Jesus and his family.

THE CULT OF PAUL

A radically new, and phenomenally successful, version of the story of Jesus was about to arise. A man from Tarsus, the son of Jewish converts, became a Roman citizen and changed his name from the Hebrew 'Saul' to the Roman equivalent 'Paul'. This Jewish citizen of the Roman Empire from Turkey set himself up as the scourge of the rebellious group of Jews in and

---

[17] Bright, J: 'Isaiah 1', *Peake's Commentary on the Bible*

around Jerusalem. It is said that Saul persecuted Christians, but this was impossible as there were no such people. The followers of Jesus and, after his death, of his brother James the Just remained Jews and did not become members of Paul's new Christian religion. Christianity was a later cult developed by Saul of Tarsus exclusively to attract pagan converts throughout the broader Roman Empire – people who were already inclined towards the nature-based dying and rising god theme.

According to the New Testament, Paul underwent a trauma after which he claimed that he alone was given special insight into the meaning of Jesus' mission directly from God. Paul claimed:

> But when it pleased God . . . to reveal his son in me, that I might preach it to the gentiles.[18]

The word 'gentiles' has become respectable in Christian thinking because it is taken as being a Jewish description of Christians, but it meant no such thing at the time that Paul was preaching his bizarre creed. It was a word used by the followers of Jesus and James to describe the pagans who did not believe in the God of the Jews.

Paul quickly found himself at total odds with James because the story he was telling about James's brother Jesus was so outrageous. It is evident that Paul was prepared to do anything to get his way; he even admits that he is happy to lie if that is what is required:

> And unto the Jews I became as a Jew, that I might gain the Jews; to them that are under the law, as under the law, that I might gain them that are under the law;
>
> To them that are without law, as without law, that I might gain them that are without law.
>
> To the weak became I as weak, that I might gain the weak: I am made all things to all men . . .
>
> Know ye not that they which run in a race run all, but one receiveth the prize?

[18] Galatians 1: 15, 16

So run, that ye may obtain . . .

I therefore so run, not as uncertainly; so fight I, not as one that beateth the air.[19]

Professor Eisenman writing in *James the Brother of Jesus* says that Paul became famous as a liar and had to make excuses for himself:

Paul was obviously being mocked by some – within the Church not outside it – as 'the Man of Dreams', 'Lies', or 'Lying', or what was also characterised in a parallel parlance as 'the Enemy' . . . It is neither accidental nor incurious that exactly where he comes to speak of 'James the brother of the Lord' and in 2 Corinthians, the Hebrew 'Archapostles', that Paul feels obliged to add: 'Now before God, (in) what I write to you, I do not lie' or, again, 'I do not lie'.

The story that Paul had created was only loosely connected to the actions of the recently dead Jesus and his followers, but it did have a great deal to do with Roman tastes in theology. In Cyprus, Egypt, Turkey and Rome Paul's followers wrote the Gospels that make up the New Testament, whilst back in Israel the people that Jesus had once led became followers of James and forceful opponents of the new religion that Paul was busily inventing.

Paul's new cult of Christianity was squarely rooted in the Canaanite peasant theology of dying and rising nature gods and only retained a few misunderstood elements of the once supreme astral cult. The Bright Morning Star that marked the birth of a Jewish messiah became just a pretty Christmas star that hovered miraculously over the stable where Jesus was born. The Sun was relegated to become a halo highlighting the heads of the righteous. Male circumcision, the great covenant with God, that was claimed to have endured from the time of Abraham, was rejected because the potential recruits of the Roman Empire were not happy to pay this particularly painful price.

The New Testament tells the story of Jesus from the perspective of Paul, and it tries to establish the idea that the followers of the crucified Jesus were Christians in their churches. They were not – they were Jews.

The Pauline version of events at this time claims that there were two,

---

[19] 1 Corinthians 9: 20–25

equally valid, ways forward for believers at that time – James's Jewish route and Paul's plan for the uncircumcised. Respected writer AN Wilson says of this:

> It is clear to us today that this division was going to happen, but even at the date when Luke was writing – let us say AD 80? – it was still a possibility that the two 'Ways' could be reconciled . . . The next few chapters of Acts have to be read gingerly . . . they are propaganda, designed to make us think that 'the early Church' was always 'Christian' – whereas in fact, of course, it belonged to an era when the word 'Christian' was simply a nickname for a sect within Judaism.[20]

The nature cult created in the name of Jesus came less from the beliefs of his real followers than it did from Paul's own upbringing in Tarsus. Every autumn the young Saul, as he then was known, would have watched the great funeral pyre on which the local god was ritually burnt. God was now dead, but he would arise again in the spring (Easter). Furthermore, it is known that Tarsians worshipped saviour gods (known as *theoisoteres*),[21] so it is little wonder that Paul's 'new' religion of the 'Risen Christ' was so easy for pagans to accept – it was far from original and built upon well-established traditions.

This can be seen very clearly in Paul's attitude to blood. The idea of crucifixion was horrific to all Jews, and blood was something to be avoided at all costs, yet Paul's concept of Jesus Christ rested on the power of his spilt blood, and also of course on the sacrificial impulse which had driven the worship of Moloch. Even today Christians ritually drink the blood of Christ.

This concept of the ritual imbibing of the blood of a sacrificial human victim is about as far removed from Jewish thinking as it is possible to get. But this nauseating idea was well accepted amongst the followers of the oldest of nature cults. Wilson comments on Paul's inspiration for such an idea:

> Just as the worshippers of Mithras, in his native Tarsus, could stand beneath a platform and catch the cascade of blood falling on

[20] Wilson, AN: *Paul, The Mind of the Apostle*, Sinclair-Stevenson, 1997
[21] Wilson, AN: *Paul, The Mind of the Apostle*

them from the slaughtered bullock, so Paul could bathe in the
blood of the crucified and find that the life of the Messiah had
become his own. He was the Christ. Just as Paul's contemporaries
in Tarsus believed that the demi-god Herakles – with one human
and one immortal parent – had, in his descent into the realms of
death, become the saviour of his people, so Jesus 'gave himself for
our sins to set us free from the present evil age, according to the
will of our God and Father'.

The Romans had to place Paul in protective imprisonment when he preached in Ephesus to save him from the Jewish community that was outraged by his distorted version of Judaism. When he went to the Temple in Jerusalem there was a full-scale riot and he was dragged out by a frenzied mob intent upon lynching him on the spot. A cohort of Roman troops from the fortress of Antonia (next to the Temple) had to intervene to save his life – a cohort in contemporary Roman terms meant several hundred men. This was a sizeable intervention by the Roman occupation forces.

As the Pauline cult multiplied in the countries around the Mediterranean, the theology of the Essenes continued, with daily prayers at sunrise and sunset. As we know from the Dead Sea Scrolls, they kept to the solar calendar because they intended to keep in harmony with God's laws, 'the laws of the great light of heaven'.[22] But their hoped-for Apocalypse was not long in coming. In 62 CE James was murdered, and Paul died soon afterwards. According to Josephus, in *The Jewish War*, the Jews finally rose up against their enemy in 66 CE. They fought a terrible war in their attempt to create the kingdom of heaven on the earth of Israel.

The scrolls found at Qumran tell us that these Essenes expected their war to last forty years – a full Venus cycle. They also believed the battle would have a cosmic dimension, with part of it to be played out in heaven. Angelic armies were under the command of 'The Prince of Light' – who was also referred to as Melchizedek (the priestly line from which the Bible says Jesus claimed descent). They expected a hard war, with interim victories going to each side three times until, after the full forty years, Yahweh would intervene to annihilate all evil.[23] We speculated that there might always be a Venusian element in all solar religion – after all, both the Sun

---

[22] 1QH 12: 5
[23] 1QM 18: 1–3 and 11Q Melch 2: 9, 13

and Venus frequently occupy the same part of the sky – but the Venusian element often takes an esoteric form, as Venus is often hidden by the light of the Sun, making it seem more mysterious. In addition the cycles of Venus are much longer than the cycles of the Sun, and so followers of Venus are forced to take a longer-term view on life.

The people who wrote these Qumran scrolls expected their final victory to be followed immediately by the messianic age, and in some scrolls the 'Prince of the Congregation' is identified as the Davidic messiah. This messiah was expected to rule as a secular king under, or with, the guidance of a priest-king who would be the 'interpreter of the Law' and who would 'teach righteousness at the end of days'.[24]

The actions attributed to Jesus in the New Testament are virtually identical to these recorded expectations of the Qumran community. Also, as we have seen, the curious figure of Melchizedek appears in both Christian and Qumranic texts. This heavenly leader is expected to exact vengeance for the people of God in the great battle that will be fought against Satan and his demonic spirits.[25]

Some of the Dead Sea Scrolls contain the idea that after this messianic period sinners will be plunged into 'eternal torment and endless disgrace . . . in the fire of the dark regions'. The righteous will be rewarded with 'healing, great peace in a long life, and fruitfulness, together with every everlasting blessing and eternal joy in life without end, a crown of glory and a garment of majesty in unending light'.[26] The righteous dead will be resurrected to share in the final glory, which accounts for the almost unbelievable bravery of the Essenes. Knowing they would return gave them no reason to fear death.

The Essenes, Zealots and the followers of James, the Jerusalem Church, were at the heart of the fighting. In the midst of this war, *circa* 68 CE, the Herodian-appointed High Priests were quickly put to the sword and Josephus describes the election by a new group of priests that he called 'the Innovators'. These were to be the last High Priests ever to serve at the Jerusalem Temple. Professor Eisenman says of this:

When describing 'the last days', that is, the last days of the Temple in the 66–70 CE events but particularly as these accelerated after 68 and the elimination of all the Herodian-appointed High Priests,

[24] CD 6: 11
[25] Golb, N: *Who Wrote the Dead Sea Scrolls?*
[26] 1 QS 4: 7–8

Josephus describes the election by 'the Innovators' of a last High Priest before the Romans invest the city, one 'Phannius' or 'Phineas', a simple Stone-Cutter. Josephus constantly refers to 'the Innovators' in this period the political and religious reformers and/or revolutionaries who have all been lumped, somewhat imprecisely, under the general heading of 'Zealots'.[27]

The High Priest, Phannius, was a Stonemason, and Eisenman identifies him as a rainmaker in the tradition of Elijah, Honi, John the Baptist and James. He says of this:

There is also a concomitant 'rainmaking' tradition associated with Phineas' name, which has links not only to similar traditions about Elijah, and through him, James, but also to another interesting character who is part of this whole complex of rainmaking Zaddiks, Honi the Circle Drawer.[28]

The rebuilding of the Jerusalem Temple initiated by King Herod in 19 BCE had continued for several decades, and the inner parts had to be constructed by hereditary priests because they were touching the very house of God: not a place where he was worshipped, but the actual location of His divine presence. Thousands of priests were trained in the craft of stonemasonry, and it seems very probable that Jesus and his father Joseph were included in this endeavour. The Bible tells us that Joseph and Jesus were carpenters, but the original word used in the Greek version was 'tekton', which meant 'builder'. As few people worked in wood in Jerusalem in those times, it seems a lot more probable that Jesus and his father were priestly stonemasons, just like Phineas.

The revolutionaries took over the Temple and installed their own high priest, no doubt believing that their God would back up their fight in the struggle for supremacy that they so vividly described in the Dead Sea Scrolls. Sadly for these Jewish revolutionaries, the war climaxed after just six years, not the expected forty, and it ended with the destruction of Jerusalem and its recently rebuilt Temple. Josephus records that one million three hundred thousand Jews died in those few years. And the secrets of the Venus cult almost died with them.

[27] Eisenman, R: *James the Brother of Jesus*
[28] Eisenman, R: *James the Brother of Jesus*

For hundreds of years the Jews had been united in their devotion to Yahweh and in their acceptance of the obligations enshrined in the Torah; but their commonality of belief was now brought to an end.

Before the destruction of Jerusalem, in 70 CE, there was no such thing as Jewish orthodoxy, only disparate groups of Sadducees, Pharisees, Essenes, Zealots and Christians. It would be another two centuries before Christians ceased to be just a strange variety of Judaism.

The Christian Bible is made up of the Old and the New Testaments. The first covers the history of the world from 'the creation' through to Malachi, the last of the prophets who spoke of the return of Elijah, who was to be a forerunner of the coming Messiah. The New Testament covers the period from just before the birth of Jesus to a period about seventy-five years later, when the Jewish War broke out.

So the Bible chronicles God's interaction with His chosen people for all time right up to their near-obliteration at the hands of the Romans. After that the Bible simply stops. But it did not stop being written: in the same way that the Dead Sea Scrolls were lost, so the ongoing story just did not get bound into the official versions.

But the families who considered themselves to have a special relationship with Yahweh continued to document their journey. The bloodlines that produced the high priests survived, and continued to record their progress towards creating the kingdom of God on Earth. We have previously put forward the argument that the priests who escaped the massacre in Jerusalem in 70 CE escaped to Europe, there to found many of the families that would become pre-eminent.[29] In France these families came to control Anjou, Champagne, Normandy and Burgundy, where they mixed with Scandinavian blood. It appears that two ancient traditions were re-converging in Europe: the Jewish strand of a Phoenician Venus cult and the Norse version of the same ancient Grooved Ware beliefs that survived in pagan Scandinavia until at least 1000 CE.

ASTROLOGY THE BIG SECRET?

It appears that the chain of events beginning with the astronomical science of the Grooved Ware People was passed down through time and, via the Canaanites, came to a focus in the beliefs and aspirations of the priests

[29] Knight, C and Lomas, R: *The Second Messiah*

who lived at Qumran, and the group led by John, Jesus and James.

But we were starting to feel very uneasy. The Jewish magi clearly understood the movements of Venus, and their entire national aspirations appear to have been centred upon a superstitious belief that the light of Venus rising before dawn in conjunction with another bright planet would allow them to win wars and to go on to greatness. By any other name this is astrology.

Is this where our journey was going to end? After twenty-six joint years of investigation into the science that we had come to believe was underpinning Freemasonry, must we now accept that it was only a foolish pseudo-science?

At the beginning of this book we referred to a fear that some elements in the Roman Catholic Church seemed to have about our investigations. They appeared to have been putting a lot of energy into attacking us and trying to prevent people from taking our findings seriously. We felt that what they feared was our finding something that they would prefer to stay hidden.

Suddenly we had a great deal of sympathy with their point of view. Our line of investigation was leading us to demonstrate that Jesus was driven by a belief in the power of the Shekinah – which turns out to be little more than astrology on a grandiose scale. The Church has always detested astrology, and now we seem to have shown that its 'saviour' was born, lived and died by the rules of an ancient prophecy based on the movements of the planets. Was the Church's Pauline myth of Jesus preferable in some ways to this unpalatable reality?

We were somewhat despondent, but our quest needed to continue, because we now had to test for ourselves if there really was any science involved, or whether the whole ritual edifice was nothing more than a tangle of empty superstitions. Was this long line of ancient astronomer-priests nothing more than a string of astrological fortune-tellers with ambitions of power? We decided to review what we had learned about the Shekinah cycle, and how it first crept into Jewish belief at the time of the building of Solomon's Temple by Hiram, King of Tyre.

DATES OF THE VENUS CYCLES

Hiram came to the throne of Tyre in 983 BCE, when according to the historian Josephus he was nineteen years old. This meant he was born in 1002

BCE. We had reasoned that if he was a true son of Venus his father would have taken care to impregnate his mother at the sexual rituals of the vernal equinox. Indeed, it might well have been one of his kingly duties, as the earthly representative of El.

When Robert checked we found that Venus rose just before the Sun at the winter solstice in the year of 1002 BCE. So Hiram's birth fulfilled criteria similar to those we knew had been applied by the Qumran priests to decide if a messiah was born.

The major difference was that the birth of a Jewish messiah was marked by a series of Venus/Mercury conjunctions which only occurred every 480 years. We thought it would have been an unreasonable and impractical condition to wait 480 years for a new king, so the Phoenicians seemed to accept the simpler idea that it was sufficient for a king to be born to the pre-dawn light of Venus to make him a suitable person to rule them.

However, this idea that kings are born when a bright star is visible on the pre-dawn horizon seemed to have been taken up eagerly by the Jews. It became linked to an idea that super-kings, who were favoured by God and so could provide people with a standard of leadership which would vastly improve the fortunes of the country, were born only when a super-bright star appeared at the correct time. What was puzzling us was our realisation that the writers of the Old Testament seemed to be aware of this extremely long cycle of earlier Shekinah appearances and that they seemed to have acquired this knowledge by the time that Solomon's Temple was dedicated in 967 BCE.

Our problem was one of prediction. We knew that these clusters of conjunctions between Venus and Mercury occurred within the normal eight- and forty-year Venus cycles with a 480-year repetition pattern. But Robert was using a computer and running quite complex astronomical software to work this out. The astronomer priests at the time of Solomon did not have these sophisticated tools, so how had they known what pattern to expect? Their careful calculations back in time to the Exodus and the Flood showed they knew about this pattern, and both the Bible and *The Masonic Testament* linked their timing of these events with the characteristic appearance of the Shekinah.

We could think of only one possible way they could have come by the necessary information to do their calculations. They must have been given access to a series of previous observations.

In itself this is a simple idea: it's very easy to establish a pattern if you simply collect enough points in sequence to see how an event repeats. But the events we were thinking about only happened every 480 years. Nobody would live long enough to see more than one occurrence of this spectacular astral display, and most people would never see it. How do you spot a pattern with events so far apart in time? The information has to be passed down at least ten or so generations from one observational point to the next, possibly crossing more than one civilisation.

Our next problem is that only two occurrences do not confirm a trend. Nobody can accurately predict the period between one Shekinah cluster and the next if they only have two observation points to work with. Two points only measure the time of one period, and so until you get a third occurrence you do not know if the cycle will repeat with the same time period. This means that a minimum of three observations are needed to confirm the period, and you need at least one additional observation in order to be aware that it happens at all, because if you don't notice it in the first place then you don't start counting.

This chain of logic convinced us that it would not be possible to have worked out the period of the Venusian generations, Venusian epochs and Venusian aeons used to construct the chronology of the Bible without at least four observations of the Shekinah Venusian epoch. This would take 1,920 years to collect.

Having completed the calculation, we then worked out the earliest possible date this process would need to have started for the information to have been available at the time Hiram started work on Solomon's Temple. It was 2892 BCE – a period that was of considerable importance.

'That's shortly before the time that the Grooved Ware People seemed to abandon their sites in Britain and left them derelict,' said Robert.

'Yes, it is,' said Chris. 'But we also need to be careful, because it's also some three hundred and fifty years after the earliest evidence of Sumerian civilisation and some two hundred and fifty years after the unification of upper and lower Egypt.'

'This information has got to have come from either Grooved Ware, or the Sumerian and Egyptian astronomer priests who were influenced by Grooved Ware traders and their beliefs – and don't forget the last two groups had the advantage of a system of writing to help them record their observations,' Robert mused. 'Just look at the time-line. Nobody else had the opportunity to collect enough data.'

We now knew from our researches that all three groups had worshipped the planet Venus, which was usually, but not always, considered a female deity. The common traits associated with this bright star are love, birth, death and resurrection. The very early writings of Sumer and Egypt make reference to Venus, but the Venus observatories of the Grooved Ware People of Western Europe pre-date both by at least two hundred years. Bryn Celli Ddu and Newgrange are prime examples.

Professor Michael O'Kelly, who excavated Newgrange, stated that carbon dating puts its completion at around 3200 BCE, and it is estimated that it took at least thirty years to build. But before its builders could undertake the construction they must have observed many Venus cycles to calculate the patterns. In this case the building probably represents a form of astronomy that was being catalogued from at least the middle of the fourth millennium BCE. A cycle of Venus/Mercury conjunctions began in 3367 BCE, and we reasoned this might well have been the inspiration to design and build Newgrange. Once complete, the layout of Newgrange is such that it would be impossible to miss further appearances of the Shekinah within the darkness of its chamber.

The Venus cycle remains constant, it is only the conjunctions of Mercury which vary, so any observatory built to monitor the movements of Venus must also draw attention to the Shekinah. The tunnel, lightbox and chamber would filter and collimate the light of the brightest conjunctions in the Shekinah cycle. Structures like Newgrange and Bryn Celli Ddu were astronomical instruments to track Venus, and they comfortably pre-date any other reference to that planet anywhere in the world.

Between 4500 and 2800 BCE the Grooved Ware culture, which built these observatories, went through a period of strong economic activity. Its success was characterised by farming surpluses and trading activities ranging over most of Britain and coastal areas of Europe, and culminating in the creation of enormous stone buildings and other structures which served ritual and astronomical purposes.[30]

As we have already mentioned, this period of widespread trade coincides with the establishment of a small trading village in Byblos and of a characteristic megalithic harbour at Lixus on the west coast of Africa, and we have suggested this was a result of the activities of Grooved Ware traders. Towards the end of this period of economic success, driven by widespread trade in specialised stone artefacts such as axes, arrowheads

[30] Dyer, J: *Ancient Britain*, Routledge, 1997

and flint knives, the fledgling civilisations of Sumer and Egypt began. As we have already mentioned, both civilisations' records tell of groups of outsiders arriving and providing the technology which kick-started these new cultures, cultures which both incorporated an interest in the planet Venus viewed as a goddess.

The Sumerians had originally worshipped Venus under the name Inanna (Queen of Heaven) with the aid of astronomer or 'baru' priests. Over time they did succeed in predicting eclipses, using counting methods and knowledge of the Saros cycle of the Moon,[31] and they contributed greatly to the later development of the laws of astronomy.

In ancient Egypt Venus' name was Hathor. She was 'The Eye of the Sun-god Ra', 'The Dweller in his Breast', 'The Goddess of Many Names'. Another name she carried was Uatchet, The Lady of Flames, when she was sent to Earth to punish mankind for their rebellion against Ra. Then she got a new name: Sekhmet, She Who Prevails. Ra called her back and then, with another name, Nut, she carried Ra away between her horns (a further reference to the horn effect of Venus's movement around the Sun). In some early accounts Isis is also associated with Venus as well as with Sirius, both being characterised by a Bright Morning Star. We also knew that the Egyptian hieroglyph for Venus was literally 'divine star', and it was itself part of the hieroglyph for 'knowledge' and for 'the priesthood'.

The Hebrews inherited Sumerian ideas from Abraham and Egyptian beliefs from Moses, and we believe that the general priesthood of the Hebrews also adopted the cyclical vegetative beliefs of the Canaanite sanctuaries, but that a royal priesthood grew out of a secret astral tradition practised by priest-kings such as Melchizedek. We have also found that many of the important events in the chronology of the Bible seem to be linked to bright, pre-dawn conjunctions of Venus and Mercury, which came to be called the Shekinah.

But we were becoming concerned that this belief in the power of the Shekinah might be nothing more than superstitious astrology.

We also believe that Christianity is built on the Canaanite model of a dying and rising nature god.

Astrology is loathed by the Church as a primitive and ignorant enemy of the 'true' faith, and the major astral bodies are mainly absent from the scriptures, despite the principles of astronomy underlying the nature worship

[31] The Saros cycle is an eighteen-year pattern of movements of the Moon caused by the interaction of the gravity of the Sun, Earth and Moon.

cycles of the Christian calendar. Christmas was originally a pre-Christian festival to celebrate the winter solstice. The Easter ritual of resurrection pre-dates Christ by tens of thousands of years, but the Church still dates the movable feast of Easter Sunday as the first Sabbath with a full moon after the vernal equinox.

The confusion about who God was talking to in the first chapter of Genesis when He says 'Let *us* make man in our own image[32] arises from a conflict between two different Canaanite traditions; one vegetative and the other astral. The vegetative cult was based on the birth and death of nature with the changing of the seasons, and may well have been aware of the movements of the Sun. But the astral cult looked at the long-term patterns of the movements of the stars, which they viewed as God's counsellors, and tried to use what its priests saw of their movements to predict the rise and fall of themselves and their kings.

The rituals of Freemasonry provide a view on this belief not found in the Bible. Chapter 1 of *The Masonic Testament* says that God was talking to the three ministers of His Eternal Council, and that there were also seven other entities in existence known as malak, or collectively as malakoth. This term is translated as 'angels'. However, the root word *malak* means counsellor, and later came to mean king.

So perhaps the Bright Morning Star, which is still celebrated at every Third Degree Ceremony of Freemasonry, does indeed date from Time Immemorial.

We needed to look more closely at what happened to the astrological implications of the idea of the Bright Morning Star, and how it came to be transmitted down to *The Masonic Testament* and so into modern Freemasonry.

CONCLUSIONS

We concluded that Freemasonic ritual aligns with the astral cultic practices of the royal lineage of Jerusalem (the city of Venus) whilst Christianity draws its basic beliefs from the religion of the peasant peoples of Canaan.

We also concluded that Jesus was not a simple peasant, and the New Testament is correct when it claims that he was proclaimed a king at birth and described as one at his death. The stories of the birth and life of Jesus

---

[32] Genesis 1: 26

have a direct connection with ancient Canaanite astral beliefs and, in particular, the 'divine' light of the Shekinah. Born under the pre-dawn light of the divine Shekinah, Jesus set out to fulfil the star-prophesied role of King of the Jews and led God's chosen people in open revolt against the Romans.

Both Christian and Jewish theologians dislike astrology, describing it as a pagan abomination, a superstition that courts the Devil, and an opposition to the teachings of God. But we have found that knowledge of the heavens and a belief in its effect on mankind is central to the Jewish group that gave rise to Christianity.

We have found evidence of an ongoing theological battle between an astral cult of Venus and the prophets of the new God, Yahweh. At times this battle was extremely violent, as when the Bible claims that Elijah personally slew 450 astral priests, whilst at other points we found Isaiah drawing on astral beliefs such as the rising of the Shekinah, just before the Sun, to predict the birth of a messiah.

Important elements of the Canaanite Venus cult, which included the construction of stone circles, rainmaking, the resurrection of the dead using whispered words, and the significance of helical risings of Venus, we found to be carried down to the time of Jesus.

The authors of the Dead Sea Scrolls recorded the fulfilment of a Star Prophecy and the arrival of a messiah. We investigated these people and found them to have very similar ideas to those preserved in the rituals of Freemasonry. We believe that Jesus was their messiah but he only accepted this role after the death of John the Baptist in 36 CE. On the balance of probabilities we accept the Jesus of the New Testament as the person described in the Dead Sea Scrolls.

After Jesus' death Paul created a new Jewish cult of Christianity that was squarely rooted in the Canaanite peasant theology of dying and rising nature gods and only retained a few misunderstood elements of the once supreme astral cult. This included the story of a bright Shekinah-like star hovering over Jesus' place of birth. The Sun's status was reduced to that of a halo to highlight the heads of the righteous. After the destruction of over a million Jews by the Romans, only Paul's new religion survived to be eventually adopted by a declining Roman Empire at the Council of Nicaea.

We calculated the number of data points needed to be sure of the existence of the Shekinah cycle and concluded that it had to have been discovered by the Grooved Ware builders of Newgrange.

Chapter Twelve

THE RETURN OF THE SHEKINAH

THE UNDERGROUND MILLENNIUM

The Romans put down the Jewish rebellion without pity. The last stand of the Jews was the siege, in 73 CE, at the dramatic mountain-top fortress of Masada which overlooks the southern end of the Dead Sea. There a thousand people committed suicide rather than surrender to the Romans.

By the time the war was over Josephus, who had conveniently changed to the winning side, reports that a total of 1,356,460 Jewish people lay dead.[1] It is impossible to know whether this is an exaggeration or not, but we can be sure that casualties reached a tremendous level for the population of this small country. The destruction of the Holy City and the consequent end of Temple worship had a paralysing effect on the Jewish people, who suffered a blow that was beyond all comprehension. At best their most cherished prophecies were proven to be horribly unreliable.

The writers of the four Gospels of the New Testament recorded the story of the life of their messiah and his developing Church up to the start of the war but made no mention of the fact that the original cast of the Jesus and James story had been slaughtered. With the destruction of the Jewish homeland and the authority of the family of James the Just gone, the way was open for the followers of Paul's 'Covenant of the Uncircumcised' to turn their pagan-like brand of Judaism into the separate cult that became Christianity.

[1] Milman, H: *History of the Jews*, Everyman, London, 1909

The cult of the Christ developed in the Roman world, and in 325 CE an ecumenical council was convened by Emperor Constantine I at Nicaea. Its aim was mainly political,[2] but it also met to settle an ongoing dispute about the real nature of Jesus the Christ. Three hundred and eighteen of the one thousand eight hundred bishops of the Roman Empire attended this council to debate the nature of acceptable beliefs within their Church.

The question that they posed was: 'Is Christ divine by nature or was his divinity brought about by his actions?' Two Alexandrian priests led the opposing points of view. Arius argued that Jesus was born a man, and that a man could not also be God. Athanasius claimed that Jesus and God were of one substance – as Father and son. Despite the inherent difficulty of sustaining the argument that a father and son are the same entity, Athanasius won the subsequent vote, and Jesus became a deity from that time forward as far as the Roman Empire was concerned. The council also fixed the celebration of Easter on the Sunday after the Jewish Pesach, or Passover.

From that time forward the Roman Church discouraged further debate, and anyone who even thought about deviating from official dogma was labelled a heretic and dealt with as such. This usually meant a slow and painful death. Not surprisingly the families of the priests who had escaped the destruction of Jerusalem lay low in Europe and became good Christians as far as the outside world was concerned. Secretly, they must have protected their Venusian tradition and, most particularly, their knowledge of the Shekinah and its Divine role in the affairs of mankind.

When the Norsemen invaded France and took control of Normandy in the eighth century, Hrolf More and his cousins decided to take the name St Clair and established themselves as dukes of Normandy. The families of the Jewish priests, who lived around the same region, must have been surprised to find that these recent incomers to France had a knowledge of Venus patterns and held a similar understanding to their own astral religion.

What happened before, and immediately after, allows us to construct a picture of the two cults identifying each other like a pair of aged twins separated since birth. Neither the Norsemen nor the priestly Jewish families knew that anyone else still placed the divine planet Venus at the centre of their theology. It must have been disturbing for the secretive priestly families such as the lords of Gisors, Payen, Fontaine, Anjou, de Bouillon,

---

[2] Knight, C & Lomas, R: *The Second Messiah*

Brienne, Joinville, Chaumont and the Habsburgs to hear these Scandinavians voice ideas similar to those they cherished in their own private thoughts, especially as there had been no previous contact.[3]

It appears to have been the More family that first set about recombining the two strands of Grooved Ware culture that had met again after more than three thousand years. They brought these strands together through marriage and celebrated the new united bloodline by taking the new name St Clair, meaning 'Holy Shining Light' – which appears to be their name for the ancient Jewish concept of the Shekinah. When it was later combined with the Gaelic word 'Roslin' we already knew it gave this family the designation:

Holy Shining Light of Ancient Knowledge passed down the Generations.

By taking this title, we believe that the family under Henri St Clair was recognising both the Norse and the Jewish generations that had protected this ancient knowledge.

The St Clairs had returned to the British Isles before the invasion of the England under the leadership of their fellow priestly lord, William of Normandy. They used the family's strong links with the kings of Norway, via Earl More of Trondheim, to establish themselves in Scotland prior to all of the families uniting, perhaps for the first time since they had left Jerusalem.

William, duke of Normandy, took England in October 1066 with the help of the Norse side of the family in the form of Harold Hårdråde, the king of Norway. We could not help but notice that this military initiative was conducted exactly one thousand years after the Jews had gone to war with the Romans. Were these families taking this as a 'pesher' – the Jewish concept of meanings repeating themselves over time?

It may be coincidence, but we also must note that the famous Bayeux Tapestry, which depicts the Norman Conquest, shows panels with pelicans rising from the ground with a star above their heads. (The pelican is widely used as a symbol of resurrection.) We could fully understand how these families considered that their ancient ideals were finally arising from their long slumber.

[3] Knight, C and Lomas, R: *The Second Messiah*

But then something very strange happened: an age-old prophecy was ful-filled.

For these families the most important book of the New Testament must have been the most Enochian, the Book of Revelation, sometimes called the Apocalypse. It finishes the Bible by looking towards the 'New Jerusalem' that will be built. It was written to prepare the faithful for the last inter-vention of God in human affairs, heralding a new age of the world. But for one thousand years the evils and terrors of the existing world order were predicted to increase and intensify. Revelation chapter 20 tells us:

And I saw an angel come down from heaven, having the key of the bottomless pit and a great chain in his hand.

And he laid hold on the dragon, that old serpent, which is the Devil, and Satan, and bound him a thousand years, And cast him into the bottomless pit, and shut him up, and set a seal upon him, that he should deceive the nations no more, till the thousand years should be fulfilled: and after that he must be loosed a little season.

And I saw thrones, and they sat upon them, and judgment was given unto them: and I saw the souls of them that were beheaded for the witness of Jesus, and for the word of God, and which had not worshipped the beast, neither his image, neither had received his mark upon their foreheads, or in their hands; and they lived and reigned with Christ a thousand years.

But the rest of the dead lived not again until the thousand years were finished. This is the first resurrection.

Blessed and holy is he that hath part in the first resurrection: on such the second death hath no power, but they shall be priests of God and of Christ, and shall reign with him a thousand years.

And when the thousand years are expired, Satan shall be loosed out of his prison, And shall go out to deceive the nations which are in the four quarters of the earth, Gog and Magog, to gather them together to battle: the number of whom is as the sand of the sea.

And they went up on the breadth of the earth, and compassed the camp of the saints about, and the beloved city: and fire came down from God out of heaven, and devoured them.

This prophecy specifically states that those who died in the destruction of Jerusalem in 70 CE will be resurrected one thousand years later when a godless power will take Jerusalem. The revitalised priests of the Bright Morning Star must have been even more convinced that history was repeating itself – and that the power of prophecy had returned – because a thousand years after the loss of the 'beloved city' and the Temple, Jerusalem was sacked by Seljuk Turks.

We believe that this event was the trigger that caused these powerful families to press the kings of Europe to mount an attack on Jerusalem to seize it back from Gog and Magog, just as the prophecy required. But this took a great deal of persuasion and organisation, and it was not until 1096 that the crusading army left for the Holy Land.

In May 1099 they reached the northern borders of Palestine and on the evening of 7 June they camped within sight of Jerusalem's walls. The city was heavily defended and well prepared for a siege, but the Crusaders attacked using newly constructed siege machines and finally took the Holy City on 15 July. They then set about massacring virtually every inhabitant, whether Muslim or Jew.

The following week the army elected Godfrey of Bouillon, duke of Lower Lorraine, as ruler of the city. Soon afterwards most of the Crusaders returned to Europe, leaving Godfrey and a small remnant of the original force to organise a government and to establish a new authority over the conquered territories. Henri St Clair returned home to Roslin but nine knights, who were to become the Knights Templar, stayed on to seek out permission for their intended excavation below the ruins of the Temple of their forefathers.

It appears that they had to wait until a friendly king was installed. After the consecutive deaths of first Godfrey and then his cousin Baldwin I, King Baldwin II of Jerusalem gave them permission to dig and financial support. In 1118 they established their camp in the part of the ruins of Temple Mount known as Solomon's Stables. It is widely accepted that they lived in poverty for nine years and then they were, quite suddenly, immensely rich and quickly became more powerful than any king in the world.

The most likely explanation for this instant extreme wealth is that these nine Frenchmen excavated the artefacts listed in the Copper Scroll. The Knights Templar soon became famous for their sponsoring of great churches and cathedrals, but their very first construction outside the Holy Land was at a place they called 'Temple' on St Clair land in Scotland – just one mile away from the current building known as Rosslyn.

As the great builders of the medieval age, the Knights Templar helped the stonemasons to form organised guilds and gave them low-level rituals to admit their apprentices in a manner similar to the first rung of members of their own priesthood. The master-masons of Europe were effectively the operative arm of Templarism, sharing some knowledge of celestial alignments and astronomy, but most of all sharing a somewhat ritualistic approach to their personal development.

When the Knights Templar went into decline in the mid-thirteenth century the relationship may have begun to weaken, but when the Order was arrested in 1307 and finally ceased to exist in 1314, the stonemasons guilds were left rudderless, continuing to practise their initiation ritual without any further reference to the people who had given it to them.

In 1441 William St Clair of Roslin contacted some of Europe's finest masons and asked them to come to build him a new Jerusalem. He even constructed the village of Roslin to house these master craftsmen from the Continent.

BREAKING THE CODE OF ROSSLYN

It was a wet Sunday afternoon as we sat together again to review the Norse and Jewish imagery in Rosslyn. As we were working through a time-line of events we needed to check some details. Chris reached up to the shelf to take down a copy of *The Hiram Key*. He opened it and read aloud: 'The first turf was cut in 1441 and all of the work was completed forty-five years later in 1486.'

When we wrote those words the date that the building works started did not mean anything to us, but now its significance shone out like a beacon. The construction of Rosslyn began in the year 1441 – and given that there was no year zero, that is the number of years in a full Shekinah cycle, a cycle we have since called a Venusian aeon.

Robert looked across at Chris. 'Read that starting date again.'

'You heard it right,' Chris said. '1441. Exactly 1,440 years after the year 1 of the Christian Era – when William thought Christ was born!'

Could this be coincidence?

We now know that Jesus was born under the Shekinah in 7 BCE, but nearly seven hundred years ago, when William Sinclair was planning Rosslyn, he could not have known this, although he would be well aware that there was no year zero. For William the year 1441CE would have represented a gap of precisely 1,440 years from the Bright Morning Star heralding the arrival of the messiah. This had to mean that he was following the pattern of Shekinah appearances which he must have believed to be true:

Solomon's Temple was begun 1,440 years after the Flood.

Jesus was born 1,440 years after Moses led the Israelites through the Red Sea.

Rosslyn was begun 1,440 years after the birth of Christ.

The St Clairs of Roslin were working to the ancient rules of interaction between pre-dawn rising astral bodies and mankind. Not only is Rosslyn a careful copy of the Jerusalem Temple, it is a carbon copy in terms of the time it was constructed.

So, we reasoned, William St Clair must have believed that he was building a final temple to do God's will on Earth as he expected the Shekinah was about to do God's will in Heaven.

We now absolutely believe beyond all reasonable doubt that the scrolls from under the Jerusalem Temple are still hidden under William's masterpiece – the scrolls that the Copper Scroll describes as being hidden below the Holy Sanctuary and that Masonic ritual states were brought to St Clair lands in 1140 CE.

The St Clair (now spelled Sinclair) connection to Scotland is of great significance to our research, and a number of the current clan members have been particularly helpful to us. The most active man in the field of Clan Sinclair history is, without doubt, Niven Sinclair, a London-based businessman with a general thirst for knowledge and a particular passion for anything connected to Rosslyn or the general history of the Sinclairs.

Niven is a charming and dynamic septuagenarian with the energy to shame the average twenty-year-old combined with an encyclopedic memory for facts and figures. He uses his personal wealth to fund all kinds of research and circulates the information in the form of books and videos that he commissions. In the past he has put substantial resources into the upkeep of Rosslyn, and he founded the Clan Sinclair Library which is now preserved at the Niven Sinclair Study Centre. This extensive library is magnificently housed in the dramatic setting of the old lighthouse at Noss Head, near to Wick in northern Scotland. The site is owned and run by another stalwart of the Clan Sinclair, Ian Sinclair.

In March 2002, when we thought all of our researches were complete, we received a letter from Niven concerning a new observation made by a Caithness businessman called Ashley Cowie. Robert was unavailable on the date that Niven suggested for a meeting at Rosslyn, but Chris was able to go to meet with Niven, Ashley and Ian Sinclair, who had travelled down from his library at Wick. Ashley runs a substantial fish wholesale business in the northern port of Scrabster, and he had driven down the three hundred miles that morning.

Ian was waiting in the bar of the Roslin Glen Hotel to greet Chris, and as he entered the lobby Ian bounded towards him. The twinkle in his eye and a broad grin were apparent despite the huge grey beard that almost completely obscures his features.

'Hello!' he boomed. 'Good to see you. Have we got something interesting for you!'

As they sipped tea, Ian explained that Ashley and his friend Dave were going to present their findings about St Clair establishments in Caithness and then go on to explain something about Rosslyn that Ashley thought tied into an observation mentioned in *Uriel's Machine*.

The meeting took place in a large room to the rear of the hotel. The researcher had spread dozens of very large maps and diagrams across several tables. His enthusiasm for his investigations was obvious as his fingers pointed to location after location on the maps to establish a series of patterns. He explained how he believes the distribution of early Sinclair sites in Caithness corresponds to significant megalithic structures.

After an hour or so he moved on to the main reason for the meeting.

'I'm going to show you some marks on the wall of the crypt at Rosslyn,' Ashley said, 'which I think are a complex diagram. The marks definitely pre-date the main "chapel", and it's a type of map you will recognise. This carving involves four lozenge shapes and I think they are latitude symbols.'

Ashley had remembered how in *Uriel's Machine* we showed that such lozenges were used by the Grooved Ware People as part of the proto-writing

273

they developed between 4000 and 3000 BCE. They used the diamond-shaped lozenge as a means of writing down a location. The angles of the lozenge were derived from the angles of the Sun's shadow cast at the time of the solstice sunrises. The nearer one goes to the Equator the flatter the lozenge. More northerly sites yield increasingly tall diamond symbols.

The party strolled through the bright spring sunshine, down the narrow lane to Rosslyn. Ashley led the way, keen to point out the actual carving.

As the building came into sight, the mass of steel scaffolding sitting over Rosslyn made it look like a living creature trapped in a cage. The engineers responsible for the building's maintenance believe that covering it over for seven years or so will help the stone to dry out slowly. We hope they are right, because every earlier interference seems to have upset the natural balance intended by William St Clair.

Once inside, the group split up for a few moments. Chris gazed for a few minutes at the intricate carvings that festoon every part of the walls and ceiling, then he rejoined Ashley. Together they walked down the freshly replaced stone steps to the lower crypt.

Rosslyn is a small structure that, ignoring the horrendous Victorian baptistry, is a single unit with a second small room at a lower level, known as the crypt. The crypt is a plain room with some painted carved figures on its walls. To the left side there is a tiny side chamber made of rougher stone.

Ashley stood by the right-hand wall and pointed to a faint carving.

'There it is,' he said.

There were four faint lozenges cut in a vertical arrangement, with each touching the next at their vertical points.

Ashley's voice reverberated round the empty chamber.

'I think it could be a map. The lines running down and across look as though they represent some kind of longitude and latitude, with Egypt at the bottom here. But it's these diamonds that I think could be significant, because they look exactly like the latitudinal lozenges that you showed in *Uriel's Machine*.'

Chris had seen the faint markings before, but had never given them particular attention because they seemed so unremarkable next to the heavy carving that covers most of the building. He looked carefully at the structure of the fine lines to try and establish if they could be fifteenth century or something recent. It was impossible to be sure without detailed tests, although it was obvious that someone had scratched into the wall in recent times along the lines as though to emphasise a pattern that already existed. But in some places the original line was intact, although he had no way of knowing for sure how old the marks were. However, they did appear to match other markings in the crypt which are generally accepted as being older than the main building of Rosslyn.

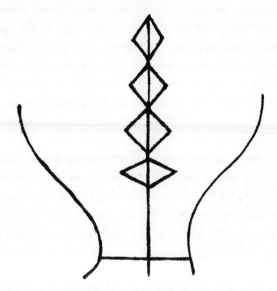

The lozenges etched into the south wall of the crypt at Rosslyn. They correspond to the four locations dearest to the St. Clair family; Jerusalem, Rosslyn, Orkney and Trondheim.

At first Chris was sceptical, because four diamond shapes on a wall can mean anything. However, he took photographs which enabled us to take accurate measurements after he returned home. The diamonds were not totally symmetrical, so the opposite internal angles of each lozenge were not exactly equal in every case, but they were very close and the averaged measurements make it clear what the author intended. In any other building, four diamond shapes could be just a decorative design, but we knew that nothing in Rosslyn is without meaning. William St Clair's great medieval mind just did not allow it.

The angles of these lozenges and their arrangement appear to suggest that Ashley could be right. If so, they are an attempt to record information in the proto-written 'language' used by the Grooved Ware People.

The bottom one is a flat shape, with internal left and right angles that gives one hundred and twenty degrees, which corresponds to the Masonic,

right-pointing equilateral triangle that we already knew to match the solstice angles at the latitude of Jerusalem.

The next symbol up this 'totem pole' is an accurate square, which corresponds to the latitude of Rosslyn itself.

This was already very interesting, because the first two shapes fitted the
known locations of the Jerusalem Temple and its later counterpart in
Scotland, but lozenges made up of two equilateral triangles and a square
are very basic geometric shapes, so it was too early to draw any firm conclusion. They said 'Jerusalem' and 'Rosslyn' to us, but they could just as
easily be a decorative device. It was the next two lozenges that would make
or break Ashley's theory. We sat down to check them, Chris with an atlas
on his lap, looking up latitudinal data, and Robert at his computer, simu-
lating solstice sunrise azimuths at different locations.

The third lozenge up was easy. It corresponded with Orkney – and
William St Clair, who designed and built Rosslyn, was the last Norwegian
Jarl (or Earl) of Orkney.

Niven Sinclair has been kind enough to pass on to us information about
the St Clair links to Orkney from Riksarkivet, the National Archives of
Norway. It says:

> Just as the year 1195 marks the subordination of the Northern
> Isles to the realms of Norway, the installation of Henry Sinclair as
> Earl of Orkney in 1379, at least in Norwegian historiography, sig-
> nals the coming transition of Orkney from Norwegian to Scottish
> sovereignty in 1468. The Sinclair earls were the last Norwegian
> earls, though of Scottish descent, and they contributed heavily to
> turning Orkney away from Scandinavia and anchoring the islands
> in the politics of northern Scotland.[4]

This transition of Orcadian sovereignty from Norway to Scotland took
place while Rosslyn chapel was being built.

We guessed that the top lozenge might be Shetland, but quickly found
that these islands are too far south to fit. But then we thought about how
the Sinclair family came to Roslin. The grandfather of Henry 'of the Holy
Shining Light of Ancient Knowledge passed down the Generations' was the
son of Rognvald, Jarl of More.

---

[4] *Historisk Tidsskrift*: Universities Forlaget, Bind 79, number 2, 2000

'Let's try Trondheim,' Robert suggested. 'I think it's about halfway up the coast of Norway.'

Chris flicked over the pages of the atlas. 'Yes, here it is. It's tucked away inside a fjord.' He read out the latitude and longitude and waited for a response. 'Well? Does it fit?'

'Almost there,' Robert said, 'I've got the two azimuths, just need to work out the angle.'

Chris looked down at the measurement of the internal angle he had taken from the photograph and waited for an age. Robert continued to click a few more keys and shuffle scraps of paper.

'One hundred and forty-eight minus twenty-five, that's one hundred and twenty-three,' he said. 'How close is it?'

'Spot on!' said Chris. 'It represents Trondheim all right.'

The top lozenge corresponds to the solstice sunrise angles of the ancient earldom of More, where the male line that made up the St Clair family originates.

Now, all of this could be coincidence, but it seems far more likely that someone carved these symbols on the wall of the crypt – using a megalithic system of proto-writing – because of the significance of the locations they describe. Everything about Rosslyn is connected to Jerusalem: its ground plan is a copy of Herod's Jerusalem Temple; its west wall is copied from the ruins of that Temple; its builders, the Sinclairs, became involved with the Knights Templar as soon as they formed in Jerusalem in 1118. Orkney belonged to the St Clair family and Trondheim was the family's ancient home.

So these are the four locations that were closest to the hearts of the St Clairs that built Rosslyn. The lozenges represent the locations in a north-to-south sequence:

Trondheim

Orkney

Rosslyn

Jerusalem

It seems that Ashley Cowie had indeed spotted something significant when he noticed this faint inscription. It's possible that the drawing itself is a diagram of something the builders planned to create within the stonework of the main building: something that has not, as yet, been discovered within this amazingly complex structure.

But we know that not everyone is going to be convinced by Ashley's observations.

Professor Alexander Thom managed to gain a huge understanding about the Grooved Ware People by applying statistical techniques to megalithic structures from Orkney to Brittany. We feel sure that reasonable people will want to make up their mind on the basis of good-quality information. We therefore decided to apply the same statistical analysis to the lozenge thesis as we did to the candidate carving. The calculation is shown in Appendix 2.

The result is a probability of at least 1:128 against those markings occurring together by chance. The case can never be proven, but it is statistically sound to assume that the lozenge arrangements are not merely coincidental. This means that we can reasonably assume the converse, which is that this set of lozenges could have been designed to represent these four locations in a Grooved Ware system of notation.

The proof of a good theory is using it to make a prediction that subsequently can be shown to be true. Ashley Cowie did not know what the angles of these lozenges would show, he just thought that they might be locations based on the technique we have shown was used by Grooved Ware People. Calculation has proved that he was right to a far greater extent than he ever imagined.

This discovery caused us to reflect on the Temple to Freyja (the Norse Venus) that the Jarls of More had built in Trondheim in around 960 CE. We already knew that this temple faced east and had two pillars at its entrance.[5] But now the year 960 CE stood out to us. This was a period equal to 2 x 480 years, which was the same length of time from Jesus' assumed birth in the year zero, as it was from the laying of the foundation stone of Solomon's Temple to the actual birth-date of Jesus.

At that time Norway was not Christian, so the date could not have been chosen for any Jesus connotation. Neither was Norway Jewish, so the timing could not be chosen to honour Solomon or the Shekinah. But the religion of the Norse did have an astral dimension, inherited from the Grooved

5 Liden, K: 'From Pagan Sanctuary to Christian Church: the Excavation of Maere Church, Trondelag', *Norwegian Archeological Review*, 2, 23–32, Oslo, 1969

Ware People who built the stone circles of Norway. For a new Temple dedicated to Freyja, the Norse Goddess who is represented by the planet Venus, the date of establishment had to be linked to the appearance of the Goddess in her role as the Bright Morning Star.[6]

THE SECRET TUNNEL

After the meeting with Ashley was concluded Chris walked around Rosslyn with his wife Caroline and Niven. No matter how many times we visit this extraordinary building there is always something new to discover, and this visit was soon to reveal new knowledge to us. The afternoon Sun was passed its zenith and their shadows were just beginning to lengthen as the three of them stood on the lawn to the southeast side of the chapel. They looked up at the turrets and spires of the medieval stonework, now shrouded in scaffolding and roofing sheets.

Then Niven began to tell the story of how he and a number of others had conducted investigations both inside and outside of the building. He recalled how, back in 1997, they had dug a number of investigative holes.

'It was here that we found the underground passageway that leads from the chapel under Gardener's Brae to the castle. We had opened up the tunnel, which was huge . . . we had a CCTV camera on a 32-foot pole, then Historic Scotland turned up and stopped us going any further.'

We knew that Niven and a number of others had conducted a series of investigations, but we had never been told any details of what they had found.

That underground passage must be very deep underground where it enters the foundation wall of Rosslyn, Chris thought, looking over the parapet and seeing how steeply the ground fell away into the valley of Gardener's Brae. He asked Niven for more details about this underground passage which Niven said 'spanned the considerable distance between the chapel and castle'.

'Did you find anything else about what's under the chapel?' Chris asked. Niven continued.

'The steps that go down from the main chapel to the crypt end on a modern floor, and most visitors assume that that is all there is to it, but it's not so.' He paused for a moment. 'There's another flight of steep steps

[6] Ellis Davidson, HE: *The Lost Beliefs of Northern Europe*

279

beneath that floor leading in the opposite direction back under the main building to a vault.'

According to Niven's information it was in this deep and centrally positioned vault that rituals of initiation with four levels or degrees were once conducted. He was not clear as to the nature of these initiations, saying that perhaps they were a secretly surviving strand of the Knights Templar or a proto-Masonic rite. But maybe these two things are the same at this point in history when Templarism metamorphosed into Freemasonry.

In Scotland today every Mason undergoes four fundamental degrees. But English Freemasonry has 'reformed' its ritual and reduced the degrees it delivers to three.

Niven also described a second staircase that was exposed just inside the north doorway when a large section of floor was lifted. Beneath the floor slabs is a six-feet-wide staircase that descends a short distance to a level below the main floor but above the lower vault. To the north at this level are the remains of several Sinclair knights laid out on slate slabs. They were interred wearing full armour. The last person lowered into this family grave was yet another Sir William Sinclair, the one who was killed at the battle of Dunbar in 1650 during the Civil War.

Niven described how the tunnel goes from a vault directly underneath the engrailed cross in the chapel roof. In *The Hiram Key* we had identified this boss, at the centre of the cross, as marking the centre of what would have been the Holy of Holies, containing the Ark of the Covenant, in Solomon's Temple. The passage continues from the hidden vault to leave the building directly below the south door just feet from the carving of the candidate being initiated by means of a ritual that we have shown statistically to be connected to modern Freemasonry.

At this point the passageway is three feet wide and five feet high where it emerges below the south door. Its roof is eight and a half feet below ground level. After a straight run of approximately twenty-five feet the passage turns ninety degrees towards the east and drops down the hillside with its roof twelve and a half feet below ground level. Parallel to the steps inside Rosslyn, there is another set of thirteen steps that lead towards the crypt. The tunnel then continues under the field towards the castle.

This is a fascinating account in its own right. As we discussed it we could not avoid asking, why would anybody spend such time and expense constructing an underground staircase to secretly join these two buildings?

One obvious answer might be that in time of siege it would provide an escape or supply route. But there seemed to be more to this than just a kind of 'super priest-hole' which would have been far more useful for making an escape had it led to the wooded river valley below the castle.

We sketched the layout of the tunnel and vaults, and as we did so we realised that we had heard this whole description of hidden chambers and secret tunnels before. It was in the ritual we used to create *The Masonic Testament*, and the story we reconstructed described exactly the same underground layout to Solomon's Temple as Niven had told us lay beneath Rosslyn.

The Fourteenth Degree of the Ancient and Accepted Scottish Rite, otherwise known as The Grand, Elect, Perfect and Sublime Mason, identifies a subterranean passageway connecting Solomon's Temple with his palace in Jerusalem, saying:

> . . . *King Solomon built a secret vault, the approach to which was through eight other vaults, all under ground, and to which a long and narrow passage led from the palace. The ninth arch or vault was immediately under the Holy of Holies of the Temple. In that apartment King Solomon held his private conferences with King Hiram and Hiram Abif.*

The degree then refers to what happened after the city was attacked:

> *After the city was taken, and the king's palace and the Temple demolished, some of the Grand Elect Masons bethought themselves of the Sacred Vault and the inestimable treasure it contained. Repairing to the ruins of the Temple at night, they found that the way which led down to the vault had not been discovered, nor the slab of marble which covered it disturbed, but upon it they found the dead body of Galaad, an eminent brother, and Chief of the Levites. He had been intrusted with the custody of the Sacred Vault and the care of the lamps that burned continually.*

So, according to Masonic ritual there was an all-important chamber underneath the Holy Temple which was connected to Solomon's palace. And we now knew that Rosslyn (the deliberate carbon copy of the last Jerusalem Temple) also had a passageway connected to the 'palace' or residence of the 'Grand Master'. The relationship between the two is remarkable.

Neither Solomon's Temple nor his palace remains even in part. However, we have explained why we believe that the subsequent temples were on the current mount and the Holy of Holies was a little distance to the west-northwest of the Dome of the Rock. It seems sensible to assume that Solomon would have built his new palace either on or very near the previous palace of the Canaanite rulers, which must have been within the original walls ascribed to King David. So as far as we can reasonably reconstruct the layout, the relationship between Rosslyn and its associated Sinclair castle is very similar to that of Solomon's Temple and his palace in terms of both distance and topology. The archaeological reality at Rosslyn fulfils the ancient dictates of the myth of Solomon's constructions in Jerusalem.

This does not necessarily mean that the ground plan of Rosslyn is a true and detailed copy of Solomon's original Temple. It might be so, or more likely this whole story was constructed around a reality established at Rosslyn and attributed to Solomon's Jerusalem. Whichever is the case, we are convinced that the accounts in Masonic ritual of a vault and a connecting tunnel beneath Solomon's Temple are directly related to the vault and tunnel beneath Rosslyn.

This fascinating information, Niven told us, links Rosslyn backwards in time to Jerusalem and forwards to modern Freemasonry.

Niven Sinclair is a wise man who understands Rosslyn at a level few others do. He has written the following about the motivation of Rosslyn's architect and builder:

> . . . Earl William St. Clair who, knowing that books could be banned or burned, chiselled out his message in the stone carvings which adorn every nook and cranny of Rosslyn Chapel. He wanted people to realise that Christianity had been hi-jacked (by Paulines) and that God and Nature was (is) ONE. He saw every leaf, every green shoot as a word of God. If there was any blasphemy or heresy it was what Man was doing to the Planet Earth from which all bounty flows. He thought that far too much attention had been paid to the Father on High and far too little attention to Mother Earth from which all bounty flows. The duality of God had to be understood. God wasn't a male deity . . . there are 'green women' in Rosslyn as well as 'green men'.

Where could such outlandish ideas have come from in the early fifteenth century – a time not noted for its liberal approach to religion?

The answer appears to be from Templarism, which itself was a merging of a Norse Venus tradition with the Jewish priests of the astral Enochian cult of the Shekinah, whose ideas lived on with the remnant who escaped to Europe. According to Jewish prophetic teaching, the purpose of Israel is to construct a community of social responsibility, of justice, compassion and brotherhood.

It is now beyond doubt that Freemasonry began in Rosslyn.

Freemasonry has always been about worshipping the Great Architect of the Universe in any way that your religion so requires you to do. Its underlying principles are clear, even if they are not necessarily embraced or demonstrated even by some of its leaders or magazine editors.

Freemasonry once taught its members:

We must be tolerant of other men's religious views, because all religions have much that is true about them, and we must combat ignorance by education, bigotry by tolerance, and tyranny by teaching true virtue.

Although we are Freemasons ourselves, we have no agenda to promote or praise it in any way. Today it is frequently criticised, but Freemasonry's own description of itself as a journey from darkness towards light seems appropriate.

THE PROBLEM OF ROSSLYN

We have made the argument that important Jewish scrolls were buried under the Jerusalem Temple around 68 CE, excavated by the Knights Templar between 1118 and 1128 CE, and brought to Kilwinning in Scotland in 1140 CE before being re-interred under Rosslyn by Earl William St Clair.

These documents are effectively the most important of the 'Dead Sea Scrolls' – of which the lesser ones were found at Qumran.

As we have mentioned, when we launched our first book together at Rosslyn Chapel one of the trustees publicly announced that the Rosslyn Chapel Trust would support an excavation if a world-class team of scholars, including some from Scotland, were to be assembled. For some reason the Trust was to change its mind.

One year later Niven Sinclair and his colleagues found vaults under

Rosslyn and a tunnel leading to the castle. Later in that same year we arranged for Dr Jack Miller, Head of Studies in geology at Cambridge University, and Dr Fernando Neaves from the Colorado School of Mines to conduct non-invasive underground radar scans around the outside of Rosslyn. But with days to go, permission for the scanning was withdrawn by the Trustees. They suggested that we might be able to work with them on future, commercially based scanning, but we would be required to agree to keep the results secret and even deny that the scans had happened if so required by the Trust.

We declined these terms on the grounds they were anti-academic. Whether the discoveries made by Niven and his team led to the sudden change of heart, or not, we have no way of knowing.

As we said earlier, in 1998 we took more world-class academics to Rosslyn, including Professor James Charlesworth of Princeton University, who subsequently submitted a detailed proposal that involved Scottish and foreign archaeologists. To the best of our knowledge he has received no reply beyond a non-committal acknowledgement.

We are also concerned at the amount of work obviously being conducted under Rosslyn, apparently as part of the restoration work, and the wide trenches dug across Gardener's Brae, to lay fairly modest drain pipes. We have no reason to doubt that the Trustees have anything but the best interests of the building at heart – but the building was designed for a purpose that cannot be ignored. We believe it was constructed to house precious documents from the second century BCE to 68 CE, which clearly takes in the all-important period of the arrival of the Christian Messiah. If we really want to understand the man who claimed to be the messiah, we must excavate Rosslyn.

Like many other professional Dead Sea Scroll scholars, Professor Charlesworth is convinced that there were other scrolls besides those found at Qumran. The evidence that they now reside below Rosslyn is irresistible. The information that we have assembled from the vast array of Masonic rituals gives us an insight into the mind of the man who last possessed these documents before he placed them deep below Rosslyn. We know that our self-set task to uncover where the rituals of Freemasonry came from, and what they mean, is not yet complete. A proper, and public, investigation of Rosslyn is still needed.

But when we sat down and reviewed what we had discovered, and completed some detailed time-lines from the dates and events, a fuller picture of the meaning of *The Masonic Testament* and its Temple of Roslin began to emerge.

CONCLUSIONS

The St Clair family which built Roslin is descended from a marriage between French noble families and the Norse Jarls of More.

Ashley Cowie, a businessman from Caithness, found a series of lozenge-type symbols in the crypt at Rosslyn, which we decoded to read Jerusalem, Roslin, Orkney and Trondheim, the main centres of political power for the St Clair family.

Niven Sinclair shared with us the results of his drilling investigation beneath Rosslyn, undertaken a year after the publication of *The Hiram Key*, and described an underground layout that fits exactly the subterranean design of Solomon's Temple which we had found in Masonic ritual.

Chapter Thirteen

NEITHER HARMLESS NOR FUN

THE GREAT SECRET OF THE ASTRAL RELIGION

So after many years of research and four books together we have found the missing link between Judaism and Christianity on the one hand and the secret Freemasonic tradition on the other. There is a hidden astral agenda, repressed in mainstream Judaism and Christianity, that has survived in the Masonic tradition and been reinforced by Norse beliefs in the power of the Bright Morning Star of Venus.

It is hardly controversial to observe that there was once a widespread belief that the movement of stars and planetary bodies control our destinies. Whilst modern astrologers have their own practices, Freemasonry harks back to an ancient form that was based on the astronomical principle that Venus is the metronome of the Earth.

We see that this might well have been what had alarmed the Church about our researches, and it was on one level an extraordinary discovery. Our research described in *Uriel's Machine* had encouraged us to believe that the Freemasonic tradition was to do with the development of real science, that it was against superstition, yet now not only Christianity but also Freemasonry seem to us to be in danger of being reduced to bunkum – and astrological bunkum at that.

Surely there must be something more to the 6,000-year-old hidden mysteries of nature and science than a superstitious belief that a bright star on the horizon at your moment of birth will ensure good fortune for the rest of your days?

Our time-line evidence showed that it must have been the Grooved Ware People who either began the study of the 'Venus effect' or certainly provide the most ancient evidence for this particular form of astronomy. What advantage could they have gained from this type of astrological belief, which had been so important that it was passed down the generations to the Phoenicians/ Jews, the Norse and finally the Freemasons?

It appears that all mainstream scientists today reject the concept of the movement of heavenly bodies having any effect on human affairs. Writing in the *Sunday Times*, Professor Richard Dawkins said this about astrology:

Scientific truth is too beautiful to be sacrificed for the sake of light entertainment or money . . . If the methods of astrologers were really shown to be valid it would be a fact of signal importance for science. Under such circumstances astrology should be taken seriously indeed. But if – as all indications agree – there is not a smidgen of validity in any of the things that astrologers so profitably do, this, too, should be taken seriously and not indulgently trivialised. We should learn to see the debauching of science for profit as a crime . . . It isn't as though it would be difficult to find evidence for astrology, if there were any to be had. A statistical tendency, however slight, for people's personalities to be predictable from their birthdays, over and above the expected difference between winter and summer babies, would be a promising start.

He makes the point that for any hypothesis to be taken seriously by rational people there has to be at least some attempt to describe a causal link behind the observed phenomena. By this he means that by now there should be some kind of observable correlation between the movement of the stars in the sky, the astronomically predicted outcome, and the fate of the individuals concerned. Quite simply, there is no evidence at all for any kind of link.

What is clear from the background research for this book, is that the driving force behind the successful expansion which spread the ideas of this Stone-Age cult was their discovery of the principles of trade and the division of labour. These economic ideas created resource surpluses which were used by astronomer-priests to build great temples in centres of wealth and civilisation.

The knowledge they amassed from long-term observation enabled them to predict the future; to know when to sow and when to reap; when to mate animals, when to sail on the tide and when to leave the boats hauled up the shingle; when there would be long hours of daylight to travel, hunt and trade, and when darkness would linger late into the morning. But then, at some time in the distant past, kings began to believe that if the heavens could predict these otherwise unknowable secrets of nature they could also give guidance on aspects of their own lives. This was when astronomy and its wanton daughter, astrology, were born.

So, in our terms, these astronomer-priests practised astrology. They or their kings wanted their children born when the Goddess was close to the Great Sun God. They presided over sexual festivals in or around their temples at the vernal equinox and 'harvested' their children the following winter solstice. And (like Abraham) some of them were prepared to burn some of their children alive to show their gratitude to the Most High.

They timed their procreation to the movements of their shining goddess as she smiled down on their intercourse from the sky. They may have believed this behaviour was scientific, but to us it is just superstitious non-sense, fascinating as history – but still nonsense. Their traders sailed into new areas, established way stations as they travelled, and by doing so carried their religious ideas to new converts. It must have been an easy religion to gain converts for, since as far as we could see it involved taking part in sexual orgies and, for the leaders at least, becoming favourites of the Goddess of the Bright Morning Star and thus destined to be rich and successful.

The Sumerians, Egyptians and Phoenicians each took elements of Grooved Ware science, economics and religion to use themselves. The intellectual principle that drove the invention of the proto-writing of the early Grooved Ware traders provided the breakthrough accounting system developed in Mesopotamia and the alphabet-based writing created by the Canaanites of Phoenicia. Their knowledge and superstitions relating to the stars and the planets entered many developing cultures from Egypt to Norway. As we have already discussed, all of these groups built great temples, aligned to the movements of the heavens, and created enormous wealth and power.

These three influences – Abraham of Sumer, founding father of Judaism; Moses of Egypt, creator of the Holy Law of the One True God; and Hiram of Tyre, Phoenician king, builder of the Temple of Solomon, and both son and husband to 'Our Lady of Heaven' – all came together to eventually form the beginning of the monotheistic religions of Judaism, Christianity and Islam.

These astrological ideas from European Stone-Age religion were the intellectual driving force behind the belief system of the Enochian Jews which said that great events happened and great leaders (messiahs) were born when the Shekinah, the visible glory of God's presence, shines just before the sunrise. And that if the Shekinah fails to appear this is a sign of God withdrawing His favour.

But the more we thought about it, the more obvious it became that this ancient cult still survives in odd remnants to this day. Freemasonry and astrology are two traditions which best preserve the belief that the position of the heavenly bodies affects the actions of individuals on Earth. At first sight these two belief systems are very different, but our research was showing that each has retained different elements of the 6,000-year-old ideas of the Grooved Ware priests.

Freemasonry has preserved much of the cult's observational science, encoded in oral traditions, modes of ritual movement and mythical tales, but this heritage is fast disappearing as Freemasons desperately try to modernise their practices and in doing so discard anything in their ritual which is hard to understand or in mild collision with intolerant Christian groups. We have found that Freemasons were at the forefront of the beginning of modern science, at the time of the formation of the Royal Society of London, but we also knew that the successful scientist-Freemasons of the seventeenth century had all been fanatical believers in astrology.[1]

Much as we disliked the idea, it was clear that we were going to have to further investigate astronomy's wayward sibling, astrology. The history of belief in astrology has been tackled by numerous observers, but where could we begin to analyse any underlying principle in a subject so entirely unscientific?

Claims to offer a scientific basis for astrology have been made in the past, for instance in the well-known series of statistical studies by Dr Michel Gauquelin. Gauquelin attempted to adopt a similar approach to astrology as Newton used with gravity. Newton could prove what was happening to the movements of the planets by analysis of many observations, but he was

---

[1] Lomas, Robert: *The Invisible College*

unable to propose a mechanism to explain it. His rules, however, did allow accurate prediction, and the return of Halley's comet proved the accuracy of his equations.

Gauquelin's study of astrology has no such predictive outcome; it merely demonstrates patterns which do not fit the horoscopes of astrology. The comment that psychologist Hans Eysenck made about the ambiguous statistical evidence of Michael Gauquelin sums up the response of most scientists.

> *Emotionally, I would prefer Gauquelin's results do not hold, but rationally, I must accept that they do.*[2]

The problem with the findings is a lack of any plausible causal mechanism to explain what has been observed. Gauquelin studied the horoscopes of a number of professions. He looked at actors, scientists, sports champions, soldiers and writers. He found statistically significant evidence that great actors tended to be born when Jupiter was rising or had just passed its zenith; sports champions tend to be born when Mars is rising or has just passed its zenith, as do soldiers; great scientists when Saturn is rising or has just passed its zenith; great writers are born to a rising or culminating Moon.

Gauquelin went to great lengths to try to identify the personality traits associated with each of these occupations, calling the traits for actors Jupiter factors; for scientists, Saturn factors; for writers, Moon factors; and for sports champions and soldiers, Mars factors. He devoted a whole chapter to discussing the effect of personality on success and character formation. He struggled with his own evidence which showed that many people shared the personality traits he identified with his successful individuals, and even when they worked in the same profession did not have the requisite planets rising or culminating in their horoscopes. Part of his difficulty stemmed from trying to define a measure of success. He resorted to categorising his sports champions as 'weak-willed' and 'strong-willed' champions. The strong-willed individuals had Mars rising or culminating, the weak-willed didn't. This approach looks very like a desperate attempt to explain data that did not fit his expectations.

But what were Gauquelin's expectations? He wanted to either prove or

---

[2] Eysenck, HJ & Nias, DK: *Astrology, Science or Supersition?*, Maurice Temple Smith, 1982

disprove astrology, so he applied the rules and techniques of astrology to trying to explain his data. He looked for Mars in the horoscope of soldiers and sports champions, because astrology predicted it would be there; he applied the same logic to Saturn, Jupiter and the Moon with respect to other professions. He did find these planets in the right place for a very large number of his 'successful' individuals, but they were in totally the wrong place, in terms of the lore of astrology, when he looked at less 'successful' exponents of the same occupation.

These results led Richard Dawkins to comment, in that same *Sunday Times* article:

If there is good evidence (i.e. better than the often quoted but non-robust Gauquelin attempt) that some other kinds of astrology work, well and good. I have to say that I'd be extremely surprised.

So Dawkins points out that without observational evidence which allows accurate and verifiable predictions to be made, there is no case for astrology.

We read the work of Dr Michel Gauquelin, outlined above, and whilst his statistics look interesting, and his methodology looks accurate, his explanations show why Richard Dawkins is so dismissive of his ideas.

Here is the reason Gauquelin gives to explain some of his findings where he shows statistical evidence that a higher proportion of actors are born when Jupiter is rising:

Within its mother's womb, the infant is also isolated from the world. Perhaps his brain is already a control center capable of receiving signals from outer space and relaying the orders throughout his entire body. Obviously, the procedure underlying parturition is not a simple one. But the infant is not deaf to the messages coming from the cosmos and he reacts to them. Nature has decided that at his birth man is to be entwined in the invisible network of forces which link the earth and sky.[3]

On reflection we decided that we agree with Professor Dawkins that this is not a robust basis for a causal principle of astrological prediction. Sadly,

[3] Gauquelin, M: *Cosmic Influences on Human Behaviour*, Aurora Press, 1994

our research finding of a belief that messiahs and leaders will be born and important events take place when the Shekinah (a Venus/Mercury conjunction) is rising just before the Sun has all the hallmarks of the superstition Dawkins condemns so succinctly.

IS IT IN OUR STARS?

Scanning through our clippings file we had one of those strokes of good luck that happen at unexpected moments. In an article taken from the *Daily Mail*, we saw the headline: 'Why I Now Believe Astrology Is a Science'. The piece was written by an old friend of ours, the author and researcher Colin Wilson (which was the main reason we had kept the clipping). Colin's article was about an anonymous woman donor who was funding a new Professorial Chair in Astrology at an unnamed British university.

Knowing that astrology had once been a respectable university subject, but had ceased to be so after Newton's discovery of the law of gravity, we were intrigued by Colin Wilson's report that there was a serious interest in reviving it as an academic subject. He had ended his article with these words:

> *The woman behind the £500,000 donation has no reason to feel ashamed of wanting to reintroduce astrology as a university subject, even though it has been dismissed by the universities for more than three centuries. I can assure her that while we still do not know quite why it works, it undoubtedly does.*[4]

With our new-found curiosity about the background to astrological belief we now took a far greater interest in what had prompted Colin to say this about his own experiences with astrology. His article continued:

> *I decided then that I ought to study astrology more closely, but never seemed to find the time. Then a Sunday newspaper asked me if I would write an astrology column and I decided this was the opportunity I had been waiting for . . . and rather dubiously launched myself on a career as an astrological journalist.*

[4] Wilson, Colin: 'Why I Now Believe Astrology Is a Science', *Daily Mail*, Thursday 22 March, 2001

It proved harder work than I had expected. There can be no guess-work involved. The position of all the planets had to be worked out, together with their aspects (oppositions, conjunctions, etc) and this took days.

But gradually I began to get a feeling for horoscopes. And this was confirmed when I received a letter from a woman whose son had committed suicide, enclosing the exact time and place of his birth. I spent a day casting his horoscope, and as I did so, the hairs on the back of my neck began to rise.

What was emerging was a personality – his enthusiasms, his hopes and his doubts about his future. It was these doubts that had led to his suicide. I sent the horoscope to his mother and she replied that the description of her son had shocked her with its accuracy.[5]

After reading this Robert just had to phone Colin and ask him if he really accepted any sort of scientific basis for astrology. Colin was very helpful and quite happy to chat about astrology. He explained that he had initially been extremely sceptical about the claims of astrology before he studied the subject, which he did in order to write an astrological column for the *Observer* newspaper. Whilst writing that regular column and reading the letters he got from his readers he became convinced that there was something real at the root of the subject.

When we pressed him what that 'something' might be, he admitted that he really did not know. His belief was based on the logical observation that the insights he gained from astrological methods were accurate far more often than he could reasonably expect by chance. About one thing, however, Colin was quite clear.

'What influences human beings is not the stars but the positions of the planets,' he said.

'But do you think it is a subject which is worth studying at university degree level?' we asked him.

'Well,' he replied. 'Some universities offer courses in subjects that make astrology sound dull and old-fashioned. You know Robert, your old university, Salford, today offers Business Economics and Gambling, De

[5] Wilson, Colin: 'Why I Now Believe Astrology Is a Science'

Montfort University offers a degree in Golf Course Studies, you can read for a BSc in Horse Studies at Nottingham, Kent has a course on the Theory and Practice of Stand-Up Comedy. The University of Plymouth, where my good friend Dr Percy Seymour works [an astronomer who also believes there is something real in astrology], can offer you degrees in the Science of Perfume or Surfing Science and Technology. Among these, astrology sounds positively conservative,' Colin finished with a chuckle.

Our stunned silence must have persuaded Colin that we weren't yet convinced, as he added a little more detail about that controversial bequest which had prompted us to phone him.

'Don't forget,' he said, 'the committee in charge of distributing that half million pounds can hardly be accused of supporting star-gazing weirdos, since some of the money is going to Professor Chris Bagley, of Southampton University, and he's using it to fund a group whose main aim is to prove that astrology is bunk.'

We quoted Professor Richard Dawkins to Colin, reminding him of the statement: 'Astrology is neither harmless nor fun, and we should see it as an enemy of truth.'

Colin, however, remained convinced that there is a link, however hard to explain, between the personalities and actions of people and the positions of the planets. We told him of our findings, and how disturbed we were that Freemasonry seemed to be largely preserving ancient astrological mumbo-jumbo in its rituals.

'My advice is not to dismiss astrology out of hand,' he said. 'I know it works, but I can only offer you anecdotal evidence and you seem to want more than that. Why not look for your own evidence?'

Robert's conversation with Colin Wilson persuaded us that he is totally sincere in his belief that there is some unknown scientific principle behind astrological beliefs. If we were to make sense of the secret stream of astral belief we had found preserved in *The Masonic Testament* we needed to know more about early astrology.

A STAR-STREWN HISTORY

In 150 BCE a Jewish writer by the name of Eupolemus wrote his account of the history of his people.[6] Dead Sea Scrolls scholar Geza Vermes, who

---

[6] Black, M & Rowley, HH (ed): *Peake's Commentary on the Bible*

translated a number of astrological texts found among the Qumran scrolls, drew attention to a claim Eupolemus made about Abraham, who the Bible assures us came from the city of Ur of the Chaldees (in the land of Sumer):

> For if many Jews frowned on astrology, others, such as the
> Hellenistic Jewish writer Eupolemus, credited its invention to
> Abraham.[7]

So around the time that the Essene community was established early in the second century BCE, there was a popular tradition that Abraham had been involved in the practice of astrology before he went to Egypt. This could only have been based on Sumerian traditions. The question we needed to return to was, what did the Sumerians believe about astral events, particularly at dawn?

We decided to look more closely at the Epic of Gilgamesh.

Tablet XXI of the epic describes how Zisudra, who survived the great flood with which the gods destroyed mankind, tells Gilgamesh the 'secret of the gods'. He describes how as he is building his Ark, on the instructions of Enki (the chief god), he is given a sign as 'on the horizon there appeared the first intimations of dawn', but at this point in the story he does not say what it is.[8]

He then describes how as the great flood begins he again watches the place where the Sun is about to rise, but a black cloud covers the horizon and he cannot see Ishtar, Goddess of Love, who he hears pleading for him in the council of gods. He continues each day to look eastwards just before dawn until the flood subsides, and then he describes how Ishtar, the Lady of the Gods (the planet Venus), arrives:

> She lifted up the magnificent jewel which Anu the Great God [the
> Sun] had made according to her desire.[9]

This appeared to us to be a description of the bright planet Venus rising just before the Sun close to another smaller bright planet, possibly Mercury. Exactly how Venus rises when it shines into the slot above the door at Newgrange.

The theme of the importance of observing the sunrise recurs in Tablet

[7] Vermes, G: Scripture and Tradition in Judaism, Penguin, 1973
[8] Temple, R: He Who Saw Everything: a Verse Translation of the Epic of Gilgamesh, Century, 1991
[9] Temple, R: He Who Saw Everything: a Verse Translation of the Epic of Gilgamesh

IX, where we are told of Gilgamesh that 'He rose just before the Sun,' and by doing this is enabled to see a garden of bejewelled shrubs. And in Tablet VIII there is again a recurrent chorus which says: '*On the horizon, there appeared / the first intimations of dawn*' (a familiar phrase from Tablet XXI). Robert Temple comments on it:

> *These two lines are repeated at intervals throughout this tablet.*
> *Their inclusion is neither accidental nor for poetic purposes but*
> *rather reflects the obsession of the Babylonian astronomer-priests*
> *with what are known as 'helical risings' of key stars and planets. A*
> *helical rising takes place when a star or planet rises over the*
> *horizon at the same moment as the 'first intimations of dawn'.*[10]

Tablet III has more information, when Gilgamesh makes a speech to the people of his city of Uruk saying:

> *The men of Uruk know, there I will be strong, I travel the wheel-*
> *rim . . . I will enter the city gate of Uruk, I will turn towards . . .,*
> *and the Akitu Festival. I will celebrate the Akitu Festival. The*
> *Akitu Festival shall be arranged and joyful singing shall be heard.*[11]

In a footnote, Robert Temple identifies the Akitu Festival as a New Year celebration, held at the time of the vernal equinox. The 'wheel-rim' that Gilgamesh refers to is the path of the zodiac, and he seems to be describing how he will move along this roadway of the gods. Later in his journey he meets with Ishtar (Venus), who asks him to become her lover, but he refuses saying she is not constant. 'In the cold seasons you will surely fail me,' he says, going on to list her lovers and to recount how they die in the autumn and are reborn in the spring. Here the mythmaker is trying to explain why some zodiacal constellations can only be seen in the summer months, and as the Sun moves south in winter these stars disappear from the sky. The tilt of the ecliptic and the movement of the Earth around the Sun were not known then, so stories of lovers who die and are reborn were substituted.

When Ishtar hears this list of her evil deeds she goes to Anu, god of the firmament, who gives her the halter rope of the great bull of the heavens which she leads to the city of Uruk:

---

[10] Temple, R: *He Who Saw Everything: a Verse Translation of the Epic of Gilgamesh*
[11] Temple, R: *He Who Saw Everything: a Verse Translation of the Epic of Gilgamesh*

With a snort of the Bull of Heaven, pits were opened and a hundred young men of Uruk fell into them, with his second snort, pits were opened and two hundred young men of Uruk fell into them. With his third snort, pits were opened and Enkidu fell into them.[12]

This seems to be describing a helical rising of Venus in the constellation of Taurus the Bull. As the bright star of the Goddess rose before the Sun, then at the time this myth was written the planet would appear to be leading the constellation of the Bull. Robert Temple states in his commentary that 'The Babylonians were well aware of this phenomenon', the precession of the equinoxes, whereby the Sun appears to rise in a different section of the sky every 2,000 years, although they did not use the same zodiac constellations as we do today. He also points out that they would have been aware that the Sun, and pre-dawn Venus, rose in the group of stars we now call Taurus between the years 4000 and 2000 BCE.[13]

The heroes defeat the Bull of Heaven and then Anu, the god of the firmament, calls together his council of Gods to decide what to do. This motif of God's Council we recognised from the first chapter of *The Masonic Testament*, where God consults with the members of this council, who are the stars of the heavens, before deciding to make Adam.

Tablet IX again describes Gilgamesh watching the sky before the rising of the Sun. '*He knows the moment of rising is near*' and as '*the day grows bright*' he once more sees an array of bejewelled shrubs. The atmospheric flickering caused by the thickness of the air layer when viewing celestial objects near the horizon is described: '*The splendour of their scintillation disturbs the mountains which keep watch over the rising and the setting of the Sun God.*'

At this point a reference to the nature of Gilgamesh's birth is made that has echoes in the Dead Sea Scrolls, which say of the messiah that '*his spirit consists of eight parts in the House of Light of the second column and one in the House of Darkness. And this is his birthday on which he is to be born.*'[14] Gilgamesh is described as '*two-thirds god, one third man*'. Robert Temple comments that this statement is significant in the Sumerian sexagesimal-based mathematics in that it links Gilgamesh with the number forty, which is two-thirds of the basic 60 units used to measure minutes and

---

[12] Temple, R: *He Who Saw Everything: a Verse Translation of the Epic of Gilgamesh*
[13] Temple, R: *He Who Saw Everything: a Verse Translation of the Epic of Gilgamesh*
[14] Vermes, G: *The Dead Sea Scrolls in English*

seconds. The number forty we already knew is closely linked with the orbital periods of the planet Venus. Temple goes on to say: '*Other aspects of the theme of two thirds relate to the planet Mercury, with whom Gilgamesh is associated*.' Of the twelve degrees of the zodiac, Mercury wanders across eight degrees, or two-thirds of the zodiacal pathway.

But we needed to know more about the obsession of the Assyrian and Babylonian astronomers with helical risings, and the place we went to look was in the Department of Western Asiatic Antiquities in the British Museum. There are stored some baked clay tablets, dated around 1500 BCE, known as the Venus tablets of Ammizaduga. The tablets themselves look a little battered, having been dropped or somehow cracked more than once in their long history. They are roughly rectangular, and tightly covered with closely impressed lines of cuneiform script.

When the text was decoded it was discovered that these tablets are a list of the morning and evening appearances of Venus over a twenty-one-year period, and the tablets show how the movements of the planet are interpreted as a means of divining the intentions of the Goddess. It contains important information such as the comment that '*when Venus stands high, love making will be pleasurable*', always a useful thing to know, we thought.

But these Venus tablets are not the earliest evidence we could find for astral religion in the Mesopotamian region. In the Louvre there is a stela, dated *circa* 2100 BCE, from the reign of Naram-Sin which shows this king as a victorious leader, standing looking out towards a horizon where the Moon and Venus are rising just before the Sun.

Historian Peter Whitfield said about the beginnings of Sumerian astrology.

There was thus in Mesopotamian thought an intimate connection between the divine realm [the heavens] and the realm of nature and man. Moreover there existed a received wisdom, a set of skills, a science, by which this connection might be understood and that science was the province of the 'ummanu'. But the ummanu were at this stage exclusively royal counsellors, neither their special wisdom nor the events they studied were of concern to the population at large, but only to the king. The omens concerned his conduct, his family, his enemies, his kingdom, his harvests and so on. There is here undoubtedly the seed of the doctrine that the microcosm and the macrocosm are linked but that link was limited and concentrated in the person of the king.[15]

Whitfield explains that the Sumerian ideas about astral kingship and the study of omens came from a tradition, explained in a document found in the library of Ashurbanipal, which said that these skills were learned from a group of divine teachers who lived on the Earth in ancient times and taught science, philosophy and law to men.[16] He also speculates that the tradition of interpreting omens was empirical, and that at some time in the past, relationships had been noted and a causal link assumed. At first this was applied just to the fortunes of the king and his kingdom.

So the basis of astrology appears to be that the priests made careful observations and recorded what they saw in the heavens. They then looked for significant events that coincided with the appearances in the sky before going on to make the unwarranted assumption that the stars and planets had actually caused those events. The power of prophecy would then rest in predicting when similar astronomical patterns would be found. When the astral event was seen, the priest could advise for and against various actions dependent on the outcome the last time the pattern was seen.

Dr Whitfield quotes a horoscope from the time of Ashurbanipal saying:

When on the fifth of the month of Nissan, the rising Sun appears like a red torch, white clouds rise from it and the wind blows from the east, then there will be a solar eclipse on the 28th or 29th day of that month; the king will die that very month, and his son ascend to the throne.[17]

He explains how dummy kings were sometimes enthroned for dangerous periods to avoid the effects of bad omens.

The Baylonian year began with the ancient Akitu Festival, at the time of the new moon after the Vernal Equinox,[18] the time we still celebrate as Easter. The Babylonian names for the Sun, the Moon and Venus were Shamash, Sin and Ishtar, and these were the three heavenly bodies that most interested the Sumerian astronomers, particularly when they all rose close together. The more we looked at the beginnings of astrology the more

---

15 Whitfield, P: *Astrology, a History,* The British Library, 2001
16 Whitfield, P: *Astrology, a History*
17 Whitfield, P: *Astrology, a History*
18 Temple, R: *He Who Saw Everything: a Verse Translation of the Epic of Gilgamesh*

it seemed to share the same roots as the Phoenician, Jewish and Freemasonic beliefs. And more to the point, it was not looking as if there was any scientific basis to it at all, beyond a need to develop basic techniques of astronomy to predict the appearance of the 'gods'.

By 1000 BCE Mesopotamian astronomers developed a star-based calendar which defined the seasons of the year in terms of the pre-dawn risings of the three brightest stars in the sky at that season. These tablets show an intense interest in the objects which rise just before the Sun. The clay plates, which can also be seen in the British Museum, are circular and divided into twelve segments by means of lines which look rather like cake slices. Each twelfth represents a month of the year, and within its segment are inscribed the details of the helically rising stars. The purpose of these 'Three Stars Each' tablets was to enable the astrologers to warn the king of impending bad fortune.

As we have mentioned, a crude form of zodiac was in use as early as 2000 BCE in Mesopotamia, but it wasn't until the Jewish king Zerubbabel was building the Second Temple in Jerusalem, mid-first century BCE, that the same people (now referred to as Babylonians) developed the zodiac into a form we would recognise today.[19] This was a major step forward because it provided a reference scale where the position of either the Sun or any of the bright planets could be described.

The zodiac is a band of shapes in the sky, formed by very distant fixed stars, which today we call constellations. In order from our modern names of Aries to Pisces, the Babylonians gave the shapes the names Luhunga, Mul, Mas, Kusu, Ura, Absin, Zibanitu, Girtab, Pa, Suhur, Gu and Zib.[20] Each constellation marks a segment of sky, but not all of the star shapes are equally big, and to compensate for this difference in size the Babylonian astrologers also invented the concept of zodiac signs. In today's system each sign is exactly 30 degrees wide, no matter how much sky its marker constellation occupies.

The Babylonians used this system from about 400 BCE down to 100 BCE, but they never took account of the problem of precession (a slight wobble in the axis of rotation of the Earth which makes the sunrise at the vernal equinox appear to move one degree every 72 years, as viewed against the backdrop of the zodiac constellations). When they first set up their calendar the vernal equinox of the Sun was in Luhunga; now it has moved on one sign to Zib.

[19] Whitfield, P: *Astrology, a History*
[20] Whitfield, P: *Astrology, a History*

This oversight has survived into modern-day astrology and it means that the star signs you read in the papers don't agree with the zodiacal constellations which appear in the sky above you. This would seem to be a major problem if you are using the stars in the sky above to predict what is going to happen down on Earth. But it seems most astrologers don't actually look at the sky, and so this mismatch, between star signs used in horoscopes and the real stars above our heads, tends to be glossed over by astrology textbooks. This definition shows how the issue is fudged:

> The astrological birth chart is a map of the zodiac and the planets set up for the time and place of birth of the individual to whom it refers. The zodiac is a belt in the heavens extending about eight degrees on each side of the path followed by the sun and containing the path of the planets. It is divided into 12 equal sectors known as the signs. Each sign therefore measures 30 degrees and is named after one of the constellations. The signs and constellations do not coincide, though they slightly overlap.[21]

More advanced astrological texts try to address this point of the difference between star-sign dates and the stars in the evening sky. But we were interested to note that these more aware astrologers seem to be claiming that it is the sidereal position of the Earth in its orbit around the Sun that really matters, not the backdrop of stars. That certainly tied in with everything we knew about the timing of festivals at the vernal equinox. Commenting on the problem of precession, astrologer Robert Parry said:

> While acutely aware of the distinction, almost all astrologers from the time of Ptolemy in the 2nd century AD have chosen to employ the zodiac based on the moving equinoctial points, the tropical zodiac, as it is called, rather than on the constellations.[22]

What he seems to be saying is that many astrologers simply rehash what is written down in hoary old textbooks on astrology, rather than trying to explain what they really think is happening.

We also found that Peter Whitfield shared our view that astral cycles were observed over time, as were various outcomes, and the result was the

---

[21] Anderton, Bill: *Life Cycles*, Quantum, 1990
[22] Parry, Robert: *Astrology's Complete Book of Self-Defence*, Quantum, 1990

creation of a supposed link between what happened in the sky and human outcomes down on Earth:

> *If schemes of lucky and unlucky days were added to an obser-*
> *vation of celestial omens on the same day, then a movement is*
> *started which is moving unmistakably in the direction of personal*
> *astrology. That this movement did occur around 400 BC [in*
> *Mesopotamia], linking the influence of the planets with the idea of*
> *lucky and unlucky days, is certain from the survival of the first*
> *cuneiform horoscopes. In these tablets, positions of planets are*
> *given with the Zodiac signs, and interpretations about the future*
> *life of the child are sometimes drawn out.*[23]

It was during this period of astrological proliferation and the extension of the idea of an astral destiny to private individuals, apart from the king, that the name Chaldean (meaning Sumerian, Babylonian or Mesopotamian) became a synonym for fortune-teller or astrologer in the Bible. The main contribution the Chaldeans made to science was in the fields of arithmetic and observational astronomy, seemingly done in the interests of fortune-telling. Professor Richard Dawkins would certainly not have approved of their motives.

But these would-be fortune-tellers were the first observers to write down the results of astronomical observations in any language that we can still read. Writing, as we mentioned in *Uriel's Machine*, greatly increases the rate of innovation in a society, as it makes it far simpler to share information between a large number of people, and even between people of different generations, without the time-consuming chore of verbal rote learning. As we stood in front of the Venus tablets in the British Museum we felt very close to the astrologer-priests who collected all that dense mass of data over so many years. We knew that the Chaldeans were compulsive list-makers – they made lists of everything: astral events, medical symptoms, materials, weather patterns, political outcomes – but only when we saw the pains that went into the creation of one of these stone-hard lists did we really begin to understand just how much effort it must have taken. Peter Whitfield describes the peak of Chaldean astrology:

[23] Whitfield, P: *Astrology, a History*

The entire heavens became a tapestry upon which complex patterns of celestial meaning were constantly being woven, and which the maturing skill of the astrologer attempted to interpret. And the crucial change was that these celestial patterns affected everybody – they were no longer tied to the king and his court. The charting of celestial positions, and the ability to draw out their meaning required special astronomical and divinatory skills, and it clearly implies the existence of a set of systematic beliefs about the power of the heavens over human life. This proto-astrology therefore combined aspects of exact science with religious or philosophical principles.[24]

But it was other civilisations which profited from this groundwork. Soon after this peak Babylon was invaded, first by Cyrus the Persian in 539 BCE and later by the Greeks under Alexander. The use of cuneiform writing declined, and by 100 BCE cuneiform was used only for recording religious and astrological texts. Soon after this time the Chaldeans faded into memory. Their great cities were covered by drifting sand and their baked-clay libraries lost and forgotten until the twentieth century, when European archaeologists dug them out of the high tells of the Mesopotamian desert.

The Achaemenid empire of the Persians encompassed Egypt, where Ptolemy developed the Chaldeans' ideas about linked lists into definitive cause and effect. This is what he had to say about the way the stars affect human life in his book *Tetrabiblos*:

A very few considerations would make it apparent to all that a certain power emanating from the eternal ethereal substance is dispersed through and permeates the whole region about the earth, which throughout is subject to change, since the primary sublunar elements, fire and air, are encompassed and changed by the motions of the ether.[25]

It sounds very like Michel Gauquelin's description, that we mentioned earlier, of the way the stars control a baby's time of birth by sending 'cosmic messages'. Interesting yes, scientific no. And we couldn't help being disturbed by the fact that some modern astrologers, publishing books within

[24] Whitfield, P: *Astrology, a History*
[25] Kitson, A (ed.): *History and Astrology*, Mandala, 1989

the last few years, still cite Ptolemy as a valuable source of astrological wisdom. Perhaps Ptolemy's thinking influenced Dr Gauquelin's ideas. Then as we looked more closely at the Greek development of astrology we began to realise why. The ancient Greeks developed modern astrology, and it hasn't changed much at all since.

The Greeks fused ideas from Mesopotamia, Persia, Egypt and Palestine. We already knew about the influence of Greek ideas in the writing down of the New Testament, but they also established astrology. Greek astrology developed away from its Chaldean roots, as a means of predicting the destiny of the kingdom, and became the personal fortune-telling tool it is today.

But where did this leave our quest for understanding? Was the pattern of the Shekinah, which we had found in *The Masonic Testament*, early observational science? Or was it just the beginnings of the ornate system of gimcrack fortune-telling the Greeks later systematised? One thing we were unsure about was if there was anything real to find or not. Colin Wilson had assured us that he thought there was, but so far we had not discovered anything to convince us that any practical science underlay astrology. Astrology seemed to have preserved all the superstitions and emotional appeal of this ancient astral cult, but did not appear to have much original science. Then we found a recent statistical study which made us think again.

LOOKING FOR PATTERNS

In 1994 the film-maker and photographer Gunter Sachs decided to undertake a statistical and mathematical investigation into the claims of astrology, an empirical approach such as we imagine the ancients had taken. He is not an astrologer, nor are any of his collaborators. In fact they admit that when they began their study, motivated purely by curiosity, none of them 'knew much about astrology'. But they did draw up a series of guidelines which they then followed very carefully. We will quote their terms of reference in full, as we found the results of their work to be extremely important.

Their seven main aims were:

1   *To examine by means of a broadly structured scientific study the possible effect of star signs on human behaviour;*

2 *Not to try to prove that there is such a thing as astrology above and beyond mythology, but to investigate whether it exists, allowing for an open result;*

3 *To publish their study even if it failed to prove the existence of non-mythological astrology. That would also be of interest;*

4 *To base their research exclusively on empirical data and not to interview any astrologers;*

5 *To examine and explain scientifically any factors which might distort their statistical results;*

6 *To indicate as significant any noticeable deviations from expected results which could not be explained as pure chance;*

7 *To have their calculations and their results checked by a suitable neutral authority such as a university.*[26]

They worked with an extremely prestigious European Research Institute, which acted as their independent adjudicator, the Institute für Demoskopie, at Allensbach, and used Dr Rita Kunstler, a statistician from the Institute of Statistics at Ludwig-Maximilian University in Munich, to advise on statistical methodology, and their results are as fascinating as they are unexpected.

They took their raw data from public authorities, insurance companies and market research surveys. They collected a vast database about the birth dates of criminals, traffic offenders, marriages and divorces, sick people, suicides and much more. The data-protection rules prevented them identifying individuals, but they were able to obtain dates of birth linked to outcomes. When they had the raw data Sachs's team set about analysing it and publishing the results. He was amazed at the level of hostility he met.

It was as though I had opened the flood gates. I was engulfed by torrents of abuse and insults. 'Stick to what you're best at, playboy – chasing good-looking women!' I never imagined what academics

[26] Sachs, Gunter: *The Astrology File*, Orion, 1997

could come up with. Time and again they accused me of getting my terminology confused. I studied mathematics at university in French-speaking Switzerland. The fact that the sums were right did not seem to interest my correspondents.

When I published a second article about our survey of 350,000 marriages, people wrote to me by the hundred. Our calculations were incorrect, they claimed, since so many marriages between two star signs were classic cases of self-fulfilling prophecies. Men and women who believe in astrology go to marriage bureaux with the firm intention of finding an Aries partner, or scan the personal ads in search of a Libra lady. Maybe. But none of these smart alecs could say how many such cases there were. We examine this phenomenon in our chapter on marriage. Hopefully, nobody will accuse us of making self-fulfilling prophecies of suicide, which we also researched. Surely no one could suggest that there are such people as suicide counsellors?[27]

When we read this comment we did begin to wonder if this hostile response is a general rule for anybody who tries to look at any sort of non-standard interpretation. We certainly have also experienced criticism from the establishment for coming up with unwanted conclusions, and testable evidence is not admissible for these people if you have not found it by means they define as conventional.

Sachs's study used very large samples, and when he carried out significance tests the Institute of Statistics at Ludwig-Maximilian University, Munich, verified his method. One thing was very clear: he carried out his tests in an unbiased manner and went to great trouble to eliminate systematic sampling bias. Sachs started by looking at publishers' sales of astrological star-sign books and compared the sales figures with the proportion of individuals born under those signs in particular sales areas. He found statistically significant differences in ten out the twelve star signs, a result that would occur by chance only once in every ten million trials. (This level of significance is way beyond the 1 chance in 99 used for most workaday statistical tests, such as engineering quality control.) He based his data on a sample of 313,368 sales of star-sign books over the period from 1991 to 1994. If you are interested in which signs are more sus-

[27] Sachs, Gunter: *The Astrology File*

ceptible to the charms of astrology then read Sachs's book. We are only interested in the fact that he found statistically significant differences in behaviour.

Sachs next looked at ten different areas of life where he could obtain data. When we are not collaborating in our historical investigations we are both research professionals, and we cannot quarrel with his methods or his analysis. Here is a summary of his main findings.

1 *Who marries whom?* He took a sample of 717,226 married people and looked at their star-sign matches to see if they fulfilled astrological expectations. His null hupothesis (the expected result) assumed that the matches would be randomly distributed between star signs. They were not. He identified 144 possible star-sign combinations and in these he found 25 pairings that deviated significantly from the expectations of chance. When he checked the probability of this result occurring by coincidence the odds were 1 to 50,000 against. This means that it is 49,999 times more likely to be due to some unknown factor than it is to mere chance.

2 *Who divorces whom?* The sample size for this test was 109,030 couples. The method used was the same as that used to test marriages. Once more, of the 144 possible combinations he found 25 significant deviations, but this time there was a much lower level of significance. Once in every 26 tests the result could be expected to occur by pure chance. This was not at a level that made it statistically meaningful.

3 *Who is single?* This test was based on census data from 1990 covering the entire population of Switzerland, 4,045,170 people. This gave a sample size of 2,731,766 people in the chosen age range. For this test he only looked at people of marriageable age, which he defined as between 18 and 40. He found that certain star signs are more prepared to commit to marriage than others. The seven significant deviations from random behaviour were statistically significant at a level of 1 in 10,000. This shows that there is a definite behaviour pattern within this sample.

4 *Who studies what?* For this test the data came from the Universities Clearing House and covered 231,026 applicants for ten restricted entry courses. The null hypothesis was that the star signs would be randomly distributed across the range of disciplines. There were 120 possible star

sign/degree course combinations and he found 27 significant deviations from chance. The odds on obtaining this result by coincidence were 1 to 10,000,000. This result is nothing less than monumental. People have been condemned to death on the basis of DNA evidence with a lower statistical significance than this.

5 *Who does what job?* The sample was taken from the 1990 Swiss census of 4,045,170 entries and 47 categories of occupation. This gave 564 possible combinations of job and star sign. Sachs found 77 significant variations at odds of 1 to 10,000,000 against it being coincidence. Again, only a fool would deny he had a correlation here.

6 *Who dies of what?* This test was conducted on all registered deaths in Switzerland between 1969 and 1994, a sample size of 1,195,174. To make the test meaningful, only deaths from natural causes were tested, with violent and accidental deaths excluded from the study. This reduced the sample to 657,492 individuals. The 240 possible death/star sign combinations revealed 5 significant deviations from chance, at a significance level of 1 to 270. This result seems modest compared to some of Sachs's results, but it is still of statistical interest.

7 *Who commits suicide?* From the above death register Sachs was able to extract a sample of 30,358 people who committed suicide. He found five significant deviations from chance expectations of star-sign distributions, with a likelihood of the result being coincidence of only 1 in 1,000.

8 *Who drives how?* The sample was taken from the British car insurers' VELO database and covered 25,000 claims made during 1996. Once more Sachs found significant deviations for four star signs at a significance level of 1 to 10,000,000. He also took a sample of 85,598 Swiss traffic offenders from the Swiss Central Crime Register and again found the same four star signs showing statistically significant deviation from chance at odds of 1 to 5,000 that it was coincidence.

9 *Who commits what crimes?* The sample was 325,866 convictions for 25 different type of offence. The data came from the Swiss Central Criminal Records Office. The test combinations were 300 possible crime/star sign matches. Six of these combinations were found to vary from the expected

level and were statistically significant at odds of 1 to 10,000,000 against coincidence.

10 *Who plays football?* From a sample of 4,162 professional footballers in Germany Sachs found nine star signs deviating significantly from the expected chance value. The odds on this being coincidence are 1 to 10,000,000

Having completed these startling statistical tests Sachs then asked his statistician advisers to carry out an extremely logical data check. The previous data sets were scrambled and the dates arranged into twelve artificial star signs before repeating the tests. In simple terms he used a random number generator to group the 365 days of the year into twelve completely arbitrary blocks. Here is his own description of the process.

The statisticians were able to mix the data at random and create artificial star signs in the same order with the year but provided these with artificial (ie false) birth dates. In this way an artificial year resulted beginning with 6 April, for example, followed by 11 Nov etc.

If the astrologers' statements about the effects of star signs were invalid there would be significant findings here too. However, there were no significant correlations between the artificial signs.[28]

Sachs summed up his work as follows:

The main purpose of our study was not to produce interesting individual results – these were, in fact, no more than entertaining by-products of our project. Rather, the declared aim of our research was to establish whether there was a correlation between star signs and human behaviour and predispositions.

We have proved it – there is a correlation.[29]

In our lives outside of our collaboration to investigate the ancient mysteries of Freemasonry we both work every day with research issues. Robert

[28] Sachs, Gunter: *The Astrology File*
[29] Sachs, Gunter: *The Astrology File*

teaches statistics and information systems to postgraduate students and Chris is a member of the leading market research professional bodies. We can appreciate the magnitude of what Sachs has detected here, although we would interpret his conclusions slightly more cautiously, saying that this study shows that a mapping between astrological birth signs and variations in behaviour cannot reasonably be rejected. What Sachs proved was the significance of his correlation, not that astrology works. Despite some excellent work he could not satisfy the criteria for acceptance that Professor Stephen Hawking put forward:

> *The real reason most scientists don't believe in astrology is not scientific evidence or the lack of it but because it is not consistent with other theories which have been tested by experiment.*[30]

Perhaps this is why the study is largely ignored by both the scientific and astrological communities. The scientific community is entrenched against it because they see it as conflicting with other theories, and the astrological enthusiasts doubt it because its findings do not confirm what they want to believe. It seems very few people are looking at the facts in a neutral manner.

But here was our first evidence that there might be a real observational science behind the astral lore of the ancient Jews and *The Masonic Testament,* even though the data did not seem to relate directly to anything we had been researching.

We had proposed a word for an astral science we suspected might exist, 'cosmocology', which broadly means the study of heavenly events at dawn. But all our research so far had suggested that it might be nothing more than superstitious nonsense and pretty myth concocted around the appearance of rare astral events. Our scepticism had now been shaken by Sachs's findings that there are patterns in human behaviour that can be detected using an astrological sorting filter.

Here was our first external supporting evidence to encourage us to see if there was some ancient science to find hidden in the myths and ritual of Freemasonry, but we were still a long way away from believing the claims that successful leaders were born when the Shekinah appeared as a pre-dawn shining light. There were no data banks to test the periods we were interested in, so we would need to look for some other supporting evidence if there was a case to be made. The task looked impossible.

[30] Hawking, Stephen: *The Universe in a Nutshell*, Transworld, London, 2001

CONCLUSIONS

Our research was leading us to the conclusion that Freemasonry might be nothing more than a receptacle for astrological mumbo-jumbo. Our previous research had suggested that there might be a secret tradition of basic observational science leading back to ancient times, but our most recent findings forced us to ask if this was merely astrological pseudo-science.

After consulting writer and researcher Colin Wilson, we were prompted to look at the development of astrology and the possibility that it might be an accurate fortune-telling tool. We found that it seemed to share exactly the same roots as the Jewish Messianic belief and the Freemasonic tradition. We did not find any secret thread of early science.

Then we came across Gunter Sachs's wide-ranging statistical investigation of astrological signs and behaviour patterns. He showed a significant statistical correlation between star sign and behaviour but offered no reason why this should be. We then set ourselves the task: if there is a statistically significant pattern of change in the behaviour of large groups of people according to the season of the years they were born, can we find evidence to show what this could mean in terms of effects on society?

Chapter Fourteen

THE STAR ACHIEVERS

LEARNING AND STRIVING

After thirteen years of research into the origins and meaning of Masonic rituals, it appeared that the whole thing was little more than institutionalised astrology. Yes, Freemasonry had developed out of very ancient astronomy, and its members had been at the forefront of kick-starting modern science, but the rituals were apparently driven by a superstitious belief that planetary conjunctions directly affected the world. Even Jesus Christ seemed to have conducted his life's mission on this basis, despite the fact that it ultimately failed him. But then the results of Sachs's investigations turned things around by demonstrating that there was a very marked correlation between human behaviour and the date on which the individual was born.

As we reviewed our situation we began to see a new way forward.

'The movements of the stars and planets may or may not be the cause in these phenomena, but do you think they might be involved, even if it's only as a marker?' Chris asked, tapping his wristwatch with his index finger as he went on: 'When we read the time of day we know our watch is not actually creating time, but it's a good indicator of how time is passing. Perhaps in the same way the stars and planets may not cause effects on human behaviour but they might provide a natural calendar of something else which does.'

'Yes,' Robert replied. 'There seems no other way these people could have developed the ideas we keep finding, except by making observations, then keeping and comparing lists of outcomes. I think it's pretty unlikely that the stars and planets are causing the patterns, but our ancient brethren probably believed that they did.'

We continued to discuss how thousands of years of observation could have led to a very good understanding of the heavens, and decided it was natural that the leaders of men would want the knowledge to work for them. Priests would identify holy days, kings demand to know when to be crowned or when their army should march into battle. The power of the priest and king could affect a whole nation, and the appearance of the Shekinah would therefore lead to great events such as the building of Solomon's Temple or a belief that the Messiah of Israel had been born. The conjunction of Venus and Mercury had not caused these events directly, but it might have driven powerful men to make them happen.

As we talked through the range of points Robert remembered another set of interesting research findings. 'The situation we are seeing here reminds me of the theory of motivation which underlies the technique of "action learning" we use at Bradford,' he remarked.

Robert teaches at Bradford School of Management, one of Europe's leading graduate business schools, where 'action learning' is a technique for helping postgraduate students acquire and use knowledge in an efficient manner. An important part of the teaching methodology is to identify each student's preferred means of learning and then try to make sure that individuals build on their strengths and strengthen their weaknesses. The success of the technique hinges on identifying and utilising a student's motivation to learn.

Robert explained: 'The original piece of research work which underpins this extremely successful way of educating mature students is a study carried out at Harvard University into what motivates people to learn how to improve their business skills. I need to look up his work in more detail – but from memory I think it could be very relevant. The basis of the work was an observation that some cultures and societies are economically extremely successful and others are not. And the difference lay in the levels of motivation of the people involved.'

A couple of days later we met again, and Robert pulled out a thick red paperback with a bold white title.

'Here it is,' he said. 'The definitive work on the subject of motivation: *The Achieving Society*, by David C. McClelland.'

'So let's see if it can help us.'

'Over the years behavioural scientists have noticed that some people have an intense need to achieve; others, perhaps the majority, don't seem to be as concerned about achievement.' Robert flicked the pages open to the yellow post-its he had inserted earlier. 'McClelland was fascinated about the motivation to achieve, or lack of it, in individuals. This book is a distillation of twenty years of study by top-notch behavioural psychologists from Harvard University.'

'I assume that McClelland's work has been widely accepted,' Chris said, suspicious that behavioural psychology is sometimes seen as less than hard-edged.

'Oh, he's squeaky clean,' Robert replied. 'His work is the ultimate source in the area of learning motivation and his techniques have become a standard tool for business psychologists.'

McClelland's book describes how his research led him to believe that the need to achieve is a distinct human motive that can be distinguished from other needs. More importantly, the achievement motive can be isolated and assessed in any group. He called the phenomenon *n-achievement*, an abbreviation of his concept of an in-built *need to achieve*. He went far beyond the normal bounds of psychology in his quest for understanding, developing innovative methods of analysis for the achievement levels of a whole range of societies right from ancient Greece down to the USA in the first half of the twentieth century.

McClelland was convinced that people's level of *n-achievement* motivation could be improved and increased, and he developed training programmes for business people that were designed to increase their achievement motivation. But he never quite managed to account for the levels of inherent *n-achievement* that he was able to measure in a whole range of different societies. What was very clear from his work was that societies went through a cycle of economic growth followed by decline, and that this cycle was closely related to the level of *n-achievement* that he measured in those societies. In his own words:

Suppose we accept, for the sake of the argument, that a part of the 'push' for economic development comes from a psychological characteristic which is roughly reflected in our measures of n-achievement. What then? Why do some people have more n-achievement at some times than other people? Is it a question of racial heredity, challenge from the environment, or perhaps certain economic, political or social disadvantages?[1]

Perhaps McClelland could help us understand the characteristics of 'successful' people and indirectly of messiahs.

He proved his methodology in existing societies by carrying out detailed interviews with groups of individuals in a range of different cultures and comparing his results with those predicted by his method of accessing literature and artefact decoration. He went on to generalise about the characteristic behaviour of people with high *n-achievement* scores, and he was able to show that those factors which distinguish high levels of *n-achievement* are found across all the cultures he studied. McClelland describes the behaviour patterns of high *n-achievers* as follows:

1 They are associated with a greater frequency of expressive movements, including a tendency to avoid repetition. (This helped him identify such people in non-literate societies, by their use of characteristic decoration.)

2 They always produce a higher level of performance when they are offered achievement incentives.

3 When using colours they prefer to utilise blues and greens in preference to reds and yellows.

4 They have a greater level of geographical and social mobility than individuals with lower *n-achievement*.

5 They place a greater emphasis on competitive games than individuals with lower levels of *n-achievement*.

6 They have a faster perception of time when compared to individuals with lower levels of *n-achievement*.

He ended his summary by saying:

People with high n-achievement behave in certain characteristic

[1] McClelland, David C: *The Achieving Society*, The Free Press, New York, 1961

ways, but if asked, they do not consistently respond with the atti-tudes and beliefs that their behaviour seems to imply.[2]

McClelland describes an experiment where a group of children, whom he had previously tested for levels of *n-achievement*, were asked to throw a ring over a peg. They were allowed to stand as close to or as far from the peg as they wished during the experiment. He found that the children with high *n-achievement* scores chose to stand a moderate distance from the peg, but the children with low *n-achievement* scores stood either very close to, or very far from, the peg.

He explained this result by saying that high *n-achievers* prefer to take 'moderate' risks, and so they stand where their skill is most likely to pay off in subjective feelings of success. If they stand too close to the peg, the task is too easy and gives them no personal satisfaction. However, if the high *n-achievers* are too far from the peg they are less likely to hit it and less likely to get satisfaction from any success, as they are more likely to regard any 'hits' as down to luck, rather than skill.[3]

So high *n-achievers* set moderately difficult but potentially achievable goals. But do people with a high need for achievement behave like this all the time? McClelland concluded that they only behave in this way if they can influence the outcome. In tests of pure chance and gambling situations they behave no differently from anybody else. So achievement-motivated people are not gamblers; it is just that they prefer to work on a problem rather than leave the outcome to luck.

Low *n-achievers* will either veer towards gambling and take a big risk because the outcome is beyond their power, and therefore they can easily rationalise away their personal responsibility if they lose. Or if they are conservative they will choose tiny risks where the gain is small but secure, because there is little danger of anything going wrong for which they might be blamed.

High *n-achievers* take the middle ground, and take a moderate degree of risk because they feel their efforts and abilities can influence the out-come. In business and economic activity generally, this aggressive realism is the mark of the successful entrepreneur.

McClelland also studied how high *n-achievers* liked to be rewarded. He found that they were not motivated by what economists call the 'profit

[2] McClelland, David C: *The Achieving Society*
[3] McClelland, David C: *The Achieving Society*

motive'. He looked at the histories of groups of high achievers, such as the Quakers and Dissenters of England, and found that although they were frequently successful in business they did not seem to be very interested in the money they made, certainly not for its own sake. Often they would plough their large profits back into further business expansion. He pointed out that the Quakers were forbidden by their religion from ostentatiously enjoying wealth, and so unless they were total hypocrites money could not have been the driving force which encouraged them to achieve. He pointed out that their behaviour showed no evidence of being driven by greed, so the accumulation of money must have had a different purpose. He suggested that personal money income plays an important role in society because it is taken as a symbol of achievement. *'A man with a large income is likely to gain respect, not because of the income itself but because of the presumption that it is an index of his competence.'*

But McClelland's work went beyond individual motivation into group, and even national, motivation. He had noticed that there was a variation in the level of achievement motivation in various societies throughout history and had plotted levels of achievement motivation against degree of economic activity. All his curves show cycles of growth, peak and decline in the economic activities of societies, cycles which may then be repeated some time later.

McClelland used various techniques, including literature analysis which showed a close correlation to the degree of economic activity in the same society approximately fifty years later. For example the time of Queen Elizabeth I produced many great authors and playwrights, including Shakespeare, Marlowe and Ben Jonson, at a time of widespread national success and development, whilst the economic peaks occurred in the mid-seventeenth century.

McClelland's work was certainly fascinating, but what was in our minds was the question of whether there was any way we could use behavioural analysis of the characteristics of particular societies to make sense of our findings about the Messiah/Shekinah myth.

The successful leaders and 'captains of industry' he talked about seemed to be similar types of people to the kings, priests and messiahs we have been studying. The main difference was that we had found a belief that 'successful' individuals were born when the Bright Morning Star was on the eastern horizon just before sunrise, while McClelland had isolated factors which drove individuals to achieve. But he had also found the same pattern of periods of high activity followed by periods of poor performance before the whole cycle started over.

It seemed to us entirely reasonable that the leaders who believed in the power of the Shekinah would use its appearances as a 'permission to achieve'. But it was not until we plotted the dates of McClelland's peaks of successful achievement-orientated behaviour against our time-line for Shekinah events that we spotted an overlap.

RIDING THE CYCLES OF SUCCESS

McClelland's research had initially concentrated on the importance of his *n-achievement* index as a way of explaining successful economic growth, but he was conscious that he had limited his investigations to modern economic development, where cultures had adapted to technology, division of labour and the factory system. He was looking for a general theory of motivation which could apply under any circumstances. He wondered if economic growth in the past might have been different in some way, and possibly caused by different motivational influences. As he explained, the question was of particular interest to him:

> It was after all an historical case, the connection between the Protestant Reformation and the rise of capitalism, which gave rise to my general hypothesis. Can we collect any data that bears more directly on this interpretation? . . . did a rise in achievement motivation precede economic growth in various countries in the past and did its fall precede economic decline?

> Fortunately the method exists for collecting data to answer such questions. The system of content analysis for n-achievement applied originally to individually written stories and then to folk tales and children's stories can also be applied to whatever imaginative literature has survived from past civilizations. Furthermore, with a little ingenuity our requirement for some kind of quantitative index of economic activity can normally be satisfied so that we need not get embroiled in disagreements as to whether or when a country was growing or declining in the economic sense. The present chapter brings together the efforts that have been made to

date to apply the approach used in the previous chapter to histor-
ical problems.[4]

In particular he made detailed studies of the proportion of *n-achievers*
active in societies in the past and what was happening to the economic
success of those societies. He choose four very different cultures in order
to cover a fairly wide range of historical epochs. These were ancient Greece,
Spain in the late Middle Ages, England from the late Middle Ages to the
Industrial Revolution, and the United States from 1800 to 1950.

His technique was ingenious. He needed two statistical measures, one
for the general level of *n-achievement* and the other for the general level
of economic development, so that he could compare the two patterns. When
he had looked at modern-day individuals he was able to use a question-
naire. But for at least three of his chosen periods all the members of society
concerned were long dead. This meant they could not be questioned directly,
so instead he decided to study the writings, and artefacts, of those societies and developed his technique for scoring the literature content on the
assumption that various samples of written material could be selected to
adequately represent the strivings and hopes of at least the portions of the
population significant for economic growth. He went on to successfully
extend this index to the use of ceramic decorations.

He had already identified a common pattern of growth, climax and
decline in many ancient civilisations, but assigning exact dates for the presence of this pattern in the development of a civilisation was problematic.
Here is how he describes his process for Greece:

> *Ancient historians are in full agreement that Athens reached her*
> *highest point of development in the 5th century B.C., during the*
> *'Golden Age' of Pericles. The development of Ionia, where Homer*
> *may have lived, was earlier and that of Sparta and Boeotia, home*
> *of Hesiod, was perhaps a little later, at least to judge by their sub-*
> *sequent military successes over Athens. Consequently the year 475*
> *B.C. was chosen rather arbitrarily as the precise date dividing the*
> *period of growth from the period of climax as a time that would*
> *not be too late for Ionia and Athens or too early for Sparta and*
> *Boeotia. It also corresponds to the time when Athens succeeded in*

[4] McClelland, David C: *The Achieving Society*

organizing the league of Delos, a great maritime federation of Greek city-states which finally succeeded in chasing the Persians definitively out of the Aegean. By the end of the 5th century Athens had lost the Peloponnesian War to Sparta and had begun her decline. Sparta in turn was defeated by the Thebans of Boeotia under Epaminondas in 369 B.C., but with his death in 362 B.C. the Thebans lost their influence to Philip of Macedon from the 'backwoods' up North. So 362 B.C. was arbitrarily chosen as marking the end of the period of climax for the city-states under consideration though it comes a little late for Athens and Ionia. These decisions set the time limits for the three periods as follows:

Period of growth – 900 B.C. to 475 B.C.

Period of climax – 475 B.C. to 362 B.C.

Period of decline – 362 B.C. to 100 B.C.

This finding was fascinating for us, as it showed that Greek culture, which we already knew had been a great influence on the Jews from the era of Zerubbabel's Temple down to New Testament times, had gone through a period of growth, peak and decline that fitted the pattern of the appearances of the Shekinah. The Shekinah, after a long period of absence attributed to the faults of Solomon's successors, started a new cycle of appearances in 487 BCE. We already knew that the Jews benefited from their interaction with Greek traders, and the rise of the Greek city states as a military balance to the Persians must have encouraged Cyrus and Darius to allow the reconstruction of Jerusalem as a buffer state against expansion from the Greeks.

Here was a possible explanation of why the ancient myth of the Shekinah was taken so seriously at the time the Old Testament was written down. The Shekinah, the glory of God's Presence in the pre-dawn sky, had last been seen at the biblical triumph that had just been celebrated in the newly recorded Book of Kings as the dedication of Solomon's Temple. The return of the Shekinah coincided with a period of economic and political turbulence, which happened to benefit the Jews, just as the ancient myths said it should.

We could easily see how these people saw events, both good and bad, as God's Will. The Shekinah appears and they feel confident and set out to achieve. It goes away and they become afraid, leading to a self-fulfilling prophecy for failure. Unfortunately, if they become unrealistically confident (like standing way too far back in the hoop-and-peg game) they will fail anyway.

McClelland said of his study of the peaking and decline of *n-achievement* in ancient Greece:

> The chi-square tests show that such differences over time could hardly have arisen by chance . . . What do the results mean? Is n-achievement a kind of 'first cause' that appears and disappears out of nowhere which makes civilisations rise and fall? Clearly it is not. By now we know a good deal about what makes n-achievement levels rise and fall and practically all of the determinants are social in origin . . . Economic wealth, no matter how high the n-achievement, cannot be built up for a whole society in one generation. But the sequence of interactions between man and society should be described no matter how many generations it takes.[5]

McClelland's definitive study of motivation and economic success describes in detail how he measured this effect, and we do not intend to discuss his methods, which are totally accepted by the academic community. We are far more interested in discussing what he discovered whilst carrying out his analysis.

Now we moved on to the next period that McClelland had studied. In particular we noticed that it coincided with another Shekinah peak, the one that inspired Sir William St Clair to plan and commence building Roslin in 1441 CE. McClelland had looked at the levels of *n-achievement* in medieval Spain covering a period from 1200 to 1700 CE. Here is the summary of his findings:

Period of economic growth/growth in *n-achievement*: 1200–1492 CE

Climax: 1492–1610 CE

Decline: 1610–1730 CE

[5] McClelland, David C: *The Achieving Society*

McClelland says of these findings:

The result was very like that obtained for Ancient Greece and confirms the connection between achievement motivation and economic growth in another time period for a totally different culture . . . The results of these two studies are sufficiently encouraging to warrant a closer examination of the relation between successive 'waves' of achievement motivation and 'pulses' of economic growth within the same country.

We knew that Sir William St Clair, the builder of Rosslyn and the founder of Freemasonry, had in his youth travelled the pilgrim route to Compostela, in Spain, before returning to Scotland.[6] So William personally experienced the buzz of high motivation which was erupting in Spain at this time. Being aware of the impending return of the Shekinah, predicted by both the Enochian and Norse beliefs, could hardly have failed to inspire his own ambition to mark the occasion with a suitable new temple and a new Order to preserve the ancient traditions. And can we really blame him for believing that the evidence of his own eyes confirmed the truth of the secret teachings of the Bright Morning Star? No wonder this powerful myth pervades *The Masonic Testament*.

The next period McClelland looked at was a time we knew very well, but it was not a period that fitted our Shekinah pattern. However, it was a time when there was an all-consuming interest in astrology amongst the Freemasons of Scotland and England. The period covered was 1500 to 1800 CE and the place was England. Here are his findings for the *n-achievement* level in England:

Growth to a peak: 1600–1690 CE

Period of stagnation: 1700–1780 CE

Growth to new peak: 1790–1833 CE

The rise in over achievement [first peak in above table] represented by the estimate of 1600–1690 occurred most probably in

---

[6] Wallace-Murphy, T & Hopkins, M: *Rosslyn, Guardian of the Secrets of the Holy Grail*

the last half of the 16th century . . . The result is an interesting
and potentially important confirmation of the theoretical expecta-
tion, not tested in Greece or Spain, that n-achievement has to rise
to the high point at the beginning of the phases of economic
growth.[7]

This has no link with the Shekinah but it suggests that the expectations
of society were reflected in the political and economic events. This is the
period we already knew to be a time when the expectations of Freemasonry
founded modern science in the shape of the Royal Society.[8]

McClelland then looked at a period which was very interesting, as far
as we were concerned: the USA over the period from 1800 to 1950 CE.
Now the patterns of *The Masonic Testament* predicted that a peak of economic and political activity should have happened in the forty years following 1913. This period ends in 1953. We were well aware these dates
covered the Wall Street Crash of 1929 and the depression that followed,
as well as two world wars. McClelland saw this period in a broader context:

What has been happening to achievement motivation in the United
States in the past century is not only of great topical interest, it
also fills an important gap in [our study of] the Western historical
record which runs more or less continuously from 1300 to the
present time. First, we noted a brief wave of achievement motiva-
tion in Spain in the late 15th century, followed by a similar wave
of somewhat longer duration in England in the mid-16th century,
then a pause and a very much larger wave preceding the English
Industrial Revolution. There the record leaves off until we pick it
[the pulse of economic success] up again around 1920 [in the USA]
and find a major wave of achievement motivation occurring prim-
arily in the underdeveloped countries of the world in the decade
1950–1960.[9]

This would suggest that the Shekinah pattern does coincide with the
longer-term rhythms of social development – but not for the reasons given

[7] McClelland, David C: *The Achieving Society*
[8] Lomas, Robert: *The Invisible College*
[9] McClelland, David: *The Achieving Society*

in the Bible or *The Masonic Testament*. If you want to understand the patterns of human behaviour which McClelland says underlie the cycles then we heartily recommend reading his book. He goes into great detail about causes, and how these causes can be manipulated to improve economic performance.

But David McClelland had one more surprise up his sleeve for us. He also looked at the variations in the level of *n-achievement* in pre-Inca Peru over the 1,500 years from 800 BCE to 700 CE. He did it from a study of the markings and quantities of funerary urns, of which some 254 had been found from the culture which lived on the north coast of Peru and could be placed in a reliable sequence. His reason for carrying out this exercise was to 'provide a tool for investigating civilisations which did not leave written records, but did leave markings'. (He had developed a technique of rating 'doodles' and the style of ceramic decoration, for level of *n-achievement*, which he tested on his other data using Greek ceramics. The idea worked, so he wanted to test it on civilisations which left no writing.)

His data show a steady decline in *n-achievement* from the earliest samples around 900–800 BCE. This drops to a low level until between 400 and 500 CE, when it again peaks. 987 BCE is a Shekinah peak, as is 473 CE. Interestingly no samples existed in his study for the period 700–300 BCE, so if there was a Shekinah peak in Peru at this time his study found no data to identify it.

Of the six achieving societies McClelland had studied, no fewer than five had reached peaks of achievement which coincided with appearances of the Shekinah as a bright morning star rising just before the Sun. We decided to check out the likelihood of this being random chance, so Robert computed a chi-square statistic to see what the chances were that five out of six achieving societies of the past should just happen to peak at times during the Venus cycle when the Venus/Mercury conjunction of the Shekinah appeared in the dawn sky. His calculation showed that any null hypothesis, saying that these peaks were randomly distributed across the whole 480 years of the Shekinah cycle, could be rejected at a significance level of 0.001. So there is less than one chance in a thousand that these peaks of achievement occurred randomly at the same time as the Shekinah.

Of course, this analysis does not suggest that the Shekinah causes the peaks of achievement McClelland found, and we have to leave open the question of why these peaks occur in such a seemingly predictable pattern.

McClelland commented on his work that it 'should be useful in helping decide which cultures were growing and which declining in energy and who was most likely to have conquered whom'.[10] We made a mental note to check if the method could be used to study the Grooved Ware proto-writing, as it suggested a way forward for understanding this valuable resource, but so far we have not had a chance to try it.

So, we wondered, is there something real behind the observational patterns which *The Masonic Testament* and the Bible have passed down to us? Our research shows that peaks of political and economic activity appear to have occurred disproportionately often at times when the Shekinah, the 'Bright Morning Star', appeared in a helical rising.

McClelland was convinced that people's level of *n-achievement* motivation could be improved and increased, and he developed training programmes for business people that were designed to increase their achievement motivation. Was he unwittingly rediscovering a 6,000-year-old technique – a technique perhaps used by the highly successful astronomer-priests of the Grooved Ware People?

His work was that most societies go through cycles of economic growth followed by decline, and that this cycle was closely related to the levels of *n-achievement* which he measured in those societies. The Grooved Ware priests controlled the economic surpluses their predictive science created, and with those resources came power, growth in population and a drive to find more exploitable resources. Their civilisation expanded and their success motivated their children, who in turn motivated their own children, born under the benevolent light of the goddess. It would seem that they managed to create one of McClelland's waves of economic success by tapping into a motivating belief in a divinely inspired destiny.

We had found that the Jewish Old Testament reflects a cyclical view of history that McClelland showed to be real. The key founding events of Judaism, the Flood, Abraham's Covenant, Moses and the Exodus, Solomon's Temple, rebuilding the Temple, the birth of Jesus, as we knew, were all keyed into the Shekinah cycle by the recorders of the Bible.

This belief gave the writers of *The Masonic Testament* a structure for the universe, and it did lay down the foundations for modern science by suggesting that God decreed laws of nature which might be discovered by man. The underlying message has remained the same: it says God has a

[10] McClelland, David: *The Achieving Society*

purpose if you look for it, and mankind's lot is not independent of the hidden mysteries of nature and science. Science may no longer have a role for God, but it still has a major role for His purpose, which it has renamed 'the laws of Physics'.

It would seem to us that there are two mechanisms at work here. One is a 480-year-long pattern of Bright Morning Stars, blazing in the pre-dawn sky. The other is a series of waves of motivational achievement which sometimes seem to coincide with these appearances. We were now aware that McClelland has also shown that these waves could appear at other times, when the Venus/Mercury Shekinah was not in the sky, thus showing there is no simple causal link, and it would be very frightening if all human endeavours were completely linked to some unseen pattern of planetary movements. But there does seem to be a correlation that transcends coincidence.

We find it impossible to accept the argument that God set up the basic orbital cycles of the solar system billions of years ago with the prime intention of using conjunctions of Venus and Mercury just once in the many thousands of millions of repetitions to send a message about a messiah in 7 BCE. The Star of Bethlehem is a wonderful motivating myth, not a scientific argument.

We have not, as yet, changed our minds about astrology. We can offer no logical basis for it to work, and even Sachs's excellent study fails to prove its reality. But something is happening out there. Something does affect human behaviour by driving ambition and achievement.

The concept of astrology has a childlike simplicity which can be applied to the problems of grown-up life. Yet the Grooved Ware power-brokers and the Sumerians were very sophisticated people – matchless observers of the sky. Their patience, the precision of their calculations and the accuracy of their observatories have led the world to an understanding of nature, the very mind of God. But they also felt the problems and terrors of being exposed to the dangers and mystery of the world, and so they created idols, which they hoped to propitiate. And their idols took the form of lists and links. After all, when the world is a collection of mysteries it is the business of the wise to establish reliable correlations and answer the question – how? The question why can be left for later discussion. Remember, they had no Lucasian Professor of Mathematics to remind them that their theological theories were 'not consistent with other theories which have been tested by experiment'.[11]

[11] Hawking, Stephen: *The Universe in a Nutshell*

But why did they place the divinities of their faith in the sky? Our simple answer: the heavens are the visual guide to understanding our own environment. Grooved Ware Britain and ancient Mesopotamia shared a climate where clouds rarely covered the stars; and faced with their wonderful sparkling, men found it easy to believe that the shining planets were themselves gods and goddesses. So these Bright Morning Stars, appearing to lighten the darkest hour before dawn, were thought to share man's feelings and fears, and to control his destiny. Small wonder that Hiram, king of Tyre, wanted to marry one and father her children.

No doubt some people who read this book will want to believe that the surges of economic success that David McClelland discovered were really caused by the stars and planets on the horizon affecting the destinies of the individuals who benefited. McClelland also considered this possibility, as he had noted that the Jewish people seem to be well above average in terms of their levels of *n-achievement* motivation, saying: 'Judaism is a Messianic religion which stresses that living up to God's Commandments will ultimately help bring about the day when God will reward His chosen people . . . that we found to be a characteristic of people with high *n-achievement*'. After conducting an extensive survey of Jewish boys in a number of American cities, he added: 'our prediction that Jewish boys should have higher levels of *n-achievement* is clearly supported by the facts'.[12]

He went on to say this about the general effect of Jewish religious belief on levels of achievement:

All that this present research adds to the controversy is that if the Jews had a higher level of n-achievement in the past, as they appear to have now in the United States, then their concern with business and commercial matters could be predicted on the basis of all the findings already reported.[13]

McClelland adds that the Jews were not alone among religious groups in having success in inculcating increased levels of *n-achievement*. He also studied Quakers, Calvinists, Catholics, Jains, Vaishnava Hindus and Parsees, and summed up his views on the effect of religion on societal levels of motivation thus:

[12] McClelland, David: *The Achieving Society*
[13] McClelland, David: *The Achieving Society*

327

Our research has refined much more closely the core religious values associated with high n-achievement . . . the person with high n-achievement wants to be responsible for his own decisions and the very act of making a decision implies some uncertainty as to the outcome. He is therefore 'on his toes' in the same sense as the believer is in individualistic religions. In formal ritualistic ecclesiastical systems, on the other hand, the individual is 'safe' if he does exactly what he is supposed to do, performs correct rituals, says his prayers often enough, calls in the right priest at the right time, etc. But here we run into the old chicken-and-egg problem: which came first, individualistic religion or n-achievement? No clear answer to the question can be given that would cover all cases. However, theoretically either factor could 'come first' and influence the development of the other. That is, Quaker parents with the religious views just described would certainly tend to behave toward their sons in ways that would be conducive to the development of high n-achievement. In this case the religion clearly comes first, and in fact since religion is one of the more stable persistent elements in many societies, it may often have 'come first.'

Freemasonry is just such an 'individualistic religion'. So was the cause of McClelland's cycles of achievement the motivation provided by the practice of religion? We do not think mysticism provides a complete explanation, although it may have contributed to the patterns we found. There may be some unknown third factor, such as changes in the environment, which correlates with both patterns and provides a causal link. But we do not at the moment have any further suggestions about this strange linkage.

During the early days of the Royal Society, one of its founders, Sir Robert Moray, worked with the Dutch scientist Christiaan Huygens to try and develop an accurate pendulum clock for use at sea in order to determine longitude.[14] As part of the trials Huygens made a series of identical clocks, and whilst they were being tested in his workshop he noticed a strange phenomenon. When he stood two of these identical clocks on the same shelf and started them at separate times, so that their pendulums swung out of time with each other, by the following morning the movements of their pendulums would have become synchronised. Yet if the two clocks

[14] Lomas, Robert: *The Invisible College*

were placed on different benches on opposite sides of the room they stayed permanently out of synchronisation.

The reason for this is simple. When the two clocks were on the same shelf the movement of the pendulum also slightly moved the shelf, so transmitting a slight jolt to the other clock. When the pendulums were moving in opposition to each other the little jolts slowed the pendulums, by transferring energy between them. As they both slowed slightly they eventually came into phase, at which point they no longer jolted each other and so they moved together.

Perhaps this mechanism can help explain the strange phase-lock between McClelland's data and the appearance of the Bright Morning Star. If you believe in the Shekinah, as Jesus did, you act accordingly, and so time your actions to match what you perceive as the Divine Will. A nice thought, but we are aware that it doesn't go nearly far enough to satisfy Professor Hawking's criteria for acceptance of astrological belief.

But, strangely, this ancient astral cult that gave rise to the great monotheistic religions of the world, which share the Old Testament it inspired, still survives in odd remnants to this day. As we have already commented, Freemasonry and astrology are two traditions which best preserve the age-old belief that the position of the heavenly bodies affect the actions of individuals on Earth.

Modern astrology is frozen into the form that Ptolemy dreamed up almost 2,000 years ago, where the Earth was considered to be at the centre of numerous crystal spheres that carried the material of stars and influenced the destiny of man with their harmonies. We are convinced that newspaper astrology is worthless, and even individually prepared horoscopes are probably no more meaningful than reading tea leaves.

But science says something is happening to affect human behaviour – and Freemasonry appears to be the memory of something historically important. It has preserved much of astronomy's observational science, but it is buried deep in weird verbal traditions, odd modes of ritual movement and mythical tales.

THE END OF THE JOURNEY

It is now thirteen years since we set out on our mission to find the origins of Freemasonic rituals. It was then a private endeavour, entirely for our own satisfaction. We began with a clean sheet of paper and, despite being

Freemasons ourselves, we had no preferences for the outcome. If our findings showed the Craft to be some sixteenth-century eccentric invention – so be it. If we had concluded that Freemasons were evil or wrongdoers we would have spelled it out to our readers. And if we had found that the official line, that it all sprang out of the medieval guilds of stonemasons, was true we would have said so.

The journey has been far longer and more arduous than we ever imagined, but we have made many friends along the way. This alone has made the 20,000 hours or so that we have invested worthwhile. Unfortunately, and perhaps inevitably, the reporting of our findings has caused some people to resent or even despise us, and some have attacked us in a variety of ways.

As we have already recorded, the most venomous attacks have come from people who do not appear to have read our books, yet feel threatened by our interpretation of events described in the Bible. For them Jesus is God and the son of himself – and he died to save us 2,000 years ago yet he lives on today in a place called heaven.

We openly admit that we have difficulty with such concepts, and to us he was a charismatic leader of men and women who revolutionised the world despite his personal failure. Although we do not accept much of the traditional interpretation of biblical stories at face value, we have great admiration for the Church in general and for people of religion. It is our view that the world can only benefit from open and frank discussions on the subject of human belief and our interaction with the power that underpins the universe – the power that many people call God and scientists call the Laws of Physics.

Freemasonry claims that it is not a religion and that it is compatible with the belief systems of all religions. We entirely accept this, although it does provide a focal point for many people who are not active in any particular faith – and for them it is a replacement for religion, in that it provides spiritual values without a requirement to subscribe to an entire belief system.

Perhaps some of the strangest people we have met are those men who consider themselves to be 'experts' on Freemasonry. By far the majority of Freemasons have welcomed our input and valued the debate we have set running in lodges across the world. But we are aware that some of these 'experts' are outraged by our daring to question the standard history and then publish our findings for anyone to read. Some of them refer to their belief that there is a requirement for secrecy, even though the most senior lodge in the world, the United Grand Lodge of England, has expressly said that there are no secrets save the actual words and signs used for recognition – which we have no need ever to mention.

There is something of a 'Masonic Mafia' made up of men who consider themselves to be well-informed gentlemen and conduct endless meetings and seminars to discuss the standard view of Masonic History. Whilst we are giving talks all over the world in public and to Grand, and sometimes less than grand, lodges, they hold their 'academic' discussions in the quiet comfort of their faith that Freemasonry sprang out of the Medieval guilds of stonemasons. They generally refuse to look at our findings, and the few that do use a process of 'extract and compare'. This is a simple process of taking one element of our findings and checking its fit for accuracy against their own framework of history. Understandably they conclude that the finding in question is wrong because they assume that their fundamental paradigm is correct.

In response we would say that the idea that Freemasonry sprang out of stonemasons' rituals is nothing less than silly. To accept it is to make huge assumptions by accepting the 'authority' view, when there are no facts to substantiate such a belief. Our research tells us that the guilds of stonemasons did have an involvement, but the reason is that they were originally attached to those proto-Freemasons, the Knights Templar.

The Knights Templar were responsible for the huge upsurge in cathedral building in Europe in the twelfth and thirteenth centuries, and they naturally organised the stonemasons into guilds. We believe that they would have given their stonemasons rituals of a certain kind to bind them to the Order of the Knights Templar. When the Templars were arrested in 1307 the stonemasons of Europe had little option but to continue with their rituals, which were eventually to re-merge with non-operative Masonry from 1441 and the building of Rosslyn. The same tendencies can also be detected in London in later times.

When we give talks at assemblies where these people are present they look on with an expression of confusion, because we describe an audit trail that spans thousands rather than hundreds of years. For them it is far more comfortable to assume that everything in history sits in its own little box, untouched by wider events. This allows them to endlessly catalogue Masonic documents and call it research.

We give talks to Freemasons all around the world, and they are usually greeted enthusiastically. Whilst we were finishing off this book, the Grand

Master of one country was recently so impressed with our work that he proposed Chris be made an honorary member of their Grand Lodge after he had delivered a full day's talk. We were both delighted at this recognition.

We welcome probing questions and relish informed debate – but sometimes we find that people prefer not to think about new ideas. After giving a talk at an annual Masonic seminar held in Scotland, Chris spent much of the evening with a very charming but somewhat myopic member of this 'Masonic Mafia'. Although he was the Worshipful Master of a lodge of Research he had not read our books, because he somehow just knew they contained nothing but fanciful nonsense. He did admit to hearing through the grapevine that, surprisingly enough, we were actually 'regular guys', but during the generally enjoyable conversation he constantly assumed what he believed to be the 'serious high ground' by stating that he would need to see the steps leading to new conclusions, implying that we jump to casual conclusions as the fancy takes us. Any attempt to introduce an idea that was not part of his standard dogma, he deemed to be inadmissible.

Here was a man who took it for granted that his existing view of Masonic origins was definitively correct, and that any variation or development would have to start with his assumptions before proceeding. When Chris suggested that his adoption of the United Grand Lodge's standard explanation might be seriously flawed, he simply looked confused.

The problem is one of paradigm collision. The standard explanation for the existence of Freemasonry is based on the idea that the bizarre rituals are simply 'morality plays' borrowed from the initiation rites of guilds of working stonemasons by philosophic gentlemen for their own betterment. In our view this starting point is inherently silly, and any steps leading from it are likely to be deeply flawed. Our research started from scratch and was built up slowly, looking at the broadest possible context. The two views on Masonic origins have points of commonality, but they have to be evaluated independently for their own self-consistency.

But Freemasonry is listening, even if self-appointed 'experts' in England prefer to turn a deaf ear. Only a month earlier Robert had been invited to speak about the formation of the Royal Society to a lodge of Installed Masters in the North of England, a lodge which also takes a serious interest in research. Many of its members also belong to the local university lodge and so are also academics. He has been asked if he will return to give further lectures about our work. So we are heartened to think that our research findings, and personal enthusiasm, for Freemasonry is not being entirely ignored and there are many groups of open-minded brethren who want to hear new ideas about the history of their Order.

There are very few absolute proofs in history, and we accept that we must have got a number of things wrong. But however wrong we might be, we see a pattern that strongly suggests that we are less wrong than all the others. As one professor put it when he looked at our work, 'I can't say for certain that you are right, but you have joined up the dots of history better than I have ever seen anyone do before.'

In the course of our journey we have travelled backwards in time many thousands of years, and our 'blank sheet of paper approach' has caused us to solve major problems such as the riddle of the Megalithic Yard. This result proved that Professor Alexander Thom was right all along about the existence of this incredibly precise prehistoric unit of measurement that was used from northern Scotland to western France. We have demonstrated that some of the main megalithic structures of the British Isles are advanced astronomical devices to track the movements of Venus and shown the huge social and economic benefits that this would have given to prehistoric man. These findings are testable and have been accepted by leading academics (although not by the Masonic Mafia). For example we were delighted to be sent a reprint of a study on the alignment of early churches in Britain, carried out by the University of Hong Kong's Department of Earth Sciences, which cited our research in *Uriel's Machine*.[15]

We have shown the existence of the Shekinah patterns in the Bible and produced the first credible explanation for the Jewish fixation with the numbers 40, 480 and 1,440.

Several people in the past have attempted to explain the reality of the Star of Bethlehem by looking for any bright object in the sky at the time, but we have demonstrated exactly what it was through analysis of Canaanite and Hebrew traditions as well as a variety of Jewish texts, together with astronomical cross-checking. We believe that we have painted a picture of the man we remember as Jesus Christ that helps improve our understanding of his mission as a Jewish Messiah.

The strange building of Rosslyn has been explained as a copy of the ruins of Herod's Temple, and analysis of a single carving has demonstrated that it is unreasonable not to accept that there is a connection between it and the First Degree ritual of modern Freemasonry. We have shown how

[15] Ali, JR & Cunih, P: 'The Orientation of Churches: Some New Evidence'

the layout of the building fits precisely with the description of King Solomon's Temple in *The Masonic Testament*. However, we still await the promised excavation to be conducted by the world-class team proposed by Professor Charlesworth.

We have collated as many old Masonic rituals as we can lay our hands on, and we have published them on a huge website, hosted at Robert's university as a general academic resource for researchers, which is available for the free use of anyone interested in Freemasonry and its teachings. We have also put together a chronological sequence for the historical information contained in Freemasonry, and produced *The Masonic Testament* as a book that is complementary to the books of the Bible, and that we publish here as Part Two of *The Book of Hiram*.

For a time it seemed to us that the rituals of Freemasonry were really corrupted science, and that they might be little more than astrological superstition. Then we found patterns from well-accepted studies that suggest that Freemasonry is a memory of something that worked in the past and may have significance for the future. Whatever is driving the relationship, Sachs has shown that there is a correlation between the time of an individual's birth and their subsequent behaviour. And social and economic cycles suggest that there may be some reality to long-term behavioural effects that have a tendency to coincide with planetary events.

Ultimately, Freemasonry appears to have been an ancient memory of a science that drove human ambition and achievement. And that is undoubtedly what it achieved. The men who built the world's largest democracy and today's only superpower were either Freemasons or subscribed to the values of the Order. The great renaissance of science that gave birth to the modern age was driven by Freemasons such as Sir Robert Moray, Benjamin Franklin and Sir Christopher Wren. Freemasonry was an attitude that was waiting to emerge, an ancient science that had to wait its time before it could become modern science.

And what of the future?

We started this book by stating that Freemasonry is dying, and that remains true so long as those people that run it continue to use it as a gentlemen's dining club. They change ritual where and when it suits them, and they have no idea of its origins, let alone its purpose. The Craft deserves to live on, but it has always belonged to men who have dared to achieve, who have sought out a better way forward by believing in God's purpose and in science.

The modern tension between God and science is, in our opinion, a short-lived issue. There is no difference between the Almighty, His works and science – it is simply a different way of expressing the same thing. Science is not an end-product, it is merely an approach to the human condition that seeks to explain the world in rational terms that can be tested against other observations.

The way forward for mankind must surely be to continue to seek out and embrace the hidden mysteries of nature and science. In this endeavour the Western world has never seen a better way of achieving it than the real principles upon which Freemasonry rests.

We truly hope it can survive.

But to close our quest we need to return to the question we asked when we first began.

WHAT IS FREEMASONRY?

In Masonic ritual the question '*What is Freemasonry?*' requires the answer '*a peculiar system of morality, veiled in allegory and illustrated by symbols*'. This is undoubtedly true, but it is also entirely inadequate, particularly as any sort of description of why the organisation exists.

Having immersed ourselves for many years in a search for the origins of the rituals used by Freemasons, we have finally arrived at a new understanding of the Order. We broadly understand its origins and we know how and why it became a global success story for so long, before gradually descending to a point where it is now largely a subject for public ridicule.

Time and again when we have been interviewed by the press or broadcast media the interviewer has expressed amazement that we are prepared to admit that we are Freemasons, let alone state that we are proud of the fact. The general view is that Freemasons are secretive, elitist and possibly evil in both creed and deed.

This highly negative view has been cemented by decades of poor leadership that fostered unnecessary secrecy and promoted the arrogant belief that the world should mind its own business. The attempts to be more open have come too late and been too poorly executed to hold back the tide of public disquiet.

In England members of the Labour government have recently sought to change the law to force Freemasons in the judiciary, or in the employment of other public bodies, to declare their membership of the Order. Nothing like it has been seen since the persecution of Freemasons in Nazi Germany.

Freemasonry blossomed from the end of the sixteenth to the middle of the twentieth century. Before its decline it was at the heart of society, counting the kings of England and many of the archbishops of Canterbury as senior Freemasons. Despite heads of the Church of England, such as King George VI, being members it is now popular amongst certain Christian groups to claim that Freemasonry is incompatible with Christianity.

So, what is Freemasonry?

And why should it be trusted?

Our answer is that Freemasonry was an engine of achievement that drove the world from darkness to light.

Freemasonry was once an organisation that was the epitome of *The Achieving Society* described by David McClelland. Its members were the great and the good, the people who ran the Church, the country, industry, the armed forces and academia. They were the entrepreneurs and the intelligentsia who made the industrial revolution and who pioneered social and scientific advancement.

Europe thrived on Freemasonry, and the Order was spread by travelling military lodges to every corner of the planet. The oldest universities such as Oxford and Cambridge were proud of their lodges, the great shipbuilders and the men who took the American railroads westwards mingled with the judges and the generals to work together for a better society. Ambition was in their bellies and achievement was their only acceptable outcome.

The American Constitution and the Royal Society came into existence because of Masons like George Washington, Benjamin Franklin, Sir Robert Moray, Alexander Bruce and Elias Ashmole. The city of Washington was designed by Freemasons and London raised from the ashes of the Great Fire due to the inspiration of Grand Master Mason, Sir Christopher Wren. Even the 'Wild West' was tamed by Freemasons Davy Crockett, Jim Bowie, Buffalo Bill and Pat Garrett, to name but a few.

In every town throughout the Western world, Masonic Temples provided the meeting ground for the men who set out to achieve. In the West Yorkshire town of Halifax, the world's largest building society was brought into existence by Freemasons who met in the Old Cock Inn. Now a major bank, this institution, named after the town, provided the financial structure to give hundreds of thousands of ordinary people the new opportunity to own their own home.

At a time when leading thinkers and doers in England were either Christians or Jews, Freemasons of all religions met on equal terms in the lodge to share their enthusiasm for progress on the road to making life better for themselves, their families and the community at large. They worked in harmony with their church or synagogue as any religious differences evaporated in the atmosphere of tolerance that is central to the Order.

As they achieved ever-greater success, their towns and their countries grew more prosperous and new, more specialist, ways of working together came along. Freemasonry had fought for and attained an age of reason and personal freedom. Now people could develop themselves and their communities without the need to meet in darkened rooms, wear strange regalia and recite odd-ball ritual.

No longer are Masonic lodges the meeting place of 'movers and shakers'.

The people who would once have been the backbone of the Order, now would not dream of asking to join. They have better things to do in their life – careers to build, families to rear, social commitments to take up their time. Everyone from businessmen to police officers, from councillors to academics, gives the Order a wide berth. These days membership of the local lodge is either irrelevant or positively detrimental to a young person's career.

When our first book came out, we were not exactly popular with the United Grand Lodge of England. But when a journalist from a national magazine interviewed the leading lights at Masonic Hall in Great Queen Street, London, they were initially stumped when he asked if he could meet a Mason who worked at a senior level in a modern industry. The only person they knew of was Chris Knight, who was the chairman of an advertising and PR company – as well as one half of the writing partnership along with the academic Robert Lomas who had so recently penned the Masonically heretical book, *The Hiram Key*.

Membership of modern Masonry does not carry any benefits, and the result is that most Freemasons are no longer social drivers. Lodge members no longer talk of ambition and social development. They make donations to charity but they talk little of philosophy or physics, and spend hours toasting the symbols of a bygone age.

Freemasonry is a victim of its own success. It has achieved the social and scientific change it set out to establish, but now it is like an old soldier, a spent force representing a great past that demands respect, not for what it is now, but for what it once did.

Freemasonry can be trusted.

Despite unfounded rumours to the contrary, it has always demanded the highest standards of honesty and decency. Today, the sad fact is that it could not be other than benign even if it wanted to, because it has no power, no money and no influence.

But, in the final analysis, Freemasonry has earned its special place in history because it was one of the working tools used by the Great Architect of the Universe to build our modern world.

Part Two

THE MASONIC TESTAMENT

TO THE READER

The general opinion of Masonic ritual is not positive. Writing in the British *Times* newspaper on the subject of American sororities and fraternities, one journalist said:

> The Freemasons have elaborate initiation mumbo-jumbo, with blindfold, trouser leg rolled up, and compass point pressing the bare chest.[1]

The Chambers Dictionary defines mumbo-jumbo as 'foolish ritual' or 'baffling jargon', which is a fair assessment of Masonic ritual when viewed without understanding. The big question is whether there is meaning behind the ritual, in the same way that the Bible cannot be dismissed just because it has some rather bizarre sections. Most things in life tend to become considered 'sensible' through familiarity, and only rarely through genuine understanding.

Masonic ritual has only been written down for perhaps two hundred years, but it would be wrong to assume that the content only dates from that time. Freemasonry was once an entirely oral tradition – and theoretically it still is, as most lodges conduct their ritual from memory. The Old Testament was first written down over a thousand years after the supposed time of Abraham and several hundred after Solomon, but it is wholly accepted that this was just a formalisation of oral traditions.

Another example can be seen in the loss and recovery of the Book of Enoch. Now believed to have been written at Qumran around 200 BCE, yet it records elements which we argue are a tribal memory of real events that took place some three millennia before that time. When Freemason James Bruce returned from Ethiopia in the late eighteenth century with copies of the Book of Enoch, which had been lost for over 1,400 years, the world in general thought it must be a terribly corrupted version because it seemed to make no sense. Only when a number of copies of the book were found at Qumran amongst the Dead Sea Scrolls was it proven that Bruce's version was quite correct. And it took analysis by non-theologians like Robin Heath and ourselves to extract the lost layers of meaning.

The problem with all oral traditions is that meaning can become lost over time, leaving the ritual to appear as charming nonsense. Consider the

[1] Howard, Philip: 'Ritual ordeal is all too human', *Times* (London), 19 October 2002

341

nursery rhyme '*Ring a ring of roses . . . a pocket full of posies*'. It sounds pleasant, but it makes no sense because most people today do not realise that it is a story of the plague, with attempts at prevention followed by the final line '*atishyoo atishyoo . . . we all fall down*' playing out an infection and death scene.

As the meanings of individual words evolve and terminologies change, oral material usually stays frozen in the past. Another example taken from nursery rhymes demonstrates this point further:

> *Half a pound of tuppenny rice,*
> *Half a pound of treacle,*
> *That's the way the money goes,*
> *Pop! goes the weasel.*

Originally this was a lament about the cost of living in early Victorian London, where 'pop' was the term for taking something to the pawnbroker's and 'weasel' a corruption for 'whistle', which itself is Cockney rhyming slang for a suit (*whistle and flute = suit*). Apparently it was very common for men to pawn their best suits two centuries ago just to get enough money for food, but it is something that would be unusual today.

Printed Masonic ritual may be relatively recent, but its content is not. For example, Masonic ritual has always described a dormer window in the east face of King Solomon's Temple, when there is no mention of such a device in the Old Testament. Freemasonic ritual talks about this dormer without any understanding of its function, although it does describe the light of the Shekinah entering through it. As we have shown, this must be very old knowledge indeed.

The close statistical correlation between the appearances of the Shekinah and peaks of achievement in various societies, the reality of which has been confirmed by the research of Harvard Professor David McClelland, shows a strand of observational knowledge which can be traced back over at least 3,000 years through the descriptions of the significance of the Shekinah contained within the ritual. Knowledge of this link was certainly not available to the Masons who first wrote down the verbal myths of the Craft, but it was to the Phoenician builder of Solomon's Temple. This particular verbal myth survives only in the rituals of Freemasonry.

We believe that the rituals of Freemasonry are a major source of historic information for those with eyes to see it. To help all researchers to clarify this vision, 'The Web of Hiram' has been constructed and opened to all as an academic resource, courtesy of the University of Bradford website. And we have extracted from this plethora of material the logical storyline that we have called *The Masonic Testament*.

This testament has been laboriously reassembled from across the rituals of the 160 degrees of Freemasonry which we have become familiar with since we published *The Hiram Key*. It is in the nature of Masonic ritual to be repetitive – every item is repeated three times over, usually by three separate officers, using very similar words. There are also many common elements across all the degrees and orders, which involve opening and closing the assembly, checking that all officers know their duties and responsibilities, and ensuring that only initiated members of the degree are present. We have not included these elements with this compilation. What we have concentrated on is the wonderful stories which are told to candidates as part of their initiation into this wide range of degrees. Sometimes the stories are acted out, with the candidate playing the role of one of the Masonic heroes. At other times the stories are told to the assembled brethren in the form of a carefully memorised 'traditional history'. The ritual is always verbal and often includes gestures, and steps to be performed during the re-enactment.

In this way, by telling and retelling ancient stories since time immemorial, Freemasons have preserved and nurtured their myths and legends. Until recent times, that is, when some individuals took it upon themselves to 'improve' and 'simplify' the stories passed to their care. So politically incorrect oaths and penalties are removed from ceremonies, the names used to describe the 'Most High' are changed to 'more suitable' ones, and many degrees are awarded in name only, without their ceremonies being worked in open lodge. In this way ignorant and unlearned bigots destroy an ancient verbal heritage without any care for its possible meaning.

We have been careful to preserve the stories exactly as they are told in the oldest copies of the ritual we have been able to find. This means that the style of the language often changes, but we have decided to accept this in order to keep the subtlety of the Masonic verbal record.

Some claims, such as that made in Chapter 14 that the Roman Emperor Constantine was born in York, may have more to do with the need of the Grand Lodge of York to claim a glorious ancestry, rather than with historical truth but we have consistently reproduced the Masonic claims of the ritual without adding any editorial comment. Our comments have been confined to Part One of the book. In this *Masonic Testament* we have collected together the great myth of Freemasonry and presented it in a logical order. We have adopted the chapter and verse convention of other testaments to make reference to particular sections simple. Now, for the first time since 1813 and the attempted destruction of Masonic ritual by the Duke of Sussex, it is possible to read once more the vast sweeping story that was once the secret knowledge that the Order of Freemasonry taught to its adepts.

Why leave the East and go to the West?

In search of that which was lost.

What was that which was lost?

The genuine secrets of a Master Mason.

How became they lost?

By the untimely intervention of the Duke of Sussex.

How do you hope to find them?

By the reconstruction of the Masonic Testament.

Read on, and as you learn the genuine secrets of Freemasonry enjoy that daily advancement in Masonic knowledge and tolerance that the Craft has all but forgotten.

Chapter One

GOD MAKES MANKIND

1. When God in His eternal council conceived the thought of Man's creation, He called to Him the three ministers that continually waited upon the throne. And their names were Justice, Truth, and Mercy.

2. And He addressed them saying: 'Shall we make Man?' Justice answered: 'O God, make him not, he will, trample on Thy laws;' and Truth also answered: 'O God, make him not, for he will pollute Thy sanctuaries.' But Mercy, dropping on her knees and looking up through her tears, exclaimed: 'O my God, make him and I will watch over him with my care through the dark and dreary paths he will have to tread.'

3. And hearing Mercy's pleas God made man and called him Adam, and said to him: 'O Man, thou art the child of Mercy – go and deal with thy brother.'

4. When Adam first presented himself before God under the celestial canopy of divers colours that is heaven he presented himself in humble posture, with uplifted hands and bended knees betokening at once his humility and dependence on the blessed author of his being. Again did he thus present himself before his offended Judge when he endeavoured to avert His wrath, and conciliate His mercy,

and this expressive and contrite form he has handed down to posterity forever.

5. From that time this penitential sign has denoted that state of heart and mind, without which our prayers and oblations can never be acceptable at the throne of grace, before which a frail and erring creature of the dust should present himself to his maker.

6. And Adam's place was in the east facing west, clothed in a saffron-coloured robe, and with head covered. In his right hand he held a sceptre, its handle gilded, and on the top a globe of gold. His jewel was a sun of gold, suspended by a chain of gold, worn around his neck. On the reverse side of the jewel was inscribed a hemisphere of gold, showing the northern half of the ecliptic and zodiac, with the signs from Taurus to Libra.

7. In God's eternal council the minister called Truth resided in the West. His robe was rose-coloured and he held a white rod, at the end of which was an eye of gold.

8. Also there were seven lesser beings collectively known as Malakoth [meaning Angels]. Individually they were called Malak [meaning Angel] and their names were Gabriel, Uriel, Michael, Raphael, Zarakhiel, Hamaliel and Tsaphiel. They wore bright flame-colour robes and an apron, from their collar hung a seven-pointed star of gold.

9. Gabriel was placed in the northeast, having on his right his banner, square in shape, of crimson silk, having upon it the figure of an eagle, and the sign of the planet Jupiter.

10. Michael in the southeast, having on his right his banner of black silk, of like shape, bearing the figure of a lion, and the sign of the planet Saturn.

11. Uriel in the southwest, his banner of flame-coloured silk, of like shape, on his right, bearing the figure of a bull, and the sign of the planet Mars.

12. Raphael in the northwest, his banner of green silk, of like shape, on his right, bearing the figure of a man, and the sign of the planet Mercury.

13. Zarakhiel in the east, his banner of purple silk, of like shape, on his right, bearing the sign of the sun.

14. Tsaphiel in the east, in front of Truth, his banner of white silk and on his right, bearing the sign of the Moon.

15. And Hamaliel in the South, his banner of blue silk bearing the sign of the planet Venus.

16. Gabriel also wore bracelets of pure tin; Michael, of lead; Uriel of steel; Raphael, of hollow glass, partly filled with quicksilver; Zarakhiel of gold; Tsaphiel of silver; and Hamaliel, of polished copper. The banners of Michael, Gabriel, Uriel and Hamaliel were fringed with silver; those of the others with gold.

17. The other members of the Council were termed Aralim [plural of Aral, meaning Lion of God; or hero]. Their jewel was a five-pointed star, suspended by a flame-coloured ribbon on the left breast.

Chapter Two

ENOCH MEETS GOD AND ENGRAVES HIS TRUE NAME

1. Jared, who was the sixth in descent from Adam, had a son whose name was Enoch, meaning city. Enoch was filled with the love and fear of God, he strove to lead men in the way of honour and duty. And in a vision God appeared to him in visible shape, and said to him: 'Enoch, thou hast longed to know my true name: arise and follow me, and thou shalt know it.'

2. In this vision Enoch saw a mountain and a golden triangle showing the rays of the sun. From that time this device became known as The Delta of Enoch.

3. Enoch, accepting his vision as an inspiration, journeyed in search of the mountain he had seen in his dream, until, weary of the search, he stopped in the land of Canaan, then already populous with the descendants of Adam, and there employed workmen. Then, with the help of his son Methuselah, he excavated down into the ground, creating nine apartments, one above the other, and each roofed with an arch as he had seen in his dream, the lowest being hewn out of the solid rock.

4. In the crown of each arch he left a narrow aperture closed with a

square stone, and over the upper one, upon ground level, he built a modest temple. It was built of huge unhewn stones and roofless so as to view the celestial canopy that is the work of God; the Grand Architect of the Universe.

5. Enoch then created a triangular plate of gold, inlaid with many precious gems, on which he engraved the ineffable NAME OF GOD, and sank the plate into one face of a cube of agate. This most precious of objects was placed in the vaults beneath the temple.

6. None knew of the deposit of the precious treasure; and, that it might remain undiscovered, and survive the Flood, which it was known to Enoch would soon overwhelm the world in one vast sea of mire, he covered the aperture, and the stone that closed it, and the great ring of iron used to raise the stone, with the granite pavement of his primitive temple.

7. Then, fearing that all knowledge of the arts and sciences would be lost in the universal flood, he built two great columns upon a high hill – one of brass, to resist water, and one of granite, to resist fire. On the granite column was written in hieroglyphics a description of the subterranean apartments; on the one of brass, the rudiments of the arts and sciences.

8. And Enoch knew that the Lord was great in Zion. Let all the earth praise Him for His great and terrible name, for it is holy. Exalt the Lord our God, and worship on His holy hill.

9. He spake from the cloudy pillar and from the fire; and from the depth cometh forth the riches of secret places. Exalt the Lord our God, for He is holy; and His name, for it is from everlasting to everlasting.

10. We are but of yesterday, and know nothing. Our days are but a shadow: they flee and we know not.

11. Canst thou, by searching, find out God? Canst thou find out the Almighty to perfection? He is as high as heaven. What canst thou do? He is deeper than hell. What canst thou know?

12. Mark the perfect man, and behold the upright: for the end of that man is peace. 'Mine eyes shall be on the perfect man.' saith the Lord. 'The perfect of the land shall dwell with me: they shall walk in my name, and serve me forever.'

13. Let us give thanks unto the Lord, who hath given us the treasures of darkness and the hidden riches of secret places.

14. Oh, thou real and eternal Lord God, source of light and of love – thou Sovereign Inspector and Mighty Architect of the wonders of Creation – who from Thy throne in the highest heaven in mercy looketh down upon all the dwellers of the earth – lend, we beseech thee, Thine ears to the prayers and petitions of Thy unworthy servants now assembled in Thy presence, to teach the mysteries of that Sublime Edifice which is erected and dedicated to Thy Most Holy and Glorious Name.

15. The holy and blessed One raised Enoch from the world to serve Him, as it is written, for God took him God, showed him all the repositories of the superior and inferior kingdoms, and He showed him the tree alphabet of life, respecting which Adam had received his command, its leaves and its branches we see all in his Book.

Chapter Three

NOAH BUILDS THE ARK TO SURVIVE THE FLOOD

1. Before the General Deluge, which is commonly called Noah's Flood, there was a Man called Lamech, who had two wives, the One called Ada, the other Zilla.

2. By Ada, he begat two sons, Jabal and Jubal, by Zilla he had one son called Tubal and a daughter called Naamab. These four children found the beginning of all crafts in the World; Jabal found out geometry, and he divided flocks of sheep. He first built a house of stone and timber. His brother Jubal found the Art of Music. He was the father of all such as handle the Harp and Organ. Tubal-Cain was the instructor of every artificer in brass and iron. And the daughter found out the art of weaving. These children of Lamech knew well that God would take vengeance for sin either by fire or water; being warned by their grandfather Enoch.

3. In his old age Lamech begat Noah, and God warned Noah about the coming deluge, telling him to build an Ark.

4. With the deluge expected, Noah built the Ark using an axe with which he cut down trees and squared them; a saw, with which he sawed those trees into planks; and an auger, with which he made holes in the planks.

Also with the axe he cut out pins and drove in the pegs by which means the planks were kept together.

5. These tools have other meanings. The axe felled the trees, and they, being cut down, are emblematic of the fall of the old world. The saw, dividing the timber into planks, is emblematic of the separation of Noah and his family from the rest of mankind by the Lord. The auger, making holes in the planks, teaches us the use of affliction in producing self-abasement and searchings of the heart.

6. As the Ark was built by these tools, so we are shewn that by perseverance in faith, hope and love, we may be shut into an Ark of safety, when the elements shall melt with fervent heat, and the whole earth shall be dissolved.

7. Wisdom, Strength and Beauty were displayed in the construction of the Ark. By the wisdom and cunning workmanship of Noah, that beautiful structure, the Ark, was formed, the strength of which proved the temporal salvation of himself and his family and all the living creatures contained therein.

8. The Antediluvians, sentenced to the watery abyss, endeavoured to frustrate the wrath of Heaven by pulling each other to the summit of hills, to the tops of trees and all other places which presented a temporary relief from the justice of Him who was pouring down destruction upon their heads.

9. The granite column, which had been erected by Enoch before the Deluge, was overturned and swept away by the Deluge, but that of brass stood firm, and was later found by his grandson, Noah.

10. After the Deluge the men and animals came out of the Ark on the mountains of Armenia. They had been dispersed over the whole earth, and have rested wherever the providence of God was pleased to direct them.

11. Noah stood with an erect posture when he offered up the sacrifice to God in thanksgiving for his safe deliverance from the Deluge. God then

fixed His rainbow in the sky and established His covenant with Noah that the waters should no more become a flood to destroy all flesh.

12. Listen to the promise given by God as a covenant with Noah:

13. In a little wrath I hid my face from thee for a moment: but with everlasting kindness will I have mercy on thee, saith the Lord thy Redeemer. For this is as the waters of Noah unto me: for as I have sworn that the waters of Noah should no more go over the earth; so have I sworn that I would not be wroth with thee, nor rebuke thee.

14. For the mountains shall depart, and the hills be removed; but My kindness shall not depart from thee, neither shall the covenant of My peace be removed, sayeth the Lord that hath mercy on thee.

15. That promise of God will comfort us in trouble, cheer us in the hour of our death and make us happy for all eternity.

16. The Olive Branch is an emblem of hope and commemorates the abatement of the waters.

17. At that ancient time the survivors of the Flood founded their places of worship using the mysterious Porphyry Stone. They used the Porphyry Stone and not the Sacred Scriptures because at that time the Sacred Writings were not yet in existence.

18. The traditions connected with Porphyry Stone are three in number. First: Upon this Stone the Patriarch Noah reposed when he daily returned from his pious labour in building the Ark, and it was placed by him in the centre of the Ark when finished. Second: With this Stone did Noah fix the station of the Ark when it rested on Mount Ararat. Third: Upon this Stone Noah made his offering to the Lord in thankfulness for safe deliverance; and he desired that it should be fixed at the foot of Mount Ararat until the first of his descendants should be called upon to travel again by either land or water.

19. Upon the Porphyry Stone our Ancient Brethren placed a golden triangle with its apex towards the East.

20. The Delta, which stands on the Mysterious Porphyry Stone, is emblematical of the Sun, Moon and Stars.

21. Those in the high sphere of life have the largest province wherein to do good, but those of an inferior degree will be eminently distinguished if they move regularly and prove useful members of society. The highest is he who performs his part best, not he who fills the most exalted position: for the Moon, although reflecting her light from the Sun, evidently sets forth the glory of God; and the flowers of the field declare His power equally with the Stars of the firmament.

22. The three points of the Triangle are synonymous with Wisdom, Strength and Beauty.

23. Man, in his ignorance at the commencement of his pilgrimage believes himself secure, and, often times discarding the use of the unerring compass, strays from the true course, and thus incurs the risk of being overwhelmed by the waters.

24. Since the providence of God preserved our ancient brethren from the overwhelming waters, they have observed and obeyed God's voice in being fruitful and multiplying on the earth and so they have kept up the memorial of so signal a deliverance.

25. By coming into the Ark, they proved true and faithful brothers and since that time have been known by the name, Noachida.

Chapter Four

THE TOWER OF BABEL DESTROYED BY GOD

1. Be it known notwithstanding the recent vengeance which the Deity had taken upon mankind for their iniquities, by causing universal deluge, notwithstanding the Deity had given the rainbow as a sign of reconciliation, vouchsafing that favour declared that the world should not be again destroyed by waters, the descendants of Noah, from their want of faith in the Divine prediction, being apprehensive of a second deluge, said: Let us build a city whose top may reach the heavens, and let us make a name lest we be scattered abroad upon the face of the earth.

2. To accomplish their designs, they began to erect an high tower in the plain of Shinar; but this enterprise being displeasing in the eye of their Maker, as tending to frustrate or delay the execution of His design, that mankind should not always continue together, He obliged them to discontinue the project by confounding their language, so that one could not understand another.

3. From this circumstance the city took its name of Babel, which signifies confusion; and a dispersion of the people and a planting of nations ensued. It was on the night of the full moon that the Lord worked this wonder.

4. The architect was named Peleg; at least, it was he who gave the idea of this building.

5. As a punishment for his contumacy, and the presumption of his fellow builders, he was deprived of his speech; and to avoid the outrages of his companions, who considered him as the cause of the failure of their design, he travelled into countries remote from Shinar, and from thence, only by moonlight, as he was fearful of massacre if his person were recognised.

6. His place of retirement was in a dark forest, where, having erected a triangular dwelling, he, by humiliation, and contrition for the part he had taken in the plain of Shinar, obtained remission for his sins, and had his speech restored to him. In this dwelling of Peleg's was found a stone of white marble, on which was inscribed the following epitaph: Here repose the ashes of the grand architect of the tower of Babel. The Lord had pity on him because he became humble.

Chapter Five

MELCHIZEDEK, KING OF SALEM, MAKES ABRAM A GRAND HIGH PRIEST

1. And it came to pass in the days of Amraphel king of Shinar, Arioch king of Ellasar, Chedorlaomer king of Elam, and Tidal king of nations; that these made war with Bera king of Sodom, and with Birsha king of Gomorrah, Shinab king of Admah, and Shemeber king of Zeboiim, and the king of Bela, which is Zoar.

2. All these were joined together in the vale of Siddim, which is the salt sea.

3. Twelve years they served Chedorlaomer, and in the thirteenth year they rebelled.

4. And there went out the king of Sodom, and the king of Gomorrah, and the king of Admah, and the king of Zeboiim, and the king of Bela (the same is Zoar); and they joined battle with them in the vale of Siddim;

5. With Chedorlaomer the king of Elam, and with Tidal king of nations, and Amraphel king of Shinar, and Arioch, king of Ellasar; four kings with five.

6. And the vale of Siddim was full of slimepits; and the kings of Sodom and Gomorrah fled, and fell there; and they that remained fled to the mountain. And they took all the goods of Sodom and Gomorrah, and all their victuals, and went their way.

7. And they took Lot, Abram's brother's son who dwelt in Sodom, and his goods, and departed. And there came one that had escaped, and told Abram the Hebrew; for he dwelt in the plain of Mamre the Amorite, brother of Eschol, and brother of Aner: and these were confederate with Abram.

8. And when Abram heard that his brother was taken captive, he armed his trained servants, born in his own house, three hundred and eighteen, and pursued them unto Dan. And he divided himself against them, he and his servants, by night, and smote them, and pursued them unto Hobah, which is on the left hand of Damascus. And he brought back all the goods, and also brought again his brother Lot, and his goods, and the women also, and the people.

9. And the king of Sodom went out to meet him after his return from the slaughter of Chedorlaomer, and of the kings that were with him, at the valley of Shaveh, which is the king's dale.

10. And Melchizedek king of Salem brought forth bread and wine: and he is the priest of the Most High God. And he blessed him, and said: Blessed be Abram of the Most High God, possessor of heaven and earth: And blessed be the Most High God which hath delivered thine enemies into thy hand. And he gave him tithes of all.

11. And the king of Sodom said unto Abram: Give me the persons, and take goods to thyself.

12. And Abram said to the king: I have lift up mine hand unto the Lord, the Most High God, the possessor of heaven and earth. That I will not take from a thread even to a shoe latchet, and that I will not take anything that is thine, lest thou shouldest say, I have made Abram rich: Save only that which the young men have eaten, and the portion of the men which went with me, Aner, Eschol, Mamre; let them take their portion.

13. And Melchizedek, Prince of Jerusalem, and King of Salem, sat in state in his Royal tent in the valley of Saveh, which is known as the King's Dale. As Abram approached his tabernacle Melchizedek stood at the entrance, drew his sword and aimed a downward blow at Abram, who parried the blow and knelt before him.

14. Melchizedek asked who the stranger was and in reply was told that the person before him was his friend and brother Abram, saying: 'Behold the captives and the spoils: I give thee tithes of all.'

15. And Melchizedek said: 'Blessed be Abram of the Most High God, possessor of heaven and earth; and blessed be the Most High God, which hath delivered thine enemies into thy hand. Arise, my friend and brother Abram. Enter my Tent, eat of my bread and drink of my wine.'

16. And Melchizedek stood with his drawn sword in his hand in the centre of his Tabernacle and fed Abram bread from the point of his sword saying: 'Behold, how good and how pleasant it is for brethren to dwell together in unity. Eat with us this bread, which you receive at the point of the sword, to teach you that you should ever be ready to divide your last loaf with a Companion Anointed High Priest, and should his necessities demand it, even though he be a personal enemy, to feed him at the point of the sword.'

17. Holding his sword across his chest, Melchizedek then offered Abram his goblet from the flat of his blade saying: 'Behold, bless ye the Lord, all ye servants of the Lord, which by night stand in the house of the Lord, Lift up your hands in the sanctuary, and bless the Lord. The Lord that made heaven and earth bless thee out of Zion. Drink with us this wine, which you receive over the sword, to teach you that you should ever be ready to divide the luxuries as well as the necessities of life with a Companion Anointed High Priest. If he hunger, feed him; if he thirst, give him drink, if he be naked, clothe him; if he be sick or afflicted, visit him and minister unto him; sympathise with him in his sorrows, and rejoice with him in his joys. These things do unto him and never forsake him.'

18. Melchizedek ordered his companions to form themselves into the sides

of an equilateral triangle. He placed Abram in the centre of the triangle and stood in the East at the apex whilst they all kneeled as he prayed:

19. May the Supreme High Priest of Heaven and Earth grant His blessing to this our companion, so that he may teach the laws and commandments of the Lord and perform the duties of his office with fervency, fidelity and zeal.

20. And he blessed Abram saying: The Lord bless thee and keep thee. The Lord make his face to shine upon thee and be gracious to thee. The Lord lift up his countenance upon thee and give thee peace.

21. And Melchizedek spoke to Abram, who remained kneeling in the centre of the equilateral triangle, saying: I will now explain to you the secrets of this Holy Order. Anointing with oil is the principal and divinely appointed ceremony in the inauguration into each of the three typical offices of the Jewish Commonwealth – Prophet, Priest and King. It is received as a symbol of sanctification, and of dedication to the service of the Most High God.

22. When I Melchizedek, king of Salem, made Abram a Grand High Priest I anointed him first three times with oil, and then three times with wine: both these triple anointings are in allusion to the Triangle, a symbol of the Deity. Thus are you reminded that the true brother should so dedicate himself to the service of the Most High God.

23. As the unchangeable Priesthood of Melchizedek is superior to that of Aaron, which passed away, so do we look forward, after the close of this earthly existence, to an entrance into that Tabernacle 'not made with hands, eternal in the Heavens'.

24. Remember that the responsibilities of this Holy Order rest not alone upon the Officers, but equally upon the individual members of the Order, a dereliction of duty being equally destructive in the one case as in the other.

25. As you value, then, your honour as a man and a brother; as you prize

the purity and permanency of the Order; as you fear to displease the Almighty, Whose Name you have solemnly invoked; so keep inviolate every pledge you have made, and perform with fidelity every duty to which you have become bound.

26. Let the Lion of the Tribe of Judah be the symbol of your strength and boldness in the cause of truth and justice. Be as patient as the Ox with the foibles and errors of your Brethren, and as swift as the Eagle to do every good work. Set before your Companions of the Royal Craft the bright example of an upright and perfect Man, and especially of a Companion Anointed High Priest.

27. Let Holiness to the Lord be engraven upon all your thoughts, words and actions.

28. Finally, after this painful life is ended, may the Most High God, Who dwelleth between the Cherubim, admit you into His glorious and everlasting Sanctuary, there to adore Him for evermore.

Chapter Six

THE SECRETS OF MOSES

1. The true name of God remained unknown until He said unto Moses in Egypt, when He ordered him to go to Pharaoh, and cause him to send forth the children of Israel out of Egypt: 'I am that which I was and shall be: I am the God of thy fathers; the God of Abraham, of Isaac, and of Jacob. Thus shalt thou say unto the children of Israel. He who is hath sent me unto you, I am the Lord, that appeared to Abraham, to Isaac, and to Jacob by my name, AL-SHEDI, but my name I did not show them.'

2. Moses engraved the ineffable name upon a plate of gold, and deposited it in the ark of the covenant. Moses made the name known to Aaron and Joshua, and afterwards it was made known to the chief priests.

3. The word being composed of consonants only, its true pronunciation was soon lost, but the word still remained in the ark; and in the time of Othniel in a battle against the King of Syria, those who bore the ark were slain, and the ark fell to the ground. After the battle, the men of Israel, searching for it, were led to it by the roaring of a lion, which, crouching by it, had guarded it, holding the golden key in its mouth. Upon the approach of the High-priest and Levites, he laid down the key, and withdrew. Hence, upon the golden key worn by the treasurer,

you see the initials of these words: 'In ore leonis verbum inveni' – 'In the lion's mouth I found the word.' This plate of gold was melted down, and made into an image of Dagon by the Philistines, who took it in battle.

4. The First or Holy Lodge was opened after the Exodus of the Israelites from their Egyptian bondage, by Moses, Aholiab and Bezaleel, on consecrated ground at the foot of Mount Horeb, in the Wilderness of Sinai, where the host of Israel had assembled and pitched their tents, to offer up prayers and thanksgivings for their signal deliverance from the hands of the Egyptians. In this place the Almighty had thought fit to reveal Himself before that time to His faithful servant Moses, when He commissioned him His High Ambassador of Wrath against Pharaoh and his people, and of Freedom and Salvation to the House of Jacob. Here were delivered the forms of those mysterious prototypes, the Tabernacle and the Ark of the Covenant; here were delivered the Sacred Laws, engraven by the hand of the Most High, with those sublime and comprehensive precepts of civil and religious polity, which, by separating His favoured people from all other nations, consecrated Israel a chosen vessel to His service; for these reasons this is denominated the First or Holy Lodge.

5. This favour was signalled to the brethren by the appearance in the East of the Divine Shekinah which represents the Glory of God appearing on Mount Sinai at the deliverance of the Sacred Law.

6. The rods, we use as emblems of power; as such they have been employed by all nations, but we use them in commemoration of the Rod wherewith Moses wrought so many wonders in the land of Egypt and in the wilderness.

7. Bezaleel was the inspired workman of the Holy Tabernacle which he built to house the Ark of the Covenant and to allow the light of the Divine Shekinah to shine upon it. His design afterwards became the model of King Solomon's Temple, and conforms to a pattern delivered on Mount Horeb by God to Moses, who afterwards became the Grand Master of the Lodge of Israel.

8. In after times when the Lord God appeared to Moses at the foot of Mount Horeb, in the burning bush, unable to support the dazzling radiance of the Deity, Moses thus shielded his eyes from the divine splendour, at the same time placing his hand on his heart in token of submission and obedience.

9. This Penitential sign denotes that state of heart and mind, without which our prayers and oblations can never be acceptable at the throne of grace, before which how should a frail and erring creature of the dust present himself, but with uplifted hands and bended knees betokening at once his humility, and dependence. In this humble posture Adam first presented himself before God, and blessed the author of his being; again did he thus present himself before his offended Judge when he endeavoured to avert His wrath and conciliate His mercy, and this expressive and contrite form he has handed down to posterity for ever.

10. Moses created Princes of the Tabernacle. The especial duties of a Prince of the Tabernacle were to labour incessantly for the glory of God, the honour of his country, and the happiness of his brethren; and to offer up thanks and prayers to the Deity in lieu of sacrifices of flesh and blood.

11. The Court of the Princes of the Tabernacle was presided over by Moses, the Most Puissant Leader, its High Priests were Eleazar and Isthamar, the sons of Aaron. Aholiab and Bezaleel supported Moses when he held this court. Eliasaph, son of Lael, of the house of Gershom, was the orator to the court. Its secretary was Eliazaphan, the son of Uzziel, of the house of Kohath, and the treasurer was Zuriel, son of Abihael, of the house of Merari. Caleb, the son of Jephunneh, was the Master of Ceremonies and Joshua, son of Nun, was the Captain of the Guard. All Princes of the Tabernacle are Levites.

12. When the Pentagram, or Blazing Star, was to be seen in the east Moses called the Court together to initiate new Princes. As the initiate entered Eliasaph addressed the Court saying: My brother, the initiate is he who possesses the lamp, the cloak, and the staff. The lamp is reason enlightened by science; the cloak is liberty, or the full and entire possession of one's self, which isolates the sage from the currents of instinct; and

the staff is the assistance of the occult and eternal forces of nature.'

13. Then Moses said: 'My brethren, the power of darkness has prevailed over the prince of light. The earth mourns, and is wrinkled with frost. The leaves drop from the trees; snow shrouds the mountains, and cold winds sweep over the shuddering skies. All nature laments; and we share the common sorrow. Let prayers be offered up in the tabernacle for the return of light and the reascension of the sun, and of that moral and spiritual light of which He is the type.'

14. Moses said: 'We, like our ancient masters, mourn Osiris, the type to us of the sun, of light, of life. The scorpion and the serpent rule the winter waves, on which the frail ark tosses that contains his body. Weep, my brethren, for Osiris! Weep for light lost, and life departed, and the good and beautiful oppressed by evil! Man hath fallen from his first estate, and is lost, as the sun hath sunken into the icy arms of winter. Weep for Osiris, type of the good, the true, the beautiful! How shall his body be recovered from the embraces of the hungry sea; and earth again be gladdened by his presence?'

15. Eleazar said: Brethren, behold a new Priest of the Tabernacle, to be instructed and prepared to fulfill all his duties as a Prince of well-doers in this frail Tabernacle of life, that he may be raised on the great day of account, a shining monument of God's glory, in the tabernacle of eternity.

16. When the new moon occurred in the vernal equinox during the fortieth year of the wandering of the children of Israel in the desert, Aaron died. Moses pitched his camp at Punon, on the eastern side of the mountains of Hor, Seir or Edom, in Arabia Petraea, on the confines of Idumaea, and there he held a council.

17. Moses presided over the council which consisted of Joshua, son of Nun, and Caleb, son of Yephanah. The council's orator was Eleazar, son of Aaron. His brother Ithamar was the council's scribe. In front of Moses stood two short columns, one to the east and one to the west. On one column is a winged globe encircled by a serpent and atop the other is a basilisk, his body coiled in folds and his head and neck

erect. In the East was erected a tau cross with a coiled serpent inter-twining it.

18. Moses spoke to the council: 'So much of the truth as it is given to mortals to know, is within the reach of those alone whose intellects are unclouded by passion or excess. To attain it, to comprehend the delicate distinctions of the thought in which the truth is embodied, the intellect, like a keen instrument of the finest steel, must be able to dissect the thought, and distinguish one from the other its invisible nerves. The edge of the instrument is blunted by the indulgence of the sensual appetites, or of the intemperate passions of the soul Therefore it is that the sages have always required of those who sought to scale the heights of philosophy a preparatory discipline, of long-continued temperance and self-restraint; and fasting is enjoined, as well as prayer. If thy intellect is dull and coarse by nature, or clouded and confused by indulgence, the sacred symbolism will have no meaning to thee; and we shall address thee in a foreign tongue. Thus it is that true Masonry has always been, and always must be, confined to a few; since to the mass its truths are foolishness and valueless.'

19. Eleazar replied: Most Puissant Leader, the soul of the people was discouraged, because of the way, journeying from Mount Hor, by the way of the Red Sea, to compass the land of Edom; and they spake against Adonai and against thee, saying: 'Why hath AL-Shadai and his servant Moses brought us up out of Egypt, to die in the wilderness? There is no bread nor any water, and our souls loathe this light manna. We go to and fro these forty years; and as Aaron died, in the desert, so also shall we all die here. Let us put trust in Adonai no longer; but let us call on the great gods Amun and Astarte, Osiris and Isis, to deliver us from this misery.'

20. And as the children of Israel cried aloud, Lo Adonai sent fiery serpents among us, by whom much people hath died. And those that remain have repented and saith: 'Put chains upon thy neck in token of our penitence, and go unto Moses our leader, and beseech him to pray unto Adonai that he take away the serpents from us,' and Eleazar did as they desired.

21. He only is worthy of initiation in the profounder mysteries who has overcome the fear of death, and is ready to hazard his life when the welfare of his country or the interests of humanity require it; and to die even an ignoble death, if thereby the people may be benefited.

22. I have prayed for the people, and Adonai hath said unto me: 'Make thee an image of a venomous springing serpent, and set it upon a pole; and it shall come to pass that every one that is bitten, when he looketh upon it, shall live. The plague of serpents is stayed; and as they have fled to their caves, so the celestial serpent flees, with the scorpion, before the glittering stars of Orion. The great festival of the vernal equinox approaches, and it is time to prepare ourselves by purification for the Passover. Light will soon prevail once more over darkness; and the pulses of life again beat in the bosom of the earth, long chilled by the wintry frosts.'

23. 'Let the brazen cross and the serpent be borne before the congregation, and be forever a symbol of faith, by the dying out whereof in the hearts of nations, they fall into decay; and lest the knowledge of its true symbolic meaning should in time be lost, and the people hereafter imagine, it to be something divine, and worship it, we will perpetuate the remembrance of this day's events, and the true meaning of this and our other symbols, and of the fables of Osiris and Ormuzd, and Typhon and Ahriman, as the last degree of those sacred mysteries which Joseph, the son of Jacob, like myself, learned from the Egyptians, and which I have taught to you; such as our forefathers practised on the plains of Chaldea.'

24. 'The Father sends fiery serpents to sting and slay his children. Yet he commands us to forgive those who trespass against us. And this law is not the mandate of His will, but the expression of His nature. Who will explain this great mystery?'

25. Below, upon the earth, the serpent is the minister of death. Its image, lifted on high, heals and restores life. The first sages who sought for the cause of causes saw good and evil in the world; they observed the shadow and the light; they compared winter with spring, old age with youth, life with death, and said: 'The first cause is beneficent and cruel. It gives life and destroys.'

26. 'Are there, then, two contrary principles a good and an evil?' cried the disciples of Manes.

27. No! the two principles of the universal equilibrium are not contrary to each other, though in apparent opposition; for it is a single wisdom that opposes them one to the other. The good is on the right, the evil on the left; but the supreme good is above both, and makes the evil subserve the triumph of the good, and the good serve for the reparation of the evil.

28. Wherefore this first cause has always revealed itself by the cross; the cross, that one composed of two, each of the two divided, so that they constitute four, the cross, that key of the mysteries of Egypt, the tau of the patriarchs, the divine symbol of Osiris, the keystone of the Temple, the symbol of occult Masonry; the cross, that central point of junction of the right angles of four infinite triangles; the four in-one, the divine tetragram.

29. The Universe is the Temple of the Deity whom we serve. Wisdom, Strength and Beauty are about His throne as pillars of His works, His Wisdom is infinite, His Strength omnipotent, and Beauty shines through the whole of the creation in symmetry and order. The heavens He has stretched forth as a canopy; the earth He hath planted as His footstool; He crowns His Tabernacle with Stars as with a diadem, and His hands extend their power and glory.

Chapter Seven

THE BUILDING OF SOLOMON'S TEMPLE

1. David intended to build a temple to God, but bequeathed the enterprise to Solomon, his son, and Solomon selected a place near Jerusalem; but finding overthrown columns of Enoch's temple, and supposing them to be the ruins of a heathen temple, and not wishing to select a desecrated spot, selected Mount Moriah for the site of his Temple to the True God.

2. Our three Grand Masters, Solomon king of Israel, Hiram king of Tyre and Hiram Abif, being in possession of the writings of Moses and the Prophets, well knew that if the Children of Israel deviated from the laws therein contained, their enemies would be let loose upon them, their cities and holy Temple sacked, ruined and destroyed and all the sacred treasures contained in the Sanctum Sanctorum would be forever lost.

3. In order to prevent this evil, they agreed to construct a secret vault underground, leading from King Solomon's most retired apartment and ending under the Sanctum Sanctorum or Holy of Holies.

4. King Solomon builded a secret vault, the approach to which was through eight other vaults, all under ground, and to which a long and

narrow passage led from the palace. The ninth arch or vault was immediately under the Holy of Holies of the Temple. In that apartment King Solomon held his private conferences with King Hiram and Hiram Abif.

5. This Secret Vault was divided into nine arches or crypts. The ninth arch was constructed by our three Grand Masters as a place wherein to deposit all the holy vessels and sacred treasures which would be contained in the Sanctum Sanctorum above; and also as a place wherein the three Grand Masters could meet and confer the Degree of Master Mason when the Temple had been completed.

6. Each Mason will apply our symbols and ceremonies according to his faith. In no other way could Masonry possess its universality, that character which has ever been peculiar to it from its origin, and which enabled two kings, worshippers of different Deities, to sit together as Grand Masters while the walls of the first Temple arose; and the men of Gebal, who bowed down to the Phoenician gods, to work by the side of the Hebrews, to whom those gods were an abomination.'

7. There were employed to work on the other eight arches, twenty-two men of Gebal, a city of Phoenicia, together with Adoniram and Ahishar, all of whom were skilled in the arts and sciences generally, but particularly in sculpture.

8. Their hours of labour were from nine at night until twelve, the time when all prying eyes were closed in sleep. On completion the twenty-four Menatzchim were given the recognition secrets of a Master Mason and were chosen as Select Masters. After the sacred vault was used as a cabinet room wherein the three Grand Masters together with the twenty-four Select Masters formed a Council of twenty-seven to discuss matters of high policy and when necessary to confer the Select Master degree. It was, however, agreed that the Council should never exceed a membership of twenty-seven.

9. Whereas all Overseers were in possession of the necessary trade secrets, a Mason's Word was essential to enable anyone to negotiate contracts, employ craftsmen and talk on equal terms with other Masters. It was at first arranged by Grand Master Hiram Abif, that the Select Masters

would lead the first parties of Craftsmen to leave the Temple site when the building was complete. In order to preserve the secret of the vault, the Select Masters wore no special badges of rank but carried on in public as ordinary senior overseers.

10. Nevertheless, in spite of official secrecy, rumour persisted as to certain Menatzchim with special status. This, not unnaturally, engendered much heart-burning among those who considered themselves eligible for the secrets of a Master Mason, which would have qualified them to lead parties of Craftsmen in search of work when the Temple was finished.

11. Among these was one Zabud. He, from having had frequent contact with King Solomon, had become known as 'the king's friend' and one day, emboldened by familiarity, asked the king what his chances were of receiving the Word. The king told him to be patient, assuring him, metaphorically, that a door would soon be opened to him. Zabud took this assurance literally and on a certain day, having a confidential report to make to the king, went to the latter's private apartments in the palace. Entering the room and finding the king absent he determined to wait. Presently he noticed a door standing ajar and immediately jumped to the conclusion that this was the door to which the king had referred. Passing through the door he found himself in a tunnel and eventually came to another door, also partly open. Entering, he found himself in the presence of what proved to be the Council of Twenty-seven.

12. Zabud was immediately seized and condemned to death as an intruder. Explanation and discussion followed, upon which Zabud was exonerated of the charge of trespass but the careless brother who had failed to close the door was executed while Zabud was chosen to fill the consequent vacancy.

13. When the ninth arch had been completed, our three Grand Masters deposited therein an exact copy of the Ark of the Covenant, containing the pot of manna and Aaron's rod, also a true copy of the Book of the Law, or all the writings of the Bible up to that period. And that it might be known by whom and for what purpose it was deposited, they placed on three sides of the Ark the initials of their names, and on the fourth, the date, meaning deposited in the year of light 3000 by

Solomon, king of Israel, Hiram, king of Tyre, and Hiram Abif, for the good of the Craft in general, and of the Jewish nation in particular.

14. When the deposit had been made thus far our Grand Master Hiram Abif was assassinated, and it was at first supposed that the Master Word was lost. But owing to the information received from Adoniram that it was Hiram Abif's wish that, in case of his death, the Master Word should be deposited beneath the Sanctum Sanctorum or Holy of Holies of the Temple, our two remaining Grand Masters agreed to deposit it in the ninth arch of the secret vault, on top of the Ark of the Covenant, in a triangular form and in three languages, Syrian, Chaldean and Egyptian, so that if the children of Israel should ever be carried into captivity and remain so long as to forget their mother tongue, yet on their return it might, if found, be restored by means of the other languages.

15. And that it might, when found, be known and distinguished as the Mason's Word, they placed on the top of the Ark of the Covenant, the three Grand Masters' jewels, inscribed one in each language, knowing that the descriptions thereof would be handed down to latest posterity.

16. After the death of Hiram Abif the two kings ceased to visit it, resolving not to do so until they should select one to fill his place; and that, until that time, they would make known the sacred name to no one.

17. Solomon proposed to erect a Temple of Justice, and selected as a site the spot where Enoch's temple had stood, and to that end directed that the fallen columns and rubbish should be removed. Gibulum, Joabert and Stolkin were selected to survey the ground and lay off the foundations.

18. Whilst clearing the rubble they discovered the secret vault prepared by Enoch in which were deposited treasures which they took to King Solomon. The king took the treasures of Enoch, consisting of a golden delta inlaid in a cube of agate and the fragments of the pillar containing the arts and science of the world, and placed them in the sacred vault of the ninth apartment on a twisted column of white marble, and in this apartment he held his private conferences with King Hiram of

Tyre and Hiram Abif, they only knowing the way by which it was approached.

19. After Adoniram, Joabert, and Stolkin had discovered the cube of agate and the mysterious name, and had delivered it to King Solomon, the two kings determined to deposit it in the secret vault, permit the three Masters – who discovered it to be present, make known to them the true pronunciation of the ineffable word, constitute the last degree of Ancient Craft Masonry, and term it Grand Elect Mason.

20. At the building of King Solomon's Temple and before the institution of the degree of Master Mason there were 80,000 operatives employed, part of whom were at quarries of Zeredathah, and part builders of the Temple; besides these there was a levy of 30,000 in the forests of Lebanon.

21. In order that each of the 110,000 workmen might be known to his superior officers, every part of the workmanship subjected to the nicest scrutiny, and each faithful labourer receive with punctuality the reward of his industry and skill; this immense number was divided into 1100 Lodges of Fellow Crafts and Entered Apprentices, the latter being Lodges placed under the superintendence of the former, who taught them the work.

22. Over the whole presided 3,300 Mentzchim, Overseers, or Mark Masters, three over each Lodge. Each Fellow Craft had a mark peculiar to himself by which his work was known to his immediate Overseers, and while the Overseers had but one mark in common by which they signified their approval of the Fellow Craft's work, they had other marks by which they denoted the juxtaposition of any two stones. Thus without any difficulty was each individual's work known and recognised as perfect, and its proper place in the building indicated.

23. The Fellow Crafts were allowed to choose any mark, not previously fixed on by another in their own Lodge. It consisted of three, five, seven, nine, or any other odd number of points connected by lines so as to form any figure they pleased except that of the equilateral triangle.

The Overseers, as already said, had but one mark in common, the Equilateral Triangle alluding to the Triune essence of the Deity, as revealed to Enoch. These 3300 Overseers were again divided into 100 Lodges, with 33 in each, over which presided 300 Harodim or Rulers. These are now called Right Worshipful Master, Senior and Junior Warden respectively. They were appointed by Hiram Abif himself, and on them devolved the duty of paying the others their wages.

24. When the Fellow Crafts and their Overseers or Mark Masters received their wages they put in their hands in a different manner, and at different wickets, so that if a Fellow Craft presumed to put in his hand at the Mark Master's wicket he was instantly detected as an impostor, and the Junior Harodim, or Warder, stood within with an axe ready to inflict the penalty of striking off his offending hand. This constitutes part of the penalty of a Mark Master, and, as well as the other part, was an ancient punishment among the Sidonians.

25. The Mark Master's degree was constituted in Joppa by Hiram Abif before he came to Jerusalem, and the timber for the Temple was carried there on floats by sea, and, as Masonic traditions inform us, the shore at that place was so steep that it was impossible to ascend from the rafts without assistance from above. This was effected by Brethren, being stationed there for that purpose, giving a strong grip to assist Brothers ashore.

26. The grip copied the mutual adaptation of the stones to each other, joint to joint, and the peculiar mark of the Mark Masters. The ancient brethren were known as Companions of the Mark.

27. It was the Master's business to prove each stone, not only as to its soundness by giving it three blows with a mallet, as to its finish by turning it over, but as to its being made exactly according to the working plan with which each Mark Master was provided. If found perfect in every way, it received the Mark Master's mark, and was sent on to the Temple; but if not, it was condemned and thrown among the rubbish. This was effected by two or more of the Brethren taking it between them and after swinging it backwards and forwards three times it was heaved over among the rubbish.

28. Every sixth working day it was the custom of the Overseers or Mark Masters to wait upon the acting Grand Master Hiram Abif in order to receive instructions, as also the necessary plans for carrying on the work and keeping the men employed. Part of one of these working plans appears to have been lost, but an ingenious and intelligent Fellow Craft, having either seen the portion of the imperfect plan in the Overseer's possession before it was lost, or forming a good idea of it from the nature of the work, perceived that a stone of a very peculiar form and construction was wanting to complete the design, and probably thinking to gain honour to himself for displaying a superior knowledge of his work, he immediately commenced blocking out such a stone.

29. After spending much labour on it, he ultimately finished it by putting his own mark upon it. When the imperfect working plan was examined no place was found for this particular stone, and the Fellow Craft instead of honour received nothing but angry words and reproaches for idling away his time, and in the heat of passion the Overseer ordered the stone to be heaved among the rubbish, which was accordingly done by two Brethren, probably well pleased at what they considered the humiliation of their companion's vanity. The sorrowful Fellow Craft who had cut the stone, on seeing this unworthy treatment of his work, placed his hands to his head, and reclining in a disconsolate manner, exclaimed his despair.

30. The stone long lay neglected among the rubbish. At last, however, the time drew near when the Key Stone of the Porch of King Solomon's Temple was required, to which the portion of the working plan alluded to referred. Search was made at the Temple, but no such stone could be found, and, on further inquiry, it was ascertained that no stone of the requisite form had ever been brought there. The Overseers of that portion of the building immediately sent to the Overseers at the quarries, who had not received the plans and orders for that portion of the work, to inquire the reason why this stone had not been forwarded with the others. The latter declared they knew nothing about it, and that there was no plan for any such stone among those entrusted to their care.

31. The work came to a standstill, and the reason was speedily demanded

by Hiram Abif, who not only recollected drawing the plan, and writing instructions about this stone, but also giving them himself to the Mark Overseer of the Hewers. The latter being sent for was reprimanded for his carelessness in losing that portion of the plan, and, on learning the shape of the stone required, it came to his recollection that one of that description had been cut by one of his workmen. He informed Hiram Abif of this, and added that, owing to his not finding it noted in his plan, he had refused to mark it, and had caused it to be rejected. Hiram Abif instantly sent for the Fellow Craft who had cut the stone, and questioned him concerning it, when, from the answers and description of it, he immediately perceived that it must be the very stone required. Instant and careful search was ordered to be made for it among the rubbish, where it was at last found uninjured.

32. As the Mark Overseer had displayed such ignorance of his working plans as not to be able to discover the use of the stone, Hiram deposed him from his office and deprived him of the badge and insignia thereof, which he conferred on the humble Fellow Craft, whom he made a Mark Master, and raised to fill his place.

33. The Fellow Craft, or newly made Mark Master, was ordered to cut the Mark Master's mark on the stone around his own on the small end, and outside of it. The stone was conveyed to the Temple with great pomp and parade, and while it was being fixed in its place, the newly made Mark Master in an ecstasy of joy clasping his hands together and looking up, exclaimed: 'All Glory to the Most High.'

34. When the Temple was almost completed King Solomon, with the Princes of his household, went to view it and they were so struck with its magnificence that with one simultaneous emotion they raised their arms and exclaimed 'O Worthy Masons.'

35. The ornaments of the Temple were the Porch, Dormer, and Square pavement. Their uses were as follows. The Porch was the entrance to the Sanctum Sanctorum; the Dormer the window that gave light to the same; and the Square pavement for the High Priest to walk on.

36. The High Priest's office was to burn incense to the honour and glory

of the Most High, and to pray fervently that the Almighty, of His unbounded wisdom and goodness, would be pleased to bestow peace and tranquillity on the Israelitish nation during the ensuring year.

37. The labour force employed on the Temple project were organised in lodges, each ruled by three Menatzchim. As the building neared completion and various trades became redundant, a lodge would be closed and its members, in parties led by a qualified overseer, would take the road in search of other employment. The term 'qualified overseer' meant one who, in addition to all necessary trade secrets of his guild, was also in possession of the Mason Word which would enable him to talk on equal terms with other Masters, accept contracts, arrange terms and generally organise the welfare of his men.

38. Overseers considered by the Grand Masters to be suitable leaders were honoured with the rank of Royal Master, and it is not difficult to appreciate the state of mind of an overseer who, having made tentative arrangements to lead a party, had not yet received the Mason Word.

39. Such a one was Adoniram, overseer of a gang of metal workers engaged on finishing touches to the Sanctuary. Knowing that he and his men would shortly be laid off, he was worried because he had not yet become a Royal Master. One morning as the hour of High Twelve approached, he took a richly chased bowl to Hiram Abif for approval, and as the latter was in the act of passing it the trumpets sounded for the midday break.

40. The Craftsmen went off and Hiram Abif repaired to the Sanctuary to pray and to deposit the newly approved bowl. Adoniram, instead of accompanying his men, lingered behind and, as the Master, having finished his devotions, prepared to leave the sanctuary, he waylaid him and inquired when he was likely to be honoured with the rank of Royal Master. Hiram Abif exhorted Adoniram to be patient, well knowing that Adoniram was already on the list, and (somewhat irregularly) hinted that if he should die before Adoniram received the secrets, the Mason Word would be found buried below the spot where they two were standing, i.e., in the sacred vault, of which Adoniram knew nothing. Only partially satisfied, Adoniram retired while Hiram Abif,

rejoining his two colleagues, related the incident and confessed his indiscretion. After discussion a day and time were fixed for the next meeting of a Council of Royal Masters for the purpose of conferring the degree on Adoniram. But he was not the only anxious aspirant for the secrets of a Master Mason: and shortly after the above-mentioned interview, Hiram Abif was slain, so that the degree of Royal Master had to be given to Adoniram by the two surviving Grand Masters.

41. There must have been many trades employed, e.g., blacksmiths to make tools, carpenters to erect scaffolding, make templates and gauges, also painters, decorators and many ancillary trades. Nevertheless, stonework being the principal trade it was customary for the head of any building project to be styled Master Mason. Consequently a Craftsman honoured with the rank of Royal Master received the recognition secrets of a Master Mason.

Chapter Eight

THE ASSASSINATION OF HIRAM ABIF

1. To the just and virtuous man death has no terrors equal to the stain of falsehood and dishonour. Of this great truth the annals of Masonry afford a glorious example, in the unshaken fidelity, and noble death, of our master, Hiram Abif, who was killed just before the completion of King Solomon's Temple, at the construction of which he was the principal Architect.

2. As Master Masons we come from the East directing our course towards the West. We were induced to leave the East and go to the West to seek for that which was lost, which, by our instruction and our own industry, we hope to find, the genuine secrets of a Master Mason. They came to be lost by the untimely death of our master, Hiram Abif.

3. Fifteen Fellow Crafts, of that superior class appointed to preside over the rest, finding that the work was nearly completed, and that they were not in possession of the Secrets of the Third Degree, conspired to obtain them by any means, even to have recourse to violence; at the moment, however, of carrying their conspiracy into execution, twelve of the fifteen recanted, but three of a more determined and atrocious character than the rest, persisted in their impious design, in the prosecution of which they planted themselves respectively at the East, North

and South entrances of the Temple, whither our master had retired to pay his adoration to the Most High, as was his wonted custom at the hour of high twelve.

4. Having finished his devotions, he attempted to return by the South entrance, where he was opposed by the first of those ruffians, who, for want of other weapon, had armed himself with a heavy Plumb Rule, and in a threatening manner demanded the secrets of a Master Mason, warning him that death would be the consequence of a refusal.

5. Our Master, true to his Obligation, answered that those secrets were known to but three in the world, and that, without the consent and co-operation of the other two he neither could, nor would, divulge them, but intimated that he had no doubt patience and industry would in due time entitle the worthy Mason to a participation of them, but that, for his own part, he would rather suffer death than betray the sacred trust reposed in him. This answer not proving satisfactory, the ruffian aimed a violent blow at the head of our master, but being startled at the firmness of his demeanour, it missed his forehead, and only glanced on his right temple but with such force as to cause him to reel and sink on his left knee. Recovering from the shock, he made for the North entrance where he was accosted by the second of those ruffians, to whom he gave a similar answer with undiminished firmness, when the ruffian, who was armed with a Level, struck him a violent blow on the Left temple, which brought him to the ground on his right knee.

6. Finding his retreat cut off at both those points, he staggered faint and bleeding to the East entrance, where the third ruffian was posted who received a similar answer to his insolent demand (for even at this trying moment our master remained firm and unshaken), when the villain, who was armed with a heavy maul, stuck him a violent blow on the forehead, which laid him lifeless at his feet.

7. The death of our master Hiram Abif was a loss so important, being that of the principal Architect, that it could not fail of being speedily and severely felt. The want of those plans and designs, which had hitherto been so regularly supplied throughout every department of the work, was the first indication that some heavy calamity had befallen

our Master. The Menatschim or Prefects, or more familiarly speaking, the Overseers of the work, deputed some of the most eminent of their number to acquaint King Solomon with the utter confusion into which the absence of Hiram had plunged them, and to express their apprehension that to some fatal catastrophe must be attributed his sudden and mysterious disappearance.

8. On the same day the twelve Craftsmen who had originally joined in the conspiracy came forward before the King and made a voluntary confession of all that they knew up to the time of their having withdrawn themselves from the number of the conspirators. His fears being awakened for the safety of the chief artist, the King selected fifteen trusty Fellow Crafts and ordered them to make diligent search after the person of our Master, to ascertain whether he were yet alive or had suffered death in the attempt to extort from him the secrets of his exalted Degree.

9. Accordingly, a stated day having been appointed for their return to Jerusalem, they formed themselves into three Fellow Craft Lodges and departed from the three entrances of the Temple. Many days were spent in fruitless search; indeed, one lodge returned to Jerusalem without having made any discovery of importance, but a second lodge was more fortunate, for on the evening of a certain day, after having suffered the greatest privations and personal fatigue, one of the Brethren who had rested himself in a reclining posture, to assist his rising caught hold of a shrub that grew near, which, to his surprise, came easily out of the ground.

10. On a closer examination he found that the earth had been recently disturbed; he therefore hailed his Brethren, and, with their united efforts, succeeded in reopening it and there found the body of our Master Hiram very indecently interred. They covered it again with all respect and reverence, and in order to distinguish the spot stuck a sprig of Acacia at the head of the Grave; they then hastened to Jerusalem, to impart the afflicting intelligence to King Solomon, who, when the first emotions of his grief had subsided, ordered them to return and raise the body of our Master to such a sepulchre as became his rank and exalted talents; at the same time informing them that by his untimely death the genuine Secrets of a Master Mason were lost; he therefore

charged them to be particularly careful in observing whatever casual signs, tokens or words that might occur among them while paying this last sad tribute of respect to departed merit.

11. They performed their task with the utmost fidelity, and on reopening the ground one of the Brethren looking round observed some of his companions in a position expressive of the horror of the afflicting sight, and others viewing the ghastly wounds still visible on his forehead smote their own in sympathy with his sufferings: two of the Brethren then descended the grave, one of them endeavoured to raise our Master by the Entered Apprentice grip, which proved a slip, the other tried the Fellow Craft's grip, which proved a slip likewise; having both failed in their attempts, a more zealous and expert Brother descended, and, using the strong or lion grip of a Master Mason, with their assistance raised him on the Five Points of Fellowship, while others, still more animated, exclaimed words having a nearly similar import; King Solomon ordered that these casual signs, tokens, and words should designate all Master Masons throughout the Universe, until time or circumstances should restore the genuine ones.

12. The body of our Master was ordered to be re-interred as near to the Sanctum Sanctorum as the Israelitish laws would permit, there in a grave from the centre three feet East, three feet West, three feet between North and South and five feet or more perpendicular.

13. He was not buried in the Sanctum Sanctorum, because nothing common or unclean was allowed to enter there, not even the High Priest except once a year and not even then until after many washings and purifications, against the great day of expiations of sins, for by the Israelitish law all dead bodies are deemed unclean. The same fifteen Fellow Crafts were ordered to attend the funeral, clothed in white aprons and gloves as emblem of their innocence.

14. Immediately after the assassination of Hiram the builder, the Temple was but partially constructed. King Solomon selected seven of the most worthy and expert brethren, made them Master Masons, and appointed them special guardians of the Sanctum Sanctorum and of the sacred furniture of that Holy Place. They were called Secret Masters.

15. In the grey dawn of morning, even before the sun rising over Mount Olivet flushed with crimson the walls of the Temple, the chosen few, awe-stricken and grave, had assembled. The light from the seven-branch candlestick in the East was reflected back from the golden floor, from the brazen laver of water, with hyssop and napkins, but fell sombrely on the heavy drapings of the sack-cloth on the walls. Amidst the prayers and exhortations, and the solemn chanting of the Levites, the seven entered into a mystic bond, and the duty of secrecy and silence was laid upon them.

16. And then the doors of cedar and olive wood heavily carved and gilded were opened, the veils of blue, and purple, and scarlet, and richly embroidered white linen were drawn aside, and the mysteries of the Holy of Holies revealed to them.

17. None but the Priests and Levites had entered the Sanctum Sanctorurn since the Sacred Ark had been brought thither, and now as the Seven Secret Sentinels put off their shoes and washed their feet, and stepped over the golden threshold, they stood in silence blinded with the light that burst upon them. The spreading wings of the Cherubim covered the Ark of the Covenant, but from all sides the walls glittered with gold and precious stones.

18. King Solomon spoke saying: 'what is the hour?' and Adoniram, son of Abda replied. 'The morning star is driving away the shades of night, and its rosy light begins to gladden our Lodge.'

19. And King Solomon spoke again saying: 'As the morning star is the forerunner of the great light which begins to shine on our Lodge, and we are all Secret Masters, it is time to commence our labours. Who so draweth nigh to the contemplation of the Ineffable mysteries, should put off the shoes of his worldly conversations; for the place whereon he stands is holy ground. Set a watch, O Jehovah, before my mouth, and keep thou the door of my lips.'

20. O Jehovah! our Adonai, how excellent is thy name over all the earth! Thy name declares the glory of Elohim. There appears to be power in Thy name which revealeth secrets.

21. Permit me now, my brothers, to receive you as Secret Masters, and give you rank among the Levites. By the rank you now hold among the Levites in the quality of Secret Master, you have become one of the guardians of the Sanctum Sanctorum, and I place you in the number of seven.

22. Brother Adoniram, it is our order that you cause to be erected a tomb or obelisk, of white and black marble, west-southwest of the Temple, wherein shall be deposited the embalmed remains of our lamented Grand Master Hiram Abif. The white marble shall denote the innocence and purity of our departed Grand Master, and the black the untimely death of him we mourn. See, therefore, that the solemn duty is speedily executed, and let the obsequies be performed with becoming and imposing ceremonies.

23. King Solomon opened a Lodge of sorrow for the departed worthy brother. He opened the Lodge of Perfect Masters in the darkness of dawn as the blazing star in the East cast its lurid red light over the black-draped coffin on which were laid the jewel and apron of Grand Master Hiram Abif.

24. King Solomon stood before the coffin of our Master Hiram and prayed to the Most High:

25. O Almighty and Eternal God! there is no number of Thy days or of Thy mercies. Thou hast sent us into this world to serve Thee, but we wander far from Thee in the path of error. Our life is but a span in length, and yet tedious, because of the calamities that enclose us on every side. The days of our pilgrimage are few and evil; our bodies frail; our passions violent and distempered; our understandings weak, and our wills perverse. Look thou upon us, our Father, in mercy and pity. We adore Thy majesty, and trust like little children to Thine infinite mercies. Give us patience to live well, and firmness to resist evil, even as our departed brother resisted. Give us, O most merciful Father, faith and confidence in thee; and enable us so to live, that when we come to die we may lie down in the grave like one who composes himself to sleep, and that we may be worthy hereafter to be remembered in the memories of man. Bless us, O God: bless our beloved fraternity:

may we live and emulate the example of our departed brother; and finally, that we may in this world attain a knowledge of Thy truth, and in the world to come, life everlasting. Amen.

26. This ceremony was established by King Solomon to commemorate the death of our Grand Master Hiram Abif, whose labours at the building of the first Temple, and whose tragic death furnish so much of the mystical knowledge of Ancient Craft Masonry. It is a lesson both useful and instructive. Let us look forward to brighter scenes, when our deceased brother, who had been smitten down by the resistless hand of death, shall be raised from his prostrate state at the word of our Supreme Grand Master, and admitted to the privilege of the Perfect Lodge above.

27. Happy to have the poor consciousness of having found the precious remains of so great and so good a man as Hiram Abif, and having an opportunity of paying a just tribute of respect to his memory, King Solomon ordered the noble Adoniram, his Grand Inspector, to make suitable arrangements for his interment. The brethren were directed to attend with white gloves and aprons, and he forbade the marks of blood which had been spilled in the Temple to be effaced until the traitors should be discovered and punished.

28. In the meanwhile, he directed the noble Adoniram to furnish a plan for a superb tomb or obelisk, of white and black marble, which plan was accepted and the work finished.

29. Three days after the funeral ceremonies had been performed, King Solomon repaired with his Court to the Temple, and all the brethren being arranged as at the funeral, he proceeded with his brethren to see and examine the tomb and obelisk, with the inscription thereon. Struck with astonishment and admiration, he raised his eyes and hands to heaven and exclaimed 'It is accomplished and complete!'

30. King Solomon upon the death of the Grand Master, Hiram, found it necessary to appoint several Judges, in order that justice might be administered among the workmen upon the Temple, their complaints heard, and their disputes decided; for difficulties and disturbances were

now more frequent, pending the temporary cessation of work and the period of mourning. This duty of judgement had devolved upon the lamented Hiram, and his loss caused the appointment of Tito and his associates to listen to and adjust the complaints that might be brought before them.

31. King Solomon appointed Tito, Prince of Herodim, to be the chief Provost and Judge, Adoniram, and Abda, his father, and four others learned in the Law of Moses, to complete the number and constitute the Tribunal. They held their sittings in the middle chamber of the Temple, where the records of the Tribunal were kept, in a box of ebony, studded with precious gems, the key of which was committed to the Provosts or Judges; and there they considered and adjusted the demands and differences of the workmen, and determined all appeals from the judgement of a single Provost and Judge administering the same laws to the Phoenician as to the Hebrew, and endeavouring to do entire justice, according to the law of Moses, between man and man.

32. The necessity for a Court of Judges did not exist until after the death of the Grand Master Hiram, as the number of difficulties and dissensions among the workmen was not so numerous, and judgement was arrived at by the ready decisions of Hiram, which all quietly acquiesced in.

33. The death of Hiram, the Chief Architect, threw the workmen of the Temple of King Solomon into great confusion; and for a time the construction of the building was stayed, for the want of essential plans and an expert director of the work. The period of mourning having expired, King Solomon, upon consultation, determined to appoint five Superintendents – one for each of the five Departments of Architecture – and under their supervision the building progressed.

34. King Solomon called together, Adoniram, the son of Abda, who he made the Head of the Board of Architects; Joabert, a Phoenician, who he made Chief Artificer in Brass; Stolkin, a Hebrew, who he made Chief Carpenter; Selec, a Giblemite, who he made Chief Stone-Mason; and Gareb, a Hebrew, who he made Chief Worker in Silver and Gold and Engraver. And King Solomon addressed them.

35. 'My Brethren, to become an Intendant of the Building, it is necessary that you be skilful architects and learned in the knowledge of the East and Egypt. But it is equally necessary that you should be charitable and benevolent, that you may sympathise with the labouring man, relieve his necessities, see to his comforts and that of his family, and smooth for him and for those who depend upon him the ragged way of life, recognising all men as your brethren, and yourselves as the almoners of God's bounty.'

36. After the death of the Grand Master, the assassins having made their escape, a great assembly of Masons was convened by King Solomon, to consult as to the best means of discovering and apprehending them. Their deliberations were interrupted by the entrance of a herdsman, who demanded to speak to the king. On being admitted to an interview, he acquainted King Solomon that he had discovered persons concealed in a cave near the coast of Joppa, answering the description given of the traitors; and he offered to conduct those whom the king should select to the place of their concealment. This being communicated to the Masters, they one and all eagerly requested to be made participators in the vengeance due to the assassins. Solomon checked their ardour, declaring that only nine should undertake the task; and to avoid giving any offence, ordered a selection of nine of the brethren by lot, to accompany the stranger. At the first hour of the night, Stolkin, the favourite of King Solomon, and eight others, conducted by the stranger, travelled onward through a rough and dreary country toward the coast of Joppa.

37. On the way Stolkin, the most ardent of the nine, learning that the murderers were hidden in a cavern not far from where they then were, pressed on ahead, found the cavern and entered it with the shepherd, where, by the dim light of the lamp, he discovered one of the assassins asleep, with a dagger at his feet. Inflamed at the sight, and actuated by an impatient zeal, he immediately seized the dagger and stabbed him, first in the head and then in the heart. The assassin had only time to say 'Necum' [pronounced nay-coom], or 'vengeance is taken,' and expired. The avenger then quenched his thirst at the fountain.

38. When the eight arrived at the spot, they asked him what he had done.

He replied: 'I have slain the assassin of our Grand Master, and have performed a feat for the honour and glory of the Craft, for which I hope to be rewarded.' He then severed the head from the body, and taking it in one hand and his dagger in the other, with the eight returned to Jerusalem. In his zeal, however, he hastened into the presence of the king, passing the guards at the entrance. Solomon was at first very much offended that it had been put out of his power to take vengeance, in the presence of, and as a warning to, the rest of the workmen, and ordered the guards to put his favourite to death; but by the intercession of his brethren he was pardoned for his zeal, and they became reconciled. King Solomon established the grade of Master Elect of Nine, and conferred it upon the nine companions.

39. About six months, it is said, after the execution of the assassin, Bengaber, an intendant of King Solomon, in the country of Gath, which was tributary to him, caused diligent inquiry to be made if any person had lately taken shelter in that region who might be supposed to have fled from Jerusalem. He published at the same time an accurate description of the traitors who had made their escape. Shortly afterward he received information that persons answering the description had lately arrived there, and believing themselves to be perfectly secure, had begun to work in the quarry of Ben-Dekar.

40. As soon as Solomon was made acquainted with this circumstance, he wrote to Maaka, King of Gath, to assist in apprehending them, and to cause them to be delivered to persons he should appoint to secure them, and have them brought to Jerusalem to receive the punishment due to their crimes.

41. Solomon then selected fifteen Masters in whom he could place the greatest confidence, and among whom were those nine who had been in the cavern, and sent them with an escort of troops in quest of the villains. Five days were spent in the search, when Zerbal, who bore King Solomon's letter to King Maaka, with Stolkin and another of his companions, discovered them cutting stone in the quarry. They immediately seized them, and, binding them in chains, conducted them to Jerusalem. On their arrival they were imprisoned in the tower of Achizar, and the next morning received the punishment which their crimes deserved.

42. After punishment had been inflicted on the murderers, King Solomon instituted a degree, both as a recompense for the zeal and constancy of the Elus of the Fifteen, who had assisted him to discover them, and also to enable him to elevate other deserving brethren from the lower degrees to those of places in the higher, which had been vacated by their promotion. Twelve of these fifteen he elected Sublime Knights, and made the selection by ballot, that he might give none offence, putting the names of the whole in an urn. The first twelve that were drawn he formed into a Chapter, and gave them command over the twelve tribes. He gave them the name of Emeth, which is a Hebrew word signifying a true man. He exhibited to them the precious things which were deposited in the tabernacle.

43. After the murderers of the Master Hiram Abif had been discovered, apprehended, tried, and punished, his monument and mausoleum completed, and the matters which concerned the revenue of the realm provided for, King Solomon, to assure uniformity of work and vigour in its prosecution, and to reward the superior and eminent science and skill of Adoniram the son of Abda, appointed him to be chief Architect of the Temple, with the title of Grand Master Architect, and invested him with that office, as sole successor and representative of the deceased Master Hiram Abif, and at the same time made him Grand Master of Masons and the Masonic peer of himself and King Hiram of Tyre. Afterward the title was conferred upon other Princes of the Jewish court as an honorarium, and thus the title became established.

Chapter Nine

THE COMPLETION OF THE FIRST TEMPLE OF JERUSALEM

1. King Solomon held the installation of Adoniram in the Chamber of Designs, within the partially completed Temple, when the sun had just set and the evening star had appeared.

2. Before the starting the building of the Temple King Solomon had built a secret vault, the approach to which was through eight other vaults, all under ground, and to which a long and narrow passage led from the palace. The ninth arch or vault was immediately under the Holy of Holies of the Temple. In that apartment King Solomon held his private conferences with King Hiram and Hiram Abif. After the death of Hiram Abif the two kings ceased to visit it, resolving not to do so until they should select one to fill his place; and that, until that time, they would make known the sacred name to no one.

3. Gibulum, Joabert and Stolkin had been selected to survey the ground and lay off the foundations for Solomon's Temple of Justice, and during the work they discovered the secret chambers beneath the ruined Temple of Enoch. They explored the depths, and discovered hidden deep in the darkness of the earth the delta or golden plate upon which Enoch had engraved the ineffable name of God.

4. They took the delta to King Solomon, who said, 'Companions let us give thanks unto the Lord who hath given us the treasures of darkness and the hidden riches of secret places.' King Solomon determined to deposit it in the secret vault, permit the three Masters, who discovered it, to be present, make known to them the true pronunciation of the ineffable word, constitute the last degree of Ancient Craft Masonry, and term it Grand Elect Mason. The cube of agate was so deposited.

5. Afterward the twelve Princes of Ameth, the nine Elect, and the Chief Architect were admitted to this degree. This vault was thereafter called the sacred vault, and was originally built by Hiram Abif, and none but Grand Elect Masons knew of its existence, or knew other than the substituted word.

6. Six and a half years after the laying of the foundation stone, King Solomon's Temple was completed and plans were made to transfer the Ark of the Covenant from the temporary tabernacle, in which it had been housed by King David, to its new home in the Holy of Holies, also to dedicate the Temple to the Most High. To celebrate the occasion King Solomon decided to institute the degree of Most Excellent Master and to confer this on those senior Menatzchim who so merited special recognition, particularly the twenty-four who, unknown to the generality, already held the rank Select Master: a step which enabled King Solomon to give public distinction to those worthies without revealing the existence of the sacred vault.

7. The furniture of the Sanctum Sanctorum included many holy vessels made of pure gold, but the most important was the Ark of the Covenant, called the glory of Israel, which stood in the middle of the Most Holy place under the wings of the Cherubim.

8. It was a small chest or coffer, two cubits and a half in length and one cubit and a half in width and depth. It was made of wood, excepting only the mercy seat, and overlaid with gold both inside and out. It had a ledge of gold surrounding it at the top, into which was let the cover called the mercy seat. The mercy seat was of solid gold, the thickness of a hand's breadth; at the ends were two Cherubim looking inward towards each other, with their wings expanded which, embracing the

whole circumference of the mercy seat, met in the middle on each side. All the Rabbis say it was made out of the same mass without any soldering of parts.

9. Here the Shekinah or Divine Presence rested and was visible in the appearance of a cloudy light over it. Hence the Bath-Kol issued and gave answers when God was consulted. And here it was that God was said to dwell between the Cherubim; that is between the Cherubim on the mercy seat; because there was the seat or throne of the visible presence of His glory amongst them.

10. Before the date fixed for the ceremonies, however, Hiram Abif was slain and the said ceremonies had to be delayed while Israel and its king mourned the death of the Master.

11. The Temple was completed in the year 3000 – six years, six months and ten days after King Solomon had laid the first cornerstone; and its completion was celebrated with great pomp and splendid magnificence.

12. And the rulers of the surrounding nations sent ambassadors to congratulate King Solomon on the completion of the stately edifice, whose regal splendour and unparalleled lustre are said to have surpassed all imagination. But one sovereign from the East was not content to send an ambassador, as others had done, she came to Jerusalem to be received by King Solomon within the Holy Temple.

13. To dedicate the Temple King Solomon called a general assembly of Masons and dedicated it with solemn prayer and costly sacrifice, while to the strains of the finest music the vast congregation raised their praises to the Most High. Upon placing the Ark in the most Holy Place the glory of the Lord filled the House. And when the singers and trumpeters were to make one sound in praise and thanks to the Lord, saying, 'Praise the Lord, for he is good: his mercy endureth forever,' that the Temple was filled with a cloud, and the name was fully pronounced.

14. It was during the ceremony of dedication that the Divine Shekinah entered the Temple and shone her light into the Holy of Holies as a sign of the approbation of the Most High.

15. The first and highest honour ever conferred on Freemasons is this descent of the Divine Shekinah from the East, first at the consecration of the Holy Tabernacle, and afterwards at the dedication of the Temple of the Lord by King Solomon, placing itself on the Ark or Mercy-seat of the Holy of Holies, covered by the wings of the Cherubim, where it continued to deliver its oracular responses for fourteen generations.

16. The Blazing Star symbol represents The Glory of God appearing as the Divine Shekinah as it had previously appeared on Mount Sinai at the deliverance of the Law received by Moses.

17. Subsequently, during the ceremony of the dedication of the Temple, King Solomon conferred this sublime degree on twenty-five brethren.

18. On the second day, an audience was given to all Masons, from the degree of Master to the Royal Arch, and all vacancies were filled. On the third day, King Solomon devoted his time to advancing and raising Fellow Crafts and Entered Apprentices.

19. Thus far the wise King of Israel behaved worthy of himself, and gained universal admiration; but in process of time, when he had advanced in years, his understanding became impaired; he grew deaf to the voice of the Lord, and was strangely irregular in his conduct. Proud of having erected an edifice to his Maker, and much intoxicated with his great power, he plunged into all manner of licentiousness and debauchery, and profaned the Temple by offering incense to the idol Moloch, which only should have been offered to The Living God.

20. The Grand Elect Masons saw this, and were sorely grieved, being fearful that his apostasy would end in some dreadful consequences, and perhaps bring upon them those enemies whom Solomon had vainly and wantonly defied. The people, copying the follies and vices of their king, became proud and idolatrous, neglecting the true worship of God for that of idols.

Chapter Ten

THE RETURN FROM THE BABYLONIAN CAPTIVITY

1. With the death of King Solomon in B.C. 938 the Jewish empire began to disintegrate. Israel promptly asserted its independence, leaving Judah, comprising only the tribe of that name, with its capital at Jerusalem.

2. The Divine Shekinah descended so its light shone upon the Ark or Mercy seat as it stood in the Holy of Holies, until the Israelites proved unfaithful to the Most High. And so may the light of Masonry be removed from all who prove unfaithful to their God!

3. The Council of Twenty-seven fell into desuetude: vacancies among the Select Masters were no longer filled, and the existence of the Sacred Vault lived only as a legend known only to the few worthy brothers.

4. The Masons continued to hold annual meetings of the Council of Princes of Jerusalem on the 20th day of the tenth month Tebet: and elected Officers at every annual meeting: these they installed on the 23d day of the eleventh month – Adar. It was the province of the Council of Princes of Jerusalem to inspect and watch over, with due care and fidelity, the few remaining Lodges of Perfection, and see that their 'work' was done in conformity with the regulations and land-marks of the order.

5. As an adequate punishment for the defection of King Solomon, God inspired the heart of Nebuchadnezzar, King of Babylon, to take vengeance on the kingdom of Israel. This prince sent an army, with Nebuzaradan, captain of the guards, who entered Judah with fire and sword, took and sacked the city of Jerusalem, razed its walls, and destroyed that superb model of excellence, the Temple. The people were carried away captive to Babylon, and the conquerors carried away with them all the vessels of gold and silver.

6. Israel disappeared in B.C. 734 and by B.C. 597, the kingdom of Judah was itself on the point of extinction.

7. Ten years previously Jerusalem had been captured by Nebuchadnezzar (heir to the throne of Babylon). Leaving the city and Temple intact (except for the temple treasures) Nebuchadnezzar took ten thousand of the principal citizens into exile in Babylonia. The prophet Ezekiel accompanied the exiles while Jeremiah remained in Jerusalem. The kingdom of Judah was reduced to the status of a Babylonian province, with Zedekiah on the throne as satrap (tributary king).

8. After eleven years of vassalage Zedekiah rebelled, whereupon Nebuchadnezzar (now king of Babylon) sent his general Nebuzaradan to capture and destroy Jerusalem and the Temple and to devastate the province. Having dealt with other strong points, Nebuzaradan laid siege to Jerusalem and when Zedekiah saw that the situation was hopeless he attempted to escape to Egypt with a few followers. He was intercepted, his eyes put out (the usual punishment for treason in those days), and taken to Babylon in chains of brass.

9. It is at this juncture Gedaliah, governor of Jerusalem, presided over a Council of Super Excellent Masters to consider last-minute plans. That Word supposed to have been lost when Hiram Abif was assassinated was actually lying in the sacred vault beneath the Council Chamber over which Gedaliah was presiding. And it remained there, lost to living memory, after the temple was destroyed.

10. The meeting was convened within the besieged Temple and Gedaliah spoke, asking the Keeper of the Temple: 'Are we secure?' He received

an affirmative answer. Gedaliah opened the meeting by offering a prayer to the Most High saying: 'Companions, let us offer up our fervent prayer to the Almighty that He may be pleased to vouchsafe to us His protecting care and favour.'

11. Oh Lord and Supreme Master of the Universe, we humbly beseech Thee to bless us in all our undertakings help us to worship Thee worthily; fill our hearts with Thy fear, and make us steadfast in Thy service that hereafter we may praise Thee to all Eternity.

12. He then ordered that the Ark of the Covenant be unveiled at which point a herald sought entry to the lodge with an urgent message. Gedaliah ordered him to be admitted and the Herald spoke: 'Companions, the sword of the enemy prevails, the innumerable forces of Nebuchadnezzar, king of Babylon, advance and fill the city, the king has fled, and the army of the Chaldeans has pursued and overtaken him on the plains of Jericho.'

13. Gedaliah stood and urged the assembled Masons to remain calm and he said: 'In this extremity, let us repair to the Holy Altar and there pledge our faith, renew our vows and demonstrate once again the ties that bind us for ever to the Most High.'

14. Gedaliah then called the assembled Masons to form a Square around the Ark of the Covenant. And he said to them: 'This square represents the encampment of the Israelites, with the Ark of the Covenant in the centre, and three tribes on each side. On the East side, towards the rising sun, shall they of the standard of the camp of Judah, pitch with Issacher and Zebutun. On the South side, the standard of the camp of Reuben with Simeon and Gad. On the West side, the standard of the camp of Ephraim with Benjamin and Manasseh, and on the North side, the standard of the camp of Dan with Asher and Naphthali. Then the tabernacle of the congregation shall be set forward with the camp of the Levites in the midst of the camp.'

15. Gedaliah then said: 'Companions, you will form triangle round the Ark of the Covenant. The triangle or delta is an emblem of the Deity, and represents His Omniscience, Omnipresence and Omnipotence it also

represents the triple duty we owe to God, our neighbours and ourselves. Companions, you will form a circle round the Ark of the Covenant. The circle is an emblem of friendship; the Ark of the Covenant in the centre as the blazing star. It is also emblematical of the circle of our moral virtues, as inculcated in the Degree of Entered Apprentice by the point within the circle embordered by two parallel lines. It is further an emblem of eternity, having neither beginning nor end. The first, the emblem of friendship, may be broken; the second, the emblem of our moral virtues, may be changed; but the third, the emblem of eternity, will never alter. This emblem encourages the hope that, through faith in the Divine promises, we may attain to the full fruition of a glorious immortality. We are the guardians of the traditions of the Council of Twenty-seven. We solemnly promise we will never bow down to other gods, or pay religious adoration to idols, but will faithfully and zealously worship only the One, True and Living God. We swear this under no less a penalty than that of having our thumbs cut off, our eyes poked out, and our bodies bound with chains of brass.'

16. Gedaliah closed the council with another Prayer: 'Almighty and Eternal God, the Protector of all who trust in Thee, save us, we beseech Thee, in all difficulties and dangers. Keep us faithful to our vows, and true to our obligations so that we may never waver nor be cast down, but through Thy mercy may at length be admitted to that immortal Temple eternal in the heavens.'

17. Soon afterwards Gedaliah was assassinated by the Babylonians, and Nebuzaradan again invaded Judea and carried away the people. After destroying Jerusalem, Nebuzaradan took the remnant of the people to Babylon, leaving only a few agriculturists and vine-dressers to work on the land.

18. When the Jews returned after the Exile they found what had been a fertile land had been reduced to a wilderness of about a thousand square miles.

19. By his capture of Babylon in B.C. 538 Cyrus, king of Persia, became master of an empire stretching from the Caspian to the Mediterranean

and, with a view to subsequent conquest of Egypt, decided that a friendly power, based on Jerusalem, would be a considerable strategic advantage. This object could be attained by repatriating the Jews who had been deported to Babylon under the previous regime.

20. King Cyrus was sitting in council in his Tower of Audience when a stranger approached. The guard at the entrance asked: 'who goes there?' to be answered 'A Stranger, The First amongst equals, a Mason of rank and captive by misfortune.'

21. The stranger sought admission to the presence of the great King, but before he was admitted Cyrus spoke to his council: 'Generals and Knights, this Sheshbazzar is the Prince of Judah, known among the Jewish captives by the name of Zerubbabel (meaning the Exile or Stranger in Babylon), but, before admitting him, I wish to relate to you the particulars of a dream I had last night'.

22. 'While I slumbered, methought I perceived a lion ready to attack and devour me, and at a distance my predecessors Nebuchadnezzar and Belshazzar in chains. They were contemplating A GLORY, which Masons interpret as the sign of the Great Architect of the Universe. In the clouds appeared an Eagle, from whose beak issued an order to RENDER LIBERTY TO THE CAPTIVES, otherwise my crown would pass into foreign hands. I was astonished and confounded. The dream vanished, but my tranquillity is disturbed. It has long been my desire to set the Jewish captives at liberty, for I am tired of hearing their heart-wrung yearnings for home. This dream has now deter-mined me. You will not, therefore, feel surprised at the reception I intend to give this Jewish Prince. Do you consent to his being admitted?'

23. The Knights of the Council rose, stepped forward with right foot, drew their swords, and indicated their consent. Cyrus then ordered: 'Let the captive be introduced, that we may interrogate him.'

24. Cyrus spoke. 'Stranger, as thou callest thyself, for what purpose do you appear before us?' The stranger replied: 'I implore your goodwill and justice.'

25. Cyrus enquired upon whose account he asked for goodwill and justice, and the stranger replied that it was his own, and that of his companions who had been seventy years in bondage.

26. The king then enquired what favour did he request, and the reply came that he asked that his people be granted liberty and be permitted to return to Judea to rebuild the Temple of the Most High.

27. Cyrus spoke: 'Since motives so just and honourable have brought you here, you shall be admitted to our grace. Arise, worthy Prince, I have long witnessed the weight of your captivity, and am ready to grant your request this instant if you will communicate to me the mysteries of your Order of Masonry, an Order for which I have always had the most profound veneration.'

28. The stranger whispered to the guard, who then spoke to the king saying: 'Most potent Sire, I am desired by the Prince to say that your situation tenders it impossible for him to entrust you with them, for Solomon when he first laid down the principles of the Order taught that Equality, Fidelity and Brotherly Love were ever to be the criteria among Masons. Your rank, your titles, and your court are incompatible with the humble mansions where the sacred mysteries of the Order prevail. His engagements with his Brethren are inviolable, and he dare not reveal to you their secrets. If his liberty is to be thus purchased, he prefers captivity.'

29. Cyrus replied: 'I admire your zeal and courage. Generals, Knights, this worthy Prince merits liberty for his fidelity to his engagements. Zerubbabel, I grant your request, and consent to your being set at liberty. You are free.'

30. The king ordered his Guards to strike off the chains which bound the stranger, saying: 'may these emblems of slavery never again disgrace the hands of a Mason, more particularly a Prince of the house of Judah.'

31. Cyrus then addressed Zerubbabel saying: 'Zerubbabel, return to your country of Judea. I permit you to rebuild the Temple of Jerusalem destroyed by my predecessors, and your treasures shall be returned to you before the sun is set. I appoint you chief among your Brethren and

to preside over your equals, and I command that they shall honour and obey you as they have hitherto honoured and obeyed me. The tribute I shall exact will not be oppressive, but will be an evidence to your neighbours that you are still under my protection. It will be three lambs, five sheep, and seven rams. Henceforth you will be to me, and I will be to you, a friend; in token of which approach and kneel.'

32. 'I create you a Knight of the Sword. Rise, Zerubbabel, Knight of the Sword. I now arm you with this Sword, as a mark of distinction among your companions. Consider it as the same Sword that Nebuchadnezzar received from your King Jehoiakim when taken captive. I am persuaded that you will only use it in your own defence, or in that of your country, religion or laws, or the cause of justice. Take it, and let it remain in its scabbard until it is consumed by rust rather than draw it in the cause of injustice and oppression. I also decorate you with this ribbon, which, although not accompanied with any mysteries like those of your Order, I grant as an honour to the Princes of my Court. You will henceforth enjoy the same privileges and distinction. Go into your own country. You shall get from my treasury the sacred vessels and relics belonging to your former Temple. Take this olive branch as a symbol of peace between us. I will give instructions to my Guards to allow you and your companions to pass through my dominion.'

33. Turning back to the Council he said: 'Generals, the audience is over. The captivity has ceased from this hour.'

34. As Zerubbabel returned to Judah he said the following words: 'Brothers, we are now returning to Jerusalem from Babylon, where we have been held in captivity many long years. Thanks be given to King Cyrus, by whose proclamation we have been liberated and permitted to return to our native country to assist in rebuilding our City and Temple. We have left the domes and spires of Babylon behind us, and I can now just see them glittering in the sunlight over the hills and plains of Chaldea. Our trust is in the great I AM, and although our journey may be long, tedious, and dreary, and our pathway rough, rugged, and dangerous, yet we will endeavour to overcome every obstacle, endure every hardship, and brave every danger, to promote the great and glorious work upon which we have entered.'

35. Zerubbabel told his brothers that the routes diverge; one leading in a direct line through the deserts of Arabia the other up the banks of the river Euphrates, and round by the way of Tadmor and Damascus. The Desert route is less frequented by travellers, owing to its extensive sandy plains, its intense heat and great scarcity of provisions and water. The other route is much more pleasant, though longer and more mountainous. On this route there is also plenty of fresh water and fruits.

36. They took the more pleasant route, but before reaching the banks of the Euphrates they had to pass over a rough and dangerous place. Before they undertook its passage they did as all good men ever do before entering upon any important undertaking, and knelt to invoke the blessing of the Deity.

37. They passed over the green banks of the ever-running water of the Euphrates and onwards through Syria towards Damascus. They passed near the ancient city of Tadmor or Palmyra, and through many beautiful groves and vineyards. Before reaching Damascus they had to cross a bridge over a deep ravine which they examined and found to be a very difficult and dangerous place. Therefore, before they proceeded they knelt to pray.

38. The travellers managed to cross the bridge just before its rotten structure collapsed and they were able to travel on to arrive at Damascus. This was a famous resting place, and here they sat down to refresh themselves amongst the vineyards and cool fountains. 'Arise, brothers!' Said Zerubbabel, 'Let us be going. We must not tarry longer, for we have one hundred and twenty miles further to travel before we shall reach Jerusalem.'

39. Eventually they passed through the forests of Lebanon, where their fathers felled and prepared the timbers for King Solomon's Temple, but then they came to another very difficult place, more dangerous than the others. Once more they knelt to pray before continuing the journey to the plains of Jordan, between Succoth and Zaredatha, where our ancient Grand Master Hiram Abif so faithfully wrought in casting all the holy vessels for King Solomon's Temple. It was here that those two famous brazen pillars, Jachin and Boaz, were cast.

40. Zerubbabel bade his followers to be cheerful as their journey was almost at an end. The ruins of Jerusalem could be seen in the distance, and the glistening tents of their brethren. Rough and rugged had been the road; long and toilsome had been their march; but sustained by a firm trust in the great I AM, they arrived at their journey's end.

41. And then Zerubbabel said: 'I can see the tabernacle just before. Look let us hasten on. Look, brothers, look.'

42. In the spring of B.C. 517, the seventieth year of first deportation, a caravan of 42,000 Jews; men, women and children with their flocks and herds, together with the Temple treasures, set out for Jerusalem under the leadership of Zerubbabel, Prince of Judah, and Joshua the High Priest. They came along the banks of the Euphrates to the ancient town of Mari, thence across the desert to Damascus and south via the Sea of Galilee. The journey occupied two years, and on arrival the repatriates found nothing but a dreary desert unoccupied except for the tents of nomad tribes with their goats and camels.

43. Shelter there was none, but it was decided that priority should be given to the building of the Temple; the people to make do with temporary shelters for the time being. One or more tabernacles were erected, on lines of that made by King David when he brought the Ark from Kirjath Jearim. One tabernacle served as a treasury and storehouse, another was the Headquarter Offices, accommodating the Grand Sanhedran, presided over by the three principals. This august body, otherwise known as the Grand and Royal Lodge, directed the work, and as necessary conferred the degree of Excellent Master.

Chapter Eleven

THE REDISCOVERED SECRETS OF KING SOLOMON'S TEMPLE

1. A small group of three Masons who were still captive in Babylon wished to return to help in building the Temple in Jerusalem, but they had first to be given permission by the Grand Lodge of Babylon, which conferred on them the degree of Excellent Master. They had first to approach the Right Worshipful and Excellent Master and each make the following petition:

2. 'I now wish to avail myself of the decree of Cyrus, and to return to Jerusalem to assist in rebuilding the House of the Lord God of Israel, and I approach the Grand Lodge of Babylon with a request to grant me permission and such tokens as shall be satisfactory to my Brethren who have already set out from here and arrived at Jerusalem. I make this request in the name of the Pentagram, or Blazing Star.'

3. The Right Worshipful and Excellent Master offered up a prayer to Most High saying: 'Oh Thou Eternal and Omnipotent God, who didst aforetime appear to Thy servant Moses in a flame out of the midst of a bush; enkindle we beseech Thee in our hearts devotion to Thee, love to our Brethren, and Charity to all mankind. Comfort us and all Thy people with Thy divine grace, guide and assist us in rebuilding a Second Temple to Thy Holy Service, and grant that when the Veil of this earthly

Tabernacle shall be rent asunder we may be received into that Holy Sanctuary where Thou reignest for ever and ever. Amen.'

4. He then continued: 'During the 470 years that have elapsed since the building of King Solomon's Temple, we have been widely spread, and as the decree of Cyrus only effects the descendants of those who were brought captive to Babylon. We, previous to the departure of Zerubbabel and our Brethren, in order to prevent others from sharing in the great and glorious work now commencing, have instituted a new degree.'

5. 'For so doing we have the example of our ancestors, who, at every building of importance adopted particular marks of recognition known only to those employed at it. We only communicate this degree to those who have been found qualified to preside over Operative or Fellow Craft Lodges.'

6. At the building of King Solomon's Temple the workmen were divided into lodges according to trade. On the second Temple, however, where the design was a smaller scale, lodge organisation was unnecessary. All skilled men were members of a common building trade and, as a pre-caution against cowans, it was decided that only those holding the degree of Excellent Master could become members of the 'Union', but to gain this degree the candidate had to prove himself master of his trade.

7. When the three sojourners arrived in Jerusalem they discovered that Zerubbabel had convened a meeting of the Sanhedran. They approached the Council Chamber and identified themselves as they had been taught, and so gained admission to the Chamber where Zerubbabel, Haggia and Joshua sat as the three principals of the Sanhedran. As they were brought into the chamber Zerubbabel asked them where they had come from.

8. They replied that they had travelled from Babylon, the land of cap-tivity, and Zerubbabel then enquired as to why they had left Babylon, the land of captivity, to come to Jerusalem, the city of promise. They replied: To assist in rebuilding the Temple of the Lord. Having heard that you are about to rebuild the Temple, we have come with the hope that we may be permitted to sojourn among you and contribute

our best services to forward that great and glorious work.

9. Zerubbabel demanded to know how they hoped to obtain admission. They replied: By virtue of certain signs, tokens and words received in Babylon, and then they gave the proofs as required and were admitted to the centre of the chamber.

10. Joshua prayed saying: Let the brightness of Thy Majesty, O Lord our God, shine upon us; Prosper Thou the work of our hands; Yea, prosper Thou our handiwork and may all that we do be to the honour and glory of Thy Most Holy Name. Amen.

11. Zerubbabel spoke: We highly commend your intention, but we wish to know more particularly who you are?

12. They replied: We are of your own nation and people, sprung from the same tribes, and branches of the same original stock, being, like yourselves, descendants of the Patriarchs Abraham, Isaac and Jacob, but the transgressions of our Ancestors having called forth the displeasure of the Most High, our people (as was foretold by the mouth of the prophet Jeremiah,) were given captive into the hands of the King of Babylon, for the space of 70 years -an event which took place in the fourth year of the reign of King Jehoiakim; but the years of the captivity being expired and the anger of the Lord appeased, He hath stirred up the heart of Cyrus, King of Persia and Babylon, to issue a decree liberating us and granting us permission to return to our native land and rebuild the Temple of the Lord.

13. Zerubbabel spoke: 'Our own knowledge of these facts, and the candour with which you have related them, leave no doubt of your sincerity, but we wish to know who were your immediate ancestors.'

14. They replied that their immediate ancestors were princes and rulers in Israel, whose fidelity to their king and country caused the King of Babylon, as a punishment, to carry them into Captivity.

15. Zerubbabel asked them: 'In what branch of the work do you wish to be engaged?'

16. They replied that they deemed the lowest service in the work of the Lord to be an honour, and therefore only begged employment.

17. Zerubbabel spoke saying: 'Your humility bespeaks your merit, and we do not doubt that you are qualified for the highest offices, but these are already filled. You will report yourselves to the Superintendent of Works, who will provide you with tools and direct you what to do; but we have this particular injunction to give you, that should you find anything belonging to the old Temple, you will immediately report the same unto us. Go, and may the God of our Fathers go with you and prosper your work.'

18. The following day the three Sojourners again presented themselves before Zerubbabel and the Sanhedran, where he asked them about a discovery they had made.

19. They replied that they had indeed made a discovery, four hundred and seventy years, six months and ten days after the dedication of the Temple. Pursuant to Zerubbabel's instructions they had reported to the Superintendent of Works and were directed by him to clear the ground previous to laying the foundations of the Temple. During their work at an early hour that morning one of their number, on breaking the ground with his pick-axe, struck on something which, from the sound, was judged to be hollow underneath; and on calling on another companion to clear away the loose earth with his shovel, they found a large brazen ring fixed to a broad flat stone with the words 'AM – B' - 'TSAPN' engraved thereon.

20. This was in the tongue of the workers and in the language of one of the Provinces of Babylon, where the companions had sojourned. The words signify 'the Way to hidden treasures', implying as it were, an instruction to search at or around it. The stone was accordingly raised; and found under it the crown of a perfect arch, but not being able to find any way into it, the workman loosened the keystone with his crowbar, and having drawn it forth discovered a cavity beneath.

21. This discovery incited their desire to know what it contained, and they resolved to explore it, but being apprehensive of danger from foul air

or other unknown causes, they cast lots among themselves as to who should descend. They agreed on proper signals, and one of their number was lowered down by his companions, by the help of a cable tow round his waist and steadying himself by holding it with his left hand above his head. The bottom was reached without impediment.

22. The sun, however, at that early hour in the morning only peeping from the porticoes of the east, and darting its beam parallel with the plane of the horizon, and the aperture being extremely small, the worker found himself enveloped in almost total darkness, and beginning to suffer from the foulness of the air, he made the agreed on signal – being three gentle pulls on the cable tow – and was drawn up. On examining the Keystone they were surprised to find on it certain characters which proved to, from the knowledge they already possessed, show that the vault must be the secret vault of King Solomon.

23. They therefore set to work and removed another stone in order to admit more light and air, and another of the companions was let down. In groping about he laid his hand on something which appeared to be wrought into due and regular form, on the top of which was a Roll; wishing to ascertain what this was he made the signal and was drawn up. On inspecting the Roll it was found to be the Book of the Holy Law; which gave them much joy, and they resolved to extend their search.

24. Having enlarged the opening by drawing forth another (that is a third) stone, and the sun having by this time reached its meridian altitude, another companion was now let down. On examining the place he found it to be a splendid apartment supported on seven pillars; round the architraves were the twelve signs of the Zodiac, and the names of the twelve tribes of Israel, and what had formerly been found, wrought into due and regular form, proved on inspection to be an Altar of pure white marble, in shape a double cube, and rich in sculptured ornaments, erected to the Lord God, for at that moment the meridian sun, darting his rays through the aperture, on to the top of the Altar, brilliantly illumined a circle of gold, on which was the grand, peculiar and mysterious name of Deity; and on a triangle of the same metal within the circle were inscribed other characters, of which they could not

understand the meaning, although they did not doubt that they were connected with the Sacred Word itself.

25. They further told Zerubbabel that on the front of the Altar were the initials of the three Grand Masters who presided at the building of the glorious Temple of King Solomon. Considering that they had made a discovery of much importance, and, having closed the aperture with care, the workers came, as in duty bound, they had come to report the circumstance to the king.

26. The first worker stepped forward saying to Zerubbabel: 'This is is the Roll which I now present; and this is a drawing of the Chamber as it appeared at High Meridian.'

27. The sojourners handed over the Roll and drawing to Zerubbabel, who told them that the discovery they had made was of the very greatest importance, saying: 'It is no less than the Book of the Holy Law, long lost but now found. Holiness to the Lord!'

28. In case anything may have been misunderstood or unobserved, Zerubbabel instructed them to return to the vault with Ezra the scribe, who was well skilled in languages to report what he observed. After a further examination of the vault the Sojourners and Ezra returned to the Sanhedran.

29. Ezra spoke: 'All has been correctly stated by the Sojourners, and in addition at the base of the Altar I found this Jewel, having carved on it the mark of Hiram Abif, and it appears to have belonged to that eminent person.'

30. Zerubbabel then asked how the Sojourners had been engaged during their captivity. They replied that they had been much employed in masonry, following which the king further enquired, what did they mean by masonry.

31. They replied that they meant that great and universal science which includes almost every other, to the several parts of which they had given their attention, but they had more particularly studied that part

which taught them their duty to God and to their neighbours, and a knowledge of themselves. From the knowledge they had thus acquired of the traditions of their people they believed that they had been the humble instruments, in the hands of the Most High, in restoring to light that which was lost by the untimely death of Hiram Abif, the Widow's Son.

32. Zerubbabel then said: 'It shall be our care to reward your discoveries, and also to show their importance. We invest you with these Sashes as badges of honour, and with these Jewels as a reward for your eminent services; we also place these rods in your hands as emblems of power and authority, and constitute and appoint you Princes and Rulers in Israel. To ennoble you still more we clothe you with these Aprons and receive you amongst us as Brethren and Companions, and if you continue faithful, and act with honour, it shall be our care to instruct you in every branch of our mystical knowledge.'

33. He then preceded to instruct them as follows: 'Companions, the discovery which has been made is of the greatest importance, and you see that the world is indebted to Masonry for the preservation of the Book of the Sacred Law. Had it not been for the wisdom and precaution of our first Grand Master in constructing under the Temple a secret vault, which remained proof against the devouring flames, and fury of the enemy, this the only remaining copy of the Law, would have been lost at the destruction of the Temple. The characters on the triangle – the meaning of which the Sojourners could not understand – represent, as has been suggested to us by the learned Sanhedran, the name of God in three different languages; and all indicate, in our opinion, the true and long-lost method of pronouncing the Sacred Word inscribed upon the circle; for it is of too essential a nature to be comprehended by human wisdom, or pronounced by the tongue of any individual. Lastly, Masonic tradition informs us that the ancient Master Mason's word lost at the building of King Solomon's Temple would, one day be recovered, and as the Jewel which the Sanhedran discovered bears the mark of Hiram Abif there can be no doubt that the characters on the triangle signify that lost word and the manner of pronouncing it, for we know that it could only be imparted when the three Grand Masters were present, and consented to give it.'

34. 'That we can do no good nor acceptable service but through strength-ening power and mercy of the Most High, without whose special favour we must ever be found unprofitable servants in His sight. Therefore, according to the manner adopted by our holy ancestors and like prac-tised by the atoning Priests, we shew by this, the outward form of con-trition and humility, as if we would prostrate ourselves with our faces to the earth, and throw ourselves upon the mercies of the Living God, looking forward with a becoming confidence to the accomplishment of His gracious promises by which alone we shall be enabled to pass through the ark of our redemption into those mansions of bliss and glory, and into the presence of Him who is the Great I Am, the Alpha and Omega, the First and the Last.'

35. Work on the second Temple, had begun in the year B.C. 535, and it had been beset with difficulties. The Samaritans, successors of the ten tribes which had seceded from the kingdom after the death of King Solomon, asked to be allowed to take part in the work but were refused, not only because they were not true Jews but because, once admitted, they would have installed pagan altars in the Temple. As a consequence of this refusal the Jews found themselves under continuous harassment, and found it necessary to keep weapons close at hand while at work. Furthermore, the Samaritans, through their representatives in Babylon, were able to induce the reigning monarch, Cyrus being dead, to stop the work.

Chapter Twelve

THE HONOURING OF ZERUBBABEL

1. For seven years the Temple site stood open and deserted. Then, in the year B.C. 521, Prince Darius succeeded to the throne of Persia. By a fortunate chance, Darius and Zerubbabel had been comrades-in-arms in earlier years, and it so happened that the former had sworn that if he ever came to the throne of Persia he would do anything in his power for his friend.

2. A Council was convened at the Temple in the second year of the Reign of Darius of Persia, to deliberate upon the unhappy state of the country during the Reigns of Artaxerxes and Ahasuerus, and to devise some means whereby they might gain the favour of the new sovereign in the work of rebuilding the Temple. Zerubbabel, Haggai and Jeshua acted as principals. Ezra and Nehemiah were also officers of the Sanhedran, the whole present being seventy-two. It was decided to approach King Darius.

3. Zerubbabel travelled once more to the Hall of Audience in Babylon. King Darius was seated on a low couch in the East of the chamber as Zerubbabel was announced as a Prince of the house of Judah, who sixteen years ago, having found favour in the sight of your predecessor, obtained liberty from him to rebuild the Temple of the Most High at

411

Jerusalem. It was explained that Cyrus had conferred on him the honour of Knighthood of the Sword and that he now came to demand justice from the king.

4. Darius asked why he did not wear the emblems of that Order, and take his place among the court by right of them? The king was then told that on his return to Judea, Zerubbabel had been attacked by the enemies of his nation, despoiled of his decoration, and only obtained liberty to pass the bridge which crosses the river on the confines of Babylon, by means of the sword, which Cyrus had previously bestowed upon him.

5. Darius then enquired why he had returned to Babylon, and was told in reply that having returned to Jerusalem, he and his countrymen had been at divers times interrupted in their labours by the malice of their enemies, and at length it has been resolved by the elders of the Jews to lay the matter before the great King, and in corroboration of these statements, two of Darius' own governors, Tattenai and Shetharbozenai, had sent letters which were then read out.

6. Unto Darius the King. All peace . . . Be it known unto the King, that we went into the province of Judea, to the house of the Great God, which is builded with great stones, and timber is laid in the walls, and this work goeth fast on, and prospereth in their hands. Then asked we those elders, and said unto them thus: Who gave you a decree to build this house, and to finish this wall? We asked their names also, to certify thee, that we might write the names of the men that were at the head of them. And thus they returned us answer, saying: We are the servants of the God of heaven and earth, and build the house that was builded these many years ago, which a great King of Israel builded and set up. But after that our fathers had provoked the God of heaven unto wrath, He gave them into the hand of Nebuchadnezzar, King of Babylon, the Chaldean, who destroyed this house, and carried the People away into Babylon. But in the first year of Cyrus the King of Babylon, the same King Cyrus made a decree to build this house of God. And the vessels also of gold and silver of the house of God, which Nebuchadnezzar took out of the Temple that was in Jerusalem, and brought them into the Temple of Babylon, those did Cyrus the King

take out of the Temple of Babylon, and they were delivered unto one, whose name was Sheshbazzar, whom Cyrus had made governor; and said unto him: Take these vessels, go, carry them into the Temple that is in Jerusalem, and let the house of God be builded in its place.

7. Then came the same Sheshbazzar, and laid the foundation of the house of God which is in Jerusalem; and since that time even until now hath it been in building, and yet it is not finished. Now, therefore, if it seem good to the king, let there be search made in the king treasure house, which is there at Babylon, whether it be so, that a decree was made of Cyrus the king to build this house of God at Jerusalem, and let the king send his pleasure to us concerning this matter.

8. Darius instructed his generals and councillors to instruct that a search be made among the records of their predecessors as to this matter. Following the search the Chancellor produced the roll and said to Darius: 'This roll, which was copied from one found among the records at Ecbatana, in the palace that is in the province Media, shows that Cyrus granted permission to rebuild the Temple of Jerusalem, as declared by this Stranger.'

9. Darius invited Zerubbabel to retire, while an answer was prepared to the letter from the governors. Darius then dictated to the Chancellor, who wrote the king's words on sheets of paper or parchment. Darius then instructed that Zerubbabel should again approach, telling him that he admired the zeal and perseverance with which he had endeavoured to promote the work he had undertaken. He told Zerubbabel that he had written the following letters to his governors.

10. The king's Chancellor then read aloud: Darius, the King – to Tattenai, Governor beyond the river, and Shethar-bozenai, Greetings. I have here sent you a copy of the decree which has been found among the records of Cyrus. Let the house be builded. Let the expenses be given out of the king's goods, even the tribute beyond the river, and offerings for the priests to sacrifice and pray to the God of heaven for the life of the king and his sons. Whosoever shall alter this word, let a beam be pulled out from his house, and let him be lifted up and hanged thereon; and let his house be made a dunghill for this. And the God, that hath

413

caused His Name to dwell there, destroy all kings and people that shall put to their hand to alter and to destroy this house of God which is at Jerusalem. I have decreed it. Let it be done with speed.

11. Darius then told Zerubbabel that the letters were to be despatched immediately, and will ensure the future protection of Zerubbabel's people whilst rebuilding the Temple, and as a mark of his esteem and favour he was to create Zerubbabel a Knight of the East.

12. Zerubbabel approached and knelt on one knee. Darius placed his sword on Zerubbabel's shoulder, and said: 'Rise Knight of the East. When you return to Jerusalem, you will pass safely through my dominions, but my request is that you remain some time at my country. In the meantime, I appoint you one of my bodyguards, and as an additional mark of my approbation, I invest you with this Sash. (Darius placed around Zerubbabel's waist a watered-silk pale green Sash fringed with gold lace, the end hanging down on the left side.) Wear this in token of the victory obtained over your enemies at the passage of the river.'

13. Zerubbabel took his place near the throne, along with the other two Guards.

14. One of the guards spoke to Zerubbabel saying. 'The great King makes known his pleasure through me, that we three should each of us give his opinion in answer to this question, Which is strongest, Wine, the King, or Women? And he that shall overcome, and whose sentence shall seem wiser than the others, unto him shall Darius give great gifts, and great things in token of victory. As, to be clothed in purple, to drink in gold, and to sleep upon gold, and a chariot with bridles of gold, and a head-tire of fine linen, and a chain about his neck: And he shall sit next to Darius because of his wisdom, and shall be called the cousin of the King.'

15. 'Each of the three of us wrote our word on a slip of paper, sealed it with his private seal, then folded and placed it under the head of Darius.' Then they retired to the extremity of the room. Later Darius awoke, rose up, and took the slips from under his pillow, and instructed

that the young guards be called so that we could each declare our own sentence. 'The King then told us to declare unto him our minds concerning which is strongest, Wine, the King, or Women.'

16. The guard then told Zerubbabel that each of the three answers were to be read from a Roll in turn.

17. The first guard spoke saying, 'Oh ye men, how exceeding strong is wine it causeth all men to err that drink it; it maketh the mind of the king and of the fatherless child to be all one; of the bondsman and of the freeman, of the poor man and of the rich. It turneth also every thought into jollity and mirth, so that a man remembereth neither sorrow nor debt. And it maketh every heart rich, so that a man remembereth neither king nor governor; and it maketh to speak all things by talents. And when they are in their cups, they forget their love both to friends and brethren, and a little after draw out swords But when they are from the wine, they remember not what they have done. O ye men, is not wine the strongest, that, enforceth to do thus?'

18. The second guard then gave his answer to the riddle: 'Oh ye men, do not men excel in strength, that bear rule over sea and land, and all things in them? But yet the king is more mighty, for he is lord of all these things, and hath dominion over them; and whatsoever he commandeth them they do. If he bid them make war, the one against the other, they do it: if he send them out against the enemies, they go, and break down mountains, walls and towers. They slay and are slain, and transgress not the king's commandment; if they get the victory, they bring all to the king, as well the spoil, as all things else. Likewise for those that are not soldiers, and have not to do with wars, but use husbandry, when they have reaped again that which they had sown, they bring it to the king, and compel one another to pay tribute unto the king. And yet he is but one man, if he command to kill, they kill; if he command to spare, they spare; if he command to smite, they smite; if he command to make desolate, they make desolate; if he command to build, they build; if he command to cut down, they cut down; if he command to plant, they plant. So all his people and his armies obey him; furthermore he lieth down, he eateth and drinketh, and taketh his rest. And these keep watch round about him, neither may any one

depart, and do his own business, neither disobey they him in any thing. O ye men, how should not the king be mightiest, when in such sort he is obeyed?'

19. Then Zerubbabel spoke. 'O ye men, it is not the great king, nor the multitude of men, neither is it wine, that excelleth who is it then that ruleth them, or hath the lordship over them? Are they not women? Women both borne the king and all the people that bear rule by sea and land. Even of them came they; and they nourished them up that planted the vineyards from whence the wine cometh. These also made garments for men; these bring glory unto men; and without women cannot men be. Yea, and if men have gathered together gold and silver, or any other goodly thing, do they not love a woman which is comely in favour and beauty? By this also you must know that women have dominion over you; do ye not labour and toil, and give and bring all to the woman? Yea, a man taketh his sword, and goeth his way to rob and to steal, to sail upon the sea and upon rivers; and lookest upon a lion, and goeth in the darkness; and when he hath stolen, spoiled, and robbed, he bringeth it to his love. Wherefore a man loveth his wife better than father or mother. Yea, many there be that have run out of their wits for women, and become servants for their sakes. Many also have perished, have erred, and sinned for women. And now do you not believe me? is not the king great in his power? Do not all regions fear to touch him? Yet did I see him and Apame, the king's concubine, the daughter of the admirable Bartacus, sitting at the right hand of the king. And taking the crown from the king's head, and setting it upon her own head, she also struck the king with her left hand. And yet for all this the king gazed upon her with delight; if she laughed upon him, he laughed also; but if she took any displeasure at him, the king was fain to flatter her that she might be reconciled to him again. O ye men, how can it be but women should be strong, seeing they do thus?'

20. 'Oh ye men, are not women strong? great is the earth, high is the heaven, swift is the sun in his course, for he compasseth the heavens round about, and fetcheth his course again to his place in one day.'

21. 'Is He not great that maketh these things? therefore great is The Truth, and stronger than all things. All the earth calleth upon the Truth, and

the heaven blesseth it; all works shake and tremble at it, and with it is no righteous thing. Wine is wicked, the king is wicked, women are wicked, all the children of men are wicked, and such are all their wicked works; and there is no truth in them; in their unrighteousness also they shall perish. As for the Truth, it endureth, and is always strong, it liveth and conquereth for evermore. With her there is no accepting of persons or rewards; but she doeth the things that are just, and refraineth from all unjust and wicked things; and all men do well like of her works. Neither in her judgment is any unrighteousness and she is the strength, kingdom, power and majesty of all ages. Blessed be the God of Truth.'

22. Darius then embraced Zerubbabel by placing his left hand on the right shoulder and Zerubbabel doing the same, and both said: 'Great is The Truth, and mighty above all things!'

23. Darius then said: 'Ask what thou wilt, more than is appointed in the writing, and we will give it thee, because thou art found wisest. Thou shalt sit next me. Thou shalt be called my cousin.'

24. Zerubbabel answered: 'Remember thy vow, which thou hast vowed to build Jerusalem, in the day when thou camest to thy kingdom. And to send away all the vessels that were taken away out of Jerusalem, which Cyrus set apart, when he vowed to destroy Babylon, and to send them again thither. Thou also hast vowed to build up the temple, which the Edomites burned when Judea was made desolate by the Chaldees. And now, O lord the king, this is that what I require, and which I desire of thee, and this is the princely liberality proceeding from thyself: I desire therefore that thou make good the vow, the performance whereof with thine own mouth thou hast vowed to the King of heaven.'

25. Darius said: 'Zerubbabel, all shall be granted according to thy desire.'

26. Zerubbabel returned to Jerusalem where he presented himself to the Council of the Sanhedran. The Most Excellent Chief, was seated in the East, two Wardens in the West. The Brethren called Knight Masons of Jerusalem were in the body of council room, which was hung in red.

27. The Most Excellent Chief asked: 'What hour is it?' and the Knights replied: 'The morning star has driven away the shades of night, and its great light begins to gladden our Lodge. It is the hour of the rebuilding the Temple.'

28. As Zerubbabel approached the guard asked: 'Who comes here?'

29. Zerubbabel replied: 'A Brother who obtained permission from Cyrus to rebuild the Temple. He afterwards received a confirmation of the same from Darius. He has now returned to reside with his brother masons in Judea.'

30. The guard asked: 'What is his name?' And was told his name was Zerubbabel.

31. The Guard announced to the Sanhedran that it was Zerubbabel, who obtained permission from Cyrus to rebuild the Temple, and afterwards received a confirmation of the same from Darius, who had now returned to reside with his brother masons in Judea, and await the welcome of the Sanhedran.

32. The Most Excellent Chief said: 'Brethren and Knights. It is our own Prince. Let the doors be opened for his approach. This is our worthy Prince, who, when the years of our captivity had expired, appeared before the Throne of Cyrus, who, admitting the justice of our claim, granted us our liberty, and armed him with the Sword he still wears and the insignia of a Knight of the Sword. In the battle which ensued between us and our enemies in crossing the bridge over the river Euphrates, he lost his ribbon, but with his sword he forced a passage for us. After arriving at Jerusalem preparations were made for rebuilding the Temple, and you are aware that in clearing the ground for its foundation three worthy brethren who followed us from Babylon made a discovery of so great an interest as to induce the Sanhedran to commemorate it by forming that exalted degree in Masonry, the Most Holy Royal Arch, of which Prince Zerubbabel himself is acknowledged to be the First Principal. Being afterwards interrupted in our labours, Zerubbabel was requested by the Sanhedran to repair to Darius, who graciously received him and created him a Knight of the East, of which

the sash or scarf he now wears is the emblem. Having prevailed upon that monarch to send letters to his governors not to molest us any more, he, at the King's request, remained with him some time longer in the hope of being further useful to his countrymen. Being afterwards so fortunate as to solve successfully a question put to him and others by Darius, the king has sent back with him many valuables belonging to the Temple, which had not been returned when we were freed by Cyrus. Having learned that there is an Order of Knighthood which has been occasionally conferred on Royal Arch Masons, he now presents himself before the Knight Masons of Jerusalem, and requests to be admitted one of your number.'

33. 'The zeal and perseverance you have shown in the good cause merits a participation in the highest honours we can bestow. Your integrity and fortitude have been put to the test. Cyrus in giving you the ribbon was actuated by a noble spirit, but not that of equality, which invariably actuates us. The loss of the ribbon at the bridge must convince you that pomp and grandeur are not so permanent as the honours of Masonry. You also merited the sash you now wear and the friendship conferred on you by Darius, but had it not been for the masonic wisdom you displayed in solving his question, your services to your country would not have come to so successful an issue.'

34. The Knight Masons of Jerusalem, led by Zerubbabel, Haggia and Joshua, rebuilt the Temple and became the Princes and rulers of Jerusalem.

35. The Grand Feast-day of Princes of Jerusalem they celebrated on the 23rd day of the eleventh month, Adar, which is the anniversary of the day when thanks were given to the Almighty for the reconstruction of the Temple. Their other Feast-days are as follows:

36. The 20th day of the tenth month, called Tebet, when 'the ambassadors made a triumphant entry into Jerusalem, on their return from Babylon.'

37. The equinoxial days, in the months of March and September, in memory of the Temple having been built twice.

38. Five members constitute a quorum: a Council cannot be opened with a less number.

39. If a Prince gives another Prince a challenge, he should be excluded forever.

40. Princes are strictly to observe the rule enforcing justice and good order, and their conduct in life should be irreproachable.

41. If any member of a Council or Lodge shall be present at, or aid, or assist in giving or receiving any of the sublime or symbolic degrees in a clandestine or irregular manner, contrary to the true intent and meaning of the statutes and regulations of the Supreme Council, or of the constitutions and laws of true Ancient, Free and Accepted Masonry, he subjects himself to expulsion.

42. A Prince of Jerusalem who visits an inferior Council or Lodge should present himself clothed with the dress and ornaments of a Prince; and when his approach is announced, the presiding officer sends a Prince of Jerusalem to examine him, and if he reports in his favour, he should be received under the arch of steel, and be escorted by four Brethren, and seated on the right hand of the presiding officer. An entry of his name and rank should be made on the engraved tablets, that he may thereafter receive due honours without examination; the same ceremonies should be observed when he retires as when he entered.

43. Princes have the right of being covered in all subordinate Lodges, Chapters, or Councils, and of addressing the Chair without first asking permission. If at any election of officers, a Prince of Jerusalem solicits votes for himself or any other person, he should be forever expelled.

Chapter Thirteen

THE GREAT ARCHITECT OF THE CHURCH

1. After the building of the second temple the masons neglected their labours, and abandoned to the ravages of time the valuable buildings which they had raised with so many pains; so that the wisdom of their workmanship, the strength of the materials, and the beauty of their architecture, were alike exposed to confusion, destruction and decay.

2. But the Eternal Most High God determined to manifest His Glory, and to replace the fallen material structures by that sublime and spiritual geometry whose existence human power should not be able to affect, and whose duration should be everlasting.

3. And the Eternal Most High God gave us the Perpend-ashlar to represent the Son of Man, who was born when the Divine Shekinah appeared to the Eastern Magi. So the Perpend-ashlar is symbolic of the Great Architect of the Church who called Himself the Rose of Sharon and the Lily of the Valley.

4. As Freemasons we were told to commemorate the Redemption of Man, to show the Glory of God. To Whom be all Honour, Glory and Praise, now, henceforth and evermore.

5. And we were instructed to travel the wide world in quest of the Holy Rock, or Mount of Adamant.

6. When we arrived over mountain tops, through deserts wide and perils great we saw the Holy Rock of our salvation and from the side of the rock a fountain issued and the voice of the Lamb said: 'Come and drink.'

7. And upon this Rock was builded a great Church in a great City. And the City was founded neither in blood nor in iniquity, but in Righteousness and Truth. Because it is said: 'The stone shall cry out of the wall, and the beam out of the timber shall answer it. Woe to him that buildeth a town with blood and establisheth a city by iniquity. Righteousness and Truth are stable as a Rock.'

8. The City was inhabited by kindreds and tongues and nations and it was guarded by a band of Angels with flaming swords and the City was called 'The Lord is there' or 'Jehovah Shammah'.

9. In the centre of the City was situated a great Church in the form of a regular square Cross. From East to West in length, because the Glory of God appears in the East and disappears in the West, and therefore all Churches, Chapels and places of Religious Worship are, or ought to be, so situated. In breath it was from North to South and in height immeasurable. Its depth was unfathomable.

10. And we heard the voice of the Grand Architect saying 'Come unto me, all ye that labour and are heavy laden, and I will give you rest.' And we worked and laboured at the building of the Church and our wages were the hopes of a Kingdom, not of this world.

11. May every Brother so labour and work that we may come unto Mount Sion, and unto the city of the living God, the heavenly Jerusalem, and to an innumerable company of angels, to the general assembly and church of the first-born, which are written in Heaven, and to God the judge of all, and to the spirits of just men made perfect, and to Jesus the Mediator of the new covenant: where our sun shall no more go down neither shall our moon withdraw itself, for the Lord shall be our everlasting light, and the days of our mourning shall be ended.

12. And as we approached the tower of the great Church we were called into the Middle Chamber by three wise men who lead us to the Cabinet of Wisdom by following a Blazing Star appearing in the East.

13. And we saw that the Cabinet of Wisdom was an ox's stall and there we did meet a most glorious Brother, his most Holy Spouse and the ever-blessed Word; and their names were Joseph, Mary and Jesus.

14. And soon after this time St John the Baptist made his appearance in the desert, near the shores of the Dead Sea, to distinguish Masonry from all the old philosophical and religious systems which were approximating to each other.

15. The Word lived forty years and a half upon earth, left a bright and shining example for us to follow, and suffered a painful and ignominious death for our salvation.

16. Then was the stone, the corner of the building, torn from the temple by the workmen and thrown among the ruins.

17. Almighty and Everlasting Father, we thank Thee that Thou didst send into the world Thy dear Son, and that, after having set a bright and glorious example for us to follow, suffered for our transgressions on the Cross.

18. As the Mystic Rose, the Word was sacrificed upon a Cross planted on the summit of a mountain, which is elevated above the surface towards the celestial spheres by three squares, three circles, and three triangles. At the instant the veil of the temple was rent, the earth was covered with darkness, the day-star of mercy was obscured, and the word was lost.

19. When the Word was lost it may easily be imagined into what a depth of misery every true mason was plunged. The stars disappeared, the light of the sun and the moon was obscured, and darkness fell upon the face of the earth.

20. The ninth hour arrived and Masonry was overwhelmed with grief and the deepest sorrow and consternation spread horror over her brow.

21. The earth quaked, the rocks were rent, the veil of the Temple was rent in twain, darkness overspread the earth, and the true Light departed from us. Our altars were thrown down, the Cubic Stone poured forth blood and water, the Blazing Star was eclipsed, our Shepherd was smitten, the Word was lost, and despair and tribulation sat heavily upon us.

22. Some of the brethren, who possessed relics of the former temple, wandered among the woods and mountains in the deepest obscurity. Others sought the sacred tomb in which the Word was hidden, and watched in silence for the space of three days. Never before was such perplexity experienced by the human heart.

23. On the first hour of the third day, being the first day of the week arrived the hour of the Perfect Mason.

24. At the hour of the Perfect Mason the Word was found and the Cubic Stone changed into the Mystic Rose. The Blazing Star reappeared in all its splendour, our altars were renewed, the true Light restored to our eyes, the clouds of darkness dispersed; and the New Commandment was given to love one another.

25. The Star and circling Glory declare the Shekinah, wherever it appear, whether on Sinai, Salem, or the place where the Eastern Magi saw the blessed Word.

26. And the Word ascended into the Lodge of Heaven, where he continues with the Holy Ghost to make intercessions for us with the Father. Three Persons in One Godhead.

27. But it was held by a vast number, that the writings of the Apostles were incomplete, that they contained only the germs of another doctrine, the mysteries handed down from generation to generation in our Masonic tradition, and proclaimed in the desert by St John the Baptist.

28. From the birth of the Word we learn that the Great Captain of our Salvation was born to redeem fallen mankind.

29. From the life of the Word we learn that it is requisite for us to follow the way of Truth.

30. From the death of the Word we learn that our debt of nature is fully paid and the rigour of the law satisfied.

31. From the resurrection of the Word we learn that the Day-Star of Mercy will rise to conduct our feet into the paths of truth and peace.

32. We must not undervalue the importance of any Truth. We utter no word that can be deemed irreverent by any one of any faith. We do not tell the Moslem that it is only important for him to believe that there is but one God, and wholly unessential whether Mahomet was his prophet. We do not tell the Hebrew that the Messiah, whom he expects, was born in Bethlehem nearly two thousand years ago; and as little do we tell the Christian that Jesus the Nazarine was but a man, or his history the revival of an older legend. To do either is beyond our jurisdiction. Masonry, of no one age, belongs to all time; of no one religion, it finds its great Truths in all.

Chapter Fourteen

EARLY CHRISTIAN
DEGREES

1. Caius Flavius Valerius Aurelius Claudius Constantine (c. 274–337 AD) was a son of Flavius Valerius Constantinus Chlorus and Helena, a British princess and a daughter of Caylus. Constantine was born in the English city of York. He succeeded his father as Governor of Spain, Gaul and Britain, and was proclaimed Emporer of the West by the Roman Legions at York and by the defeat of Maxentius.

2. Constantine was the first Roman Emperor openly to encourage Christianity, and we celebrate his conversion in the foundation of the Order of the Red Cross.

3. Candidates who enter this illustrious Order are duly admitted upon the equilateral triangle and they must obey the New Law, to take up the Cross and follow in the footsteps of the Lamb, by which means can they hope to rebuild in their heart the Temple of the Most High God.

4. They seek Immanuel. They are directed hither by Hiram the Widow's Son. They hope to rest in Shiloh, the City of God. And they are descended from Uzziah, king of Judah, famous for his military successes.

5. The inscription of the Order is 'In Hoc Signo Vinces', meaning 'In this sign thou shalt conquer'.

6. This Illustrious and Chivalric Order was founded by Constantine after the battle of Saxa Rubra in the year 312 AD in which he finally defeated the rival emperor, Maxentius. He founded it as a memorial of the Divine miracle which led to his conversion to the Christian Faith, and as a reward of the valour and constancy of certain of his soldiers.

7. The Order of the Red Cross is therefore not only a most ancient but a most honourable Institution of Masonic Knighthood; and it behoves the knights of the Order to prize the privileges descended from those worthy brethren, and ever to remember the watchwords of the Order; which are Faith, Unity and Zeal.

8. Before his conversion to Christianity, Constantine had been initiated into the Mysteries of the Collegium Artificium, or College of Artificers, at Rome and had attained to the position of Magister, or Master. This training doubtless had enlightened his mind and predisposed him eagerly to desire a more complete Knowledge of the Most High God, the worship of Whom formed the core of one of the Ancient Mysteries, so that when he assumed the Imperial Purple not even the cares of Empire or the responsibilities of command could eradicate early impressions or restrain his profound research after Truth and Wisdom.

9. The manner of his conversion is thus related: Upon an evening, during the march of his army on Rome, Constantine was meditating on the fate of sublunary things and the dangers of his expedition, and, sensible of his own inability to succeed without Divine assistance, he supplicated Heaven to grant him inspiration and wisdom to choose the right path. The Great Architect of the Universe heard his prayer for, as the sun was setting, suddenly there appeared in the heavens a Pillar of Light in the shape of a Cross with the inscription 'In Hoc Signo Vinces'.

10. So extraordinary a phenomenon created the utmost astonishment in the minds of of the Emperor and his army, and the Pagans deemed it a most inauspicious omen: but the next day Constantine, reassured by

the visions of the night, caused a Royal Standard to be made bearing as a device a Cross like that which he had seen in the heavens, and he ordered that it should always be carried before him in his wars as an Ensign of Victory and Celestial protection.

11. The tradition then relates that thereupon several Christian Masons among the soldiers came forward and openly avowed their Faith; and that the Emperor, to commemorate the event, directed them to wear on their armour a Red Cross with sixteen stars denoting the sixteen letters of the mystic words.

12. On reaching the Capital, Constantine, with the assistance of Brother Eusebius, is said to have opened a Conclave of Knights of the Order, and thereafter these valiant and illustrious men formed the personal Bodyguard of their Sovereign.

13. The Rose and Lily were adopted by our Royal Founder as emblems of the Divine Being he had learned to adore. Mystically, they represent the Rose of Sharon and the Lily of the Valley.

14. Among the other acts of Constantine, his encouragement of learning is conspicuous; he also ordered that the Scriptures should be carefully kept and frequently read in all churches; and he devoted a fourth part of his revenues to the relief of the poor and to other pious purposes. On this account his memory will abide in the minds of good men and Masons until Time shall be no more.

15. In 329 AD, St Helena, daughter of Caylus, King of Britain, Consort of Constantius and mother of Constantine the Great, made a journey to the Holy Land in search of the Cross of our Redeemer.

16. After levelling the hillocks on Mount Calvary and destroying the Temple of Venus three crosses were discovered; but it was difficult to determine which of the three had borne the divine form of the Lamb of God.

17. The Pontiff Marcellinus, being consulted, commanded them to be carried to the bedside of a woman who had long been visited by sickness

and lay at the point of death, and their virtue and efficacy to be tested by placing her hands upon each of the crosses. The Pontiff's orders were obeyed; two of the crosses rendered her no service, but when her hand was laid upon the third she was miraculously restored to health, and instantly arose, giving glory to God, saying: 'He was wounded for our transgressions, He was bruised for our iniquities, the chastisement of our peace was upon Him, and with His stripes we are healed.'

18. On the spot where the crosses were found St Helena and Constantine erected a stately church, one hundred paces long and sixty wide, part of it covering the site of the crucifixion; and by the levelling of the hillocks the Sepulchre is above the floor of the church, like a grotto, it being twenty feet from the floor to the top of the rock. There is a superb cupola over the Sepulchre; and in the aisle are placed the tombs of Godfrey, Defender of the Sepulchre, and Baldwin, the first Christian King of Jerusalem.

19. St Helena then, with the sanction of Constantine, instituted the Order of Knights of the Holy Sepulchre. The Order was confirmed by the Pontiff Marcellinus, and the Patriarch of the Holy City was appointed Chief of the Knights, who were selected from Brethren of the Red Cross fraternity and, kneeling on the Sacred tomb, were bound by a solemn vow to guard the Holy Sepulchre, protect pilgrims, and to repel the attacks of all infidels and enemies of the cross of Christ.

20. According to our Masonic tradition, the Degree of Knight of Constantinople was also founded by the Emperor Constantine the Great, in order to remedy certain evils which threatened his sovereignty. The pride and arrogance of the nobility, and their power, had greatly increased under the weak rule of several of his predecessors: he foresaw that his throne would be endangered unless he could bring them into a state of submission.

21. In order therefore to curb the nobility and bring them to a proper level with his more humble subjects, he instituted an order of knighthood, which he conferred upon some of his common people, the artisans and labourers. The Emperor then bound himself by a solemn engagement that he personally would never again confer this knighthood upon any

man: whosoever desired to obtain it must have it awarded by those common people who had already been created Knights of the Order.

22. He also agreed that he would not show his favour to any but the Knights of Constantinople. And he gave them orders to put to instant death any person who received the Degree and would not acknowledge that all men were equal in the sight of God.

23. The nobles said of the Masons: These are the common people; they are beneath our notice; it would be degrading for us, the nobility, to speak to them.

24. They spoke to Constantine saying: Will your Majesty confer the Degree of Knight of Constantinople upon us your humble servants? Constantine replied: I confer it on no man.

25. The nobles asked: From whom then can we expect to receive it? Constantine replied: From these builders and labouring masons whom you have just observed to be your inferiors, the Knights of Constantinople.

26. The nobles quickly perceived that they had lost the confidence of their Sovereign. A deputation was informed that his favour would only be shown to the Knights of Constantinople.

27. The realisation that they could not survive without the favour and friendship of their Emperor caused the honour to be eagerly sought. Many of the nobility, having complied with the requirements of the Degree, received this Order of Knighthood from the duly constituted Masonic authorities. Thus Constantine succeeded both in humbling his haughty subjects and in preserving the authority of his throne.

28. This Degree inculcates the virtue of humility. It teaches us to hate arrogance and pride, to remember that those who occupy a lower station of life may have more intrinsic merit than ourselves, and above all never to forget that he that exalteth himself shall be abased, but he that humbleth himself shall be exalted.

29. Constantine and Helena insisted that our Order should for ever acknowledge that all men are equal in the sight of the Most High God.

30. May the ever-blessed Sovereign of the Universe take the members of this Council into His holy keeping throughout the watches of the night and the labours of the day, so that they may be prepared for the coming of that night when no man can work.

31. After the death of Constantine a Brother Knight who was sent to visit the ruins of the ancient temple returned from there, having found the Scriptures of our Holy Patron. These are the circumstances thereof.

32. Having proceeded to the ruins of Herod's Temple, he found that the Emperor Julian had commenced the erection of another building on that ancient site. He was compelled to assist the labourers who were working on the foundations and, on the removal of one of the stones, a vault was discovered.

33. As the interior could not be clearly seen owing to its great depth, he was ordered to descend and ascertain its contents. His fellow workmen lowered him by means of a rope, when he found that a considerable quantity of water had accumulated on the floor of the vault, while in the midst, and scarcely above its surface, there rose a column on the top of which lay a book wrapped in a fine linen cloth.

34. He made no further discovery, and taking possession of the book was drawn up again to the light. No sooner was the volume opened than a great fear fell upon all present, both Jews and Greeks, for at the very beginning, in large characters, were written the words: 'In the beginning was the Word, and the Word was with God, and the Word was God.' It proved indeed to be a manuscript copy of our holy writings.

35. Now this incident, together with other miracles sent from heaven about the same time, made it evident that the prophecy of the desolation of the temple would never become void, for the Book declared that He who had ordered this was the Most High God, the Creator of all things. It showed moreover that they who were toiling at that building laboured in vain, for a divine and immutable sentence had decreed its final

destruction. These and similar circumstances caused all immediately to declare that it was not pleasing to the Most High God that the temple should be restored.

36. The tradition which has just been made known to you should ever impress upon your mind that the decrees of the Most High God cannot be reversed by the hand of man. Julian the Apostate attempted to rebuild the Jewish temple, but failed signally to accomplish his design; and as a punishment for sin, we find that his end was a miserable scene of blasphemy.

37. It is narrated that when wounded by Persian dart he endeavoured to mount his horse for a second charge on the enemy, but fell back exhausted into the arms of his attendants. Filling his hands with the blood gushing from the wound, he cast it into the air and died exclaiming bitterly: 'Thou hast conquered, Oh Galileen.'

38. After the death of Julian, the Christian religion spread apace, except in the East.

Chapter Fifteen

THE KNIGHTS TEMPLAR AND THE KNIGHTS OF ST JOHN OF JERUSALEM

1. The city of Jerusalem was rebuilt and ornamented in the second century A.D. by Publius Aelius Hadrianus, Emperor of Rome, and given to the Christians in the fifth century. The Persians captured it from them in 614, and a few years later fell into the hands of the Moslems, under whose oppressive rule it long groaned, until Peter the Hermit encouraged the western princes and Knight Masons to liberate the distressed Church.

2. The Word has been again lost and the Third Temple, in the heart of man, is to be built and dedicated to the Most High God of Truth.

3. When the Knights and the Princes of Jerusalem united to conquer the Holy Land, they took an oath to spend, if necessary, the last drop of their blood to establish the true religion of the Most High God.

4. Finally, when the time arrived that the Christian Princess entered into a league to free the Holy Land from the oppression of the infidels, the good and virtuous Masons, anxious for so pious an undertaking, offered their services to the confederates, upon condition that they should have a chief of their own election, and whose name was only made known in the hour of battle; which being granted, they accepted their standard and departed.

433

5. It is said that the Knights and the Princes of Jerusalem, finding themselves unable to expel the Saracens from the Holy Land, agreed with Godfrey de Bouillon to veil the mysteries of our religion under emblems, by which they would be enabled to maintain their devotions in secret, and secure themselves against the intrusion of traitors or pretended friends.

6. The valour and fortitude of these Elected Knights were such, that they were admired by, and took the lead of, all the Princes of Jerusalem, who, believing that their mysteries inspired them with courage and fidelity to the cause of virtue and religion, became desirous of being initiated. Upon being found worthy, their desires were complied with, and thus the Royal Art, meeting the approbation of great and good men, became popular and honourable, and was diffused to the worthy throughout these dominions, and thus continued to spread, far and wide, through a succession of ages to the present day.

7. Hence it follows that the mysteries of the craft are in reality the mysteries of religion. The Knights were, however, careful not to entrust this important secret to any whose fidelity and discretion had not been fully proved. They therefore invented different degrees to test their candidates, and gave them only symbolical secrets without explanation, to prevent treachery and solely to enable them to make themselves known to each other. For this purpose it was resolved to use different signs, words and tokens in each degree, by which they would be secured against the Saracens, cowans or intruders.

8. Godfrey de Bouillon unfurled the banner of the Cross, and in 1099 expelled the invaders. His companions thereupon elected him King of Jerusalem; but, as he thought not meet to wear a royal crown where his Blessed Saviour had worn a crown of thorns, he consented for the common good to be called the 'Defender and Baron of the Holy Sepulchre', which title he held until his death in 1100.

9. They have, ever since their first establishment, adhered to their customs and forms of reception. In the year 1118, the first knights of the Order, in the number eleven, took their vows between the hands of Armelfo Guavi Mundos, Prince and Patriarch of Jerusalem, who hailed from the province of Amiens in France.

10. Peace having been made, they could not practically fulfil their vows, and therefore on returning to their respective countries they resolved to do in theory what they could not do in practice. They took the name of Princes of Jerusalem and Knights of the East and West, in memory of the place where our Order was first instituted, and because their doctrines came from East and West.

11. Do not despair because you have often seemed on the point of attaining the inmost light, and have as often been disappointed. In all time truth has been hidden under symbols, and often under a succession of allegories – where veil after veil had to be penetrated before the true light was reached and the essential truth stood revealed.

12. During the period of the Crusades our Order of the Holy Sepulchre flourished, and since the loss of the Holy Land it has continued to exist in many countries of Europe. There is no longer any temple, because the light of the Lord is universally diffused, and the world has become one holy house of wisdom. The hour cometh, and now is, when the true worshippers shall worship the Father in Spirit and in truth.

13. There was a direful catastrophe which befell our Order about two centuries after its formation in Palestine. During this period the Order had flourished greatly, and been of essential service to the cause of Religion; yet, strange to say, its overthrow was to be effected by men professing the same Faith, but actuated by the base motive of possessing themselves of the treasures and lands of the Order.

14. To effect this, Philip the Fair, King of France, and Pope Clement V, in the year 1307, entered into an unholy league, binding themselves to destroy the illustrious Order. On the night of 10th October of that year, when the Grand Master and the Knights were reposing in confidence in the Christian capital of Paris, Philip, with his armed satellites, seized them in their house of the Temple there, and at break of day all the Knights throughout the Province of France were arrested and thrown into prison.

15. An act of accusation was soon after presented against them, in which they were designated as wolves, perjurers, idolaters, and in general as

the vilest of men. The astonished and unoffending Brother Knights protested their innocence, dared their enemies to the proof and asserted the integrity of their Order. But their doom was predetermined.

16. Many were put to the torture to force them to confess crimes of which they were innocent, and those who survived the rack were condemned to pine in prison for years without aid in their cause, and with scarcely sufficient sustenance to support existence. At length they were led out in bands, at one time fifty together, and were burned to death upon faggots.

17. Jacques de Molay, our illustrious Grand Master, together with four of his Priors, were the last victims of this relentless persecution. After remaining nearly seven years in prison, these illustrious Brother Knights were, on the 11th March 1314, led out for execution before the Cathedral of Paris; and after the decree and sentence of the bloody Philip were read, were burned alive before the assembled citizens, the glorious martyrs of our glorious Order.

18. The following is the prayer of Jacques De Molay, just prior to his execution.

19. Forgive, O God, those false accusers who have caused the entire destruction of the Order whereof thy Providence has made me the head. And if it please thee to accept the prayer which we now offer, grant that the day may come when the world, now deceived, may better know those who have sought to live for thee. We trust to thy goodness and mercy to compensate us for the tortures and death which we are now to suffer; and that we may enjoy Thy Divine Presence in the mansions of happiness. So mote it be.

20. All over Europe the same persecution took place with more or less barbarity, and although King Edward II of England, who was then in possession of a great part of Scotland, did not attempt to perpetrate any cruelties of the kind in this country, owing to the advance of Bruce and his army, by whom the Templars were protected, yet even here our Order was at last stripped of its privileges and possessions.

21. The physical hardships to which our Order has been subjected were hard enough to appal the stoutest heart. Poverty, chastity and obedience were the three great task-masters to whose uncompromising and unrelenting sway the whole existence of our predecessors of worthy memory was subjected.

22. We must remain familiar with the history of the Knights Templar; of their rise and progress; their great and glorious exploits; their numbers, wealth, and high standing in every kingdom of Europe; their persecution and fall, and the sufferings of the Grand Master, Jacques de Molay, and his brave Knights, by order of Pope Clement V, the cruelty and barbarity of Philip the Fair and the potentates and governments of Europe; the history of our Order of the Knights of Malta.

23. In the year 1048 some pious Masons from Amalfi, in the Kingdom of Naples, built a Monastery and Hospital at Jerusalem dedicated to St John. These Masons were known as the Brethren of St John of Jerusalem, or Hospitallers, and it was their duty to assist the sick and needy Pilgrims whom a spirit of piety had led to the Holy Land.

24. Having rapidly increased in numbers and in wealth, in 1118 they became a Military Order under Grand Mastership of Raymond du Puy, who added to their vow of Chastity, Obedience and Poverty, the obligation to defend the Church against the Infidels.

25. When Jerusalem was captured by Saladin they left the Holy City in 1191 to become a Sovereign Order with their headquarters in Acre.

26. By 1290 only Acre remained of the conquests of Godfrey de Bouillon. Appeals were made to the Christian Kings to defend and retain at least this one City upon the sod of the Holy Land, but the Monarchs were too much occupied with their mutual quarrels and jealous to listen.

27. In 1291 Acre was captured by the Saracens under Melik de Serif, who utterly destroyed the city and put 60,000 of its inhabitants to the sword. The small remnant of our Knights who escaped first took refuge in Cyprus, but decided to settle in Rhodes.

28. The Grand Master of the Order, Fulco Villaret, landed on the Island, but met with fierce resistance and after a struggle of four years took the principal city in 1310.

29. The Order remained in Rhodes for over 200 years, despite repeated attempts by the Turks to remove our Brethren.

30. In 1522, the island was besieged by Suliman the Magnificent with an immense army, and although the Knights, under Grand Master Philip de Villiers de L'Isle Adam, fought well, they were eventually forced to surrender on honourable terms.

31. For seven years our brother Knights wandered homeless, going successively to Castro in Candia, to Messina, in Sicily, and to Viterbo, near Rome.

32. In 1530 the Emperor Charles V bestowed upon our Order the Island of Malta, so that the Knights might protect and defend it and do their utmost to suppress Moorish pirates, who at that time infested the southern Mediterranean.

33. Accordingly our Brethren went to Malta and approached the shore rowing in their galleys, two men to an oar, facing each other, each Knight with his sword in his right hand and the oar in his left. As they neared the land they sang a hymn embodying the 16th verse of the 19th chapter of the Apocalypse, the refrain of which is 'Rex Regum et Dominus Dominorum'.

34. The inhabitants of the island, seeing their approach in a warlike guise, hailed them, in Arabic, saying: 'Do you come in peace?' The Knights responded in the same tongue saying: 'We come in peace,' to which the islanders replied: 'Then come in peace.'

35. Now settled in Malta, the Order again became a Sovereign Military Power, amassed great wealth, and established its Priories throughout Europe, whilst its members maintained the traditions of fortitude and valour which they inherited from our Ancient Brethren.

36. Until the year 1723 they fought an almost constant war with the Turks, who vainly expended vast quantities of blood and treasure to try to subdue the magnanimous and undaunted heroism of our brother knights.

37. But soon was a new order to come. The armies of Napoleon overran Europe, and all over Europe thrones tottered to their fall. The little domain of the Knights of St John did not escape unscathed.

38. On 9th June 1798 the French Fleet appeared before Malta with Napoleon himself on board, and our Grand Master, Ferdinand von Hompesch, was obliged to capitulate. Thus the existence of the Order as a Sovereign Power came to an end, and it now only exists as our peaceful Masonic Society.

Chapter Sixteen

EVOLVED FREEMASONRY

1. Masonry will help you to approach those ancient religions which once ruled the minds of men, and whose ruins encumber the plains of the great past, as the broken columns of Palmyra and Tadmor lie bleaching on the sands of the desert. They rise before you those old, strange, mysterious creeds and faiths, shrouded in the mists of antiquity, and stalk dimly and undefinedly along the line that divides time from eternity; and forms of strange, wild, startling beauty mingle in the vast throng of figures, with shapes monstrous, grotesque, and hideous.

2. The religion taught by Moses, which, like the laws of Egypt, enunciated the principle of exclusion, borrowed at every period of its existence from all the creeds with which it came in contact. While by the study of the learned and wise, it enriched itself with the most admirable principles of the religions of Egypt and Asia, it was changed in the wanderings of the people, by everything that was impure or seductive in the pagan manners and superstitions. It was one thing in the time of Aaron and Moses, another in that of David and Solomon, and still another in that of Daniel and Philo.

3. At the time when John the Baptist made his appearance in the desert, near the shores of the Dead Sea, all the old philosophical and reli-

gious systems were approximating to each other. The Jews and Egyptians, before then the most exclusive of all people, yielded to that eclecticism which prevailed among their masters, the Greeks and Romans. It was held by a vast number, even during the preaching of Paul, that the writings of the Apostles were incomplete, that they contained only the germs of another doctrine, which must receive from the hands of philosophy not only the systematic arrangement which was wanting, but all the developments which lay concealed therein, mysteries handed down from generation to generation in our Masonic tradition.

4. If anywhere brethren of a particular religious belief have been excluded from our Order, it merely shows how gravely the plans and purposes of Masonry may be misunderstood; for whenever the door of any one degree is closed against him who believes in one God and the soul's immortality, on account of the other tenets of his faith, that degree is no longer Masonry, which is universal, but some other thing, that is exclusive, and accordingly intolerant.

5. Each degree erects a platform on which the Israelite, the Mahommedan and the Christian may stand side by side and hand in hand, as brethren. Whatever your religion, your birthplace, or your language, you are among brethren. One language is spoken in common, the language of the Masonry, which speaks directly to the heart.

6. Masonry is the handmaid of religion. The Brahmin, the Jew, the Mahommedan, the Catholic, the Protestant, each professing his peculiar religion, sanctioned by the laws, by time, and by climate may retain their faith, and yet may be Masons. Masonry teaches, and has preserved in their purity, the cardinal tenets of the old primitive faith, which underlie and are the foundation of all religions.

7. The natural form of Masonry is goodness, morality, living a true, just, affectionate, self-faithful life, from the motive of a good man. It is loyal obedience to God's law.

8. The good Mason does that which is good, which comes in his way, from a love of duty; and not merely because a law enacted by man or

God commands his will to do it. Not in vain does the poor or oppressed look up to him.

9. You find such men in all Christian sects, Protestant and Catholic; in all the great religious parties of the civilised world, among Buddhists, Mahometans, and Jews. They are kind fathers, generous citizens, and unimpeachable in their business: you see their Masonry in their works and in their play.

10. The true Mason loves not only his kindred and his country, but all mankind; not only the good, but also the evil among his brethren. Though the ancient and the honourable of the earth bid him bow down to them, his stubborn knee bends only at the bidding of his manly soul. His Masonry is his freedom before God, not his bondage unto men.

11. The old theologies, the philosophies of religion of ancient times, will not suffice us now; there are errors to be made away with, and their places supplied with new truths, radiant with the glories of heaven. There are great wrongs and evils in Church and State, in domestic, social and public life, to be righted and outgrown.

12. Masonry cannot in our age forsake the broad way of life; she must journey on in the open street, appear in the crowded square, and teach men by her deeds, her life, more eloquent than any lips.

13. Masonry is much devoted to Toleration, and it inculcates in the strongest manner that great leading idea of the Ancient Art, that a belief in the one true God, and a moral and virtuous life, constitute the only religious requisites needed to enable a man to be a Mason.

14. It has ever the most vivid remembrance of the terrible and artificial torments that were used to put down new forms of religion or extinguish the old. It sees with the eye of memory the ruthless extermination of all the people, of all sexes and ages – because it was their misfortune not to know the God of the Hebrews, or to worship him under the wrong name by the savage troops of Moses and Joshua.

15. It sees the thumbscrews and the racks; the whip, the gallows, lows,

and the stake; the victims of Diocletian and Claverhouse; the miserable covenanters; the nonconformists; Servetus bound, and the unoffending Quaker hung. It sees Cranmer hold his arm, now no longer erring, in the flame, until the hand drops off, in the consuming heat.

16. It sees the persecutions of Peter and Paul, the martyrdom of Stephen, the trials of Ignatius, Polycarp, Justin and Irenaeus; and then, in turn, the sufferings of the wretched Pagans under the Christian emperors and all that in all ages have suffered by hunger and nakedness, peril and prison, the rack, the stake, and the sword – it sees them all, and shudders at the long roll of human atrocities.

17. Man never had the right to usurp the unexercised prerogative of God, and condemn and punish another for his belief.

18. Born in a Protestant land, we are of that faith: if we had opened our eyes to the light under the shadows of St Peter's at Rome, we should have been devout Romanists; born in the Jewish quarter of Aleppo, we should have contemned Christ as an imposter; in Constantinople, we should have cried: 'Allah il Allah – God is great, and Mahomet is his Prophet.' Birthplace and education give us our faith.

19. Few believe in any religion because they have examined the evidences of its authenticity, and made up a formal judgement, upon weighing the testimony. Not one in ten thousand knows anything about the proofs of his faith. We believe what we are taught; and those are most fanatical who know least of the evidences on which their creed is based.

20. What is truth to me is not truth to another. The same arguments and evidences that convince one mind, make no impression on another: this difference is in men at their birth. No man is entitled positively to assert that he is right, where other men, equally intelligent and equally well informed, hold directly the opposite opinion. Each thinks it impossible for the other to be sincere; and each, as to that, is equally in error. 'What is truth?' was a profound question, the most suggestive one ever put to man.

21. Many beliefs of former and present times seem incomprehensible. They

startle us with a new glimpse into the human soul, that mysterious thing, more mysterious the more we note its workings.

22. Here is a man, superior to myself in intellect and learning, and yet he sincerely believes what seems to me too absurd to merit confutation; and I cannot conceive, and sincerely do not believe, that he is both sane and honest; and yet, he is both. His reason is as perfect as mine, and he is as honest as I am. The fancies of a lunatic are realities to him. Our dreams are realities while they last; and in the past, no more unreal than what we have acted in our waking hours. No man can say that he hath as sure possession of a truth as of a chattel.

23. When men entertain opinions diametrically opposed to each other, and each is honest, who shall decide which hath the truth, and how can either say with certainty that he hath it? We know not what is the truth.

24. That we ourselves believe and feel absolutely certain that our own belief is true, is, in reality, not the slightest proof of the fact, seem it never so certain and incapable of doubt to us.

25. Therefore no man hath, or ever had, a right to persecute another for his belief; for there cannot be two antagonistic rights; and if one can persecute another because he himself is satisfied that the belief of that other is erroneous, the other has, for the same reason, equally as certain a right to persecute him.

26. The truth comes to us as the image of a rod comes to us through the water, bent and distorted: an argument sinks into and convinces the mind of one man, while from that of another it rebounds most quickly. It is no merit in a man to have a particular faith, excellent and sound and philosophic as it may be. It is no more a merit than his prejudices and his passions.

27. The sincere Moslem has as much right to persecute us, as we to persecute him; and therefore Masonry wisely requires no more than a belief in one great, all-powerful Deity, the Father and Preserver of the universe. Therefore she teaches her votaries that toleration is one of the chief duties of every good Mason.

28. The Masonic system regards all the human race as members of one great family, as having the same origin and the same destination; all distinctions of rank, lineage, or nativity, are alike unknown.

29. Yet Masonry is eternally vigilant that no atheist or base libertine contaminates with his unhallowed tread the sanctum sanctorum of our temple; such can never gain admission there, without the grossest violation of vows the most sacred and solemn. It requires the acknowledgement of the existence of the Grand Master of the Universe, and to reverence His great and sacred name, irrespective of sectarian ideas; in a word, to practise every virtue which adorns and ennobles the human character, and fly every vice which sullies and degrades it. It inculcates a generous love for all mankind, it matters not of what religious creed.

30. No evil hath so afflicted the world as intolerance of religious opinion; the human beings it has slain in various ways, if once and together brought to life, would make a nation of people, which, left to live and increase, would have doubled the population of the civilised portion of the world; among which civilised portion it is chiefly that religious wars are waged.

31. No man truly obeys the Masonic law who merely tolerates those whose religious opinions are opposed to his own. Every man's opinions are his own private property, and the rights of all men to maintain each his own are perfectly equal. Merely to tolerate, to bear with an opposing opinion, is to assume it to be heretical, and assert the right to persecute, if we would, and claim our toleration as a merit.

32. The Mason's creed goes further than that; no man, it holds, has any right, in any way, to interfere with the religious belief of another. It holds that each man is absolutely sovereign as to his own belief, and that belief is a matter absolutely foreign to all who do not entertain the same belief; and that if there were any right of persecution at all, it would in all cases be a mutual right, because one party has the same right as the other to sit as judge in his own case, and God is the only magistrate that can rightfully decide between them.

33. To that Great Judge, Masonry refers the matter; and, opening wide its portals, it invites to enter there, and live in peace and harmony, the Protestant, the Catholic, the Jew, the Moslem, the Hindu, every one who will lead a truly virtuous and moral life, love his brethren, minister to the sick and distressed, and believe in the One, All-Powerful, All-Wise, Everywhere Present God-Architect, Creator, and Preserver of all things, by whose universal law of Harmony ever rolls on this universe: the great, vast, infinite circle of successive death and life; to whose ineffable name let all true Masons pay profoundest homage. For whose thousand blessings poured upon us let us feel the sincerest gratitude, now, henceforth, and forever.

34. As a Mason in search of light and truth; many journeys made in the different degrees are symbolical. But the search is not for the truth of any particular creed or religion, that search would be in vain, for what is truth to one is not truth to another; often by argument and evidence, but almost always by the accidents of birth, education and circumstances, our religious belief is formed; and argument and testimony strike the mind of man, when arrived at his religious creed and faith, only to glance off and leave no impression.

35. Masonry's symbols and ceremonies envelop the great primitive truths, known to the first men that lived: with whatever particular meaning they may have peculiar, or believed to be peculiar, to particular creeds, and differing, as the faith differs of those who receive them, Masonry has nothing to do.

36. Masonry conducts initiates through certain forms and ceremonies, to display certain symbols and emblems; it does not give in advance their interpretation, but only indicates their general tendency; it places the thread in the hand that will guide a Mason through the labyrinth; it is for each person to apply and interpret the symbols and ceremonies of the degree in such manner as may seem the truest and most appropriate.

37. A vast multitude of men believe that the Redeemer of man has already appeared upon the earth: many believe he was a man; many, the Son of God; and many, the Deity incarnate: a vaster multitude still wait

for the Redeemer: each will apply our symbols and ceremonies according to his faith.

38. Like the story of our Grand Master Hiram, in which some see figured the condemnation and sufferings of Christ; others, those of the unfortunate Grand Master of the Templars; others, those of the first Charles; and others still, the annual descent of the sun at its winter solstice to the regions of darkness: in no other way could Masonry possess its universality, that character which has ever been peculiar to it from its origin, and which enabled two kings, worshippers of a different Deity, to sit together as Grand Masters while the walls of the first Temple arose; and the men of Gebal, who bowed down to the Phoenician gods, to work by the side of the Hebrews, to whom those gods were an abomination.

39. Pythagoras said: 'God is neither the object of sense nor subject to passion, but invisible, only intelligible, and supremely intelligent. In His body He is like the light, and in His soul He resembles Truth. He is the universal Spirit that pervades and diffuses itself over all nature. All beings receive their life from Him.'

40. There is but one only God, who is not, as some are apt to imagine, seated above the world, beyond the orb of the universe; but being himself all in all, he sees all the beings that fill his immensity; the only Principle, the Light of heaven, the Father of all.

41. He produces everything, He orders and disposes everything; He is the Reason, the Life, and the Motion of all being.

42. Each of us makes such application to his own faith and creed, of the symbols and ceremonies of each degree, as seems to him proper.

43. But the will of Him who rules all events has caused the light to shine again; the day-star of mercy to appear in greater brilliancy; and the word of God to be found.

44. The elect brethren, who had followed the hallowed footsteps of the redeemer, then taught others that it was necessary to practise faith,

hope and charity, and to obey the new law before they could resume the mystic labours of the Order.

45. It was only by means of those sublime principles that Masonry reappeared to the gladdened eyes of man, and from this period Masons no longer built material edifices, but occupied themselves in spiritual buildings. Their works were sustained by temperance, prudence, justice and strength, and they feared no more the vicissitudes of life, or the shadowy terrors of the grave.

TIME-LINE

BCE

4600 Astronomical myths begin to appear

4500 Professional priesthood established in Neolithic Britain
       First small village established at Byblos

4000 Viewing platform set up at Maes Howe
       Ditch and carved stone set up at Bryn Celli Ddu

3500 Boyne Valley complex in Ireland started to be built

3300 Uruk, the first Sumerian city, is established as a small settlement

3200 Newgrange completed
       Bryn Celli Ddu chamber built

3150 Skilled builders called 'Lords of Light' arrive in Egypt from an unknown island
       Unification of Upper and Lower Egypt into a single kingdom

3000 Earliest reference to the city of Jerusalem

2900 Byblos expanded to become a town

2800 Many Grooved Ware sites in Britain are abandoned

2750 Earliest versions of the Epic of Gilgamesh written down

2700 First ziggurat built in Sumer
       Old Kingdom of Egypt ends
       Bronze artefacts in Wiltshire but not in Scotland

2655 Skara Brae abandoned

2650 First pyramid built at Sakkara

2600 First large temple mounds built in Peru

2528 Phoenician boats buried at pyramid of Khufu

2500 Megalithic building stops in Orkney
       Avebury Stones set up

2407 Biblical Flood (traditional Jewish dating)

2300 Byblos is burnt by invaders

2100   Naram-Sin Stela from Sumer shows king with Venus, Moon and Sun on horizon together
2000   Bronze artefacts appear in Scotland
1900   Earliest probable date for Abraham and Melchizedek meeting in Jerusalem
1800   Egyptians take control of Phoenicia
1500   Sumerian Tablets of Venus recorded
1447   Moses leads the Hebrews out of Egypt (traditional Jewish dating)
1350   Phoenician maritime trading well established in Mediterranean
1300   Period of drought in Middle East – lasted for 300 years
1100   Phoenicians gain independence again
1020   Saul becomes first king of Israel
1002   David king of Israel
1000   Phoenicians set up copper mines in Cyprus
       Tyre rebuilt as an offshore defensive harbour
       Sumerian tables of three-star helical risings recorded
980   Hiram destroys his mainland temples and builds them on his island fortress of Tyre
967   Solomon builds his Temple
740   Isaiah sees the Shekinah return and makes the prophecy of a future Messiah
630   Babylonian list of astral omens recorded
622   Documents found under the Jerusalem Temple
609   King Necho II of Egypt/Phoenicia sponsors Phoenician voyage round Africa
600   Venus still worshipped by the Jews as the Queen of Heaven
600   Phoenicians sail around the African continent
586   Destruction of Solomon's Temple
539   Start of Zerubbabel's Temple
460   Herodotus writes of temples of Venus in Tyre and records temple prostitution
400   The start of personal astrology in Chaldea
250   Manetho compiles Egyptian king-lists
166   Qumran founded by priests from Jerusalem
150   Eupolemus claims Abraham invented astrology
120   Lucian writes of temple prostitution in Byblos
66   Jews begin the war with the Romans
19   Herod's Temple begun

CE

7	Jesus born under the light of the rising Shekinah on 25th December
34	Jesus commences his Messianic mission as he becomes 40 years old
36	Latest possible date for the crucifixion of Jesus
68	Dead Sea Scrolls buried at Qumran and under the Jerusalem Temple
70	Jerusalem and the Temple destroyed by the Roman army under Titus
1099	Crusaders take Jerusalem
1118	Founders of Knights Templar begin to excavate under the ruins of Herod's Temple
1128	Knights Templar excavations under the Temple completed
1140	Documents from under the Jerusalem Temple taken to Scotland
1307	Knights Templar arrested as heretics
1441	Rosslyn commenced
1598	First minutes of a Masonic lodge meeting
1714	First recorded minutes of a meeting of the Grand Lodge of York
1717	Establishment of a Grand Lodge in London
1725	Grand Lodge of Ireland formed
1736	Grand Lodge of Scotland formed
1813	The United Grand Lodge of England formed

Appendix 1

THE MYSTERY OF THE MEGALITHIC YARD REVEALED*

*And I saw in those days how long cords were given to two angels
. . . 'Why have they taken those cords and gone off?' And he said
to me; 'They have gone to measure.'*

–The Book of Enoch

THE DISCOVERY OF THE MEGALITHIC YARD

When the late Professor Alexander Thom surveyed over a thousand megalithic structures from Northern Scotland through England, Wales and
Western France he was amazed to find that they had all been built using
the same unit of measurement. Thom dubbed this unit a megalithic yard
(MY) because it was very close in size to an imperial yard, being exactly
2 feet 8.64 inches (82.966 cm). As an engineer he could appreciate the fine
accuracy inherent in the MY, but he was mystified as to how such a primitive people could have consistently reproduced such a unit across a zone
spanning several hundreds of miles.

The answer that eluded the late Professor lay not in the rocks, but in the

---

*A Paper given by Dr Robert Lomas, University of Bradford, Mr Christopher Knight, and
Professor Archie Roy, University of Glasgow, at the Orkney Science Festival, September 2000.

stars. The MY turns out to be much more than an abstract unit such as the modern metre. It is a highly scientific measure repeatedly constructed by empirical means. It is based upon observation of three fundamental factors:

1   The orbit of the Earth around the Sun

2   The spin of the Earth on its axis

3   The mass of the Earth

MAKING YOUR OWN MEGALITHIC YARD

These ancient builders marked the year by identifying the two days a year when the shadow cast by the rising Sun was perfectly aligned with the shadow of the setting Sun. We call these the spring equinox and the autumn equinox, which fall around 21 March and 21 September respectively. They also knew that there were 366 sunrises from one spring equinox to the next, and it appears that they took this as a sacred number.

They then scribed out a large circle on the ground and divided it into 366 parts. All you have to do is copy the process as follows:

Stage one – Find a suitable location

Find a reasonably flat area of land that has open views to the horizon, particularly in the east or the west. You will need an area of around 40 feet by 40 feet with a reasonably smooth surface of grass, level soil or sand.

Stage two – Prepare your equipment

You will need the following items:

1   Two stout, smooth rods approximately 6 feet long and a few inches diameter. One end should be sharpened to a point.

2   A large mallet or heavy stone.

3   A short stick with neatly cut ends of approximately 10 inches. To make life easier this should have small cuts made into it to mark out 5 equal parts.

4 A cord (a washing line will do) approximately 40 feet in length.

5 A piece of string about 5 feet long.

6 A small, symmetrical weight with a hole in its centre (e.g. a heavy washer).

7 A straight stick about 3 feet long.

8 A sharp blade.

Stage three – Constructing a megalithic degree

A megalithic circle was divided into 366 equal parts, which is almost certainly the origin of our modern 360-degree circle. It seems probable that when mathematics came into use in the Middle East they simply discarded 6 units to make the circle divisible by as many numbers as possible. The megalithic degree was 98.36% of a modern degree.

For purposes of creating a megalithic yard you only need to measure one sixth part of a circle, which will contain 61 megalithic degrees. This is easy to do because the radius of a circle always segments the circumference exactly six times.

So, go to a corner of your chosen area and drive one of the rods vertically into the ground. Then take your cord and create a loop that can be slipped over the rod.

Originally the megalithic builders must have divided the sixth part of the circle into 61 parts through trial and error with small sticks. It is highly probable that they came to realise that a ratio of 175:3 gives a 366th part of a circle without the need to calibrate the circle.

Your next step is to make sure that your cord is 175 units long from the centre of the first loop to the centre of a second loop that you will need to make. The length of the units does not matter, but in this case, for convenience, use a stick about 10 inches long, but to avoid too large a circle mark the stick into 5 equal units (you can cheat and use a ruler for this if you want). Next use the stick to measure out 35 lengths (= 175 units) from loop to loop, which will give you a total length of approximately thirty feet.

Now place the first loop over the fixed rod and stretch out the cord to its full length in either a westerly or easterly direction and place the second rod into the loop. You can now scribe out an arc of a circle in the ground. Because we are using the ratio method there is no need to make out an entire sixth part of a circle's circumference; a couple of feet will do.

Next take your piece of string and tie it neatly to the weight to form a plumb line.

You can then drive the second rod into the ground somewhere on the arc you have scribed, using the plumb line to ensure that it is vertical. Now take your measuring stick and mark out a point on the arc that is 3 units away from the outer edge of the second rod. Return to the centre and remove the first rod, marking the hole with a stone or other object to hand. This rod has now to be placed on the spot that you have just marked on the circle's arc, making sure that it is vertical and that its outer edge is 3 units from the corresponding edge of the second rod.

Return to the centre of the circle and look at the two rods. Through them you will be able to see exactly one 366th part of the horizon.

Stage four – Measuring time

You have now split the horizon so that it has the same number of parts as there are sunrises in the course of one orbit of the Sun. Now you need to measure the spin of the Earth on its axis.

You will have to wait for a clear night when the stars are clearly visible. Stand behind the centre point and wait for a bright star to pass between the rods. There are twenty stars with an astronomical magnitude of 1.5, which are known as first-magnitude stars.

The apparent movement of stars across the horizon is due to the rotation of the Earth. It follows that the time that it takes a star to travel from the trailing edge of the first rod to that of the second, will be a period exactly equal to one three hundred and sixty-sixth part of one rotation (a day).

There are 86,400 seconds in a day, and therefore a 366th part of the day will be 236 seconds, or 3 minutes 56 seconds. So your two rods have provided you with a highly accurate clock that will work every time.

When you see a first-magnitude star approaching the first rod, take your plumb line and hold the string at a length of approximately 16 inches, and swing the weight like a pendulum. As the star appears from behind the first rod count the pulses from one extreme to the other.

There are only two factors that effect the swing of a pendulum; the length of the string and gravity – which is determined by the mass of the Earth. If you swing a pendulum faster it will move outwards further but it will not change the number of pulses.

Your task now is to count the number of pulses of your pendulum whilst the star moves between the rods. You need to adjust the length until you get exactly 366 beats during this period of 3 minutes 56 seconds. It is likely to take you several attempts to get the length right, so be prepared to do quite a bit of star-gazing.

Stage five – Making your megalithic yard measure

Once you have the correct length of pendulum, mark the string at the exact point that it leaves your fingers. Next take the straight stick, place the marked part of the string approximately in the centre, hold it in place there, and stretch the line down the stick. Mark the stick at the point where the centre of the weight touches it. Now swing the pendulum over to the other end of the stick, ensuring that the marked part of the string stays firmly in place. Mark the stick again to record the position of the centre of the weight.

Discard the pendulum and cut through the stick at the two points that marked the position of the weight.

Congratulations. You now have a stick that is exactly one megalithic yard long.

It is interesting to note that the curious British measurement unit known as a 'rod' or a 'pole' is equal to 6 megalithic yards to an accuracy of 1 per cent. There are 4 rods to a chain and 80 chains to a mile. Could it be that the modern mile of 1,760 yards is actually based on the prehistoric measure of the megalithic yard?

Appendix 2

THE STATISTICAL
EVALUATION OF THE
ROSSLYN LOZENGES

In this test our purpose was to establish a null hypothesis consisting of the idea that these lozenges were not intended to indicate the latitudes of Jerusalem, Rosslyn, Orkney and Trondheim. We will therefore give the balance of probabilities, in each aspect, to the idea that these are random markings. This is a standard technique used to investigate the likelihood of a sequence of occurrences happening together by chance.[1]

We believe that everything carved into the fabric of Rosslyn is universally accepted as being there for a reason, and that this image is not decoration, but for the purpose of analysis we will assume that there is an equal chance that it is. We therefore will put a 50-50 probability to each of the following conditions happening by chance:

1   That the lozenges are simply a meaningless doodle.

2   That the angle of the bottom lozenge corresponds with the Jerusalem solstice sunrises.

3   That the angle of the second corresponds with Rosslyn's solstice sunrises.

[1] Lomas, R & Lancaster, G: *Forecasting for Sales and Material Management*, Macmillan, 1985

4   That the angle of the third corresponds to the Orkney solstice sunrises.

5   That the angle of the fourth corresponds to the Trondheim solstice sunrises.

6   That all four of these lozenges are in a correct north to south sequence of places of known prime importance to the St Clair family.

7   That the diagram complies with the rules of Grooved Ware symbolism.

Clearly, we are being very fair to the null hypothesis by giving a 50-50 probability to each being a complete coincidence. The result, however, is 1:128, which means that the null hypothesis is well below 1 per cent, the usual minimum threshold for plausibility, so we can reject it.

Appendix 3

THE NAMES FOR VENUS IN VARIOUS TRADITIONS

Anat	Hebrew
Asherah	Canaanite
Asherat	Canaanite
Ashtar	Canaanite
Ashtoreth	Phoenician
Astart	Hebrew
Astarte	Canaanite
Baalat	Phoenician
Baalat-Gebal	Phoenician
Bright star of the morning	Masonic
Freyja	Norse

Frigg	Norse
Hamaliel	Masonic
Hathor	Egyptian
Inanna	Sumerian
Ishtar	Sumerian
Matrona	Hebrew
Morning Star	Masonic
Nut	Egyptian
Salem	Canaanite
Sekhmet	Egyptian
Shachar	Canaanite
Shalem	Canaanite
Uatchet	Egyptian

BIBLIOGRAPHY

A Companion to the Bible: published by T & T Clark, Edinburgh, 1939

Ackerman, Susan: 'Sacred Sex, Sacrifice and Death', *Bible Review*, vol. VI, no. 1, February 1990

Albright, WF: *From the Stone Age to Christianity*, Johns Hopkins Press, 1940

Ali, JR & Cunih, P: 'The Orientation of Churches: Some New Evidence', *The Antiquaries Journal*, 81, pp. 155–93, 2001

Allegro, John Marco: *Lost Gods*, Michael Joseph, London, 1977

Allegro, John Marco: *The Treasure of the Copper Scroll*, Routledge & Kegan Paul, London, 1960

Anderson, James: *The Book of Constitutions of the Grand Lodge of London*, 1738

Anderton, Bill: *Life Cycles*, Quantum, 1990

Baramki, D: *Phoenicia and the Phoenicians*, American College Press, Beirut, 1961

Bellesort, Marie-Noel: 'Le Jeu de Serpent: Jeux et Jouets dans l'Antiquité et le Moyen Age, *Dossiers d'Archéologie*, 1992

Black, M: *The Book of Enoch or I Enoch*, A New English Edition, Leiden, EJ Brill, 1985

Black, M: 'The Development of Judaism in the Greek and Roman Periods', *Peake's Commentary on the Bible*

Boccaccini, G: *Beyond the Essenes*, Eerdmans (Grand Rapids), 1998

Bonnet, H: 'Skarabaeus', in *Reallexikon der ägyptischen Religionsgeschichte*, Berlin, DeGruyter, 1952

Brandon, SGF: *The Fall of Jerusalem and the Christian Church*, SPCK, London, 1951

Brown, RE: *The Semitic Background of the Term Mystery in the New Testament*, Philadelphia, 1968

Butler, A: *The Bronze Age Computer Disc*, W. Fulsham & Co, 1999

Cassell's Concise Bible Dictionary: Cassell, 1998

Charles, RH: *The Book of Jubilees*, OUP, 1902

Charles, RH: *The Book of Enoch*, OUP, 1912

Cohn, Norman: *Cosmos, Chaos and the World to Come*, Yale University Press, 1993

Cross, FM: 'King Hezekiah's Seal Bears Phoenician Imagery', *Biblical Archaeology Review*, March/April 1999

Crossan, JD: *The Essential Jesus – Original Sayings and Earliest Images*, Castle Books, 1998

Crossan, JD & Watts, Richard G: *Who Is Jesus?* New York, HarperCollins, 1996

Crossley-Holland, K: *The Norse Myths, a Retelling*, André Deutsch, 1980

Dawkins, R: *Unweaving the Rainbow*, Penguin, 1998

De St Clair, L: *Histoire Généalogique de la Famille de Saint Clair*, Paris, 1905

Deutsch, R: 'First Impression – What We Learn from King Ahaz's Seal', *Biblical Archaeology Review*, May/June 1998

Dictionary of National Biography, ed. Sidney Lee: Smith, Elder & Co, London, 1903

Dinely, M, The First Orkney Brewery, Orkney Science Festival, 2001

Dunand, M; *De l'Amanus and Sinai*, Beirut, 1953

Dyer, J: *Ancient Britain*, Routledge, 1997

Eisenman, R: *James the Brother of Jesus*, Faber and Faber, 1997

Eisenman, R: *The Dead Sea Scrolls and the First Christians*, Element, 1996

Eisenman, R & Wise, M: *The Dead Sea Scrolls Uncovered*, Element, 1992

Ellis Davidson, HE: *The Lost Beliefs of Northern Europe*, Routledge, 1993

Eogan, George: *Knowth and the Passage Tombs of Ireland*, Thames and Hudson, 1986

Evans-Pritchard, EE: *Theories of Primitive Religion*, Oxford University Press, 1965

Eysenck, HJ and Nias, DK: *Astrology, Science or Superstition*, Maurice Temple Smith, 1982

Fohrer, G: *History of Israelite Religion*, SPCK, London, 1973

Frankfort, Henri: *Kingship and the Gods*, University of Chicago Press, 1978

Furneaux, R: *The Other Side of the Story*, Cassell, 1973

Gauquelin, M: *Cosmic Influences on Human Behaviour*, Aurora Press, 1994

Golb, Norman: *Who Wrote the Dead Sea Scrolls?* BCA, 1995

Gould's History of Freemasonry, Caxton, 1902

Graves, R: *The White Goddess*, Faber and Faber, 1948

Grimal, N: *History of Ancient Egypt*, Blackwell, Cambridge, 1992

Hackwell, W John: *Signs, Letters, Words. Archaeology Discovers Writing*, Charles Scribner's Sons, New York, 1987

Hawking, Stephen: *The Universe in a Nutshell*, Transworld, London, 2001

Heath, Robin: *Sun, Moon and Stonehenge. Proof of High Culture in Ancient Britain*, Bluestone Press, 1998

Hedges, John: *The Tomb of the Eagles*, Tempvs Reparatvm, 1992

Henshall, AS: 'The Chambered Cairns', in *The Prehistory of Orkney*, Edinburgh University Press, 1993

Herm, Gerhard: *The Phoenicians*, Victor Gollancz, 1975

Herodotus, *The History*, trans. George Rawlinson, New York, Dutton & Co., 1862

Herodotus: *Histories*, Wordsworth Classics of World Literature, 1996

Hertzberg, Arthur, *Judaism*, George Braziller, New York, 1962

Heyerdahl, Thor: *The Ra Expeditions*, George Allen & Unwin, 1971

Historisk Tidsskrift: Universities Forlaget, Bind 79, number 2, 2000

Hoffman, Michael A: *Egypt before the Pharaohs*, Michael O'Mara Books, 1991

Hunter, RH: *Cassell's Concise Bible Dictionary*, Cassell, 1996

Hyde, D: A *Literary History of Ireland*, T. Fisher Unwin, 1899

Jagersma, H: *A History of Israel to Bar Kochba*, SCM Press, 1985

Johnson, AR: *Myth, Ritual and Kingship*, Clarendon Press, 1958

Kitson, A (ed): *History and Astrology*, Mandala, 1989

Knight, C & Lomas, R: *Uriel's Machine, The Ancient Origins of Science*, Arrow, 1999

Knight, C & Lomas, R: *The Second Messiah*, Arrow, 1997

Knight, C & Lomas, R: *The Hiram Key*, Arrow, 1997

Layish, Dov Ben: *A Survey of Sundials in Israel*, 1969

Lehner, Mark: *The Complete Pyramids*, Thames and Hudson, 1997

Levy, A: 'Bad Timing', *Biblical Archaeological Review*, July/August 1998

Liden, K: 'From Pagan Sanctuary to Christian Church: the Excavation of Maere Church, Trondelag', *Norwegian Archeological Review*, 2, 23–32, Oslo, 1969

Lockyer, N: 'Some Questions for Archaeologists', *Nature*, vol. 73, 1906, p. 280

Lockyer, N: *Stonehenge and other British Stone Monuments Astronomically Considered*, Macmillan, 1909

Lomas, R: http://www.bradford.ac.uk/acad/mancen/lomas Ref Seminar Number 9

Lomas, Robert: *The Invisible College*, Headline, 2002

Lomas, R & Lancaster, G: *Forecasting for Sales and Material Management*, Macmillan, 1985

Lucian: *Dialogues of the Gods*, Penguin Classics, 1960

Mackenzie, D: *Pre-Columbian America*, Gresham Publishing Company, 1922

Mackie, E: *The Megalithic Builders*, Phaidon Press, 1977

Man, John: *Alpha Beta, How Our Alphabet Shaped the Western World*, Headline, 2000

McClelland, David C: *The Achieving Society*, The Free Press, New York, 1961

Mcfadyen, JH: *Introduction to the Old Testament*, Hodder and Stoughton, 1905

Milman, H: *History of the Jews*, Everyman, London, 1909

Montet, P: *Byblos et l'Egypte*, Paris, 1928

Oesterley, WOE & Robinson, TH: *Hebrew Religion, Its Origin and Development*, SPCK, 1952

O'Brien, W: *Bronze Age Copper Mining in Britain and Ireland*, Shire Archaeology, 1996

O'Kelly, Michael J: *Newgrange; Archaeology, Art and Legend*, Thames and Hudson, 1982

Palsson, H & Edwards, P (ed.): *The Orkneyinga Saga*, Penguin Classics, 1981

Parry, Robert: *Astrology's Complete Book of Self-Defence*, Quantum, 1990

Peake's Commentary on the Bible, Thomas Nelson and Sons, 1962

Pixner, Bargil: 'Jerusalem's Essene Gateway', *Biblical Archaeology Review*, vol. 23, no.3, May/June 1997

Polano, H (ed): *The Talmud*, Frederick Warne, 1936

Rappoport, A S: *Myths and Legends of Ancient Israel*, Senate, 1995 (3 vols)

Ray, TP: *Nature*, vol. 337, no. 26, 345–346, Jan. 1989

Raymond, EAE: *The Mythical Origin of the Egyptian Temple*, Manchester Univ. Press, 1969

Renan, E: *Mission de Phénicie*, Paris, 1864

Renfrew, C: *Before Civilisation*, Jonathan Cape, 1973

Renfrew, C: *Archaeology, Theories, Methods and Practice*, Thames and Hudson, 1996

Robinson, HW: *The History of Israel, Its Facts and Factors*, Duckworth, 1938

Robinson, J: *Born in the Blood, The Lost Secrets of Freemasonry*, Guild Publishing, London, 1989

Robinson, TH: *The History of Israel (A Companion to the Bible)*, T & T Clark, 1939

Russell, DS: *The Method and Message of Jewish Apocalyptic 200 BC – AD 100*, SCM Press, London Sachs, Gunter: The Astrology File, Orion, 1997

Schonfield, Hugh: *The Passover Plot*, Element, 1965

Schultz, J: *Movements and Rhythms of the Stars*, Floris Books, 1987

Schwarez, HP: 'ESR Dates for the Hominid Burial site of Qafzeh in Israel', *Journal of Human Evolution*, 17, 1988

Sinclair, A: *The Sword and the Grail*, Century, 1993

Steiner, R: *The Festivals and Their Meaning*, Rudolf Steiner Press, 1981

Stevenson, David: *The Origins of Freemasonry*, Cambridge University Press, 1988

Stiebling, WH: 'Did the Weather Make Israel's Emergence Possible?', *Biblical Review*, vol. X, no. 4, August 1994

Sturluson, S: *Helmskringla*, Parts 1 & 2, translated by Samuel Laing, Everyman Library, 1961–1964

Sturluson, Snorri: *The Prose Edda*, translated Jean L Young, Cambridge Univ. Press, 1954

Sykes, B: *The Seven Daughters of Eve*, Corgi, 2001

Szekely, EB (translator & ed.): *The Essene Gospel of Peace*, Book One, International Biogenic Society, 1931

Tacitus: *The Histories*, Penguin Classics, 1962

Temple R: *He Who Saw Everything: a Verse Translation of the Epic of Gilgamesh*, Century, 1991

Thom, A & AS: *Megalithic Rings*, BAR British Series 81, 1980

Thom, Alexander: *Megalithic Sites in Britain*, Oxford University Press, 1967

Thom, AS: *Walking in All the Squares*, Argyll Publishing, 1995

Thompson, WPL: *History of Orkney*, The Mercat Press, 1987

Thouless, RH: *An Introduction to the Psychology of Religion*, Cambridge Univ. Press, 1971

Turville-Petre, EOG: *Scaldic Poetry*, Oxford University Press, 1976

Twohig, ES: *Irish Megalithic Tombs*, Shire Archaeology, 1990

Vermes, G: *Scripture and Tradition in Judaism*, Penguin, 1973

Vermes, G: *The Dead Sea Scrolls in English*, Penguin, 1995

Wallace-Murphy, T & Hopkins, M: *Rosslyn, Guardian of the Secrets of the Holy Grail*, Element, 1999

Ward, JSM: *Freemasonry and the Ancient Gods*, Cassell, 1928

Whiston, W. (ed. and trans.): *The Works of Flavius Josephus*, William F Nimmo, 1890

Whitfield, P: *Astrology, a History*, The British Library, 2001

Wickham-Jones, CR: *Scotland's First Settlers*, Historic Scotland, 1994

Wilson, AN: *Paul, The Mind of the Apostle*, Sinclair-Stevenson, 1997

Wilson, Colin: 'Why I Now Believe Astrology Is a Science', Daily Mail, Thursday, 22 March 2001

Wilson, I: *Jesus: the Evidence*, Weidenfeld and Nicolson, 1984

Wise, M, Abegg, M & Cook, E: *The Dead Sea Scolls, a New Translation*, Harpert SanFrancisco, 1996

Wolters, Al: *The Copper Scroll, Overview, Text and Translation*, Sheffield Academic Press, Sheffield, 1996

Woolley, Sir Leonard: *Ur of the Chaldees*, Pelican, 1929

Zertal, A: 'Israel Enters Canaan', *Biblical Archaeology Review*, vol. XVII, no: 5, Sept./Oct. 1991

INDEX

Virgin Mary, 76, 97
Von Hompesch, Ferdinard, 79, 439

W
Waite, AE, 217, 218, 220, 221
Wales, 13, 14, 27, 33, 35, 103, 104,
  178, 452
Wallace, William, 57
Ward, JSM, 54, 56
Warren, Lieutenant, 86
Washington, George, 55, 336
Web of Hiram, 7, 20, 23, 51, 55, 70,
  343
White Wall, 37, 109, 134
William of Normandy, 67, 268
William St Clair, 58, 64, 66, 67, 70,
  77–79, 153, 190, 271, 272,
  274–276, 283, 321, 322
William the Seemly, 67
Wilson, AN, 254
Wilson, Colin, 292–294, 304, 311
Winter solstice, 16, 24, 38–40, 42–45,
  75, 88, 107, 129, 147, 153, 157,
  224, 225, 227, 233, 260, 264, 288,
  447
Wise, Michael, 30, 73, 83, 90, 164,
  184, 215, 216, 243, 245, 282, 326,
  393, 423, 440, 446
Woden, 124
Wollongong, 130
Women's Courtyard, 87
Woolley, Sir Leonard, 102, 106
Wren, Sir Christopher, 14, 334, 336

X
Xerox, 60

Y
Yahweh, 16, 18, 80, 82, 90, 98, 99,
  119, 120, 124, 129, 132, 133, 141,
  142, 144, 145, 162–164, 168, 169,
  172, 176–179, 181, 185, 187,
  189–191, 203, 244, 246, 248, 249,
  255, 258, 265
Yehimilk, 93, 98
Yehotam, 186
Yggdrasil, 73
Yishâq, 133
Yohanan, 193
Youssef, Ahmed, 113

Z
Zadok, 143
Zadokite, 191, 205, 238
Zarephath, 89
Zealot, 242, 256–258
Zechariah, 246
Zedek, 124, 131, 132, 188
Zedekiah, 211, 395
Zeredatha, 17
Zertal, Dr Adam, 137, 138
Zerubbabel, 5, 57, 86, 161, 190,
  191, 205, 300, 320, 398–402,
  404–406, 408, 409, 411–415,
  417–419
Zilpah, 147
Zion, 61, 119, 120, 128, 175, 246,
  349, 359
Zodiac, 42, 75, 132, 157, 193, 194,
  296–298, 300–302, 346, 407
Zoroastrians, 190